MW01054552

To Eunice,

With every best
wish ————————

Warm regards —
Marilyn G. Shergold
May 10, 2017

YONKERS

IN THE
TWENTIETH
CENTURY

YONKERS

IN THE
TWENTIETH
CENTURY

Marilyn E. Weigold

and the

Yonkers Historical Society

excelsior editions
State University of New York Press
Albany, New York

Cover image credit: An aerial view of West Yonkers in the 1920s. Courtesy of the
Yonkers Historical Society; Mary Hoar, Executive Illustrations Editor, Marianne
Winstanley, Assistant Illustrations Editor.

Published by State University of New York Press, Albany

© 2014 Yonkers Historical Society

All rights reserved

Printed in the United States of America

No part of this book may be used or reproduced in any manner whatsoever
without written permission. No part of this book may be stored in a retrieval
system or transmitted in any form or by any means including electronic,
electrostatic, magnetic tape, mechanical, photocopying, recording, or otherwise
without the prior permission in writing of the publisher.

Excelsior Editions is an imprint of State University of New York Press

For information, contact State University of New York Press, Albany, NY
www.sunypress.edu

Production, Eileen Nizer
Marketing, Kate R. Seburyamo

Library of Congress Cataloging-in-Publication Data

Weigold, Marilyn E.
  Yonkers in the twentieth century / Marilyn E. Weigold and the Yonkers Historical
Society.
        pages cm. — (Excelsior editions)
  Includes bibliographical references and index.
  ISBN 978-1-4384-5393-4 (hardcover : alk. paper)
  E-ISBN 978-1-4384-5394-1
  1. Yonkers (N.Y.)—History—20th century. I. Yonkers Historical Society.
II. Title.

  F129.Y5W45 2014
  974.7'3043—dc23   2014002123

10 9 8 7 6 5 4 3 2 1

**Dedicated to the memory of
Yonkers Historical Society President Emeritus John F. Prill**

Without his commitment, leadership, guidance, and passion for Yonkers history, this book would not have been possible.

Our special thanks to the Hudson Valley National Foundation and the late William E. Griffin. His leadership of the Foundation and faith in the Yonkers Historical Society and the History of Yonkers enabled us to tell this story.

Contents

Preface / xi

Introduction / xv

CHAPTER 1
"Queen City of the Hudson":
Yonkers in the Early Twentieth Century / 1

CHAPTER 2
The Great War and Its Aftermath / 45

CHAPTER 3
Years of Pain and Glory:
The Great Depression and World War II / 79

CHAPTER 4
The Remaking of Yonkers: The Postwar Years / 127

photo gallery follows page 168

CHAPTER 5
An Urban/Suburban Metropolis:
Yonkers in the Sixties and Seventies / 169

CHAPTER 6

A City in Transition:
Challenges and Opportunities in the Decade of the Eighties / 223

CHAPTER 7

Toward the Millennium:
The Nineties / 271

Notes / 295

Bibliographic Note / 313

Yonkers Speaks: Excerpts from Oral History Interviews / 321

Donors / 347

Index / 351

Every effort has been made to ensure the historical accuracy of the materials presented in *Yonkers in the Twentieth Century* and to include major events in the evolution of the city during the period covered in this volume. There are many stories still to be recounted by individuals who lived through the period, and it is the hope of everyone involved in making this book a reality that these stories will be compiled in the future.

Preface

When the uncovering of the long-submerged Saw Mill River began
in 2011, as part of a project to create a four acre park in downtown
Yonkers not far from where the Saw Mill (also known as the Nepperhan
River) empties into the Hudson River, *The New York Times* observed that
Yonkers would "be better with a river running through it."[1] At the same
time the paper noted that Yonkers was "a work in progress."[2] Although
this remains the case in the early twenty-first century, it was even more
relevant throughout the twentieth century, the period that is covered
extensively in this book. The decline of New York State's fourth largest
city, a metropolis once known as the "Queen City of the Hudson" and
the "City of Gracious Living," from the pinnacle of industrial output and
economic vitality and its rebirth, characterized by the redevelopment of a
waterfront long dominated by factories, occurred within the ten decades
highlighted in this work.

In recognition of the historical significance of the transformation
the city had undergone since 1900, in the waning decade of the century
John F. Prill, who served as president of the Yonkers Historical Society
until 1999, conceived the idea for a comprehensive history of the city's
evolution during the twentieth century. After retiring as president, John
F. Prill continued to chair and spearhead the society's book committee.
It is because of his vision and perseverance that the book became reality.

The volume for which John F. Prill deserves the gratitude of present
and future Yonkers residents was to be one of several initiatives aimed
at preserving and disseminating information about the rich history of
Yonkers. Chief among them were the efforts of the Yonkers Historical
Society, which in addition to maintaining extensive documentary and
photographic archives at its headquarters in the Grinton Will Library,
has a well-designed, user-friendly website containing interesting and

informative data, including pictures and articles from its quarterly publication. Illustrations from the society's photographic collection were utilized for *Then and Now: Yonkers* (2008), a collaborative work of the Yonkers Historical Society and the Blue Door Artist Association. This book was a welcome addition to a collection of works on Yonkers that includes Frank Walton, *Pillars of Yonkers* (1951), Yolanda Johnson, Mary E. Lawson, Lillian Reilly, Loraine Spencer, Ethel Thibault, and Emelyn Webster, *Yonkers Through the Years* (1962), Warren G. Halliburton, *A Pictorial Story of Yonkers and Its People* (1987), and the Reverend Charles E. Allison, *The History of Yonkers: Westchester County, New York* (1896).

Building upon the foundation laid by previous authors, the current project has benefited from their work and from the unstinting support of the trustees of the Yonkers Historical Society and the Society's History Committee. The individuals who have served as trustees are: Gregory Arcaro, James Blanchard, Susan Blanchard, Symra Brandon, Richard Carlson, John Constantine, Msgr. Hugh Corrigan, Mina Crasson, Carol McEwan Daly, Edward Dee, Suzanne Dottin-Ramirez, Tom Dunn, John Favareau, Elizabeth Fitzgerald, Rosalie Flynn, Tom Flynn, Ira Goldman, Joan Hanrahan, Teresa Hennelly, Mary Hoar, Joan Jennings, Jeremiah Jerome, Kathleen Kelleher, Rudy Kern, Dewey Lohrfink, Maureen McAllister, Darryl Mack, Stephen Macknowski, Mary Madden, Patricia Mangold, Phil Matthews, Elizabeth McFadden, Richard Moore, Peg Murphy, Joseph Nocca, Christine Kenney O'Rourke, Jerry Ostroff, Joyce Pidel, Terrence Price, John F. Prill, Nancy Lee Racassi, Margaret Reilly, Georgiana Reynolds, Andrew Romano, Deirdre Hoare-Rylander, Stephen Sansone, Nancy Sarmast, Nortrud Spero, Josephine Tienken, Lucia Trovato, William Watson, Jeffrey Williams, Robert Wilson, and Marianne Winstanley.

The following individuals, some of whom are trustees of the society, have served on the History Committee: John F. Prill, chairman, Mina Crasson, Benedetto "Ben" Ermini, John Favareau, Rosalie Flynn, Tom Flynn, Teresa Hennelly, Mary Hoar, Joan Jennings, Jeremiah Jerome, Elizabeth McFadden, Richard Moore, Andrew Romano, George Rutledge, Deirdre Hoare-Rylander, Jennie Tritten, Jeffrey Williams, Robert Wilson, Leonard Winstanley, and Marianne Winstanley.

Trustees and committee members, as well as members of the community, shared their recollections of Yonkers in a series of interviews. Their insights were invaluable, and for that reason the author wishes to acknowledge and thank the following individuals who were interviewed: Gregory Arcaro, Sylvia Banks, Symra Brandon, Rhoda Breitbart, Mario Caruso, Alfred DelBello, Norman Downes Jr., Dorothy Dunn, John Favareau, Tom Flynn, Anna Hawkins, Rosanna Hirschkind, Walter

Hlewicki, Mary Hoar, Milton Holst, Joan Cahraman Hull, Joan Jennings, Jeremiah Jerome, Royden Letsen, Gerald Loehr, Stephen Macknowski, Angelo Martinelli, Joseph Pastore, Edward Petti, Sal Prezioso, John F. Prill, Arlene McCann Reden, Andrew Romano, John Romano, John Rossell, George Rutledge, Nicholas Spano, Corinne Thomas, Jennie Tritten, Jeffrey Williams and Leonard Winstanley.

The author wishes to acknowledge Jeffrey Williams not only for taking time for an interview but for the support he demonstrated for the twentieth-century history project during his tenure as president of the Yonkers Historical Society. His successor, Mary Hoar, who had previously served as president beginning in 1999, following the passing of Patricia Mangold, John F. Prill's successor, has been extremely supportive and during her second term as president has devoted considerable time to reviewing the manuscript. The following individuals, to whom the author also owes a debt of gratitude, reviewed portions of the manuscript: John F. Prill, Mina Crasson, Benedetto "Ben" Ermini, John Favareau, Rosalie Flynn, Teresa Hennelly, Mary Hoar, Joan Jennings, Jeremiah Jerome, Richard Moore, George Rutledge, Deirdre Hoare-Rylander, Leonard Winstanley, and Marianne Winstanley The author is most grateful, as well, for the invaluable assistance provided by John Favareau, reference librarian at the Yonkers Riverfront Library, who not only read the manuscript but made the many archival treasures found in the library's superb local history collection available. The staff of the Grinton Will Library, where microfilms of Yonkers newspapers were consulted, were also very helpful.

In addition to all of the wonderful Yonkers people who facilitated this project, including the generous donors whose names appear elsewhere in this volume, there were several other individuals who deserve thanks: Jeff Canning, author and former senior news editor of *The Journal News,* and Roger Panetta, author and professor of history at Fordham University, read the completed manuscript and offered helpful suggestions for enhancing it. In the final production stage of the project, the expertise and efficiency of Amanda Lanne-Camilli and Jessica Kirschner of SUNY Press ensured a successful outcome. The author is deeply indebted to them and to SUNY Press for the important role its Excelsior imprint has played in preserving and disseminating information about the history of the Empire State.

Introduction

Yonkers and the world saw astonishing changes in our lives during the twentieth century. Revolutionary changes that improved our lives, made us healthier and longer-lived, and gave us a shorter workweek and more free time. Our lifestyles were dramatically changed.

Scientific research gave us treatments for deadly diseases. Typhoid, polio, smallpox, and yellow fever were controlled, and antibiotics were created. Infant mortality decreased by more than 90 percent. A man's life expectancy went from forty-six years in 1900 to seventy-four in 2000, and a woman's from forty-eight to seventy-nine.

Transportation changed from horse-drawn buggies and carriages to motorized buses. Cars became affordable, and changed not only how we lived but also where we lived. No one in 1900 could have foreseen people flying through space, walking on the moon, or spending months on the International Space Station, yet now, through the development of air transportation, people fly across the country every day.

In the early 1900s more than 40 percent of the U.S. working population would have been classified as poor. As they aged or became ill, they were unable to support themselves. They faced no other alternative but the "poor house." Social Security and retirement plans help today's workers provide for their own future. Advances in technology changed the average workweek from sixty-six hours in 1900 to thirty-five hours per week today. The National Child Labor Committee, formed in 1904, worked with those advocating compulsory education laws to keep children in schools and out of the factories.

Women obtained the right to vote. Educational and job opportunities opened up for women. In 1900, women were 18 percent of the work force; today they account for more than half. And, since 1981, more women than men have been earning Bachelors and advanced degrees. In

1900, only 1 percent of lawyers and 6 percent of doctors were women; now, women account for about 32 percent of both professions.

In 1900, only 10 percent of American homes were electrified; now it is a rare home without electric power. We would be lost without our computers, televisions, refrigerators, and microwaves.

Communication has vastly changed. In 1900, there were no movies, no radio, no television, no computers, and very few telephones. We wrote letters and mailed them to distant friends and family. We now can speak to people thousands of miles away on our cell phones, or chat with them on our computers using instant messaging and Skype. We can watch events happening thousands of miles away on television by pressing a few buttons.

Yonkers has undergone immense changes during this time, with the loss of industry, development and redevelopment, and changes in our living patterns. All these social and technological changes are reflected in the history of our "City of Gracious Living" during the twentieth century.

Why should we be interested in the history of Yonkers? Our history has some wonderful stories, some difficult stories, some uplifting stories, and some sad stories. Our city has changed dramatically in many ways, but in many other ways Yonkers remains the same. Yonkers's past allows us to see the relevance of today's events, and we hope will prevent us from making the same mistakes we have made in the past.

And, perhaps most important, the history of Yonkers is the story of our lives.

Mary Hoar, President
Yonkers Historical Society

"Queen City of the Hudson"

Yonkers in the Early Twentieth Century

Theodore Roosevelt and the Visiting Firemen

Shortly before the dawn of the twentieth century, the City of Yonkers rolled out the red carpet for a very distinguished visitor: Governor Theodore Roosevelt. The occasion was the twenty-seventh annual convention of the New York State Firemen's Association. The selection of Yonkers to host this important gathering marked the coming of age of a municipality long overshadowed by its gigantic neighbor to the south. Perhaps no one was more keenly aware of this than Mayor Leslie Sutherland who declared that the firemen's convention signaled the start of a new era for the "Queen City of the Hudson."

In preparation for the arrival of more than three hundred convention delegates the city went all out. Flags were everywhere, and not just American flags. Flying side by side with the Stars and Stripes were the flags of Ireland, Great Britain, Germany, and France. Colorful bunting adorned shops and private homes. Huge pieces of canvas bearing paintings of uniformed firefighters hung from the facades of buildings. Although the quality of these brightly colored artworks varied, the messages they bore were consistently positive. "Welcome to the Gallant Firemen," "The Town is Yours," and "Honor the Brave" were some of the memorable sayings that enlivened the banners.[1] As if this weren't enough to convince the visitors that Yonkers welcomed them with open arms, the city erected what *The New York Times* dubbed "Yonkers's crowning glory, the pride of Yonkers's heart."[2] What the *Times* described so effusively was actually a triumphal arch in Getty Square. A sizable structure fashioned from plaster and wood, the arch was flanked by four Ionic columns, each of which was topped by a white sphere. With flags of many nations adorning the arch and tricolor bunting wrapped around the columns, this must have been a sight to behold. "In the opinion of Yonkers," declared *The New York Times,* "this arch is a marvel of art, a thing of surpassing beauty, and there is general regret that it will not remain . . . a joy forever."[3]

The views of local residents notwithstanding, the delegates who gathered at the Music Hall at 10 a.m. on the morning of August 15, 1899, were less concerned with the city's festive new look than with matters directly pertaining to the state's firefighters. Following the invocation by the Reverend Dr. Charles E. Allison of the Dayspring Presbyterian Church, a rousing rendition of "The Stars and Stripes Forever" by sixty children accompanied by Murray's Military Band, and a welcoming address by Mayor Sutherland, the delegates got down to business. The first item on the agenda was the association's annual report, which painted a rosy picture of the organization's finances. Less positive was the information about the State Firemen's Home upriver in Hudson. There had been allegations about abuses at this facility and a committee of the State Firemen's Association had been appointed to investigate the charges. Its report stating that there was insufficient evidence for the allegations was presented to the assembled delegates by a trustee of the home but, then as now, suspicion of elder abuse was a serious and troubling matter.

That some of the delegates continued to mull this over even as the convention moved ahead with its agenda would not have been surprising, but the minute Governor Roosevelt arrived attention was diverted elsewhere. Accompanied by his wife, the governor had journeyed from his home in Oyster Bay, Long Island, where he had spent part of the summer, to Manhattan for luncheon, with a clergyman, at the Union League Club. At precisely 2:55 in the afternoon he boarded a train for Yonkers. At 3:31 p.m. he stepped off the train and was greeted by a welcoming committee consisting of Company A, First Regiment of the National Guard, and various dignitaries. Seated beside Mayor Sutherland, in a horse-drawn carriage, the governor proceeded to the triumphal arch and from there to the Soldier's Monument in Manor Hall Park. Standing on a specially constructed platform, Roosevelt spoke briefly to the assembled populace. From here it was on to the Music Hall, where his remarks were more substantive but not terribly lengthy. "Yours is a noble service. . . . It is not only that you save property and at times life, in the saving of property, but every man of you holds up to every one in so doing a high type of citizenship by rendering disinterested service to the public," Roosevelt told the appreciative delegates.[4]

Praise them though he did, the governor, whose visit was characterized by *The Yonkers Statesman* as "a great treat for the delegates and people generally," did not stay around to mingle with the firefighters.[5] Shortly after 4 p.m. he was aboard a train heading for New York City. An hour later the delegates were at the Getty House hotel for a hook and ladder demonstration by the Yonkers Fire Department's Life Saving Corps. Later that evening convention goers were treated to a vaudeville performance back at the Music Hall. The convention lasted another two days, ending with a parade of one hundred fire companies from all over the state. Prizes, donated by Yonkers businesses, were awarded to the oldest and youngest participants, as well as the tallest, shortest, fattest, and thinnest. The fireman with the biggest family was given a barrel of flour, while the one with the youngest wife received a box of perfume for his lady. For the grand finale, the "Queen City of the Hudson" treated the firemen to a spectacular fireworks display over the Hudson River.

A City on the Move

With a population of 47,931, which was roughly double what it had been a decade earlier, a treasury surplus, a recent reduction of its bonded indebtedness to $100,000, and not one but two cuts in the tax rate in recent years, the city could well afford to put on a good show for the visiting firemen. The financial picture was rosy, as evidenced by an array of public improvements, including new roads, an expanded sewer system, state-of-the-art garbage disposal consisting of an incinerator, new school buildings, and the erection of the second public bathhouse to serve the city's growing immigrant population. By 1910 there would be a third bathhouse, this one an imposing Spanish Renaissance building on Yonkers Avenue at Oak Street. This structure, which featured a swimming pool, reflected the evolution in public thinking about such facilities. "Initially, the bath house advocates opposed public pools as they felt that they were wasteful of space, which could be better used for showers," but by the early 1900s, the "conviction that organized public recreation not only strengthened bodies," but "also molded good citizens," led to the inclusion of pools.[6] With its tapestry brick façade and terra cotta trim, the Spanish Renaissance building had an eyecatching exterior, but the interior was equally impressive. The men's side of the bathhouse had forty-three showers and the women's twenty. There were also a half-dozen tubs set aside for senior citizens. Of these, four were for men and two for women. In addition to the bathing facilities, the building had a heated, sixty thousand gallon swimming pool, whose depth ranged from a little over four feet to seven feet. Lined in tile, the pool was surrounded by marble and Terrazza. The total cost of erecting this modern marvel was $40,884. In the opinion of many residents, and not just those who frequented the bathhouse, this was money well spent. Yonkers was, after all, a prosperous up and coming municipality, something the city's four newspapers of the early twentieth century frequently noted.

That *The Yonkers Herald, The Yonkers Gazette, The Westchester Observer,* and *The Yonkers Statesman* all managed to survive simultaneously may seem surprising, but in that pre-Internet and pre–radio and television era, newspapers were exceedingly popular as sources of information about international, national, state, and local news, as well as social news. Parties, debuts, births, betrothals, and marriages were noted in the pages of daily and weekly newspapers, with some of these events receiving extensive coverage. A case in point was the wedding of the editor and publisher of *The Yonkers Statesman* a fortnight prior to the dawn of the twentieth century. This was such big news that *The New York Times* ran two stories on the nuptials. The second piece bore the title "Aged Yonkers Editor Weds."[7] The widowed groom, John W. Oliver, was eighty-five; the bride (his third) was a tad younger—by thirty-two years. A clergyman from the Methodist Episcopal Church, of which the groom was a member, performed the ceremony in the parlor of the Oliver residence, Rose Cottage, on Warburton Avenue, and Mayor Leslie Sutherland, along with a city judge, was a witness. This was no small affair of a chilly December evening. The house was decorated with smilax and, appropriately enough, roses, and there were 130 guests. The bride wore "a dress of steel gray silk, which was very becoming" and, according to *The Yonkers Statesman,* when pronouncing their vows "the responses of the bride and groom were clear and emphatic."[8] Coming as he did from a long-lived family, the smitten bridegroom, whose father lived to the age of ninety-six, evidently expected to enjoy a decade or more with his new wife and he almost did. Oliver, who "was on duty every business day, almost to the very last," died at age ninety-three.[9]

In an era when the average life expectancy was forty, some Yonkers residents beat the odds, and when they did it was newsworthy. "Yonkers Woman Dies Aged 102 Years," proclaimed *The New York Times* in 1902 when reporting the death of Jane Russell Maxwell, an immigrant from Northern Ireland, who resided with her granddaughter.[10] In 1909 *The Times* published two lengthy articles about Alexander Herriott who was said to have looked no more than eighty but was actually 107! Mr.

Herriott appeared in Yonkers City Court to file a complaint against his daughter, who had seized his bankbook. Herriott had planned to use some of his savings to journey to his native Scotland. A merchant seaman who had been around the world, Herriott told a reporter that he had seen a number of famous people, including Napoleon Bonaparte, Prince Albert, the husband of England's Queen Victoria, and Abraham Lincoln. As for the secret of his longevity, he claimed that he did not adhere to a special diet but, instead, ate as much as he wanted, drank beer, and smoked. He also got around town quite a bit, disappearing from his daughter's residence for many hours as he roamed the city streets and tarried along the waterfront talking with people he encountered. His daughter contended that some of the men he chatted with obtained money from him, and this prompted a Yonkers judge to rule in favor of her continued oversight of his finances, lest his $4,000 savings disappear completely.

Greystone

To some Yonkers residents, a few thousand dollars constituted nothing more than small change. Among them was Samuel Untermyer, who in 1900 was busily restoring the home of the late New York State governor Samuel J. Tilden. Untermyer, a prominent attorney, had purchased the estate, called Greystone, the year before for $121,000, considerably less than the $225,000 hat manufacturer John T. Waring had paid to erect the home in 1870 and less than the $150,000 for which Samuel Tilden purchased the house in 1879. Tilden was said to have spent another $500,000 erecting various outbuildings on the property and buying land east of North Broadway. The latter, composed of fifty-five acres, remained a separate parcel and Samuel Untermyer obtained it by bidding $50,500 at an auction held at Philipse Manor Hall following a lawsuit involving the late governor's estate. After spending a total of $171,500 for a property that had seen better days, Untermyer proceeded to pour considerable money into the beautification of the house and grounds, both of which had been neglected in the years since Tilden's death. An oval lawn was created and the straight path running from North Broadway to the entrance of the mansion was replaced by a winding carriage road. The estate's greenhouses were restored and stocked with all sorts of colorful plants. For Untermyer, horticulture was "a consuming avocation, and Greystone allowed him ample opportunity to indulge in this hobby with a passion. He approached the task of landscaping his vast parkland as a therapeutic outlet for the fund of creative energy his legal duties barely tapped."[11] Although Greystone quite literally blossomed into something resembling a botanical garden, both Untermyer and his architect, J. H. Freedlander, shared the view that the estate needed more than beautiful plantings to bring it alive. Therefore, electric lights were installed throughout the grounds. To brighten up the house itself, a beautiful porch of white limestone was added to the side of the home facing North Broadway. On the other side of the house, two bay windows were installed to provide more light and additional vistas of the Hudson River. A new retaining wall was erected on that side as well. The improvements also included a new green slate roof.

Inside the house, the upgrades were equally impressive. They included a new entrance hall of white limestone, complete with carved stone benches. The home's original hall was reconfigured by eliminating partitions and replacing them with Gothic-style wooden screens used to display Gobelin tapestries. A new mosaic floor was installed and wrought iron lanterns were substituted for old lighting fixtures. Wrought iron was also used for what was described as the finest andirons and fireback in the country. They were designed by Mr. Untermyer's architect, who was also responsible for a super-sized French Renaissance fireplace, fashioned of Caen stone, in one of the large rooms opening onto the newly refurbished hall. French influence was noticeable, as well, in the Louis XV–style reception room just across the hall. A Louis XVI salon, in white and gold, continued the French theme. A nearby den for the exclusive use of the wealthy homeowner was a bit more subdued, with its ebony and gold adornments.

Impressive though it was, the first floor paled in comparison with the second, where the hall had been transformed into an art gallery, its red tapestry walls covered with paintings. The second floor was also the location of a Turkish bath, adorned with stained glass and tile, and a swimming pool. To create this spa-like area, a number of small rooms were combined for the Turkish bath and the billiard room was eliminated to make way for the pool. After a relaxing swim and some time well spent in the Turkish bath, an ascent to the mansion's third floor tower room was a breeze. Here the style was Pompeiian, and lovely though this interior space was, the real attraction was the river view, something that never failed to impress visitors. Of course, those lucky enough to be invited to Greystone found the house and grounds overwhelmingly beautiful as well. Richard Croker, leader of New York City's Tammany Hall Democratic Party club, who paid a return visit to Greystone in 1908, was positively enchanted by the place. He had been there once before, in the 1880s, to see Samuel J. Tilden but found the estate much more to his liking this time, thanks to all of Samuel Untermyer's improvements. Comparing Greystone to updated estates in Ireland, he exclaimed that the modernized home was considerably more beautiful than it had been in Tilden's day. Given the time, effort, and money Greystone's proud new owner had devoted to improving the place, inside and out, this is not surprising, but despite the grand refurbishing project he had undertaken Untermyer found time for other things, including an unsuccessful effort to have Yonkers annexed to New York City.

The Annexation Movement

The city's expansion movement was not limited to Yonkers. New Rochelle and Mount Vernon were to be part of a greatly enlarged Bronx. That borough had been created from the southern part of Westchester County as a result of two earlier annexations, one in 1874 consisting of the townships west of the Bronx River and the other, in 1895, consisting of the townships east of the Bronx River. A decade later it seemed only natural, to some people, including a former Yonkers mayor, John Peene, that the mega-metropolis to the south would just keep expanding. His motivation for favoring the dissolution of the independent city of Yonkers was a desire for rapid transit, something the New York Central Railroad would not provide. Peene's views were shared by E. K. Martin, president of the Yonkers Board of Trade, who blamed the railroad for lagging real estate prices and limited population growth. Martin insisted that Yonkers would have had 250,000 residents by 1905 had it not been for the inadequate and expensive New York Central rail service.

In all fairness, a few years earlier, in 1901, the New York Central had proposed a solution, namely direct service from the Battery, at the tip of Manhattan, to Yonkers. This plan would have entailed running trains on the tracks of the company that owned the Manhattan elevated railroad and then on the tracks of the Putnam Division of the New York Central. Before this could happen, electrification of the Manhattan elevated line had to be completed and an agreement worked out between the elevated company and the New York Central. Such an arrangement would have enabled the Central to provide better service to its suburban riders and would have alleviated congestion at Grand Central Station but, alas, this wasn't meant to be, and as a result, suburban residents suffered. By 1905 the situation was so bad that a committee composed of Yonkers citizens and members of the board of aldermen investigated the deterioration of rail service. The upshot of their work was a formal resolution demanding a fare cut. If the railroad would not accede to this demand, the next step would be for Yonkers to seek annexation to New York City.

It would be another six years before an annexation bill was introduced in the New York State Legislature. The proposed law called for making Yonkers the sixth borough of New York City, and it contained a provision for a citywide referendum on annexation. The merits of joining forces with the gigantic metropolis to its south were debated, in the spring of 1911, at the Yonkers Armory, before an audience of 2,500 "gathered from every section of Yonkers and from every class of the population."[12] In the course of the debate, Samuel Untermyer insisted that New York was "a much-slandered city," with a "government as good as any in the world . . . and better than that of any city in the United States."[13] As for the belief held by many people that New York was a crime-ridden city, Untermyer blamed the press for creating this impression. He went on to argue that the annexation of Yonkers would be a good economic move. The real bottom line, as far as Untermyer was concerned, was that Yonkers had much to gain by annexation and that its development would be retarded if it passed up the chance to become part of the great city to its south. Although the audience was divided on the subject of annexation, just a month after the debate Yonkers residents joined citizens of New Rochelle and Mount Vernon to voice their opposition to annexation before the New York State Senate's Cities Committee, and for the time being that was the end of the matter.

The Millionaire Straphanger: John Emory Andrus

Annexation wasn't the only political issue to surface in the early 1900s. Another important matter facing Yonkers was the city's status as a third-class city. This became a cause célèbre during the term of the so-called Millionaire Straphanger, Mayor John E. Andrus, who, despite his vast wealth and position as founder and CEO of the Arlington Chemical Company, one of the city's major businesses, rode the subway. Under New York State law, municipalities with populations of 250,000 were first-class cities while those with at least 50,000 inhabitants were second-class cities. Municipalities with fewer than 50,000 people were classified as third-class. Yonkers met the population requirements to become a second-class city, a designation that would have resulted in greater governmental autonomy. In 1904, Yonkers aldermen voted to revise the city's charter in preparation for securing second-class status. Mayor Andrus, who had been elected the year before, was all for it. Under the revised charter, the lines of wards or voting districts were redrawn and the number of aldermen was reduced.

This was not to everyone's liking, including the New York State Citizens Committee, which advised Yonkers to apply under the uniform charter for second-class cities. Andrus, however, branded the uniform charter "inadequate" but he conceded that "our charter can't pass"; in the end his recommendation was to "shelve the whole proposition."[14] Andrus then pushed through a measure postponing the charter issue for two years. His explanation for this about-face was that "it would have cost the city $30,000 more a year to operate" under the new charter.[15] Some of the aldermen refuted this, but Andrus was adamant.

He had demonstrated similar tenacity soon after taking office by shelving plans for a new city hall, which he deemed too costly. He also refused to sanction the long-standing practice of distributing end-of-year paychecks to city employees before Christmas. In Andrus's view it was "contrary to business practice to pay people in advance."[16] The mayor proceeded to cut municipal spending and in the process incurred the wrath of many Yonkers residents, including the president of the school board, who initiated legal action that resulted in the State Supreme Court ordering Andrus to restore funds for badly needed school repairs. Despite his fiscal conservatism, when the city found itself in the position of not being able to borrow money, except at a high rate of interest, Andrus saved the day by signing for a loan at a favorable interest rate, reflecting his own sterling credit rating.

Other positive developments during Andrus's tenure as mayor were a new sewer system and the opening of the first Yonkers Public Library. Yet, despite the praise he received for moving the library out of the high school and into a splendid new building donated by steel magnate and philanthropist Andrew Carnegie, Andrus found himself on the firing line because of divisiveness on the board and commissioners of the Yonkers Police Department. While the commissioners engaged in verbal duels, "a point of tragic-comedy was reached when the Democrats complained that the two heaviest men in the department . . . had been placed on horseback because of politics, presumably increasing wear and tear on animals bought by the taxpayers."[17] Andrus reconstituted the board and commissioners but more opposition awaited him, this time from the Anti-Saloon League, whose leaders expected the teetotaling Mayor to "crack down hard on saloons," and when he didn't they interpreted his inaction as tolerance of "the easy drinking that went on in political circles around him."[18] The Anti-Saloon League then "organized anti-Andrus factions," which persuaded some of the city's churches to designate an evening in November 1905 "as a special time to pray for the city."[19]

Despite everything he endured as mayor, John Andrus remained active in politics. From 1905 until 1913 he served in the House of Representatives where he proved to be

> a better listener than a talker. . . . Unlike many colleagues, his idea of conversation was not a filibuster . . . he was a legislative toiler, one of the troops who keep the regiments in motion. Of him, it can be pointed out that he believed in the GOP and backed it with his vote.[20]

The Industrial Elite

The Yonkers to which Andrus returned following his years in Congress was a more robust city than the one he had presided over as mayor. The Alexander Smith and Sons Carpet Company, Otis Elevator, the Federal Sugar Refining Company, the National Sugar Refining Company, the Habirshaw Cable and Wire Company, and many smaller firms manufacturing products ranging from beer to dry goods were doing well. Some of these companies had been mainstays of the city's industrial base since the mid-nineteenth century; others had been established in the late 1800s. In the early years of the twentieth century a changing of the guard occurred in some of these firms. At Alexander Smith and Sons, for example, one era ended and another began when Warren B. Smith died while on a trip to Algiers in 1903. The bulk of his $40,000,000 estate went to relatives, with five nieces and nephews receiving $1,000,000 each. There was a bequest of $50,000 to St. John's Hospital, $250,000 to his stepmother, $100,000 to his sister, Eva Cochran, $50,000 to a cousin, and sums ranging from $200 to $5,000 to his servants. Seventeen employees of the carpet company received amounts ranging from $5,000 to $200,000, with the largest sums going to a former president and a former treasurer of Alexander Smith and Sons. Warren Smith's nephew, Alexander Smith Cochran, who became head of the company following his uncle's death, received the very considerable residue of the estate.

Six years later, when Eva Smith Cochran, daughter of Alexander Smith, founder of the carpet company, and mother of Alexander Smith Cochran died, employees who had worked at the carpet company for a minimum of twenty years received $1,000. All told, after a meticulous review of personnel records by the company's paymaster, three hundred employees were rewarded for their years of service. Genuinely interested in improving the lot of Yonkers residents, Mrs. Cochran and her husband

William F. Cochran, who predeceased her, had funded local institutions, including St. John's Hospital, for which they provided the land as well as an endowment. A few years before her death, Eva Smith Cochran was characterized by *The New York Times* as "one of the best known women in Yonkers on account of her various charities and benefactions," in a front page account of a freak accident that had befallen her at her summer home in Maine.[21] While seated next to a window during an electrical storm, she was struck by lightning and blinded.

In 1900, fate dealt an even worse blow to Halcyon Skinner, the brilliant inventor of various looms for manufacturing carpet and a man "whose long connection with the Smith Carpet works made his figure a familiar one to thousands of the operatives of the factory, while his democratic and unassuming ways made him many friends."[22] As a young man working at Alexander Smith and Sons at the company's original location in West Farms, one of the communities annexed by New York City, Skinner tinkered with the factory machinery, vastly improving it. He then went on to invent a loom for weaving figures, rather than the customary stripes, into carpet. Other innovative looms followed and no sooner had he invented something new than Skinner set about improving it. In some instances he managed to double the output of looms he had invented. His inventions were of utmost importance in the expansion of Alexander Smith and Sons from approximately three hundred employees in 1874 to nearly seven thousand in the early twentieth century. Sadly, when the new century was not even a year old, Skinner was struck by a New York Central Railroad train in Yonkers and killed. The tragedy occurred when Skinner, whose home was located on the Hudson, strolled through his back gate, and as he had often done before, "went down to the tracks, either to go to his boathouse or else with the intention of walking to . . . the Corinthian Yacht Club, of which he was a member."[23] Seeing a southbound train heading in his direction, he attempted to get out of harm's way, only to be struck by a northbound train. For another famous Yonkers resident, Robert P. Getty, who had built the city's famous Getty House hotel in 1851, death came quietly, in 1902, following several years of declining health.

Less than a decade later Yonkers was mourning the passing of yet another prominent resident, Ervin Saunders, one of the principals in the firm of Saunders & Sons, Incorporated, manufacturers of machinery, a company founded by his father. Ervin Saunders was sixty-one when he died suddenly after having been "in delicate health for more than 20 years."[24] A lifelong bachelor, Saunders left his shares in the family company to his brother and small bequests to two nieces, but the bulk of his estate went to various Yonkers institutions. Saunders considered it his "duty as well as a privilege and pleasure to devote a substantial portion of my estate to what seems to me to be the best interest of my home city."[25] Toward that end, he bequeathed $50,000 to the Yonkers Public Library with the stipulation that the income from the gift be used to purchase nonfiction books. Like many other communities that received splendid new library buildings from Andrew Carnegie, Yonkers had to supply the books. In addition to funding the purchase of books, the will of Ervin Saunders provided a $450,000 permanent endowment for the Yonkers Homeopathic Hospital and Maternity Institution, in memory of his mother. To memorialize his father, he left the rest of his estate to the City of Yonkers for the creation of a trade school under the auspices of the board of education. His will required the school to offer evening classes for the benefit of students who worked during the day. The will also stipulated that $60,000 was to be used to build the new school and another $60,000 to equip it, with the remainder as an endowment for the upkeep of the institution. As a public school, what would become known as simply "Saunders" was open to all, including the city's growing immigrant population.

The Working Class

Joining English and Scottish immigrants, who were recruited by Alexander Smith when his company was in its infancy, were Irish, Poles, Slavs, and Ukrainians. As time went on, the first generation of skilled workers from the British Isles moved into supervisory jobs and unskilled newcomers were employed to tend machinery, which performed the tasks once done by skilled laborers. When economic slowdowns occurred and domestic and foreign orders for Alexander Smith and Sons carpets dwindled, unskilled workers and recent hires were especially vulnerable. During the panic or depression of 1893–97, John Masefield, who became England's Poet Laureate after returning to his native land, was one of those dismissed from the carpet company. According to Masefield's estimate, five to six thousand workers were jobless but at least double that number were affected when one took into account the impact of the layoffs on workers' families. "Most of the married men could not see beyond the mill; it was their life," Masefield declared in his book *In the Mill,* describing his experiences at Alexander Smith and Sons.[26] He went on to say: "Few of the unmarried men ever saved money. Few of either party had expected any horror of this kind; their ship went from under their feet."[27] Traumatized though they were by the sudden closing of the mill, workers and their families managed to survive, thanks to the generosity of their fellow citizens. Masefield was so impressed by this that he stated:

> I shall never forget the universal sympathy in that stricken town; how kind all people were in those days; how gladly they shared what they had, and how the tradesmen . . . lowered their rates at once, to the cutting off of all possible profit to themselves, so that their clients should not have too hard a time.[28]

Given the fact that most of the workers lived within walking distance of the mill, some of them in company housing, layoffs and strikes at the carpet company had a profound effect upon the City of Yonkers. Far less significant than the layoffs of the 1890s, which continued to influence the thinking of workers into the next century, was a lesser-known incident in American labor history, involving the Triangle Shirtwaist Company, a little more than a year before the dreadful fire that claimed the lives of 146 workers at its headquarters in Greenwich Village. When fire broke out in March 1911, Triangle workers, most of them young women from the Lower East Side, were trapped because the factory's owners had locked the doors to the fire escapes to prevent union organizers from getting into the building. Prior to the fire, in the midst of a strike called by the Shirt Waist Makers' Union in 1909, the Triangle Company opened a factory in Yonkers. The new facility was staffed by strikebreakers sent up from New York. When union pickets arrived in Yonkers, some of the girls quit only to be replaced by other strikebreakers. Yonkers police became involved after fighting broke out between pickets and strikebreakers. Everyone was hauled into Yonkers Police Court where they got off with only a warning, mainly because of conflicting testimony. At that point, the owners of the Triangle Shirtwaist Company threw in the towel and announced that they would close the Yonkers factory.

The frequently adversarial relationship between labor and management was evident not only during strikes but on one extraordinary occasion in 1903 when labor leaders accepted an invitation from industrialist John C. Havemeyer to appear on the stage of the Yonkers Music Hall for a "discussion of the principles and methods of labor."[29] Like many business leaders of the time, Havemeyer, a sugar refiner, was concerned that the balance of power between capital and labor was tipping toward the latter and he decided to challenge union leaders by publishing a pamphlet containing sixteen specific questions. Havemeyer then rented the Yonkers Music Hall and invited three prominent labor leaders to appear on the stage to respond to the questions. Havemeyer, accompanied by family members, occupied a box close to the stage and remained stoical as some of the speakers made vindictive comments about the rich. Havemeyer did not respond. Indeed, prior to the meeting, which *The Yonkers Herald* claimed was "captured by the captains of Socialism and turned into a Socialistic pow wow," an attempt had been made to persuade him to take questions from the labor leaders during the gathering but he refused, saying he might be willing to do so at a later date.[30]

In advance of the much-anticipated event, a thousand tickets were distributed and when the big day arrived, every seat in the house, including two hundred on the stage, was occupied. So many people were eager to attend that the city issued a permit for a simultaneous meeting on the street. As soon as the labor leaders replied to questions inside, other labor representatives paraphrased their answers and presented them to the crowd outside. The first few questions dealing with the rationale for unions were answered by J. T. Windell of the Federation of Labor. He noted that Standard Oil and other trusts raised their prices without consulting the public, implying that unions, which he conceded were sometimes called the Labor Trust, had the right to organize workers without consulting the management of the companies employing those workers. As for the goals of unions, Windell said that they "were to secure for those who produced the greatest part of the country's wealth a proper share in that wealth, and to protect the laborers and their families."[31] When asked whether labor's intention was to oppose the accumulation of wealth, Windell replied: "This is a foolish question. It is far from the intention of any sane man to oppose the accumulation of wealth, but we do intend properly to regulate theft. Regulating the man who can pile up a thousand millions is just as necessary as regulating pickpockets and gamblers."[32]

In answer to a question, which was prefaced by the statement that it was Mr. Havemeyer's understanding that fifteen different occupations composed the Yonkers branch of the American Federation of Labor, Windell said that if one category of workers went out on strike, other members of the Federation would not join them. Another speaker, D. L. Russell of the Commercial Telegraphers of New York, pointed out that most union members were "level-headed."[33] He also addressed the subject of child labor, noting that "the time to enjoy life is when you are young, and not when you have grown old laboring after the dollars."[34] Toward the end of the meeting, Mr. Windell looked John C. Havemeyer straight in the eye and demanded that he answer sixteen questions about the sugar trust in particular and trusts in general. Windell was amenable to Havemeyer taking his time in arranging a future meeting to respond to questions posed by labor leaders, but he was adamant that such a gathering be held. Nothing came of this, but nearly a decade later the sugar trust was subjected to public scrutiny by a Congressional committee investigating the American Sugar Refining Company, which was generally regarded as the sugar trust.

Claus A. Spreckels, president of the Federal Sugar Refining Company, which operated a huge plant in Yonkers, testified that at several of his firm's plants, including the one in Yonkers, men who were actually in the employ of the American Sugar Refining Company had damaged machinery and deposited dead animals in barrels of refined sugar. Spreckels said that his company had experienced these problems as soon as it opened the Yonkers plant in 1902. Problems persisted for a year and were so bad that one night he himself went to the plant where he had workers open sealed barrels, only to learn that they contained foreign matter. He fired the workers, who promptly demanded their pay. "I told them they better go to the people who had employed them to do the dirty work," he recounted.[35] The men threatened to sue, and Spreckels would have actually liked the judicial process to take over because it would have enabled his own attorneys to cross-examine the men, but the suit did not materialize. His problems with industrial sabotage notwithstanding, Spreckels continued to operate the Yonkers plant, producing three thousand barrels of refined sugar each day or roughly twice what another firm, the National Sugar Refining Company, made during the first decade of the twentieth century. By 1917, Federal's eight hundred employees were turning out refined sugar twenty-four hours a day. Both Federal and National closed soon after the Great Depression struck but the economic debacle wasn't the only thing that caused them to cease operations. Tariff legislation resulted in many refineries moving offshore to Cuba. In 1938, a company producing liquid sugar took over the Federal Refining Company's plant.

Strikers and Strikebreakers

At one point during its heyday the Federal Sugar Refining Company was forced to shut down, when the City of Yonkers obtained an injunction restraining the company from burning soft coal and permitting dense black smoke and cinders to escape from its soaring chimney. Extremely diligent in safeguarding the health of its citizens, the city intervened whenever the board of health felt it was necessary. In 1907, during an especially nasty strike by trolley car workers employed by the Yonkers Street Railway Company, several hundred strikebreakers imported by the company were found to be living in squalid conditions in the trolley barns. After touring the barns, the city's health officer concluded that an epidemic was likely to occur if the premises were not cleaned up immediately. The president of the company was subpoenaed that very day to answer charges of violating the Yonkers sanitary code. He was fined ten dollars but this was the least of his problems, because the day after the trolley barns were inspected, company trolleys were badly damaged as strikebreakers attempted to put them back in service.

Intending to make a bold statement, the company's president decided to run the cars in the middle of the day. The timing could not have been worse, because the streets were thronged with factory workers on lunch break. Sympathetic to the striking employees of the Yonkers Street Railway Company, they immediately began shouting when the first trolley emerged from the barns. Although a mounted police officer rode directly in front of the trolley, he and other members of the Yonkers police force were no match for the crowd, which was "in ugly humor."[36] As the trolley slowed to avoid hitting a disabled wagon, the mob hurled bricks and stones at the trolley, breaking all of its windows and sending it back to the barns. Other trolleys dispatched by the company met a similar fate. Mobs set bonfires in their paths, causing derailments, and some of the strikebreaking crews fled for their lives. An especially large bonfire had to be extinguished by the Fire Department and several injured policemen were hospitalized.

As the situation deteriorated, the entire police force was called up and officers were told, in no uncertain words, that if they failed to do their duty there would be serious repercussions. The police arrested a number of young men in connection with the attacks on the trolleys, and the youths became local folk heroes cheered by sympathizers lining their path to the police station. The Yonkers Street Railway Company attempted to run several trolleys later in the afternoon, but angry mobs once again attacked the cars. In the opinion of *The New York Times,* which reported that three thousand people had been involved in the attacks, the day would "go down as the worst, from a standpoint of rowdyism and rioting, that Yonkers has ever known."[37]

The attacks on the trolleys prompted Mayor Frank Coyne to issue a proclamation calling upon the citizenry to maintain the peace. As rumors that the Yonkers Street Railway Company was planning to ask the governor to remove Mayor Coyne circulated, the mayor requested help from the sheriff of Westchester County. The next day the sheriff conferred with Yonkers officials, who by then had been informed in writing that the Yonkers Street Railway Company would hold the mayor and the city responsible for damages suffered by the company. The mayor was reluctant to see the New York State Militia called out until other means of maintaining order were tried. With strike sympathizers filling ash cans with heavy items and installing them on trolley tracks along Warburton Avenue, Riverdale Avenue, and Main Street, as well as stockpiling rocks and other potential missiles on the Croton Aqueduct path in preparation for attacks on Tuckahoe Line trolleys, which ran through an arch in the aqueduct, it appeared that the mayor was being too cautious. Perhaps he held out hope that clergymen, who were said to have met with the strikers at Hibernian Hall, could broker a settlement between the workers and the company. The mayor's delaying tactics paid off, because a day later the Yonkers Street Railway Company threw in the towel and not only recognized the union but agreed to take back the strikers without penalizing them for anything done during the strike. A committee, which included the clergymen who had been instrumental in bringing the two sides together, was appointed to determine wage increases for the rehired employees. This proved to be a win–win situation for everyone, including five thousand Yonkers commuters who relied upon trolleys to get to their closest New York Central Railroad stations.

Three years later, commuters had to don their walking shoes again when nine trolley lines serving Yonkers were shut down by striking employees demanding wage increases. The eight-day strike ended when a judge, acting as arbitrator, recommended a two cents per hour wage increase, which the strikers accepted. In 1913, employees of the Yonkers Street Railway Company were hopeful that a strike, which began when a handful of Yonkers trolleymen were dismissed after refusing to break in a new man sent up from New York by management, would be settled by arbitration. The Yonkers Chamber of Commerce arranged a conference but the ten delegates selected to represent the striking workers withdrew, claiming that the company's president had demeaned them. A formal statement issued by the strikers characterized the president as a petty tyrant and asked him to retract statements he had made questioning the intelligence and integrity of the strikers. As the strike was about to enter its third week, hope resurfaced when the company president made a verbal promise to the Public Service Commission, in the presence of strikers' representatives and the mayor of Yonkers, to accept arbitration. Although he refused to put anything in writing, the commission's stenographer had taken everything down and when this was released to the public, the president had no choice but to abide by what he had said. This meant accepting the recommendation of the Public Service Commission that arbitration be employed to settle matters upon which the workers and the company could not agree, and that the strikers return to their jobs, without penalty, under the terms of their prior contract.

Even before the dust settled in the 1913 strike, the Yonkers Street Railway Company was amenable to the idea of a buyout by the City of Yonkers. As far back as 1906, proposals for the elimination of the company had surfaced. That year, a group of concerned Yonkers residents, led by a Wall Street attorney, investigated the possibility of forming their own company to run trolleys on the tracks of the Yonkers Street Railway Company. Since their demands for better service had been ignored, they considered taking advantage of a provision of the New York State Constitution that forbade the granting of exclusive franchises. They interpreted this to mean that although the Yonkers Street Railway Company had a franchise from the city to run its cars, other companies could use the same tracks by compensating the city. This plan was scrapped in favor of one calling for municipal ownership of trolleys, something that made sense to many residents when the Yonkers Street Railway Company experienced financial problems in the aftermath of the 1907 strike. From 1908 through 1911, the company was in receivership. Although the line regained its independence and provided new cars and upgraded tracks, Yonkers riders, who had endured three strikes in six years, were not overly impressed by these enhancements. What they really desired was reliable and safe service.

Safety was a major issue because going back to the very beginning of the century, there had been serious accidents. In 1900, at approximately 9 p.m. on a June evening, nearly two dozen passengers ended up sprawled all over the interior of a Yonkers house after the trolley in which they were riding went out of control while going downhill on Park Avenue. A mechanical malfunction rendered the brakes inoperable and the car went flying across an intersection, demolished a wall of a private home on Ashburton Avenue and came to rest inside the house. Miraculously, only two people were injured, and very slightly at that. Happily, the occupants of the home were not in the front room where the trolley ended up. Initially, they believed there had been an earthquake. Three months after this accident, two Yonkers trolleys traveling in opposite directions on the same track collided with considerable force. Three women occupying the front seat of one of the trolleys received minor injuries when they tried to jump off. Other passengers on both trolleys suffered serious cuts and bruises and a man who jumped to avoid the collision hit the ground and was critically injured.

In 1901, a motorman's decision to proceed rather than wait for a late trolley coming from the other direction to pass, led to a crash near the Dunwoodie station on the trolley line running between Yonkers and Mount Vernon. Two passengers were badly injured. In 1902, a trolley headed for Yonkers from Hastings-on-Hudson had just made it across a bridge spanning a deep ravine on Warburton Avenue when the steel superstructure of the span slipped. Heavy rains and melting snow had swollen the stream flowing through the ravine and the rushing water undermined the bridge's supports. The precipitation was so heavy that many streets in the Saw Mill River Valley were under water. The moquette works of the Alexander Smith and Sons Carpet Company, where carpet with a deep tufted pile was manufactured, were closed when water rose to the level of the firepits at the division's riverside location. The resulting uncompensated layoff was a hardship for the workers but it paled in comparison with the suffering of the sixty-one people involved in a 1906 crash of a Yonkers Street Railway Company trolley linking Fordham and Yonkers.

Heading down Horseshoe Hill in Lincoln Park, the trolley jumped the tracks after its brakerod failed. A seventh-month-old child suffered repeated head injuries as a result of being crushed underfoot by fleeing passengers scrambling to get out of the car at the bottom of the hill. The baby died a short time later. The child's mother and an older sibling had cuts, bruises, and internal injuries. Much to their credit, passengers and crew of another trolley that arrived on the scene pulled the injured from the wreckage and three drivers of a new type of private vehicle, the auto, which was still quite rare in Yonkers, piled some of the injured into their cars and drove them to St. Joseph's Hospital. One Good Samaritan, a woman who lived near the scene of the accident, arrived with sheets and linens and began bandaging the wounded. While she was working on a female passenger, someone grabbed a gold watch that had been affixed to her blouse by a stickpin. The thief ran off with both the timepiece and the pin and disappeared in the crowd. In the aftermath of the accident, the Yonkers Common Council discussed the possibility of requiring trolley companies seeking to extend their franchises to operate within the city to substitute air brakes for the less reliable hand brakes then in use.

Safety was of utmost importance, but riders were concerned about other things as well. When trolley lines linking Yonkers with the Bronx eliminated transfers and began to charge additional fares, the City of Yonkers filed a complaint with the Public Service Commission. Compounding the problem was the fact that Yonkers residents bound for New York had not only been accustomed to paying a five-cent fare for the entire trip but they had been able to remain in the same car even though it traveled over the lines of different companies. Along with the elimination of transfers came the phasing out of through service. Twenty-five thousand unhappy commuters were required to pay double fares and change cars as well.

Riding the Rails

When it came to mass transit, Yonkers residents of the early twentieth century had legitimate grievances against not only the trolley companies but the New York Central Railroad. Like the trolleys, the railroad was not immune to accidents, whether because of mechanical malfunctions or human error. The latter was responsible for the death of the driver of a wagon who was heading down to the docks to pick up a load of coal. Having stopped at the railroad's Ashburton Avenue grade crossing, waiting patiently for a southbound train to go through, he proceeded to drive across the tracks after the gateman raised the barrier only to be hit by a northbound train. The wagon driver's horses were severed in two and he himself was ejected from the vehicle and killed. The driver left behind eight children. Two years later, at the Washington Avenue crossing, a southbound express train hit an engine that was attempting to get out of a switch by going in reverse. As the engine crossed the main tracks it was hit broadside by the express train whose engine was sliced in half. A number of its passenger cars derailed, causing pandemonium. Amazingly, only one person, a Yonkers man, was injured. He suffered a concussion but came to, as did six female passengers who fainted. In 1903, two freight trains collided near the Glenwood station during a major snowstorm. The result was "tracks blockaded for two hours."[38] Given the poor visibility, one train plowed into the other and sparks from its engine ignited the second train. Although this accident was weather related, the fact that accidents at grade crossings had occurred going back to the nineteenth century resulted in a concerted effort to deal with this problem. In 1906, the New York State Assembly enacted legislation requiring public hearings on any future expansion or alterations involving the crossing of exist- ing thoroughfares. Following the hearings, the New York State Railroad Commission could either permit new grade crossings or require that the tracks be elevated with the railroad bearing the full expense.

Besides safety, commuters were concerned about fares. With Mayor Coyne taking the lead, Yonkers commuters were determined to force the New York Central to lower fares on its lines running through Yonkers: the Hudson River Division, the Putnam Division, and the Harlem Division. Toward that end, a conference involving the mayor, the Yonkers Board of Trade, delegates from taxpayers' associations, and representatives of the New York Central was held in 1906. At this gathering the railroad assured the people of Yonkers that fares would be reduced as soon as the new Grand Central Terminal had been completed. In the interim, the Harlem Division was electrified. This meant comfortable new cars, with beautiful interior lights, but when the first four trains powered by electricity left New York for Yonkers, they went only as far as Highbridge using the new source of power. From there to Yonkers steam locomotives were used because the railroad was still working on the electrification of lines in Westchester.

Before long, commuters were wondering why it was taking so long to finish the job and to replace all of the old rolling stock with new passenger cars. The continued use of antiquated equipment during the transitional period between partial and full electrification was cited as the cause of interminable delays on the Harlem Division. Dissatisfied with assurances from the railroad that its rolling stock was reliable, commuters from Yonkers and other communities on the Harlem line held a big meeting at the Tuckahoe Lyceum in January 1907. Participants decided to form a committee to campaign for better service. The plan was to distribute forms to commuters to enable them to document any problems they experienced. These forms were to be sent to the committee's secretary once a week; from there commuters' complaints would go to both the railroad and to the New York State Railroad Commission. Citing "delays costly to business and professional pursuits and vexations to social and domestic life," the lengthy resolution emerging from the meeting criticized the railroad's management for sanctioning the continued use of substandard cars that were often "overheated, overcrowded . . . and contain many broken seats."[39] If the railroad did not heed the complaints of the committee, which was formed to represent commuters, the plan was to petition the state attorney general to revoke the New York Central's lease of the Harlem line and possibly to withdraw its charter. But, instead of getting better, things got worse!

In July, Mayor Coyne felt compelled to host a mass meeting of disgruntled commuters to protest a fare hike after the Crestwood Citizens' Association passed a resolution denouncing a recent increase, contending that it was not only unnecessary but illegal. The association also complained about the New York Central's decision to close the Crestwood station at 7 p.m. Public Service Commission hearings on the fare increase were held in Albany, and Mayor Coyne kept up the pressure by demanding a five-cent fare between Yonkers and New York and better service overall. Three years later, fares were still uppermost on the minds of commuters. With a fare increase looming, Yonkers mayor James T. Lennon fired off a letter to New York State governor Charles E. Hughes in which he asserted that the fare increase would have a negative effect on the real estate market. Despite the inevitable fare increases, this was not the case. The "Queen City of the Hudson" continued to attract new residents, many of whom commuted to the city on the Central's various lines, including the Putnam Division, where conditions were so bad that *The Yonkers Herald* declared "Bryn Mawr in Despair Over Putnam R.R. Service."[40] Now and again, the railroad made some improvements on its various lines. These included a new Glenwood station. In 1911 when the New York State Public Service Commission allowed the New York Central to phase out the Glenwood Station on Point Street, it insisted that a new station, complete with elevators, be erected on Glenwood Avenue and that the fare differential between that station and the main station in downtown Yonkers remain the same.

A Little (or Not So Little) Home in the Suburbs

Affordable, safe, reliable, and comfortable transportation within the sprawling City of Yonkers and between Yonkers and the mega-metropolis to the south was a prerequisite for suburbanization. Although the service on all divisions of the New York Central left something to be desired, families seeking a better quality of life than what Manhattan, and even the outer boroughs, offered were increasingly drawn to Yonkers. Most put down permanent roots but some new arrivals were only temporary residents. Among the latter was a band of gypsies who camped in Yonkers on the eve of the twentieth century. Their sojourn in the "Queen City of the Hudson" was covered in an unusually lengthy article in *The New York Times*. The piece began with the observation that "Nepperhan Ways lies in the valley west of the high hill that is the pride of Yonkers."[41] The rather exuberant feature writer then proceeded to describe this idyllic spot as "a countryside of cottages, meadow, and winding road."[42] One can only wonder what the inhabitants of those new homes thought when a gypsy caravan pulled into their neighborhood. Soon wagons were unloaded, tents pitched, and cooking fires started. The gypsies' makeshift village was captured on film by a *Times* photographer and nine pictures were used to illustrate the article. A picture may be worth a thousand words, but the reporter couldn't refrain from using excessive verbiage to describe the encampment. "The Camp was framed thickly with trees, rarely beautiful in their foliage," he said, adding: "To the back a high hill climbed, green carpeted, with many a tree here and there."[43] Their makeshift quarters apparently suited the gypsies just fine, for, as the reporter observed: "Children, horses, and dogs alike drank in the happy hours of primeval simplicity."[44]

The gypsies' living arrangements were a far cry from those of the new suburbanites who put down roots in Yonkers in the early twentieth century. Given its proximity to New York City and its varied topography, it was only natural that the City of Yonkers would attract families yearning for the type of suburban ambience real estate developers were only too willing to provide. One of the leading developers, the American Real Estate Company, went all out in creating a model community at Park Hill. In the first decade of the twentieth century, homes sprouted on this promontory overlooking the Hudson. For a brief time, there was also a hotel, the Hendrick Hudson, on the western slope of the hill. Erected by the American Real Estate Company, the seven-story, 230 room luxury hotel was an architectural clone of Quebec's famous Château Frontenac. Sparing no expense, the developer installed a direct connection between the hotel lobby and the New York Central's Putnam Division station at the bottom of the hill. Guests arriving by train were to enter a 150-foot tunnel and then take an elevator to the hotel lobby. Just when the arduous and expensive job of building and outfitting the turreted grand hotel had been completed, fire broke out. The huge conflagration, which occurred on March 31, 1901, lit up the night sky. By morning all that remained of this magnificent building was the elevator shaft, the tunnel hewn from solid rock, stone arches, and retaining walls. The hotel was not rebuilt. The tunnel remained a place of endless fascination for Yonkers children until it was eventually sealed by the city, which acquired the site in 1929. Through the years various projects, including a South Yonkers High School and garden apartments, were proposed for the eight acre site. In 1946 the property became Leslie Sutherland Park, named for Mayor Sutherland.

By that time, Park Hill was a mature suburb. Back in the early 1900s, however, Park Hill was in its infancy and the American Real Estate Company, which had "conceived the thought of creating somewhere in the vicinity of Manhattan Island, on its direct lines of communication, an ideal community, in which every modern improvement would supplement noble natural scenery," undertook a major campaign to ensure the future of its enterprise.[45] In addition to the usual newspaper advertisements, the company funded a stunning, if somewhat effusive, four page spread in the fashionable *Country Life* magazine. The piece, heavily illustrated with nearly a dozen pictures, began with a statement about Park Hill's ideal location "less than three-quarters of a mile from the city's northern edge."[46] After a brief, introductory remark about the community's beautiful setting, the inset commented on the environment, saying that Park Hill was "perfectly healthy, ideal in summer, and comfortable and invigorating in winter, and free from the greatest of all pests, the mosquito."[47] Since mosquito-borne illnesses, including malaria, were not unknown in the New York area at the time, this was an important selling point, as was the peace and quiet of the place. Targeting middle-class buyers, the *Country Life* inset said that "this most delightful of New York's suburbs offers an escape to those of moderate income from the city's . . . crowded streets and box-like apartments, for the standard of the little community at Park Hill is refinement, rather than great wealth."[48]

Readers were then taken on a hypothetical trip to this unique Yonkers community. Using, as its premise, the notion that a New Yorker had been invited by a friend living in Park Hill to spend a weekend there, the person perusing *Country Life* began the journey with a ride on the New York Central, which resulted in the visitor being "rested and a trifle refreshed by a glimpse of woodland and stream."[49] Upon arriving at the station, he walks up the hill breathing "deeply of the pure air."[50] Once at his friend's home he is "met by a charming hostess, whose brow is not all furrowed by the strain and rush of life in a great city, and several rosy-cheeked children . . . greet him"; one of those youngsters, "the sturdy boy of the family," is immediately assigned the duty of escorting the visitor to the country club where his friend awaits him.[51] As they stroll along "the pleasant streets, past houses whose shady lawns and verandas look most inviting," the guest suddenly "remembers regretfully that he has just signed a lease for another year at $2,000 for an apartment on the upper West Side, in which he lives with his wife and pale little daughter."[52] Upon arriving at the country club, the city dweller "looks on enviously at the people who are enjoying themselves so hugely."[53] Sitting on the veranda, following a game of billiards, the visitor confides that he had no idea that this type of community existed whereupon his host "beams upon him, as this suburb is his pet enthusiasm."[54]

Of course, it was also the "pet enthusiasm" of the American Real Estate Company, which did its best to lure *Country Life* readers with its tantalizing descriptions of Park Hill's many attractions. To underscore the point that there was so much to do in this new community, the author of the *Country Life* piece had the city dweller returning to the country club in the evening for "a dance which young and old alike attend."[55] Presumably, he did not dance the night away, because early on Sunday morning he joined his host for horseback riding in nearby Van Cortlandt Park. Then it was back to the house for breakfast and down time, which both guest and host probably needed, on the veranda perusing the Sunday papers. During the afternoon, the visitor enjoyed Sunday dinner with his host's family and before bidding them farewell to head back to his little family in the overcrowded city, he was taken on a drive to observe "the magnificent trees, perfect roads and sidewalks, and inquires concerning water, gas, electricity and sewers, and finds everything complete, and as convenient as his own apartment."[56]

At this point the hard sell began, as the advertising inset noted that Park Hill's building lots were fifty feet by one hundred feet and that homes erected on those lots cost a minimum of $5,000. By imposing a bottom-line figure and excluding two-family homes, the developers endeavored to ensure the community's future as a middle-class enclave. Since the heads of household in those middle-class families would be commuting to New York City, readers were informed that one could get to Park Hill on three rapid transit lines but that the community "is protected from the encroachment of the city by its elevation," and as "saloons, stores, factories and trolleys were excluded," Park Hill was "just the place in which to bring up a family."[57] Prospective residents were assured that "children of the best families" attended the nearby public schools and that "the children enjoy the out-of-door sports—the freedom of a real home, and association with refined boys and girls, as there is no foreign element at Park Hill."[58] In other words, for native-born middle-class white families this was the ideal place to raise children. Should he move there, the hypothetical visitor would see his daughter's cheeks "grow round and rosy, and her long, little legs stout and strong."[59] What more could anyone want? Not much, if you were the visitor who vowed to bring his wife and daughter to beautiful Park Hill. Anyone else considering purchasing one of the more than one hundred lots remaining was invited to contact the American Real Estate Company for a complimentary copy of "their little booklet, Park Hill the Distinctive."[60] Free copies of the booklet must have flown off the shelves because a March 1910 New York Times article characterized Park Hill as an enclave that had "attained a high and permanent character as a choice residential community."[61]

Appealing as Park Hill was, families seeking homes in Yonkers had many areas to choose from. Given the scarcity of single-family homes and the rapid escalation of prices in such New York City neighborhoods as the West Side and Washington Heights, developers moved across the city line erecting comfortable and, at least by middle-class standards, affordable homes. In new developments, water, sewer, and gas lines were installed and roads paved before homes were built. This eliminated the need to tear up streets each time a new house went up. Moreover, unlike in New York City, the streets in new developments were not required to intersect at right angles but could be serpentine, winding around to maximize views of the suburban landscape. Whether or not they were located on winding roads, new homes in Yonkers were very appealing to buyers even if they cost a minimum of $7,500, which was the case at Van Cortlandt Terrace, where every home had fifty feet of frontage and was set back twenty feet from the street.

Regardless of the size of one's budget, Yonkers had something to offer prospective home seekers, and properties in the city represented good value, a fact noted by *The New York Times* in a lengthy article published at the height of the spring buying season. This piece began with the observation that "Yonkers particularly commends itself to the homeseeker."[62] Citing the electrification of the New York Central's main line, the planned completion of electrification on the Putnam Division within a year, and trolley connections with the subway, the *Times* declared that Yonkers was almost "within the Manhattan rapid-transit zone."[63] Aside from good public transportation, Yonkers offered a variety of housing opportunities. Land was available in many parts of Yonkers and residents could enjoy country life "without its proverbial inconveniences."[64] Getting specific, the article listed a host of Yonkers neighborhoods, including Nepera Park, Nepperhan Heights, Armour Villa Park, Crestwood, Lawrence Park West, Bryn Mawr, Park Hill, Sherwood Park and Amacassin "to choose from."[65]

Needless to say, real estate agents interviewed for the article fully agreed, especially if their own firms were doing well. Such was the case with a broker who reported making three sales in South Yonkers the previous week. He was not only bullish on that section of the city but was convinced that prices throughout the city would keep escalating. Colleagues agreed. A South Broadway broker, for example, asserted: "There is no investment so permanently safe as to income or certain to ultimate profit as good Yonkers realty."[66] Alluding to an economic downturn that had begun the previous year, a Getty Square real estate agent observed that the market for small houses, whether for sale or rental, would remain strong irrespective of the national economy. Another broker allowed that some prospective buyers would wait to see the outcome of the 1908 presidential election before making a commitment, but he insisted that both prices and values would hold up. His opinion was shared by a colleague who declared there was no indication by residents of "any pressure to sell."[67]

Such optimism was warranted in view of the fact that the economic downturn known as the Panic of 1907 was not protracted. Buying, selling, and building continued in Yonkers, and within three years, a record price was set when a three-story brick building on the southwest corner of Main Street and Broadway was sold for $200,000. Located near the Getty House hotel, several banks and the new city hall, then under construction, this was prime business property. Activity in commercial real estate was matched by a brisk residential market, especially in the lower part of the city, which was experiencing a boom thanks to the construction of multifamily, as well as single-family, homes. Fourteen two-family houses on Elliott Avenue, five blocks north of the Yonkers/Bronx border, were offered for sale in 1909. In each house, the larger of the two apartments had nine rooms, albeit one bathroom, which was standard for the time, while the smaller apartment had six rooms and a bath. The nine-room unit was actually a duplex occupying the first two floors of the house. A major selling point was the fact that each house had a private staircase leading to the top floor apartment.

In the first decade of the twentieth century, in addition to two-family homes, developers erected three-story apartment buildings in South Yonkers. What made these structures so appealing was the fact that only one apartment, with all outside rooms, occupied a floor. Nearly a dozen buildings, each containing ten modest apartments, were built on Lawrence Street while spacious seven-room units were featured in buildings on Broadway in the vicinity of Ashburton Avenue. Before the decade ended, some new apartment buildings had elevators. As comfortable as apartment living might be, however, the dream of most residents of multifamily buildings was to eventually realize the goal of home ownership. Attaining that objective did not have to mean forsaking Yonkers. One could stay put and enjoy an enviable lifestyle that included "all of the benefits sought for in suburban homes."[68]

The Advent of the Automobile

Could one wish for anything more than a suburban home and a shiny new automobile to be used for pleasure drives throughout Yonkers and environs? The auto and suburbia are, after all, inextricably linked. Leisurely Sunday drives were often the prelude to house hunting in communities surrounding great cities. Once Sunday visitors became full-time suburban residents, they used their cars for shopping trips and commuting to the railroad station. The auto was an indispensable device facilitating the suburban lifestyle. At the very beginning of the twentieth century, however, before autos had displaced horses as a mode of transportation, cars were viewed less as utilitarian objects than as status symbols of the wealthy. They were rich men's toys used for tooling around estates. As cars became more reliable, owners ventured out onto the public roads, often terrifying pedestrians and horses alike, even if they weren't speeding. Of course, racing on public thoroughfares was unacceptable, whether one was at the wheel or holding the reins. Samuel Untermyer learned this lesson the hard way. Accustomed to driving himself to the railroad station in a bright yellow carriage pulled by two horses, Untermyer was often in a hurry and people took notice. A property owner on Warburton Avenue even contacted city authorities about Untermyer's recklessness at the reins. Acting on the complaint, the Yonkers Police Department assigned an officer from the bicycle squad to be on the lookout for Mr. Untermyer, who admitted that he liked to drive quickly but denied that his speed was excessive.

Some wealthy motorists managed to escape prosecution for speeding by placing the blame on their chauffeurs. Such was the case in 1902, when the autos of several prominent bankers were stopped as they traveled south on Warburton Avenue, a thoroughfare that had become a regular speedway. Exceeding the twelve miles per hour speed limit was so common that the city stationed an officer at the north end of Warburton to observe traffic. Upon seeing vehicles breaking the law, he phoned a station house to the south and policemen on duty there ventured out onto the street and stopped suspected speeders. When the bankers' cars were pulled over for going twenty miles per hour, the autos were impounded and the professional chauffeurs arrested. The owners of the vehicles faced no charges, however, at least initially. When one of the cases was tried, it was a different story. In this instance, the chauffeur claimed that although he was manipulating levers to avoid hitting other vehicles in a more heavily trafficked part of the road, and thus appeared to be operating the car, his employer was actually driving. The banker owned up to it and paid a twenty-five dollar fine. The other cases were also settled by the imposition of fines.

Fines continued to be the standard punishment for speeders through the first decade of the twentieth century. For a first offense it was fifteen dollars, and that's what banker Henry Clews paid after his chauffeur was charged with speeding. Although the auto was clocked at thirty-one miles an hour, Clews vehemently disagreed with the assessment of the arresting officer. At the station house, where Clews demanded a receipt for the hundred dollars bail he posted for his chauffeur, he jotted down the names of every officer on duty. That same day, Ogden L. Mills, heir to a banking and railroad fortune, was picked up on North Broadway driving his low-slung sports car forty miles an hour. Having neglected to take any cash with him, young Mills handed over his pricey watch as bail. The privileged daughter of a glass manufacturer was also cashless when police apprehended her for speeding in 1909. She seemed less upset at having to put up her diamond ring as bail than having to appear in court the next day at what to her was the dreadfully early hour of 9 a.m.

The previous year, exceptionally high bail of $300 was set for a Bronx contractor who led a Yonkers Bicycle Police sergeant on a twelve-mile chase, which began in Yonkers and ended in Elmsford. The contractor was racing another driver and both vehicles were estimated to be going forty miles per hour. Realizing he was being pursued by the police, the contractor abandoned the race and fled north, coming to a stop in Elmsford when one of his tires blew out. Meanwhile, the valiant Yonkers police officer, who had been literally left in the dust, kept pedaling northward. To the surprise and dismay of the contractor, the officer approached him as he was fixing his flat tire and not only arrested him on the spot but ordered him to put the bicycle in the car and drive both the bike and the officer back to Yonkers.

By the end of the decade, Yonkers traffic enforcement officers were riding motorcycles instead of bicycles, and drivers really had to watch out. The Touring Department of the Automobile Club of America warned its members about a speed trap just beyond Getty Square. Motorists who failed to heed the club's advice could expect a hefty fine of fifteen dollars. Besides enriching the city treasury, cracking down on motorists who ignored the law helped prevent accidents. Excessive speed, however, was not always the cause of serious accidents. In the fall of 1902, the dangerous maneuvering of a professional chauffeur who, according to eyewitnesses, had weaved across the trolley tracks several times to afford his passengers a better view of the Hudson and the Palisades in their autumnal splendor led to a collision with a loaded trolley car after the automobile became entangled with the tracks and came to a halt. The trolley could not avoid hitting the auto, but fortunately for the nearly two dozen people on board, despite being "derailed, dashed against a curb and overturned," the trolley leaned away from an embankment below which were the tracks of the New York Central's Hudson Division.[69] Terrified trolley passengers were tossed about and most sustained injuries before they could be extracted from the wreckage. A few were hospitalized at St. John's Riverside. Meanwhile, the automobile, disengaged from the tracks by the force of the collision, continued on its way, but not for long. Soon after the auto had limped away on only three good tires, the chauffeur was arrested. His passengers refused to give their names, and no one was willing to reveal the identity of the vehicle's owner. The chauffeur was found guilty despite his assertion that he was only following the instructions of his passengers and that, in any event, he was unaware of the fact that the trolley was coming up behind him because the trolley's bell was inaudible. He received a six months' sentence.

Sometimes the long arm of the law caught up not just with chauffeurs but with owners of automobiles involved in accidents. In 1906, following a collision between one of two autos racing each other on Central Park Avenue and a carriage that had pulled off the road to allow the cars to pass, Yonkers City Judge Joseph H. Beall, who previously had administered a slap on the wrist to speeders, handed down prison sentences to both the chauffeur and the owner of the auto. The fact that one of the victims was former Yonkers Supervisor Thomas A. Browne may have had something to do with the harsh sentence or perhaps it was the judge's realization that accidents spared no one, no matter how prominent. In any event, the judge declared that an automobile owner who directed his chauffeur "to drive the machine, irrespective of consequences to a specified point at a highly excessive and dangerous rate of speed" was as culpable as the actual driver of the vehicle.[70] Although *The New York Times* observed, in an editorial, that the imposition of fines would have brought the case to a speedy conclusion, whereas the appeal filed by the car owner might cause the legal proceedings to be prolonged, the paper admitted that what the judge had done would serve as a warning of likely consequences "if the careless minority of automobilists do not speedily reform."[71]

Punishing "automobilists" for their wrongdoings was something that most citizens of Yonkers applauded. Something else they endorsed was the building of new and better roads. Long before the Bronx River Parkway and the Saw Mill River Parkway wended their way through portions of Yonkers, there was a concerted effort to promote the idea of a fifty-mile-long highway from Yonkers to the Catskills. The year was 1906, and the road's supporters had borrowed the idea from William K. Vanderbilt, whose Long Island Motor Parkway, an automobile road extending from Queens to Lake Ronkonkoma, was nearing completion. The proposed mainland highway was to follow the route of the new Catskill Aqueduct from the Hillview Reservoir in Yonkers to New Hamburg, south of Poughkeepsie. At that point the aqueduct crossed the Hudson. Getting cars across the river was another matter, as yet unresolved, but this challenge in no way dampened the enthusiasm of proponents of the new road, who proposed to pay for it by floating bonds and charging tolls. A former president of the Automobile Club of America conceded that the growing number of automobiles posed a serious problem but there was a solution. "Horsemen," he said, "have had their own speedways in various parts of the country, and there is no reason why automobilists should not at least have one or more highways."[72]

The Yonkers to Catskills highway did not make it off the drawing board, but "automobilists" still managed to emulate horsemen in locating a place to let loose. The venue was the Empire City Track, the forerunner of the Yonkers Raceway. As early as 1901, American and foreign drivers were testing their vehicles and themselves on the Yonkers track. In the autumn of that year, a Frenchman, driving a sixty horsepower auto, set a new world's record of one minute and six seconds for a mile. Two years later, in May 1903, Barney Oldfield, one of the most famous drivers of the early auto age, set a new world's record of one minute and one second in a two-man race. In July 1903, Oldfield bested himself by defeating a Yonkers driver and setting a new world's record of fifty-five seconds for a mile. A number of races were featured that day, and in one of them a driver behind the wheel of a sixty horsepower Mercedes came close to matching Oldfield's new record. Yonkers residents who ventured out to the track were treated to more than just exciting races. They got to see two hundred fabulous cars displayed on the lawn beneath the grandstand. Most of them were sleek new models, some with glass windows and luggage racks. Gasoline engines, electric cars, and steam-driven vehicles were all represented.

When steam vehicles first made their appearance in Yonkers a few years earlier, there was some talk about requiring operators to have a boiler license for these "locomobiles," but nothing came of this. The cumbersome steam vessels, which resembled horse-drawn carriages, were quickly eclipsed by gasoline-powered cars. The same fate befell electric vehicles, but in 1904 they were welcomed, along with other types of autos, to compete for the Yonkers Cup in a five-mile race restricted to cars selling for a maximum of $1,000. The International Cup Race was another feature at the Empire City Track. In 1904, the winning vehicle was a thirty horsepower Renault. Two years later, cars racing around the track weren't the only thing luring visitors to Empire City. In addition to enjoying the sight of sleek vehicles zooming around in circles, the public was treated to an auto show, held under a huge tent opposite the grandstand. Visitors were free to roam around inspecting more than three dozen autos, among them one and two-cylinder runabouts and four-cylinder touring cars. The highlight of the show's opening day, however, was neither the demonstration runs around the track nor the gorgeous vehicles on display, but a balloon ascension. At least that's what the organizers had in mind.

Making the trip in the enormous black balloon were a man and woman dressed in circus attire. Their role was to mesmerize the crowd by hanging from trapezes while the balloon ascended and then parachute back to earth, but things did not go according to plan. The balloon failed to gain sufficient altitude and tumbled to earth, sending spectators scurrying in all directions. The parachutists were dragged along the ground before alighting from the balloon with torn costumes. To avoid impropriety, coats were grabbed from some of the automobiles, and the man and woman, their torn tights camouflaged, were whisked away to their dressing room, actually a small tent on the Empire City grounds. The next day, luck was on their side. The balloon ascension went off without a hitch despite gusty winds, which transported the balloon a distance of four miles. Somewhere near Tuckahoe, the "aeronauts," as they were dubbed by the press, activated their parachutes and floated gracefully to a safe landing. An auto, one of five assigned to chase the balloon, gathered up the "aeronauts" while another car transported the balloon back to the Empire City grounds.

In addition to the balloon ascension, the second day of the auto show featured one-mile races. There was also a series of efficiency tests. In one of them cars competed to cover the greatest distance on a single pint of gasoline. In determining the winner, the horsepower of the autos was taken into account. A ten horsepower, one-cylinder Cadillac emerged triumphant after going nearly five miles. Fittingly, the car almost reached the grandstand before it ran out of gas. Officials calculated that the Cadillac's performance in this efficiency test indicated that the estimated mileage for this type of vehicle was an impressive forty miles per gallon. The next day featured a vibration test in which riding quality was judged by placing a pail of water in each car. The vehicles then traveled two hundred yards and the car that lost the least amount of water was declared the winner. A twenty-six horsepower Oldsmobile, whose loss was only six-eighths of an inch, took the honors. In a three-mile race that day, however, the same Oldsmobile developed a steering gear problem as it was rounding a curve and hit the fence. Before the day was over, there was a traction race, in which competing vehicles pulled five hundred pounds of sand, and several speed races. The high point of the afternoon was a speed trial. A racing car with a one hundred horsepower engine set a new world's record of a mile in fifty-three seconds, and in the process terrified spectators who went scurrying when the car swerved on a curve near the clubhouse, sending up clouds of dust.

In the fall of 1906, a huge crowd at Empire City watched as a Fiat set a new record of a mile in fifty seconds. In another event held the same day, a hundred-mile contest, one of the eight entrants lost a wheel. The car's mechanic was ejected from the vehicle and suffered a broken collarbone but the driver managed to remain in control, avoiding other vehicles until his car finally came to rest. On a more positive note, visitors to the track were given a sneak preview of a 1907 sixty horsepower touring car. It was the first of its kind to be seen in Yonkers but its price, which exceeded $3,000, made it affordable for only the select few. The same was true of vehicles participating in the New York to Paris auto race of 1908. This contest, which involved driving through North America to

Alaska and then crossing over to Siberia, began in Times Square in February 1908. A police escort accompanied the cars to Yonkers, where "Getty Square, Broadway and Warburton Avenue had for spectators thousands who were desirous of witnessing the racers whizzing through this city."[73]

Horsing Around

The New York to Paris race is merely a footnote to the history of Yonkers in the early twentieth century. Far more significant is another kind of racing, the type for which Empire City was best known. Although auto races heightened the track's visibility, Empire City was, first and foremost, a horse track, which hosted both pacers and trotters. Built by William H. Clark, a former corporation counsel of New York City who had amassed a fortune in copper, Empire City opened in 1899. From the outset it was hampered by poor transportation. Neither rail nor trolley lines operated near the track, rendering it inconvenient, if not entirely inaccessible, for would-be visitors. Thus, despite its mile-long racecourse, located on one hundred acres of land, and its imposing grandstand made of iron and steel, Empire City faced challenges from the very beginning. The death of William Clark a year after the track opened compounded those problems. The two mortgages he had on the racecourse were in arrears; other bills went unpaid as well. In August 1901, the water commissioners of the City of Yonkers terminated the track's water supply for nonpayment of bills. A few months later, in November, the track was sold at a public auction held at Philipse Manor Hall. The buyer was Frank Farrell, who was dubbed "the poolroom king" by the press. Farrell announced that he was contemplating building a railroad spur to increase access to the track, but the cost proved prohibitive. Yet, even without the spur accessibility improved thanks to the extension of the Jerome Avenue trolley line and its connection to the Yonkers-Mount Vernon line, which stopped directly in front of the track. Once the trip to Empire City became less arduous, attendance increased dramatically, especially among visitors from Yonkers itself, Mount Vernon, and the northern part of New York City.

Taking advantage of easier access to Empire City, thousands of fans turned out in 1903 to see a popular horse named Prince Alert set a world's record of a mile in one minute, fifty-seven seconds. Described as "the most sensational mile that had ever been stepped on a track," this feat positively delighted the crowd who cheered the driver, trainer, and owner, as well as the horse.[74] The enthusiastic spectators were "raised to the heights of enthusiasm by the splendid performance itself, and the realization that they had seen what no harness horse had ever done before."[75] Within two years, however, Empire City was experiencing problems. The New York State Racing Commission refused to issue a license for racing dates for the 1905 season. Although better than it had been when Empire City first opened, public transportation to the track was still problematic from the standpoint of commission members. In addition to underscoring the need for better access, the commission expressed concern about what it deemed inadequate facilities for both horses and patrons. The cost of remedying these problems was so great that it would have resulted in smaller stakes and purses which, in turn, would have discouraged horse owners from competing at the track. Empire City challenged this assessment, contending that the Yonkers track had better transportation than the Saratoga track. The attorney for Empire City also pointed out that the stables at other New York area tracks were inferior to those in Yonkers. The real issue, he asserted, was that racing had become profitable and that those who had invested in it, including members of the racing commission and The Jockey Club, which allocated the dates for racing, did not want to dilute their profits.

Persuading the New York State Racing Commission to acquiesce in Empire City's demand for a license was an ongoing effort. In 1907, James Butler, who had purchased the track following Farrell's brief ownership, took the matter to court in an effort to force the commission to show cause why it denied Empire City a license to hold a racing meeting. When a judge of the State Supreme Court ruled against Empire City, Butler refused to let the matter drop. While an appeal was pending, The Jockey Club acquiesced and agreed to allocate dates for a meeting at the Yonkers track. When the meet opened, on a sunny August day in 1907, the excitement was palpable, as enthusiastic race fans headed to Empire City. James Butler had hammered out an agreement with the New York Central for the long-sought rail spur, but it was not yet in place. Visitors were forced to rely upon the Jerome Avenue trolley. Its operator, the Union Railroad Company, simply could not handle its regular passenger load plus the race fans. Thousands of people headed for the track had to walk the last few miles on a dreadfully hot day. Fearing that this fiasco would discourage future visitors, Butler spent hours in consultation with trolley officials, finally receiving assurances that the service on the line would be augmented immediately to accommodate an expected ten thousand daily visitors to Empire City.

In November 1907, Empire City won its appeal, thereby ensuring its continued ability to host meets. Before the year ended, James Butler changed the official name of his organization from the Empire City Trotting Club to the Empire City Racing Association. This was regarded as an important symbolic step in the track's efforts to be a major institution in New York racing. Evidence of this intention were various improvements completed before the 1908 meeting. These included the addition of new stables, bringing Empire City's capacity to six hundred horses. A new chute for three-quarter-mile races and a conjoined grandstand and field stand were also in place by opening day to add to the enjoyment of visitors, many of them diehard fans who traveled to Yonkers as soon as the meeting at Saratoga ended.

Hitting Little White Balls

Despite the numerous challenges it faced in the early twentieth century, Empire City put Yonkers on the map as a racing center. During that same period, St. Andrew's, founded in 1888 and the oldest golf club in the United States, made the city famous for a game imported from Scotland. By the turn of the twentieth century, hitting little white balls across a greensward was a favorite pastime of wealthy Americans. As the game's popularity grew, tee times were in demand seven days a week. Indeed, in an era when the work ethic was strong and even CEOs, like their underlings, put in a five and a half or six day week, Sunday was often the only day one could escape to the golf course. Trouble was, though, that the City of Yonkers had rather rigid laws about what was and was not appropriate on the Sabbath. There was, for example, legislation prohibiting sporting activities on Sunday, and one fine day in the spring of 1901 a delegation of Yonkers residents, led by a number of clergymen, marched into the office of the city's police commissioner to decry the fact that baseball was being played on Sunday, in outright defiance of the law. Heeding the request of the delegation, the commissioner took action. Henceforth, there would be no more games on Sunday, this despite the fact that the Yonkers team had a complete schedule of games and had been playing on Sunday all along. Unhappy baseball players and fans struck back by insisting that if baseball was to be banned on Sunday, so, too, should golf.

At this point, the police commissioner referred the whole matter to a city judge, who ruled that the law was just as applicable to golf as it was to baseball. Anyone caught in the act of playing either game, he said, would be hauled into court. The judge's determination to enforce the law was met with considerable opposition from the golfing fraternity, especially after Benjamin Adams, a local attorney who was also a member of the Yonkers Board of Education, was arrested at the Saegkill

Golf Club for challenging the law by deliberately hitting a golf ball on Sunday. Several ladies and industrialist Walter W. Hodgman, owner of the Hodgman Rubber Company and president of the golf club, were with Adams on the links of the Saegkill Golf Club, but Adams was the only person wielding a golf club. Hodgman went along to the police station with Adams and provided bail. In the aftermath of Adams's arrest, a handful of wealthy golfers, who were as angry at the clergy who spearheaded the movement to enforce the law banning Sunday sports as they were at the police commissioner and the judge, announced that they would forfeit membership in the churches to which they belonged. Unwilling to lose major donors, two ministers who had been part of the delegation backed away saying that they had simply gone along with a fellow minister who had persuaded them to join the effort to ban Sunday sports.

Despite the ministers' change of heart, the controversy over sports on the Sabbath was not resolved until Benjamin Adams had his day in court. And what a day it was! The courtroom was packed with well-to-do citizens of Yonkers. One of them, a fellow member of the Saegkill Club who had been summoned for jury duty, appeared in golfing attire and infuriated the presiding judge by smiling at friends in the audience and winking at Mr. Adams's attorney. Since the judge was the same judicial official who had ruled earlier on the enforcement of the ban on golf, as well as baseball, he dismissed the juror. The attorney for the defendant was furious and raised a whole host of objections. The fireworks didn't end there. Contending that the game of golf was very peaceful and, therefore, did not fall into the category of activities disturbing the peace, which was the real intent of the contested legislation, Adams's attorney made a motion for dismissal. This was denied. He also argued that because the game was played on privately held club land, there was no danger of interfering with the public's right to enjoy a peaceful Sabbath. Club president Walter Hodgman testified that Saegkill's grounds were indeed private, but this mattered little to the judge who rejected another plea for dismissal.

Before the judge charged the jury, the defense attorney for the accused addressed the jurors, incorporating a humorous story about a little boy who asked his mother what heaven was. Upon being told that it was a place of perpetual Sundays, the child wasn't sure he wanted to go there! His face reddened by anger at the defense attorney for having the audacity to recount this blasphemous story, the judge nearly wore out his gavel striking it repeatedly to restore order. This action ended the merriment of Adams's supporters who had laughed, audibly, at the story. The hush that fell over the courtroom did not last long, because a juror asked whether the fact that the illegal act had taken place on private property was relevant to the case. The judge insisted it wasn't and proceeded to read aloud the law that had been violated. In so doing, he omitted the portion of the statute that referred to public sports. The attorney for the defense called him on this and the indignant judge declared that he would not allow anyone to challenge his truthfulness. In the end, though, he had to admit that he had omitted the words but, all the while, he insisted that this terminology was meant only as a guide. The jury thought otherwise. After deliberating for forty-five minutes, the jury returned a verdict of not guilty and recommended that the law either be repealed or amended.

Not everyone was pleased. *The Yonkers Statesman* declared, in an editorial titled "A Victory for the Wrong," that the negative effect of the trial would be "far reaching. It may lead thousands of young people astray, and is hailed as a victory of wrong over right."[76] The editorial proceeded to state that "the action of these Sunday golf players has done more . . . to demoralize the young people than all the lawless liquor sellers and pool rooms combined. This is because the masses, who have fewer opportunities for culture and improvement, look to those more favored for examples."[77] Local clergymen echoed the sentiments of the newspaper. Within days of the verdict the pastor of the Methodist Church delivered a sermon calling Benjamin Adams's acquittal a farce. He then referred to the clergy-led delegation to police headquarters to focus attention on illegal Sunday baseball. The objective of that initiative, he said, was to underscore the need for concerted police action in eliminating all sorts of violations of the Sabbath law. The minister was not alone in his views. A sermon delivered at St. Joseph's Catholic Church denounced the police for overlooking the rowdyism associated with saloons that operated in violation of the Sabbath law.

Recreation for the Masses

The police endured more bad press toward the end of the first decade of the twentieth century for their handling of security at the Yonkers marathon. Overwhelmed when ten thousand spectators showed up at the Empire City track for the popular event, marathon officials turned to the local police force to keep order. The chief of police obliged by personally driving a horse around the track, but some of his officers, unable to distinguish scorers and other officials connected with the marathon from the public because the former were not wearing badges, jostled marathon workers. Worse was the action of mounted police who rode through a group of scorers. The police chief was apprised of this but, according to marathon organizers, he not only ignored the complaint about his men but himself drove through a group of officials. Marathon workers were also hassled by spectators who challenged scorers. The situation was so bad that the race was called off after only seven of the fifty-one participants, who braved frigid January weather to take part, crossed the finish line.

For most Yonkers residents running a marathon, even in nice weather, held no appeal. Far more alluring were the social and recreational activities sponsored by such community organizations as the Yonkers Teutonia. With its large building housing an assembly hall, dining room, bowling alley, pool room, and meeting rooms, this club served the needs of the city's German community. Other ethnic groups, such as the sizable Polish community, had their own clubhouses. Some clubs, including the Hollywood Inn, welcomed people of all ethnic backgrounds. Founded by Episcopal churchmen as a club for working-class men, the Hollywood Inn had an impressive building donated by William F. Cochran of Alexander Smith and Sons who "furnished his dream club with every imaginable activity for men and boys. There were meeting halls, classrooms, reading rooms, lunch rooms and a well-equipped gymnasium" plus "a complete facility for billiards, pool and bowling alley in the basement of the building."[78] The facilities at the Woman's Institute weren't comparable to those at the Hollywood Inn but the institute did provide a library, an employment bureau, and courses in domestic arts and sciences for the working girls of Yonkers.

Whether male or female, in fair weather young residents abandoned even the nicest indoor club facilities and headed to the great outdoors for all sorts of activities. For young men, football games and other sporting events at Celtic Park and elsewhere were enjoyable recreational pursuits. During the summer months, Yonkers residents of all backgrounds could be found enjoying the majestic river at the city's doorstep. Whether young or old, in the summer residents flocked to the river to fish, swim, or admire the scenery from the ferry connecting Yonkers with Alpine, New Jersey, or from private boats setting forth from the Yonkers Yacht Club, the Corinthian Yacht Club, the Palisades Boat Club, and the Yonkers Canoe Club. Days spent on or near the water were usually serene, but periodically river-based recreational activities ended in tragedy.

Such was the case in the very first year of the new century, when a New York City newspaperman took his wife and two other ladies for what began as a pleasant trip across the Hudson. The foursome hopped into a rowboat and crossed over to New Jersey without mishap. On the return trip, their boat was swamped by the wake of a tugboat pulling barges. Just before a big wave hit, one of the ladies moved to the bow of the rowboat, upsetting its balance. Seconds later the boat overturned. The man, who had been rowing, was a very strong swimmer and was able to reach his wife and one of the other ladies. He maneuvered them to the boat and as they held on for dear life, he set out to save the third woman. Swimming against a strong tide, he was able to grab her and bring her back to the rowboat. As soon as they reached it, the boat flipped over and the man's wife disappeared. The other lady who had been clinging to the boat, as well as the newly rescued woman, were able to grasp the boat and hang on while the man dove beneath the surface several times until he finally located his wife. The poor woman clung to her husband so tightly that the two of them were in danger of drowning. When he tried to loosen her grip on him, she slipped below the surface. But, once again, her husband rescued her. He managed to maneuver her over to the rowboat but just as she grasped it, the boat overturned again. The other two ladies were able to hang on but the man's wife disappeared. Amazingly, he located her and brought her back to the boat, which, once again, overturned. This time she did not resurface.

While hundreds of people on the Yonkers shore witnessed the man's repeated dives, a small flotilla of boats set out from the Yonkers Yacht Club. The two ladies clinging to the overturned rowboat were hauled into small boats. Other vessels joined in the hunt for the missing woman while her husband kept diving to the point of exhaustion. He was finally pulled into a boat and immediately collapsed. Soon thereafter, his wife's lifeless body was found. She was rowed to shore at record speed by a yacht club employee. The club had summoned an ambulance from St. Joseph's Hospital and it was in readiness the minute the woman was brought ashore. Two physicians began working on her, but getting no response, they ordered the ambulance to race to the hospital, where the woman was pronounced dead.

Within weeks, another boating accident claimed two lives in the waters off Yonkers. Both victims were young men employed by the City National Bank. One of them was active in the Yonkers Canoe Club, but the other fellow was inexperienced on the water. The pair traveled in an eighteen-foot canoe from Glenwood to New Jersey where they spent a little time before setting out for the Yonkers shore. En route, they came up with what they thought was a bright idea, namely to raise a sweater on the paddle and turn the canoe into a makeshift sailboat. The consequences were dire. The sail was struck by a strong gust and the canoe overturned. Both men resurfaced only to disappear below the waves once again. As the expert canoeist tried to save his friend, a nonswimmer, he was dragged down. Ultimately, both men drowned.

Two thousand passengers on a pair of excursion barges, pulled by a tug, nearly met the same fate in July 1905. The barges had traveled up the Hudson from Hoboken, New Jersey, to Riverview Grove, a popular stop for such outings. The grove was opposite Yonkers and city residents pitched in to lend assistance after the vessels were lashed by pelting rain and wind, almost pushing them onto rocks in North Yonkers. The weather was only one factor contributing to this near mishap. The other element in this maritime drama was a stalled engine, the result of a log becoming entangled in one of the tug's propellers. The tugboat signaled for help by repeatedly blowing its whistle, and a relief tug was dispatched. All the while, the band, which had accompanied the excursionists, kept playing, but it wasn't enough to calm the nerves of terrified passengers, many of whom eagerly climbed aboard small boats sent out from Yonkers. The Yonkers Police Boat Patrol, which had been standing by, was not needed to get the excursionists to shore, however. Once safely deposited on dry land, the weary day-trippers boarded trains for New York.

Fifteen hundred people participating in a trip from Brooklyn to Riverview Grove in August 1905 also endured a mishap when the walking beam on the steamboat pulling their excursion barge broke. Barge and steamboat drifted toward Yonkers and after three hours another excursion vessel arrived to take them back to the city. Although frustrated and exhausted, they were none the worse for wear. Three months later, a small group of Yonkers residents who set out on a fishing expedition on a fine autumn day were not so lucky. They departed from the Hudson Boat Club in a big rowboat that had been modified by the addition of a sail. Since there wasn't much wind, they had to man the oars. As they were trying to maneuver the boat, there was some sort of commotion aboard and the boat, which was overloaded with gear and ballast, began taking on water. All five people aboard drowned. The victims included a boy whose anguished cries for help were audible to men in a nearby boat, which tried to render assistance. The boy's father and uncle were among those who were lost.

Working-class people in rickety boats were not the only victims of the Hudson River's swift currents. In 1907, the scion of a famous Yonkers family, whose grandfather and namesake, Edward Underhill, had founded Underhill's Brewery, went missing while on a canoe outing. In the company of other members of the Yonkers Canoe Club he traveled across the river to New Jersey. He and several other men were in single canoes and there were two tandem canoes in the group. After a pleasant day on the New Jersey side of the river everyone set out for Yonkers, but the wind and the tide were against them. The people in the tandem canoes thought it best to return to New Jersey but the single canoes persevered.

Two of them made it, but Underhill, who was believed "to have fallen out of his canoe," did not.[79] The next day, searchers came across his canoe in Piermont, but Underhill was nowhere to be found.

Looking Forward, Glancing Backward

Despite the very real danger posed by the Hudson, the river remained a popular recreational venue. It was also a tremendous economic asset. The Hudson's role as a nautical highway bringing raw materials to Yonkers factories and carrying away finished products to markets near and far was surely apparent to organizers of an industrial exposition sponsored by the Yonkers Chamber of Commerce in 1913. Held in the New York State Armory at Maple and Waverly Streets, the show highlighted Yonkers industry. As part of its preparations for the exhibition, the chamber held a slogan contest. Fully five thousand submissions were received, and the winning phrase, "Industry Unites Us With the World," became the official slogan of the exhibition. The chamber also held poster and essay contests. In addition to finding volunteers to judge the various contests, the chamber lined up representatives of the city's leading companies to head various committees. A first vice president of Alexander Smith and Sons served as chairman of the Committee on Manufactures. The committee was composed of high-ranking managers from Otis Elevator and the Waring Hat Factory. The superintendent of the National Sugar Refining Company chaired the Committee on Concessions while Louis Spreckels of the Federal Sugar Refining Company was the mainstay of the Advisory Committee. During the ten days in June that the expo was open, visitors were able to examine and purchase the myriad products on display. Many of the exhibitors, observed *The Yonkers Herald,* "have taken large orders for their goods . . . at the show," adding that "besides the great amount of advertising they receive they have netted handsome profits in the undertaking."[80] Of course, it didn't hurt that exhibit organizers provided top-flight entertainment, including musical performances and vaudeville acts, direct from New York City, each night. The imported talent included "Mr. Jean Schwartz, the well known composer, and his wife Miss Jane Dolly of the celebrated Dolly Sisters from the Winter Garden, New York."[81]

In comparison with the industrial exposition, which highlighted the present and future of the city's factory-based economy, the Greater New York Fair and Exposition, held at Empire City in August 1913, emphasized the older agrarian-based economy. This month-long event featured a variety of activities, including horse shows and horse races, but the underlying theme was agriculture, including dairying and cattle raising. Chickens of all breeds were also on display. Some of the fair's organizers were determined to reacquaint visitors with farming but with an emphasis on scientific agriculture. Convinced that a surefire way to deal with the high cost of living was to persuade people to turn their backyards into mini-farms, the director of the fair's poultry and stock department felt that residents of downstate New York were ready for a back to the farm movement. Viewing hundreds of cows and swine, and thousands of chickens, and learning a little about scientific agriculture was fine for an afternoon, but Yonkers residents had long ago jumped feet-first into the industrial age and there was no turning back.

Looking back was another story, however, and that's what the city's residents had done, not once but twice, since the dawn of the new century. In 1909, during the Hudson-Fulton Celebration, commemorating Henry Hudson's voyage to New York and the journey, two hundred years later, of Robert Fulton's North River steamboat, better known as the *Clermont,* from New York City to Albany, Yonkers was the first stop made by replicas of the two boats. Ironically, on September 29, 1909, the *Clermont* replica had as much difficulty as its namesake proceeding upriver. Its captain was determined to keep the vessel going, even after a launch pulled up alongside to deliver a message about pulling the *Clermont* out of the nautical parade if it continued to sputter along on its own. The *Clermont's* feisty captain only relented when the vessel fizzled out within sight of Yonkers. At that point he accepted a tow. The replica of Henry Hudson's *Half Moon,* on the other hand, was towed up from Manhattan, escorted by two gunboats, eight torpedo boats, and Naval Reserve and police vessels. Excursion steamboats were also out in full force. When the replicas of the *Half Moon* and *Clermont* arrived in Yonkers, members of the official reception committee were transported out to the two boats by tug, where they were entertained by the ships' crews. Yonkers returned the favor by hosting the officers of the *Half Moon* and *Clermont* at the City Club later in the day.

Less than a week after the ships' visit, Yonkers was the scene of a Hudson-Fulton parade, held in conjunction with Old Home Week. This three-mile-long, two-hour extravaganza was no small affair. Fifteen thousand people were in the line of march. The parade, which was viewed by a crowd estimated at 150,000 on a day that was "mild and partly cloudy," conditions which the *Statesman* concluded were "rather of benefit to paraders and spectators alike," also included twenty-three floats that had participated in an earlier parade in New York City.[82] These historical floats were supplemented by fifteen floats representing various Yonkers organizations. Members of fraternal and civic groups and firefighters from Yonkers and other Westchester County municipalities also participated. On hand to review the parade were New York State governor Charles E. Hughes and his wife. As he had done for the officers of the *Half Moon* and *Clermont,* Mayor N.A. Warren entertained the Hugheses at the City Club. Following luncheon at the club, the governor, accompanied by a number of staff members, enjoyed an automobile tour of Yonkers. En route through the city, they received a unique greeting from a thousand students, decked out in red, white, and blue. Positioned to replicate a flag, they stood on a grandstand outside Yonkers High School belting out patriotic tunes. Their enthusiasm, which mirrored that of the city's adult residents, was warranted, because this was the first time in a decade that a governor of New York State had come to town.

What the *Statesman* characterized as "the carnival spirit" persisted through the following night when a parade of automobiles wended its way through the city, their owners hoping to capture the prize for the best in line.[83] The winner was a vehicle covered with cotton to emulate the North Pole. Adorning its hood were a Teddy bear, a polar bear skin, and an American flag. The owner's two young sons, representing Arctic explorers, waved flags from their perches in the rear of the car. When all was said and done, *The Yonkers Herald* published an editorial commenting, in a very positive way, on the participation by foreign-born residents in the festivities. In the opinion of the *Herald,* the "largest lesson was not in the recognition of Hudson's and Fulton's accomplishments . . . but in the living testimony of the varied races that go to make up our citizenship of their corresponding growth and of the national or international character of future generations in Yonkers."[84]

As delightful as the Hudson-Fulton celebration was, for Yonkers residents looking back upon historic events, the jubilee of Philipse Manor Hall in 1912 had greater significance. This building, after all, had been the seat of Yonkers government until the new city hall was completed in 1910. In the colonial era, the imposing stone structure was the home of Frederick Philipse II, Lord of Philipsburgh Manor. When the future of the Manor House was threatened in the early twentieth century, Mrs. William Cochran spearheaded the movement to have the historic building acquired by New York State. She and her son, Alexander Smith Cochran, then funded the restoration of the property. Alexander Cochran also donated portraits of U.S. presidents for a permanent exhibition in the Manor Hall. Thanks to the generosity of the Cochrans, Philipse Manor Hall made its public debut as a New York State historic site in 1912. Local residents flocked to the new museum and came away bursting with pride because their hometown had preserved an integral part of its past. The juxtaposition of the splendid old building at the corner of Warburton Avenue and Dock Street with the modern industrial plants nearby was a reminder of the fact that the "Queen City of the Hudson" revered its past as it strode confidently into a future its citizens could scarcely imagine.

2

The Great War and Its Aftermath

Over There

The celebratory mood characterizing the dedication of Philipse Manor Hall as the state's newest, and, in the opinion of Yonkers residents, best historic site gave way to a more somber outlook when the United States entered The Great War, a conflict later known as World War I. Even before the United States declared war, Yonkers experienced the impact of events occurring in Europe. In November 1915, when an early freeze ended shipment of horses from Montreal to England and France, thousands of animals needed by Allied military forces arrived by train in Yonkers. Corrals were hastily erected on property in Dunwoodie leased from the Valley Farms Realty Company. The horses remained there for a short time before being loaded onto ships on the Yonkers waterfront. The Dunwoodie horse corrals were a reminder of the events unfolding in Europe but in May 1915, months before the Hudson supplanted the St. Lawrence as the port of embarkation for Allied equine resources, the realization that what was happening an ocean away affected the United States hit home when the Cunard passenger liner *Lusitania* was torpedoed by a German submarine off the coast of Ireland. Among the victims were 128 Americans. Although it would be another two years before the United States declared war, Yonkers was linked with the worsening conflict in Europe because of an incident involving the British cargo steamer *Rio Lages,* which picked up a cargo of sugar in Yonkers before proceeding to Halifax, Nova Scotia. From there the ship was supposed to cross the Atlantic but while at anchor in Halifax, it was engulfed by flames. The fire was believed to have been caused by an incendiary bomb that may have been smuggled aboard the ship by an enemy agent while German and Austrian longshoremen loaded the ship in Yonkers.

In Yonkers itself, the tranquility of a late fall evening in 1915 was shattered by an explosion in the vicinity of the Alexander Smith and Sons Carpet Company. Reporting the next day on the 6:30 p.m. explosion, *The Yonkers Herald* said that the incident had "police authorities baffled."[1] According to the newspaper:

> The detonation was heard for miles around, houses were shaken by the blast, windows knocked out and dishes rattled about in closets. Pedestrians in the street were nearly shaken from their feet.
>
> The noise and shock alarmed the neighborhood and hundreds of persons rushed from their homes to the streets in terror.[2]

A police officer who was only a block away from the site of the explosion blew his whistle to summon a fellow officer and the pair scoured the neighborhood. Finding part of a fuse and wires in an Orchard Street yard, they questioned residents of the largely Austrian neighborhood but failed to obtain any useful information. Two Austrian immigrants, both male, who had recently rented an apartment on Orchard Street were questioned at length and their quarters were thoroughly searched, but nothing of interest was discovered. The police conceded that incriminating items could have been discarded prior to the search and they speculated that the person or persons responsible for the blast might have been working on a new type of explosive.

While Yonkers residents wondered whether the blast was the work of German saboteurs, the issue of security at home took on new meaning as Mexican rebel leader Pancho Villa led incursions into the southwestern United States, killing several dozen Americans. President Woodrow Wilson responded by sending troops to the southern border. The U.S. force included most of New York State's mounted troops, including Squadron A, whose members assembled in Yonkers in July 1916 for a gala sendoff. The soldiers had been in camp at nearby Van Cortlandt Park and they could not have been happier to be in Yonkers, where they were not only greeted by enthusiastic residents but were treated to sandwiches, fruit, dessert, and milk by the Red Cross. Well fortified, the men loaded six hundred horses, some of them not fully tamed, and two hundred mules onto ships for the long journey to the southern border. One goat, a fox terrier, and a Pomeranian went along as mascots. As they bid farewell to friends and family who had assembled in the "Queen City of the Hudson" to see them off, the troops seemed downright jubilant. Although they had no way of knowing that Pancho Villa would remain as elusive as Osama bin Laden a century later, they were determined to capture the Mexican rebel and just couldn't wait to get to the Rio Grande.

A year later, it was a somewhat different story when Americans were drafted and sent across the ocean to aid the European Allies in their protracted struggle with the Central Powers. Within months of the U.S. declaration of war, the quota of men assigned to Yonkers was raised from 110 to 487. Word of the increase came directly from the office of New York State governor Charles Whitman, and the city's three exemption boards had to scramble to identify men who would be called up for examination. A year later, in reaction to the enormous casualties at the Second Battle of the Marne, men eagerly came forward to volunteer at a Navy recruitment event held in Glen Park. Ten thousand people attended and nearly two hundred men were accepted for the Navy.

Before the war was over, 173 of the approximately seven thousand Yonkers men who served in the military forfeited their lives fighting for democracy. Moreover, on the home front Yonkers factories turned out a variety of items needed for the war effort. The Otis Elevator Company produced 185 reinforced freight elevators powered by electricity for Army and Navy bases in the United States. The freight elevators Otis supplied to the Brooklyn Army Base were considered very advanced because they did not require onboard operators. This installation "was the first of its kind ever attempted, and made possible the economical handling and storing of vast amounts of supplies that passed through the various warehouses of the base during the war."[3] In addition to manufacturing elevators for military bases, Otis turned out gears for heavy artillery, motors for special cranes used in shipyards, steam engines, and windlasses. The company's greatest contribution to the war effort, however, was the production of recoil mechanisms for 240 millimeter French howitzers. To supply this essential part for these artillery pieces, Otis had to reconfigure its plant and "provide wholly new equipment, the larger proportion of which had to be invented, designed, and built as the work progressed."[4] Three-fourths of the Otis workforce was assigned to the howitzer project in 1918 and by the time the war ended, the method the company had pioneered for producing the recoil mechanism was being used in U.S. government arsenals.

Despite long hours at the plant, throughout the war Otis employees did various types of volunteer work. Some produced a monthly newsletter that was sent to workers fighting in Europe. Female employees joined the Otis Branch of the National Surgical Dressing Committee, which produced hospital supplies using materials purchased by their male co-workers. After working on their own for a time, the Otis volunteers joined forces with the Yonkers branch of the American Red Cross. Employees of Alexander Smith and Sons were also active as volunteers. At the request of the government, the company itself, like Otis, undertook a very difficult task. With no time to spare, as soon as the United States entered the war the government asked the carpet company to adapt its looms in order to turn out two badly needed items: blankets and duck fabric for tents. Alexander Smith and Sons complied with the request despite the fact that producing these products "on carpet looms was regarded as an undertaking of great difficulty."[5] Within two months, Alexander Smith and Sons had retrofitted its looms and had begun manufacturing one hundred thousand blankets for the United States Navy and 180,000 yards of duck to fill initial orders. With "eighty-five percent of plant production . . . converted to war needs," the company turned out very little carpet during the war.[6] Instead, it kept the looms in operation "22 hours out of every 24."[7] All told, Alexander Smith and Sons "produced 4,500,000 yards of duck, and 1,525,000 blankets . . . through the wholehearted cooperation between management and employees."[8]

Elsewhere in Yonkers, the Waring Hat Company turned out 1,500,000 hats for the military and D. Saunders' Sons, Inc. produced machinery for government arsenals, shipbuilders, Navy yards, and private companies that had received government contracts to supply various items needed for the war effort. Another Yonkers firm, the National Sugar Refining Company, was engaged in war work several years before the United States entered the conflict. Soon after fighting began in 1914, the company started producing millions of pounds of sugar for Great Britain's Royal Commission on Sugar Supply, as well as for the Red Cross and other relief organizations. Once the United States entered the war, the National Sugar Refining Company increased its output to meet the needs of the U.S. military and, like other Yonkers firms, it helped out in other ways as well. Heeding the government's plea for Americans to raise more of their own food in order to free up food for export to the Allies, National Sugar made fifteen acres of land on the Rosenbaum estate on McLean Avenue available to workers willing to cultivate garden plots. More than a hundred employees participated in the program. The company also encouraged its employees to undertake war-related volunteer work.

When they weren't at their posts at National Sugar, female employees were doing War Camp Community Service work. Established in 1918 to organize recreational activities for members of a machine gun company stationed in Yonkers to supplement the Home Guard, the Yonkers War Camp Community Service was a unit of a larger organization, which provided service both during and after the war. Following the armistice, as veterans returned home, the War Camp Community Service Information and Service Bureau, with headquarters at the Hollywood Inn, which had reopened in 1917 after a fire, was designated by the City of Yonkers as the official clearinghouse for employment and other data sought by men returning to civilian life. The War Camp Community Service also held weekly dances at the Red Circle Club in Getty Square, the meeting place of the new branch of the American Legion. The welfare of the young women who "danced with service men at War Camp's supervised dances and . . . assisted in bringing cheer to convalescent soldiers" was of concern to War Camp officials, who felt that "girls in industry needed almost as much as did . . . soldiers to have their leisure time constructively and interestingly occupied."[9] For that reason, the Service opened a community center offering classes in "gymnastics, music, dramatics and domestic science, as well as hikes, picnics and social gatherings."[10] Refreshed by these after-work activities, the young women were ready to visit hospitalized soldiers and entertain able-bodied men at those supervised dances. In recognition of their good works, performed in conjunction with War Camp Community Service, the National Sugar Refining Company presented its female employees with an American flag.

While the war was ongoing, most of the volunteer work was done in the evening, after employees of National Sugar had put in a long day. The same held true for Federal Sugar Refining Company employees who devoted their spare time to volunteering. Like National Sugar, their employer produced sugar for the Army and Navy and for the European Allies. Once a week, refined sugar was loaded onto ships on the Yonkers waterfront to begin the dangerous voyage across the Atlantic as part of a huge convoy. Ironically, despite the splendid work Federal Sugar was doing in conjunction with the war effort, the company had to deal with an unusual personnel problem after the war zone of the Port of New York was extended up the Hudson to include Yonkers in the spring of 1918. Walter P. Spreckels, assistant superintendent of the Federal Sugar Refining Company, was barred from the plant because he was considered an enemy alien. Spreckels wasn't accused of any wrongdoing, but his failure to seek naturalization, despite his residency in the United States for a decade, was enough to exclude him from the war zone.

Given the proximity of so many factories to the Hudson and the fact that employees tended to live within walking distance of where they worked, approximately ten thousand Yonkers residents dwelled within the war zone; all of them were required to obtain special permits to continue living in the zone. Complying with this regulation could be a bit cumbersome but most citizens viewed it as a necessary precaution in wartime, just as they accepted the fact that people who had emigrated from Germany were subjected to greater scrutiny than native-born Americans. Persons with German surnames who demonstrated anything but extreme patriotism and dedication to the Allied cause were particularly suspect. Such was the case when Frederick J. Heuser, an employee of a confectionary store on North Broadway, began whipping up candy sticks in the colors of the German flag. He also created table favors shaped like German military helmets. Heuser's real masterpiece, however, was brick ice cream "in the red, white and black colors of the Kaiser's flag."[11] The proprietor of the confectionary store where Heuser was hired after answering an ad the shop owner had placed in a New York City newspaper, insisted that Heuser's duties were limited to dispensing soda and that he was not involved in making any of the products sold in the store. The proprietor also said that he dismissed Heuser after learning that he was an ex-convict. During the brief time he was in Yonkers, Heuser was accused by his landlady of stealing a gold watch and other items from her apartment, but more serious were the charges brought by federal authorities who had been monitoring Heuser's activities even before he had relocated to Yonkers from New York City. The assertions of his former employer notwithstanding, Heuser was charged with "conducting a peculiar form of German propaganda" by manufacturing confectionary items in the German colors.[12] The charges also included "making disrespectful remarks about (U.S.) Government officials."[13] All of this was enough to land him in an internment camp on Ellis Island.

Expressing anti-American sentiments was not only a violation of the Sedition Act of 1918 but a despicable counterpoint to the patriotism of the war years. Feelings of national pride were particularly evident at rallies held to sell Liberty Bonds to finance the war effort. At one such event, Samuel Untermyer, who had previously subscribed large sums to the effort, offered to purchase another half-million dollars worth of bonds provided other Yonkers residents contributed enough to bring the city's total to an impressive three million. In the course of his speech, he also expressed the view that the United States should not forgive the loans made to the Allied nations. To do so would, in his opinion, be to insult those countries. On an even more controversial war-related topic, a proposal to enact legislation forbidding the publication of German-language newspapers, Untermyer opined that the German language press was the chief source of news for hundreds of thousands of loyal Americans of German extraction. He also argued against proposed legislation that would have deprived people accused of sedition of a jury trial in a civil court.

Had the legislation passed, they would have been judged by "the summary secret processes of drumhead court-martial."[14] Untermyer characterized both the proposed outlawing of German newspapers and the bill calling for secret trials of defendants accused of sedition as "outward indications of unreasoning hatred, intolerance and hysteria, masquerading in the guise of intensive patriotism, that are unworthy of the great cause to which we have unselfishly dedicated our lives and fortunes."[15]

By going public with these views, Untermyer appeared to his admirers in Yonkers and elsewhere to be a very courageous man, especially after receiving death threats from an alleged member of the Black Hand, a secret society associated with the Mafia, less than a year earlier. Untermyer was informed, by letter, that he would be killed three days hence and his home bombarded unless he deposited $25,000 in a flower pot on Odell Avenue. The Yonkers police chief made the drop and assigned two officers, dressed as gardeners, to monitor the flower pot. When the would-be killer showed up for the money, the police had to use their pistols to subdue him, but they got their man, or rather, boy, because the perpetrator was a sixteen-year-old who lived on Nepperhan Avenue.

Whether it was the Black Hand or the threat posed by Germany and her Central Powers allies, Yonkers residents realized that there was evil lurking in their midst and challenging the democratic system both here and abroad. All of this made people somber but now and again, during the war years, there were uplifting moments. Some of them were attributable to the oratory of the Yonkers Four Minute Men, formed in November 1917, as part of a national organization. Its mission was "to make known to the citizens and the populace the causes of the war, and the needs of the country to prosecute it; to arouse patriotism, to aid by public utterances and addresses all movements that supported the cause of freedom and righteousness."[16] The Four Minute Men, whose speeches were quite literally limited to four minutes, attempted to "stamp out sedition and disloyalty."[17] Four Minute Men were featured orators at Liberty Loan drives. During some Liberty Loan rallies, however, the most persuasive speakers were soldiers newly returned from the front.

At a rally held in Yonkers in May 1918, a crowd of ten thousand turned out to hear a military band from the Fort Slocum Army base in New Rochelle and to listen to a rousing speech by a soldier who had spent time in trenches on the front line. The young man was part of an elite group of fifty military men who toured the country helping to sell Liberty Bonds. The highlight of the soldier's Getty Square address was the unveiling of a wooden effigy of Germany's ruler, Kaiser Wilhelm II. Anyone purchasing a fifty-dollar bond was accorded the honor of giving the six-foot-tall cardboard dummy attached to a wooden frame pedestal a swift kick, pushing it in the direction of the Hudson River. An hour later, with $20,000 worth of bonds sold, the effigy was on the end of the city recreation pier. At that point, a rope and a twenty-pound weight were wrapped around the effigy's neck and, to the delight of onlookers who were gleeful about the ceremonial drowning of the Kaiser, the dummy was kicked into the river. This event was the highlight of an incredibly successful campaign in which Yonkers exceeded its quota of slightly under $2 million by raising more than $4 million. This placed the city in the forefront of U.S. municipalities in the Third Liberty Loan Campaign. The Yonkers Liberty Loan Committee was especially proud of the fact that more than thirty thousand people, "or practically one subscriber for every three residents," had participated.[18]

Although outdoor rallies attracting thousands were an important factor in the success of the Liberty Loan campaigns, the subscription drives undertaken by Yonkers businesses, churches, synagogues, and community organizations also figured prominently in putting the city over the top when it came to financing the war effort. Houses of worship, civic, and fraternal organizations helped out in other ways as well, thanks to their members' spirit of voluntarism. Yonkers Lodge 707, Benevolent and Protective Order of Elks, provided financial support for a Boston hospital erected to treat wounded soldiers and a base hospital in France. At home, members of Lodge 707 were instrumental in organizing the local company of the Naval Militia; the militia was quartered at the Yonkers Elks Club. The Criterion Club of the Young Men's Hebrew Association not only sent packages containing candy, cigarettes, and magazines to soldiers but club members devoted countless hours writing letters to men serving in Europe. La Rabida Council, Knights of Columbus, pitched in during the war by providing a venue where servicemen could go to play pool, cards, and shuffleboard, as well as to enjoy music, and after the war it created educational programs to train veterans in auto mechanics, bookkeeping, typing, and other subjects designed to prepare them for jobs. The Salvation Army also assisted returning veterans with the often difficult task of finding jobs, and its Yonkers branch provided direct relief to destitute families headed by veterans.

Not to be outdone by the men, female volunteers made invaluable contributions to the war effort. The Women's Suffrage Party undertook, with official authorization, a census of the city's male population to provide data utilized in determining draft eligibility. In addition to the volunteer work done by female employees of factories and refineries, members of various community organizations pitched in. The Yonkers Section of the National Council of Jewish Women entertained soldiers enrolled in training programs at Saunders Trade School, provided homemade cakes and other edible treats for men stationed at the Armory, and, in 1919, helped with efforts to find jobs for veterans. The Young Women's Hebrew Association provided various clothing items for soldiers, and during the influenza epidemic of 1918, they worked, under the direction of the Red Cross, to produce gauze masks and other badly needed medical supplies. The Y.W.H.A. also placed its clubhouse at the disposal of the Young Men's Christian Association which, in conjunction with the Girls' Social Service League, held a party for soldiers sent to the Saunders Trade School for training. On that occasion, "refreshments, tobacco and cigarettes were passed out. The evening was voted a great success, and the soldiers gave the verdict that the Yonkers way was the best way of entertaining they had met since leaving their home towns."[19]

Other women's groups devoted themselves to more passive activities, principally sewing. The Yonkers branch of the Needlework Guild of America met weekly at the Woman's Institute to make surgical dressings and garments for hospital patients, refugees, and infants in France. Clothing for Belgian refugees was produced by a group of Yonkers neighbors who also corresponded with refugees and soldiers. Female members of the Comfort Committee of Christian Scientists made clothes for French and Belgian refugees while the Yonkers branch of the American Fund for French Wounded fashioned garments for hospital patients and refugees. The Lady Borden Chapter, Daughters of the British Empire, raised money for medical supplies and equipment. The Daughters of the American Revolution provided supplies for Yonkers men who volunteered for service with the Polish Army. The D.A.R. also supplied mattresses for soldiers guarding the aqueduct. To stimulate patriotism, the D.A.R. augmented the prizes for its essay contests in the schools.

Another local group, the Yonkers Sunshine Society, sent clothing to Europe and various edible treats and reading material to military camps and hospitals. The Yonkers branch of the U.S. Navy League's Comforts Committee also shipped clothing overseas and sent Christmas gifts to children of French sailors killed in the war. At the Woman's Institute space was provided for Red Cross nursing and first aid courses, and the Woman's Institute Club provided hostesses for various social events held for soldiers. The Y.W.C.A. established a Hostess Club that entertained between eighty and two hundred men on Tuesday evenings. Before assuming their hostess duties, young volunteers were required to spend three evenings attending lectures "on conservative patriotism and hospitality," conducted by "a wise woman physician" provided by the Commission on

Social Morality.[20] When the girls took up their official duties, all decked out in "a uniform consisting of a middy blouse and white or blue skirt and a red armband," they did so under the watchful eye of "a group of older women" who functioned as chaperones.[21]

The nearly two dozen women members of the Yonkers detachment of the Westchester County Red Cross Motor Corps presumably needed no chaperones when they transported people to hospitals. All told, the Yonkers Branch of the Westchester County Chapter of the American National Red Cross, for example, had nearly four thousand volunteers who not only produced items used in the treatment of wounded soldiers but clothing for civilian refugees in the Allied nations. Volunteer knitters turned out items for American military personnel. Besides putting their expertise with knitting needles to good use, female Red Cross volunteers staffed a canteen that provided food for nearly eight thousand servicemen. Since there was no markup on the items sold at the canteen, patrons were able to enjoy a nutritious meal for between five and ten cents. Interestingly, anyone wishing cigarettes or stationery was not charged for these items. The 233 soldiers comprising one of the cohorts of men assigned to the Saunders Trade School for two months of specialized training in the summer of 1918 took their meals at a Red Cross canteen set up in the Young Women's Christian Association, or Y.W.C.A., building right across from Saunders. Forty female volunteers, along with two cooks and three dishwashers, staffed the canteen serving three meals a day to the soldiers. On Sunday nights women from various churches supplied supper and entertainment at the canteen. The Red Cross also provided a canteen at Bryn Mawr Park for the three dozen men guarding the aqueduct. Besides assisting soldiers, the Red Cross operated an emergency diet kitchen for people recovering from the influenza epidemic in 1918.

Like the Red Cross, the Salvation Army was extremely active during the war. Salvation Army volunteers knitted sweaters by the hundreds for servicemen, and Salvation Army officers paid visits to Yonkers families who had members in the military. The Young Men's Christian Association, or Y.M.C.A., also made invaluable contributions, both during the conflict, and immediately thereafter. In 1917, the organization's brand-new building was thrown open to seven thousand soldiers encamped at Van Cortlandt Park and to sailors on leave from ships on the Hudson. Servicemen were able to use the resources of the Y twenty-four hours a day. According to Y officials:

> Day after day, and week after week, these fine young fellows
> made use of our showers and swimming pool to the number

of 500 daily, and on one day by actual count, 627. After the showers and swim, our lobby, reading-room and writing-room proved popular places. Writing home to mother seemed to be the pleasant duty of many. During the evening a social program, including motion pictures, music and games, was arranged.[22]

During the initial draft, the Yonkers Y.M.C.A. hosted receptions for the men going off to war. The night before reporting to Camp Upton, the large Army training camp in Yaphank, Long Island, inductees were invited to use all of the Y's facilities. They also enjoyed entertainment and refreshments. At the end of the evening, the general secretary of the Y.M.C.A. accompanied the men to the train.

The Yonkers Y became a sort of headquarters for eighteen young local men on leave from the military. They had survived the sinking of the *U.S.S. President Lincoln* following an attack by a German submarine. In the immediate postwar period the Y provided a three months' complimentary membership to veterans. The organization also established an employment bureau to assist former soldiers in their search for jobs. Officers of the Yonkers Y were well represented on the Yonkers Mayor's Committee on Reception of Returning Soldiers and Sailors, and the grand marshal and several other leaders of the gala Victory Parade, held on June 14, 1919, were Y men. Two weeks later, a memorial honoring the Yonkers men who died in the war was dedicated at the New York State Armory in Yonkers. The mood on this occasion was somber, and it contrasted sharply with the gaiety that had engulfed the city seven months earlier when the armistice was declared.

News of the State Department's official announcement of the armistice reached *The Yonkers Herald* office by telegraph at 3:10 a.m. on November 11, 1918. Not wasting a minute, the paper distributed bulletins containing the welcome news. Meanwhile, Mayor William Wallin had been notified by phone, and he immediately sent out police officers to alert the city's factory owners who spread the good news by blowing the factory whistles. "A large portion of the city's population was aroused by the blowing of the whistles, and going out into Getty Square and environs, they saw and eagerly read the bulletins of *The Yonkers Herald* which were already pasted on the windows of all-night restaurants and hotels and on the wind-shields of automobiles and windows of trolley cars."[23] In various parts of the city strains of "The Star-Spangled Banner" and "America the Beautiful" could be heard coming from Victrolas or pianos while overjoyed residents gathered at open windows and let loose with shouts of joy. "Soon the streets, particularly in the business centre of the city were filled with a laughing, shouting, joyous throng. Bon-fires blazed until the early dawn."[24] The *Herald* noted:

> It was probably the first time in the history of the city that parades were held at 4 A.M. . . . To be sure, they were in somewhat disorganized groups. . . . But the spirit was there along with the noise, and from early morn they continued marching, the girls singing as lustily as the men and boys.[25]

Votes for Women!

When the celebrations associated with the armistice and the return of the city's World War I veterans ended, life reverted to normal, but perceptive citizens of the "Queen City of the Hudson" sensed that there was a subtle change taking place. Women were gearing up to resume their fight for suffrage, and many men agreed that they deserved the right to vote, especially in view of their outstanding contributions to the war effort. Placed on hold during the war, the women's suffrage movement resumed on a grand scale in the postwar period. Suffrage rallies and large parades attracted suffragists and their male supporters. These events were designed to make a serious political statement, and they generally lacked the light-heartedness that had characterized a particularly charming parade held in Yonkers during the war. This march was a colorful prelude to a week-long circus to benefit the Children's Pavilion at St. John's Riverside Hospital. Five hundred people participated in what was billed as the Society Circus parade, which wended its way through city streets to the Tenth Regiment Armory on Nepperhan Avenue, which had been selected as the venue for the much ballyhooed circus. With the mayor and police chief in the lead, approximately a hundred society girls and matrons, posing as bears, clowns, and Yama Yama girls—performers whose costumes suggested a bogeyman or yama—flashed brilliant smiles at onlookers along the parade route. At the armory, in addition to the circus performance, there were a sideshow, fortunetellers, and a clever but disappointing kissing booth. A pretty young lass was positioned in front of the booth selling kisses for ten cents apiece, but when eager young men forked over the money and were allowed to enter the booth where they expected to find an equally alluring girl, they were greeted by a burly man! Presumably, a good laugh was had by all!

In contrast with the hospital fundraiser, parades and other events related to the suffrage movement were serious business, both before and after the war. At an April 1913 meeting convened by the New York Men's League for Equal Suffrage, a group that supported the suffragists, both men and women addressed a large audience at Philipsburgh Hall on Hudson Street. One of the female speakers pointed out that women had "personal freedom but it would not be long secure without the ballot."[26] She then asked the audience whether they thought "women are just as much privileged to that ballot as the man. She has not more say in the running of the country's affairs than the slave and, if there is a man here who says it is just, he ought to be examined."[27]

Compared with the beautifully gowned women who acted as ushers at the Philipsburgh Hall event, more casual attire was the order of the day at the Yonkers Woman Suffrage Association's first outdoor meeting a month later. With an official city permit in hand, organizers set out for the Moose Carnival grounds on South Broadway where they made speeches while standing on the rear seats of a car. According to *The Yonkers Herald,* "A crowd of several hundred persons assembled around the machine."[28] An event held several months later was less successful. On that occasion, in August 1913, two mounted suffragists rode into town on a pair of tired-looking horses. After a grueling day that had begun on the other side of the Hudson, followed by a crossing to Tarrytown and a tedious trip for riders and horses, the suffragists arrived in Yonkers in the early evening. Determined to hold an event in the city, they scrambled to find Mayor James T. Lennon, who they hoped would give them the permit required for a mass gathering. They came upon him in Getty Square but His Honor politely explained that he did not have the form in his possession. Ever the gentleman, Mayor Lennon assured the ladies that he would phone the police chief with orders not to interfere with the suffrage rally. Ultimately, the suffragists obtained a permit from the commissioner of public safety and the rally, complete with an address to a "crowd of several hundred," went on.[29] Despite the good turnout, the speakers raised little money in Yonkers. Weary and disappointed, the women, who were staying at the Getty House, turned in for the night and the next morning "quite a crowd of the curious collected and witnessed the departure" of the suffragists.[30]

Despite the inevitable setbacks they encountered, the suffragists persisted. In November 1915, following the rejection of a suffrage amendment on the New York State ballot, *The Yonkers Statesman* headlined an article "Suffragists Are At It Again."[31] Pointing out that the women were undaunted, the paper noted that Yonkers suffragists would hold a luncheon at Stanley's on South Broadway within days to "stand shoulder to shoulder in close formation for the next marching orders."[32] In an interview with the paper "at a late hour on election night," Mrs. Carl Osterheld observed: "The campaign has left us with one of the strongest organizations on record in New York State—an organization in which thousands of women will continue to serve voluntarily, untiringly, without remuneration and without thought of personal aggrandizement."[33] The optimism of Mrs. Osterheld and other Yonkers suffragists was attributable to the fact that a majority of Yonkers voters had cast ballots for the amendment. Since the city's suffragists had initially believed that the amendment had been voted down in Yonkers, although only by fewer than two hundred votes, there was rejoicing a few days after the election when the official count was concluded. "Woman Suffrage Won Here Official Returns Show," proclaimed the headline in *The Yonkers Herald*.[34] In print only slightly smaller, the paper declared: "Board of Election Commissioners Find To-day That Amendment Enfranchising Women Carried Yonkers by 167."[35]

Although buoyed by local support, suffragists would have to wait another five years before an amendment to the U.S. Constitution granted women the right to vote. The Nineteenth Amendment was ratified in 1920, and despite a court challenge to Tennessee's ratification vote, suffragists were convinced that a judicial ruling affirming suffrage would be forthcoming prior to the November election. In an editorial titled "Suffrage Cannot Be Blocked," *The Yonkers Herald* advised election officials to "go ahead as though ratification was effected . . . making every preparation, through assessment and registration, to permit the women to vote in November."[36] And that's exactly what happened.

As they cast their first ballots that November, suffragists were mindful not only of those in their own ranks who had stayed the course until victory was achieved but of the men who supported them. One of those men was John E. Andrus, the multimillionaire CEO of the Arlington Chemical Company and former Yonkers mayor and congressman. After women had finally achieved their goal, Andrus observed that women's suffrage was one of the four most outstanding achievements in the history of the United States, the others being achieving independence from Great Britain, abolishing slavery, and implementing Prohibition.

Leading Citizens

Dedicated though he was to the cause of women's suffrage, John E. Andrus was interested in other important contemporary issues as well. The well-being of children was a special concern, and it was uppermost on his mind in 1917 when he established the Surdna Foundation. The unusual name was actually Andrus spelled backwards. The new foundation was a philanthropic entity similar to the Rockefeller Foundation and one of its goals was to provide housing for orphans, especially children of fathers killed in war. Toward that end, he established an endowment of $2,500,000, a considerable sum at the time. Nearly a decade later, in 1926, he celebrated his eighty-fifth birthday by announcing that he intended to will nearly 50 percent of his fortune, estimated at $100 million, in a trust fund earmarked as an endowment for a home for impoverished Westchester children. Money not spent on local youngsters would be utilized to assist youths in other parts of New York State and the nation.

Known as "the millionaire straphanger" because he rode the subway, Andrus claimed that he had earned his first dollar at the age of ten selling fish to Horace Greeley, the celebrated nineteenth-century reformer and editor of *The New York Tribune*. Three-quarters of a century later, Andrus was still working and earning money. On the morning of his eighty-fifth birthday, in 1926, he headed to his Yonkers office but stole away from his desk to welcome a delegation of six Yonkers mayors. The incumbent and five of his predecessors presented Andrus with a huge floral arrangement and, despite the frigid February weather, had a photo op outdoors. Andrus later dined with family members at his home on Hudson Terrace. Two years later, on the eve of another birthday, Andrus felt so fit that he challenged a *New York Times* reporter to a boxing match. The newspaperman declined, preferring instead to interview the octogenarian, whose activities had remained status quo with one exception, his mode of transportation. Andrus had forsaken the subway for an automobile when he traveled to his New York City office. To prove that his new form of transportation was not the result of any physical decline, on his actual birthday, he grabbed a shovel and did some digging at the site of a new building on the grounds of the North Broadway children's home he had founded. He also chopped wood.

The year that he turned eighty-seven, John Andrus opened a theater costing nearly $1 million. Located at South Broadway and Vark Street, the theater, which was leased to the Loews corporation, featured films and vaudeville performances. It had a capacity of 2,800 and an air cooling system. That same year, Andrus became the biggest taxpayer in the City of Yonkers, surpassing Samuel Untermyer, who, in the mid-twenties, following the death of his wife, transferred Greystone to his children. Untermyer's three offspring received an unpleasant surprise after they had taken over the beautiful estate. The assessment jumped $10,000, an increase the family deemed unjustified. They pursued a legal remedy all the way to the New York State Supreme Court and obtained the reduction they sought.

Justice had been done, but the Untermyers soon had another reason to complain. This time the issue was police protection or, as the Untermyers saw it, the lack thereof. The Untermyers filed a complaint with the Yonkers commissioner of public safety questioning whether they were actually receiving any services for the $40,000 in annual taxes paid on Greystone. They pointed out that iron fencing along the perimeter of the estate, which spanned both sides of the Albany Post Road, had been repeatedly torn down and that the public had invaded the grounds, helping themselves to fruit and even camping on the property. That the Untermyers were furious about all of this is understandable but one cannot help but wonder whether some of the people who trespassed on the property felt that multimillionaires were fair game in an era when the lifestyles of the rich and famous contrasted as much as they had in the Gilded Age with those of the middle and working classes. That fact had been very evident during an unusual late fall cold snap in 1922. While average citizens struggled financially to keep their homes heated even minimally, wealthy citizens of Yonkers dispatched chauffeur-driven limousines to city docks to pick up sacks of coal on Saturdays and Sundays, when regular coal deliveries were not available.

That wealth conferred privilege and power was a given. So, too, was the ability of the well-heeled to do just about anything they pleased and if anything displeased them, they did something about it. When sugar refiner John C. Havemeyer objected to cigar smoke at Yonkers chamber of commerce meetings, he resigned but he didn't go away quietly. Instead, Havemeyer went to the newspapers to complain about the distribution of complimentary cigars at chamber meetings and the clouds of smoke that filled the air at chamber dinners. He explained that, prior to resigning, he had voiced his views to chamber members but that they had not only been unsympathetic but downright antagonistic. Havemeyer's antismoking campaign was but one of his attempts to fight what he believed to be the good fight. As an active lay member of the congregation, Havemeyer often took the place of the minister of the Yonkers Methodist Church to sermonize on moral and political issues. Despite poor health, which had forced him to retire at the age of forty-seven, his commitment to clean living paid off. He lived to the age of ninety, dying at his home on Lamartine Avenue in 1922.

Another prominent resident of the city who died in the 1920s was Alexander Smith Cochran. Regarded as the world's most eligible bachelor in his younger years, Cochran not only inherited his parents' vast wealth but $20 million of his uncle Warren B. Smith's $32 million fortune. After graduating from Yale, he was employed at the family's carpet company, rising to the position of president. Citing ill health, he handed the management of the company over to his brother and devoted himself to yachting. In 1914, he built the *Vanitie* to challenge Sir Thomas Lipton's *Shamrock* in the America's Cup Race. Three years later, just before the United States entered World War I, he accepted a commission in the British Navy. After the war he was secretly wed, in Paris, to a Polish singer, but the marriage lasted less than two years before being dissolved by a French judge.

Although he spent many years abroad, Alexander Smith Cochran neither forgot nor neglected his hometown and its people, including the employees of Alexander Smith and Sons. He instituted semiannual bonuses for the workers and, following his yacht-racing triumphs abroad, gave hundreds of workers who had been with the company for at least a decade $1,000 each. Cochran was genuinely interested in people and their well-being, so much so that *The New York Times* stated in his obituary: "Mr. Cochran was extremely democratic, and would stop in the street to chat with persons of modest circumstances. The people of Yonkers greatly admired him, and his employees adored him."[37] Under the terms of his will, one thousand carpet company workers received up to $10,000 each. St. John's Riverside Hospital was also a beneficiary, receiving a half-million dollars. In his lifetime he had been a major benefactor of St. John's, as well as the Y.M.C.A. and the Y.W.C.A., and had donated the land on which Yonkers erected a municipal tuberculosis hospital. Cochran himself was a victim of tuberculosis, having contracted the disease in his early forties, and this was the health problem to which he alluded in announcing that he was stepping down from an active role at Alexander Smith and Sons. He suffered from the disease for the last fifteen years of his life. After spending the winter of 1928–29 in California, he returned to New York, but his condition worsened. In June, he was transported by private train to Saranac Lake to be treated by Dr. Francis B. Trudeau, whose late father had founded the Trudeau Institute, which specialized in the treatment of tuberculosis. Alexander Smith Cochran died at the age of fifty-six, soon after arriving in Saranac Lake.

The Majestic Hudson

Alexander Smith Cochran's untimely death was a reminder of the fact that tuberculosis was not exclusively a disease of impoverished immigrants and slum dwellers living in overcrowded tenements. Since contagious diseases of all types tended to spread more rapidly among the poor, however, the city's health department was ever vigilant in its efforts to detect illnesses that posed a threat to Yonkers residents. Yet, ironically, in the 1920s the city was slow to remedy the problem of raw sewage emptying into the Hudson River from a dozen outfall pipes, one of which was adjacent to a popular swimming pier. Yonkers sewage was carried downriver but was brought back by the next tide. In 1927, the New York State health commissioner traveled to Yonkers to inform city officials, in no uncertain terms, that they had to stop polluting the river. When Yonkers failed to act, the state health commissioner threatened in 1929 to turn the matter over to the office of the attorney general. If Yonkers did not want to remedy the problem itself, it could become part of a new sewer district created by the Westchester County Sanitary Sewer Commission. The county's plan was to build a trunk sewer line through the Saw Mill River Valley and a sewage disposal plant in Yonkers. Citing the burden this would impose upon the city's taxpayers, Yonkers officials were anything but enthusiastic about this plan but they nevertheless were forced to acquiesce.

Besides being a great natural resource deserving of environmental protection, the Hudson River was a nautical lifeline. All sorts of things made their way to Yonkers by boat, and anything that impeded navigation on the river posed a direct economic threat to the city. For that reason, during particularly cold winters measures were taken to keep the main shipping channel open. Usually, the federal government sent cutters to break up ice floes in the river but in February 1914 when the cutters were unable to make headway against the ice, the Federal Sugar Refining Company imported a couple of strong tugboats to do the job, thereby allowing ships, waiting off Yonkers with their cargoes of raw sugar, to reach the company's dock. The inability of coal ships to reach docks in the city caused Mayor James T. Lennon to bring in a tug to deal with the ice. Yonkers was confronted with a similar problem during another extremely cold winter in 1917–18. In January 1918 the situation was so severe that the New York Central Railroad sent a special six-car train containing coal from Manhattan to Yonkers. Lacking enough coal for its citizens to heat their homes for even a day, Yonkers was desperate. The arrival of coal-filled rail cars provided some relief, but even more significant was the arrival of the icebreaker *Poughkeepsie* to free coal barges trapped by the ice.

As difficult as cold winters were, some of the greatest challenges on the mighty Hudson River occurred during the busy summer season when private pleasure boats, both large and small, vied for space on the waterway with the ferry and excursion steamboats. Most outings on the river were pleasurable and safe, but in June 1914 the *Tourist,* a sightseeing vessel, collided with barges and canal boats, which were lashed together.

The accident occurred mid-river between Alpine and Yonkers. One of the barge captains was killed; the captain of another barge, together with his wife and baby, who were on board with him, ended up in the water but all three were rescued by a nearby tugboat. One of the canal barges sank and the *Tourist* took on so much water that only its smokestack jutted out from the river when it finally came to rest close to Alpine. Everyone on board, including some who had taken to the water in an attempt to swim to New Jersey, was rescued by the tugboat that had picked up the barge captain's family.

A month later, two canoeists landed in St. John's Riverside Hospital after their little boat was swamped by a wave from an excursion steamer. The young men were camping at Palisades Interstate Park and were heading to Yonkers for provisions when the accident occurred. One of the young men was plucked out of the water unconscious after a half-hour; his companion was in the water for an hour. A fifteen-year-old resident of Ashburton Avenue was not so fortunate. After bragging to his friends that he could swim the mile of swiftly flowing river separating Yonkers from Alpine, he took the ferry over to New Jersey late on an August day in 1914, and shortly before sunset, with an escort consisting of one rowboat, he dove into the river. A good swimmer, he evidently thought he could make the crossing quickly, but he became thoroughly exhausted halfway across. When he slipped below the waves, his companions in the rowboat tried to rescue him but to no avail. Although he was found, he was pronounced dead upon arrival in Yonkers.

Drownings and accidents notwithstanding, the Hudson River remained a popular place of recreation, attracting swimmers, fishermen, and boaters, as well as people whose only contact with the waterway was an occasional trip on the ferry to Alpine. For some Yonkers families, the crossing to New Jersey was the highlight of the summer because it was usually combined with a picnic or hiking in the Palisades Interstate Park. For travelers whose objective was not a pleasant day in the park but, rather, transportation from one side of the Hudson to the other, the ferry left something to be desired. Waiting times could be long, and in winter ice brought ferry service to a halt. Clearly, something had to be done to create a reliable, year-round connection between opposite sides of the Hudson. At least that's what a United States senator from New Jersey thought. Citing the need to relieve congestion between New Jersey and New York, he proposed a temporary solution: a pontoon bridge from the vicinity of Yonkers to the area around Alpine. Such a structure would last ten to fifteen years. It would rest on supports consisting of wooden ships retired by the federal government following World War I. The plan was to purchase fifty of these mothballed vessels and space them far enough apart to permit tow boats, private vessels, and freighters to navigate the Hudson. Larger ships would travel beneath the bridge's center span, which could be raised. A private company would undertake to build and maintain the bridge and would charge tolls for crossing the span.

With a tunnel between Manhattan and New Jersey at least five years away, a pontoon bridge requiring only a year to build was a very intriguing concept, but not everyone thought so. Steamboat companies and chambers of commerce on both sides of the river joined forces to oppose the bridge, claiming that it would impede navigation and that it might be swept away by ice during a bad winter. Proponents of the bridge argued that the span would be firmly anchored to bedrock by chains and that any ice collecting in the vicinity of the bridge would be broken up by three tugs permanently located at the bridge to fight fires on the wooden span. This argument didn't carry much weight with seasoned captains who testified at a hearing held by the Army Corps of Engineers. They pointed out that thick ice was not uncommon in the Hudson as far south as Yonkers and a pontoon bridge simply could not withstand the pressure of that ice. Despite all of the arguments against the bridge, Yonkers liked the idea. Mayor Wallin was convinced that the bridge "would prove a very great impetus to the city's trade, growth and general prosperity, and that in view of this fact, the city should stand ready to go more than half way with the Federal government in bring-ing about its construction" by "arranging the city's highway system as to have it synchronize with the traffic on the bridge."[38] But, alas, it was not to be. Only three months after the project had been proposed, the pri-vate company planning to build it bowed out because it had received an ultimatum from the federal agency selling the obsolete wooden ships. The company was told to pay for the ships immediately, but as the project was still awaiting congressional authorization, the company refused to comply with the ultimatum. Thus, the pontoon bridge that Yonkers residents were eagerly awaiting died aborning.

Parks and Parkways

Other projects, some of them quite grand, did become reality, however, in the twenties. One of them was the creation of a vast system of new parks being developed by Westchester County in conjunction with the building of parkways. Besides creating outdoor recreational spaces along the Hudson River and Long Island Sound, Westchester County provided splendid new facilities in inland areas, including the Saw Mill River Valley, where Tibbetts Brook Park opened, amidst great fanfare, in 1927. With the exception of a second athletic field, the complex was fully operational at the beginning of the summer season. A crowd estimated at between fifteen and twenty thousand people turned out for opening day ceremonies. Since county facilities were not restricted to Westchester residents in those days, visitors from New York City were in attendance. Inhabitants of the nearby Bronx would return again and again to enjoy the park's splendid facilities, which included two manmade lakes, a playground, a wading pool, athletic fields, and a cavernous concrete swimming pool that "when initially constructed . . . was the largest in the eastern United States."[39] With a capacity of three thousand people, the 430-foot-long pool proved to be a popular spot. Park patrons could not jump into the water, however, until the opening day festivities concluded. These included a pageant by students from various schools in Yonkers, patriotic songs sung by literally thousands of children, a regatta of colorfully decorated boats, and speeches by county and city officials. Yonkers Mayor William A. Walsh was effusive in his praise of the county, declaring that recreational facilities enhanced the value of a community's real estate and protected children who might otherwise be playing in the streets.

Like other Westchester County parks, Tibbetts Brook was a component of a much larger system of parks developed by the Westchester County Park Commission, a governmental body that also built parkways. The first of these new roadways, the Bronx River Parkway, spurred the suburbanization of the eastern part of Yonkers. In 1925, the year the parkway was completed, *The New York Times* published a lengthy article titled "Yonkers: A Centre of Choice Homes."[40] Citing the easy commute from Yonkers to Manhattan as an important reason for the city's post–World War I residential expansion, the *Times* quoted a real estate developer who praised the city's assets, including its parks and streets as well as the fact that it boasted "more churches and charitable institutions than most cities of its size."[41] In 1926 Yonkers was one of the twenty-five leading American cities in terms of building activity. Besides new homes on vacant parcels in the older Armour Villa Park, Cedar Knolls, and Lawrence Park West areas, most of whose residents signed a petition in 1918 requesting support from the Yonkers Board of Aldermen for the annexation of their enclaves to Bronxville, houses were going up in Crestwood. The Bronx River Parkway, "which provided easy egress to the city at all hours of the day and night, attracted many notables to become Crestwood residents. Among them was Broadway and film star Eleanor Powell, dancing partner of Gene Kelley and Fred Astaire."[42] Another noted show business figure, composer Jerome Kern, also lived in Yonkers. While residing on Dellwood Road in Cedar Knolls he produced the musical scores for *Show Boat* and other plays.

In addition to single-family homes, apartment buildings went up at a record rate in the 1920s. One truly grand project never made the leap from the drawing board to bricks and mortar, however. It was to have been an apartment hotel, costing $1,300,000 and containing one hundred units, some 350 feet above the Hudson on the Hendrick Hudson Hotel site in Park Hill. Crowned by a gold illuminated dome, the proposed structure was intended to be the centerpiece of a complex featuring exquisitely landscaped grounds, teahouses, and tennis and handball courts. As an apartment hotel, it would also have maid service. In this state-of-the-art complex, each unit was to be equipped with the very latest in appliances, including dishwashers. Kitchens, as well as baths, in each of the three- to seven-room apartments, would have tile walls, and the central, oil-fired heating plant would maintain a temperature of seventy degrees in the apartments even when it was zero outside.

Although the spectacular apartment hotel planned for the site of the Hendrick Hudson Hotel did not materialize, many other multifamily buildings were erected, so many in fact that by 1928 there was a glut of rental units available and developers were becoming anxious. Reducing the rents for vacant apartments proved to be the solution for many building owners. In new apartments along the Bronx River Parkway, however, discounts were not necessary; in South Yonkers they were. The western part of the city, however, was doing well in the 1920s. A new post office was built in the area, which became known as Larkin Plaza in honor of Mayor Thomas F. Larkin, who suffered a stroke and died, at age fifty-six, on a golf course during an outing sponsored by the Yonkers City Club in 1928. Getty Square, while still the city's business hub, was expected to benefit by the broadening of the commercial district to Larkin Plaza.

An Industrial Powerhouse

As important as it was for the well-being of Yonkers, economic activity in the downtown area was eclipsed by that of the factories and refineries, whether those along the Hudson River or those back from the water's edge. Yonkers was still a factory town in the 1920s and proud of it. Even while touting the suburbanization under way in the eastern part of Yonkers, *The New York Times* noted industry was the moving force of "the energies of a city which is growing rapidly in population, wealth and the influence which attends a great production of national value."[43] Industry certainly buoyed the city financially and during economic downturns, such as the one following World War I. Layoffs and wage cuts had a profound ripple effect upon Yonkers. In 1921 the six hundred workers at the National Sugar Refining Company saw their wages reduced from forty-five cents per hour to forty cents. That same year, 250 mainly female employees in the trimming department of the Waring Hat Company went on strike rather than accept wage cuts of 10 to 20 percent. In 1922, 1,200 employees of the Federal Sugar Refining Company left their jobs for two months, but their departure was involuntary. The president of the company, Claus A. Spreckels, furloughed the workers rather than pay what he considered artificially inflated prices for the commodity. Closing the plant was his way of trying to put a stop to speculation in the sugar market.

In the early 1920s, another major Yonkers industry, Alexander Smith and Sons, became disenchanted with foreign suppliers of machinery and decided to do something about it by constructing its own equipment. The carpet company, whose seven thousand employees were producing fifty-seven miles of carpet a day in 1923, was in the midst of a $3 million expansion, which would transform it into the largest comprehensive carpet manufacturing company on the planet. Attaining this goal was not easy. The contractor erecting a concrete weaving mill across the Saw Mill River struck quicksand and had to sink thirty-foot pilings. Coffer dams were required to protect the foundations of new buildings, but despite these obstacles the expansion went forward. By the end of the decade, when a hundred carpet distributors from throughout the United States toured the company's various buildings to view the firm's new machinery and enhanced processes for manufacturing different types of carpeting, Alexander Smith and Sons was number one in its field. The company was prospering mightily and as a result was able to continue the practice of providing bonuses to its workers. Although the profit-sharing plan introduced by Alexander Smith Cochran in 1911 had been fine tuned through the years, by the mid-1920s, more than $6 million had been distributed to employees. In 1925 almost seven thousand Smith employees shared $439,000. To be eligible, a worker had to be employed for at least a year, and the sum received was a percentage of the person's annual earnings. It ranged from 2 to 15 percent and, as *The Yonkers Herald* put it, stating the obvious, the bonuses "tended to keep" the workers.[44]

The decade of the 1920s was a period of innovation in Yonkers and not just in the carpet industry. Thanks to a local resident, the city became home to a major research facility, the Boyce Thompson Institute for Plant Research. Located across North Broadway from his estate, The Alders, the institute was established by William Boyce Thompson, a financier who specialized in mining companies. The institute's purpose was to study plant diseases in order to safeguard the food supply for a rapidly growing nation. Realizing that there would be "two hundred million people in this country pretty soon," Thompson vowed to "work out some institution to deal with plant physiology, to help protect the basic needs of the 200 million. Not an uplift foundation, but a scientific institution dealing with definite things, like germination, parasites, plant diseases, and plant potentialities."[45] Opening day in 1924 attracted distinguished scientists from the United States and abroad who were among three hundred guests inspecting the laboratory and greenhouses that constituted phase one of the institute's ambitious building program.

The outstanding scientific work undertaken by the Boyce Thompson Institute was made possible by its founder's commitment of his personal resources. To Colonel Thompson, utilizing $10 million of his fortune for the public good was the right thing to do. His approach to handling wealth, however, was in sharp contrast to the expenditures of some well-to-do Americans in the Roaring Twenties. Yet, if money was earned honestly or inherited, most people conceded that the person possessing it was entitled to do what he pleased with his riches. Ill-gotten gains were another matter, and Yonkers was the epicenter of a scheme to accumulate wealth by defrauding clueless investors.

Crime Doesn't Pay

The victims were mostly Russian immigrants; the swindlers, working from an office in New York and another in the Proctor Theatre Building on South Broadway in Yonkers, set up two companies: The Great Oriental Land Development Industrial Company, Inc. and the Iridium, Gold and Platinum Company. The Land Development company purchased a ninety-two-acre farm in Nepera Park where they claimed to have found gold. News of their "discovery" was disseminated by the Iridium, Gold and Platinum Company through a Russian-language newspaper and pamphlets, which were distributed all over the United States. The literature featured testimonials from alleged prospectors, including a man who claimed to be an experienced miner from the Ural Mountain area. When Yonkers residents got wind of this, the race was on to dig up all sorts of vacant land in the city. No gold was discovered, of course, and the man who had planted a small quantity of the precious metal on the property of the so-called Nepperhan Valley gold mine testified against the principals in the Iridium, Gold and Platinum Company. The swindlers, who were said to have stolen between $500,000 and $1,000,000 from unsophisticated investors, issued beautifully engraved stock certificates, in Russian. Purchasers of the stock were informed that after a sufficient quantity of gold had been removed from the mine, the value of each share of stock would soar to $600. This represented a six-hundredfold increase over the original one dollar value of each share. Investors were told that the Nepera Park farm where the mining was to take place contained platinum as well as gold, and that the combined estimated value of the metals was $10 billion! The company's prospectus went so far as to break down the value. It claimed that there was $8 billion in gold on the property and $2 billion in platinum. As an added inducement, the prospectus hinted at the possibility that the farm would also yield silver worth $100 million.

Some investors insisted upon visiting the farm. Once there they were met by an American, who, according to the assistant district attorney involved in prosecuting the case, had been the United States consul general in St. Petersburg for several years prior to World War I. As suspicious investors looked on, this man grabbed handfuls of dirt and tossed them into a rock crushing machine. Out came a few gold nuggets, which had been planted. The process was repeated for platinum. At one point, hundreds of Russians were at work digging on a hillside at the Nepera Park property. The red ribbon of rock they uncovered was said to be a rich vein, and this was enough to assuage some of the suspicious investors who visited the property in the early 1920s. One especially unlucky man testified that he had invested his entire savings, totaling $800. So convinced was he that the mine was a sure thing, he borrowed $1,000 to purchase additional shares with the thought that he would repay a little each week from his twenty-dollar paycheck and then pay back the bulk of the loan as soon as the mine was up and running. For this poor fellow and countless others, "Yukon in Yonkers," as this scheme was dubbed by the press, was a bust.[46]

The mining scheme was one of the more unusual crimes committed in Yonkers during the twenties. More traditional criminal activity consisted of robberies, including the theft of jewelry from the home of John Andrus in 1929. The thief entered the Andrus residence on Hudson Terrace at approximately 9 p.m. and hid until the family went to bed. Then he attempted to enter Mr. Andrus's room, but it was locked, as was the next room he tried, that of Mrs. Albert Benedict, Mr. Andrus's daughter. While trying to figure out what to do next, the burglar sat down on a couch and was soon fast asleep. Upon awakening, he found a hiding place in the house and there he stayed until the next morning. After family members got up and headed downstairs for breakfast, the crafty thief strolled through the bedrooms and left, undetected, with $12,000 worth of jewelry. Jewels and cash were not the only items stolen in Yonkers robberies during the 1920s. Early in the decade, horse thieves ran off with two prize animals owned by a local mortician and used to pull a hearse. Illegal gambling was another form of criminal activity that existed in Yonkers. From time to time it made headlines as city officials attempted to crack down on bookmaking, but far more newsworthy than the placing of illegal bets on sporting activities was criminal activity undertaken to circumvent the Eighteenth Amendment to the United States Constitution.

"Drys" versus "Wets":
The Strange Case of William H. Anderson

The Prohibition amendment outlawing the manufacture, sale, consumption, and importation of alcoholic beverages, and the Volstead Act passed by Congress to implement the amendment, were welcomed by some Americans while others had misgivings. Samuel Untermyer, who was a director of a large British brewing company and the architect of a deal in which three of the biggest breweries in Boston were acquired by British investors, believed that Prohibition would not work without strict enforcement. This would entail "search and seizure of liquor in private dwellings," something omitted from the legislation implementing Prohibition.[47] According to Untermyer, this amounted to "immunity for the rich man who can stow away his liquor for years to come . . . while the poor man who cannot afford this luxury is discriminated against."[48] In Untermyer's opinion, this was "a vicious piece of class legislation."[49]

Untermyer did not prevail, but his concerns about enforcing Prohibition proved very sound. The federal revenue agents charged with this task were involved in an uphill fight in which their lives were frequently on the line. An agent who walked into a Dock Street establishment in 1920 and ordered a drink of whiskey was in the process of arresting the bartender who served him when the owner of the place pulled out a revolver. The agent was not harmed, and he managed to apprehend both men. Despite some success in enforcing the Volstead Act, nabbing violators was a hit and miss operation. As a result, some supporters of Prohibition felt that the authorities were not doing an adequate job to enforce the law. William H. Anderson, a resident of Park Hill and state superintendent of the Anti-Saloon League of New York, charged, in the summer of 1920, that government officials were accepting monetary payments to ignore Prohibition violations. According to Anderson, "the nub of the matter" was that citizens were paying taxes and weren't getting their money's worth when it came to law enforcement.[50] His organization was determined to persuade the taxpayers "to demand an honest dollar's worth of law enforcement for an honest dollar paid in taxes."[51] A few months later, Anderson published "Morals, Taxes and Law Enforcement—Their Inter-Relationship in Yonkers"; this pamphlet was really a call to arms to the citizens of Yonkers to support aggressive enforcement of Prohibition by embracing what Anderson called the "Yonkers Plan."[52] This was to be a five-year program costing at least $5,000 a year. The money, which would be donated by honest citizens, would be placed in a Yonkers bank and paid to people who secured evidence against violators of the Volstead Act. V. Everit Macy, commissioner of charities and corrections for Westchester County, was so enthusiastic about the plan, which he felt could apply to other communities in the county, that he offered to donate $5,000 per year for five years, provided that others contributed as well. John D. Rockefeller Jr. also pledged $5,000, attaching the same conditions.

Once he had high-profile supporters, Anderson's demand for more effective law enforcement produced results. Ninety-one federal Prohibition enforcement agents descended upon Yonkers on an October day in 1920 and arrested twenty-five bartenders and bar owners. Two truckloads of liquor were also netted in the raid. The Yonkers commissioner of public safety dismissed the suggestion that this major raid was a direct response to William Anderson's crusade, but many Yonkers residents thought otherwise. A month later, Yonkers police broke down doors during raids at three saloons and two stills and hauled away seventy barrels of liquor. Federal agents also paid a return visit in November 1920. Led by Izzy Einstein and Moe Smith, agents who became celebrated as the team of "Izzy and Moe," the agents moved about the city for several days. After obtaining search warrants, they launched a series of raids, which netted two truckloads of liquor and twenty-seven people. Izzy and Moe were back in Yonkers in October 1921. This time they located twenty-two truckloads of liquor and staged raids in two dozen places in the city. Another series of raids, in March 1922, proved disappointing. One hundred agents descended upon Yonkers and, armed with search warrants, they raided forty-two locales, but found evidence in only a dozen of them. Disappointing though this was, the feds kept their eyes on Yonkers because the city was thought to be a principal distribution center for liquor smuggled in from Canada, as well as a destination for small boats transporting alcohol from the Bahamas. Moreover, William Anderson and the Anti-Saloon League kept the pressure on.

Skilled at disseminating information to the press, Anderson was constantly in the news. In 1923, he grabbed more headlines than ever before but not because of his crusade for effective law enforcement. This time, Anderson himself was under scrutiny for his handling of the Anti-Saloon League's finances. A former financial official of the league, whom Anderson had fired, charged that Anderson had taken half of the commissions he was paid as a subscription agent for the organization. The accuser also alleged that most of the payments to Anderson had been made in cash and were not listed in the league's financial records. Anderson issued a denial stating that his accuser and two other dismissed employees were out for revenge. Despite his insistence that he had done nothing wrong, Anderson was on the hot seat and in addition to defending himself, he had to defend his son, who, according to press accounts, had been expelled from Wesleyan University for a "drinking escapade."[53] Anderson informed the papers that he had been informed by Wesleyan that the story, which had been attributed to a professor, was "a fabrication."[54]

Over the course of the next few months, the always controversial William Anderson became even more so, and not only because he refused to answer questions about yet another aspect of the Anti-Saloon League's finances, a publicity fund, but because he took on Raymond B. Fosdick, a philanthropic adviser to the Rockefeller family. In a pamphlet titled "Some Facts About Rockefeller Support of the Anti-Saloon League of New York and Mr. Raymond B. Fosdick," Anderson denied that the Rockefellers had donated $100,000 a year to the league and insisted that commissions had not been paid on any of the contributions the Rockefellers had actually made to the league. He also stated that Raymond Fosdick had attempted to influence Anti-Saloon League policy and to dissuade the Rockefellers from donating to the league. Fosdick, in his view, was actually supporting the "wets," that is to say, opponents of Prohibition, because of his alleged opposition to proposed legislation calling for enhanced state and local enforcement of Prohibition. Fosdick denied Anderson's accusations and was backed up by John D. Rockefeller Jr., who issued a statement of support from the family's winter retreat in Ormond Beach, Florida. At the same time, Rockefeller urged that all of the financial records of the Anti-Saloon League be made public. Undaunted, Anderson continued to speak out and to portray himself as a victim of a conspiracy involving "not merely the criminal liquor interests alone."[55] According to Anderson, the Tammany political machine was also involved as were "wet Republican machine politicians."[56] He then asserted "the power and scope of the influences interested in 'getting' me are the best proof both of the effectiveness of my work and the failure of ordinary methods to eliminate me," adding that "it is impossible to convict me under an indictment, if one is returned."[57]

How wrong he was! In July 1923, Anderson was indicted on larceny, extortion, and forgery charges. He was charged with stealing nearly $2,000 in interest from the league on nearly $25,000 he obtained from the organization's directors to reimburse him for what he claimed were outlays from his personal funds for public relations expenses. He was also charged with doctoring the organization's books to cover up a $4,400 extortion payment from the former league employee who had made the initial accusations against him.

On the eve of the trial, the directors of the Anti-Saloon League passed formal resolutions reaffirming their faith in him, but within a month they withdrew their support. In the interim, a newsworthy court drama played out. When Anderson took the stand, he admitted that he had split commissions with his accuser. Responding to questions from his attorney, former New York governor Charles S. Whitman, Anderson explained that the idea for sharing the commissions had originated with his accuser. He also stated that since he had spent considerable time providing his accuser with suggestions for fundraising, his acceptance of part of the man's commissions "wasn't anything more than a square proposition."[58] He said that he had gone along with the split in order to eliminate the debt of nearly twenty-five thousand dollars incurred for the public relations campaign. Anderson also said that the money for this initiative had come from "a perfect stranger," whom he refused to identify further than simply saying he was a Mr. John T. King, and that someone who worked for this shadowy figure directed the campaign but did not provide documentation for campaign-related expenses.[59] Just before the defense rested its case, Governor Whitman produced a surprise witness who informed the court that he had been employed by the campaign director to write newspaper articles and public relations pieces touting Prohibition and that he had been paid in cash. The witness also revealed that he had met with William Anderson but that they did not speak about the campaign director, who had forbidden the publicist to do so. Governor Whitman also produced, as character witnesses for Anderson, a prominent Manhattan rabbi and several Protestant pastors from Westchester County.

When the day's court proceedings ended, William Anderson hopped into a taxi and headed uptown from the Criminal Courts Building to the Marble Collegiate Church for the annual union meeting of ministers. In advance of the meeting, clergymen planning to attend were informed that Mr. Anderson was going to reveal details of an alleged attempt by a Republican political figure to bribe an Anti-Saloon League employee who had been gathering evidence against breweries. Anderson supposedly was going to name names, but he didn't, claiming that to do so at that point would jeopardize work under way and alienate a major supporter of the league's work. Anderson's appearance at the ministers' meeting was his last hurrah, because the very next day he was convicted. According to *The Yonkers Herald*, "Newspaper offices were flooded with telephone calls inquiring [about] the verdict. More persons asked this information, telephone operators said, than have ever inquired the result of a World's Series baseball game."[60]

Editorializing on Anderson's conviction, *The New York Times* declared, "If ever an indicted man had a fair trial, it was had by William H. Anderson."[61] The *Times* went on to observe that the support Anderson continued to enjoy from the officers of the Anti-Saloon League "may do injury to the cause which these excellent men have at heart."[62] It didn't take the league long to come to the same conclusion. The organization's officers did an about-face after Anderson was sentenced to from one to two years imprisonment in Sing Sing for "deliberately" committing "the crime of forgery."[63] Anderson's chief counsel, Governor Whitman, made a last-minute plea for clemency, noting that his client had enjoyed "an unblemished reputation" prior to his trial.[64] Whitman also pointed out that "no injury, no loss, no fraud had been suffered by anybody" because of Mr. Anderson's actions.[65] Although Whitman made a motion for a new trial, it was denied, but Anderson was not hauled off to prison immediately. He was released on the $5,000 bail he had posted at the time of his indictment six months earlier. That he was able to return to his Park Hill home rather than take up residence in Sing Sing was attributable to the fact that the judge, responding to another motion by Governor Whitman, "granted an order for a certificate of reasonable doubt" which was to be argued in the Special Term of the Supreme Court.[66] Although Anderson was temporarily a free man, the day after his sentencing, blazing headlines announced that the Anti-Saloon League had dismissed Anderson, who, whether by choice or otherwise, had submitted his letter of resignation to the organization's board.

A few days before Anderson's next court date, *The New York Times* observed, in an editorial, that suspending his conviction would be "flying in the face of justice."[67] In a scathing criticism of the former superintendent, the paper declared that "his whole course and attitude have been impenitent, insolent and violent," and consequently the paper felt that he deserved no leniency.[68] Within days after this editorial appeared, Governor Whitman was back in court arguing that the jury had not been charged correctly. The prosecutor took issue with Whitman's assertion that a jury could not determine what constitutes legal proof. The presiding judge in the Special Term of the Supreme Court rejected Anderson's application for a certificate of reasonable doubt. Had the certificate been granted, Anderson would have remained free pending an appeal. Instead, he prepared to journey north to Sing Sing from his Park Hill home, where he had been holed up, refusing to issue any statements to the army of reporters camped outside. Before leaving Yonkers, Anderson who, days earlier, had surrendered his pistol, made arrangements for his wife to secure a weapon for what he said was the defense of their home!

Five months into his sentence, Anderson received some bad news, namely that the Appellate Division of the Supreme Court had upheld his conviction. Once again *The New York Times* weighed in on the matter. The paper termed "revolting" Anderson's "attack on the courts, the Irish Catholic Tammany Judges."[69] Referring to Anderson's Anti-Saloon League supporters who continued to defend him, the *Times* said: "Let them stop whimpering over a justly convicted criminal."[70] Neither Anderson nor his supporters heeded the advice of *The New York Times*. In September 1924 the former superintendent of the Anti-Saloon League was lashing out again in a document titled "A Message from William H. Anderson Through His Wife." Mrs. Anderson was said to have written the preface but the rest of the piece was vintage Mr. Anderson. As he had so often done prior to his conviction, he came out swinging against the "wets." Comparing himself to Christ, he insisted that God would "avenge him," and he implored his supporters to pray that the court of appeals, the next step in the judicial process, would reverse his conviction.[71] He also discussed life in prison, where he was doing some teaching, and claimed that this offered an "unusual opportunity for observation respecting immigration and education in their relation to crime."[72] For him, prison was "a rest cure combined with a most unique sociological experience."[73]

The rest cure lasted longer than he hoped when the court of appeals voted unanimously to uphold his conviction despite Governor Whitman's argument before the appeals court that technical errors had been made by the trial court regarding the issue of intent to commit fraud. Although Whitman could have attempted to move the case to the U.S. Supreme Court, the process would have been so time consuming that his client would have finished serving his sentence before the highest court in the land heard his case. There was nothing for Anderson to do but wait it out in Sing Sing. As things turned out, he didn't have to wait too long because the state board of parole reversed a ruling requiring prisoners to serve the minimum term to which they had been sentenced. The reversal meant that time off for good behavior would be taken into consideration. Although it was generally agreed that Anderson had been a model prisoner, he was questioned at length by a panel of parole commissioners. Many of their queries dealt with Anderson's views on the court system. When asked if he had "any feelings against the courts," he replied: "I believe that under a constitutional form of government the courts should be supreme."[74] This evidently satisfied the commissioners, who also took into account a letter from the prosecutor in the case. The prosecutor refrained from making any recommendation about whether Anderson should be paroled prior to completing the minimum sentence but he noted that the convict had issued numerous public statements attacking the grand jury, the prosecutor himself, and other public officials. In the prosecutor's opinion, this constituted disrespect for the courts.

To an extent, the prosecutor's letter was offset by Anderson's deft fielding of the questions and by the impressive list of references he supplied to the commissioners. Included on the list were prominent clergymen from New York City and Westchester and the general secretary of the Yonkers Y.M.C.A. All of this went a long way in convincing the commissioners to release the controversial prisoner. On Christmas Eve 1924, Anderson walked out of Sing Sing and returned to Yonkers. Despite a cold rain, "he presented a natty appearance. He had on a gray, well-fitting suit, double-breasted. A four-in-hand of blue and red silk had been carefully tied."[75] Waiting for Anderson outside the prison was the pastor of the Central Methodist Church in Yonkers. As they drove away in his pastor's car, Anderson, his "head drooped," seemed "to be depressed."[76]

Two months later, Anderson was back on his soapbox. In his first public statement since his release from prison, he charged that not only was Yonkers wet but that "liquor conditions are rotten in Yonkers."[77] Anderson's assertion was made the day a liquor-related brawl led to a shooting incident in the city. The Yonkers commissioner of public safety immediately called upon federal Prohibition agents to do something about the situation in Yonkers, while a city judge refused to reduce bail for two men nabbed on a truck used to transport bootlegged alcohol. The judge declared that he did not want Yonkers perceived "as a station on the underground road for bootleg traffic."[78] Anderson could not have agreed more, but he blamed New York State for having the least effective Prohibition enforcement in the nation. Pointing out that Yonkers had the "power to enact an enforcement ordinance," he admitted that things would not improve until New York enacted "a new State dry law."[79] Anderson was at it again in June 1925, issuing a sixty-four page pamphlet attacking the New York State management of the Anti-Saloon League. He accused the management of trying to ruin him personally and financially by refusing to turn over $6,000 given by various supporters to his defense fund and of aiding "wets," in a conspiracy against dry Protestant churches.

Bootleggers and Rumrunners

Rail though he did against his opponents, Anderson faded from the headlines. The struggle to enforce the Volstead Act continued, however, and sometimes the effort paid off handsomely. In 1926, for example, customs agents appeared in the Hudson off Yonkers and seized the steamship *Eker*. As soon as they got close to the somewhat rickety vessel, then nearly fifty years old, their nostrils were assailed by the unmistakable smell of alcohol. Once on board, they discovered approximately three hundred gallons of grain alcohol in the ship's water tank. Below decks, grain alcohol was also discovered in a tank capable of storing at least twenty thousand gallons. Although both the *Eker*'s master and engineer had jumped ship prior to the arrival of the customs agents, crew members were apprehended, as was a Yonkers man whose little boat was suspiciously close to the *Eker*. The seizure of this ship was hailed as the "most important ever made by customs men" in the war against rumrunning, presumably because, in addition to the enormous quantity of alcohol seized and its value, which was estimated to be $1 million, a document attesting to $20,000 in graft payments made for the purpose of getting the *Eker* upriver to Yonkers was found aboard the vessel.[80] This important piece of evidence listed specific amounts paid to policemen and Prohibition enforcement agents to look the other way.

In their efforts to eliminate the flow of alcohol government officials scored few victories as significant as the seizure of the *Eker*. Instead of high drama on the Hudson, the struggle to control bootlegging and rumrunning usually consisted of periodic raids at local watering holes and at some establishments that, outwardly at least, seemed to be above suspicion. The State Cereal and Beverage Company, a front company for Underhill's Brewery, for example, appeared to be complying with the law by turning out near-beer, a nonalcoholic drink. What the authorities didn't realize was that the brewery was producing real beer at night. The mastermind of this operation was believed to be the infamous Dutch Schultz. Under his direction, the company installed an ingenious system of hoses connected with the Yonkers sewer system to deliver real beer to various collection points and from there to local watering holes. There were other, less inventive, ways of obtaining alcohol in Yonkers. In February 1929, Prohibition agents discovered this when they visited a pharmacy on

Saratoga Avenue. Although they lacked prescriptions for medicinal alcohol, the agents were able to purchase liquor. Once the transaction had taken place, the pharmacy was raided and a variety of hard liquor and different kinds of wine were discovered.

During the Prohibition era, one of the more unusual apprehensions involved neither bootlegging nor rumrunning but a runaway sea lion named Jerry who abandoned his spouse, Molly-O, and "Nell, their flapper child," all of whom resided in a pool at a garden center.[81] Three-hundred-pound Jerry escaped and "ambled along Central Avenue and Tuckahoe Road, causing timid motorists to forswear the use of Westchester County cider."[82] One driver attempted to alert an incredulous police officer, but, suspicious that the motorist had been hitting the bottle, the officer warned him about "the S-curve up the road," adding: "There's a herd of elephants just round the corner of it."[83] One can only imagine the policeman's surprise when he read, in the following day's newspaper, a full account of how Jerry had made it to the Bronx River and from there all the way down to the Botanical Gardens where he successfully negotiated a fifteen-foot waterfall. But, alas, poor Jerry was captured, and returned to his family in Yonkers. Rounding him up had been such an ordeal, however, that his captors probably needed a good stiff drink once they had completed their task.

The same might be said of Yonkers residents who suffered big losses in the stock market crash of 1929. For most Yonkers residents the real issue was survival during the decade-long Great Depression, which gripped the country in the aftermath of what *The Yonkers Statesman* termed "the record down sweep of the market" on Black Tuesday, the October day in 1929 when the stock market crashed.[84] Following a precipitous decline the previous Thursday, *The Yonkers Herald* struck an optimistic note, declaring: "Stock Market In Recovery Today."[85] According to the paper, sales volume was "heavy again but panicky features are missing" but the paper also reported that the force of 110 police regularly assigned to Wall Street, almost evenly split between patrolmen and detectives, was being supplemented by more than five hundred men, including one hundred detectives.[86] This increased police presence would not remain a permanent fixture of the financial district, but while it lasted it was a stark reminder of the uncontrollable economic forces buffeting the nation. Although the full impact of the Great Depression would not be felt immediately, by the early 1930s, the pace of economic activity slowed and great industrial cities such as Yonkers were forced to grapple with unemployment, homelessness, and other problems resulting from the protracted economic downturn gripping the nation.

3

Years of Pain and Glory

The Great Depression and World War II

Brother, Can You Spare a Dime?

The lyrics of the popular song "Brother, Can You Spare a Dime?" surely resonated with the people of Yonkers during the Great Depression. Yet, for more than a year following the stock market crash of 1929, no one realized just how bad things would actually get. To be sure, it wasn't business as usual in the days and weeks after Black Tuesday. Many investors suffered immediate ruin but lots of people held onto their jobs and simply hoped for the best. Interestingly, the city's largest employers were neither laying off workers nor canceling expansion plans. In an exceptionally lengthy article about Yonkers, published five months after the crash, *The New York Times* noted that several large Yonkers companies were either planning to expand their operations or had already done so. Of special note was the Otis Elevator Company, which was "operating to capacity," having landed a contract to install elevators in the Empire State Building, then under construction.[1]

There were signs of trouble on the horizon, however. In February 1930, the American Real Estate Company was forced to liquidate, at a court-ordered auction, all of its holdings, including seventy lots in Park Hill. Still, *The New York Times* saw a glimmer of hope on the real estate front, noting that the occupancy rate for apartments had risen in the past year and "real estate operators anticipate early announcement of plans for more buildings."[2] According to the paper, the president of the Thomas S. Burke real estate company was quite enthusiastic about the arrival of the spring buying season. Touting the city's allure for potential buyers, he said: "As a home city, Yonkers has always attracted the best citizenship of the land."[3]

Industrialist John E. Andrus shared the real estate agent's enthusiasm for the city, but by 1931 he was pessimistic about the future of Yonkers and the nation. Putting a positive spin on things may have been justified a year earlier when residential real estate was stable and commercial real estate, as evidenced by the success of the Park Building, was doing well. This six-story structure on South Broadway was fully occupied within two months of its completion, early in 1930, and its owners were planning to add two more floors. By the end of the year, it was a different story. Building slowed to a trickle, and the total value of the city's real estate, including the various components of the Alexander Smith and Sons Carpet Company, which had taken legal action to have its assessment cut by more than $1 million, declined. Cognizant of this downward spiral, John E. Andrus lamented the sorry state of the economy. In February 1931, on the eve of his ninetieth birthday, he told a reporter that he felt sorry for President Herbert Hoover. "He is a sincere man, trying to do what he believes right. But it is hard to handle Congress," said Andrus.[4] Having served in the House of Representatives, Andrus knew whereof he spoke. A year later, on the eve of another birthday, Andrus declared: "The clouds on the business horizon are the darkest since Columbus discovered America."[5]

On his ninety-third birthday, Andrus revealed that his fortune, which had been accumulated through wise investments in commodities and real estate, as well as the chemical company he had founded at the suggestion of his late wife, Julia Dyckman Andrus, had declined 55 percent since the beginning of the Depression. He also stated that, in his opinion, "the greatest current problem was taxes."[6] Elaborating on this, he said: "Men who work hard to develop business may not wish to give a big share of their time to business and then give their earnings to the government."[7] Andrus, who told a reporter that he couldn't recall ever having taken a two weeks' vacation, went to his Yonkers office until the end of his life. He died, unexpectedly, of pneumonia at his Yonkers home, on December 26, 1934, after having fallen ill only three days before. A quarter century earlier, his wife had passed away on Christmas Eve. Following a service attended by hundreds of people, including twenty-five children from the Julia Dyckman Andrus Home, the orphanage established in his wife's honor, John Emory Andrus was laid to rest, beside his beloved wife, in a $500,000 mausoleum in Kensico Cemetery.

Comparing Andrus's final resting place with his Hudson Terrace home, which was believed to be worth only $50,000, a reporter noted that the mausoleum "was built like a Greek temple, crowning a knoll and surrounded by several acres of land. Its marmoreal splendor will house the body of a man who scoffed at luxury all his life."[8] So what! Prior to the Depression Andrus's fortune was estimated at from $100 million to $800 million, and throughout his life he had been exceedingly charitable. Gifts made during his lifetime and trusts established for his children, plus the Depression's impact upon the value of his holdings, reduced the net estate to a little over $9 million. Under the terms of his will, the estate was placed in a trust and the Surdna Foundation, which he had established more than a dozen years before his death, was to receive 45 percent of the income from the trust, with children and grandchildren receiving 55 percent. The same division applied to the value of the trust at the time of its expiration. In 1935, the Surdna Foundation donated varying amounts to local institutions, including St. John's Riverside Hospital and the Yonkers Y.W.C.A. and Y.M.C.A. The Foundation also gave $500,000 to the Julia Dyckman Andrus Memorial, Inc., which not only provided homes for orphaned children but specialized training as well. At the Julia Dyckman Andrus Memorial Farm in Yonkers, for example, boys received "a thorough education in animal husbandry and in the management of an up-to-date dairy plant."[9]

Besides mourning the passing of former mayor Andrus, in the 1930s Yonkersonians said farewell to other prominent residents, including G. Clifford Noble, CEO of the publishing firm Noble & Noble and a partner in Barnes & Noble, booksellers, who died at age seventy-two of heart failure, at his North Broadway home in 1936. At the beginning of the decade, in June 1930, sixty-one-year-old Colonel William Boyce Thompson passed away at The Alders, his estate on North Broadway. In poor health since the mid-1920s, Thompson had hoped to recover by spending time in Arizona and on his yachts, the *Alders*, which had the same name as his Yonkers estate, and the *Savarona*. At 294 feet, the latter was one of the world's biggest privately own recreational vessels.

Most residents of Yonkers could scarcely imagine a yacht of that size and the lifestyle it represented. As the economic downturn, which had begun less than a year before Colonel Thompson's death, grew worse, Yonkers residents were preoccupied with matters far more mundane than pleasure cruises. Rising unemployment was chief among them. With scant prospects of help from the federal government, in the early years of the Depression Yonkers had to rely upon itself. That meant, for starters at least, assessing the worsening employment situation and finding ways of dealing with it. Toward that end, the Chamber of Commerce established a committee to study the problem and launch a public relations campaign to create local job opportunities. Mayor John J. Fogarty also did his part by appointing a committee of sixteen government officials, labor leaders, and businessmen to come up with recommendations for counteracting growing joblessness. Although Yonkers had the highest number of out of work residents in Westchester County by the summer of 1930, census data for that year revealed that out of a total population of 135,123, the number of unemployed residents was 4,483. At 3.3 percent the percentage of jobless people in Yonkers was still low and was on a par with Mount Vernon and New Rochelle, where unemployment rates were 3 percent and 3.1 percent respectively. Throughout the year, factory employees constituted the single largest number of workers in the city. Out of a total of 57,942 gainfully employed individuals, 8,868 of them were toiling away in the city's traditional industries. In 1931, the situation was less favorable, and this resulted in a concerted effort to raise $150,000 through private donations, to tide unemployed residents over until jobs opened up. Using World War I bond drives as a model, a relief committee, composed of prominent citizens and chaired by the vice president of the Third Avenue Railway System, felt confident it could achieve its goal by sending out teams to every neighborhood in the city to request small contributions.

Although the majority of citizens applauded such efforts, there was a small minority who believed that the capitalist system was bankrupt. In their efforts to promote socialism and communism, some of these individuals took to the streets, organizing rallies and parades. When a handful of these so-called reds attempted to hold a gathering in Larkin Plaza in February 1931, they attracted approximately one thousand people, but according to Yonkers police, no more than fifty of them were communists. The police, nevertheless, broke up the rally because the organizers had failed to secure a permit. So off to jail they went, at least until they posted bail. Six months earlier, a group of about fifty "reds" trucked in from a summer camp in Wingdale attempted to take over Larkin Plaza for a meeting. Although they had obtained a permit to hold their gathering at the city pier, the change of venue meant that they were in clear violation of the law. After a crowd of three to four hundred people assembled, twenty Yonkers police officers assigned to the plaza moved in to break up the rally. They were immediately assaulted by the "reds," but the police soon had the upper hand. A half-dozen people, including two local women, were arrested and charged with disorderly conduct.

Besides restraining "reds," in 1931 Yonkers police had to deal with more routine matters, including the investigation of accidents. One of the most serious was a horrific collision involving a runaway trolley that "raced a quarter mile down the steep grade in Palisade Avenue north of Getty Square."[10] The speeding streetcar toppled two automobiles along the way.

One of them was ignited by the crash. Despite the valiant efforts of the motorman, aided by a passenger, a surveyor in the city engineer's office, the trolley kept on going until it encountered an immovable object, a brick building at the bottom of the hill. The streetcar ended up partially inside the structure. Its front end, where six passengers were trapped, was ablaze. The Yonkers Fire Department not only rescued the trapped passengers but, instead of waiting for ambulances to arrive at the scene, firemen transported the injured to St. John's Riverside Hospital in a firetruck. Extracting the operator of the trolley from the wreckage proved especially difficult. In the end, an acetylene torch was used to free the motorman. Almost all of the thirty-one people on board the runaway trolley were injured; one of them, a fifty-six-year-old Orchard Street woman, was killed. In the immediate aftermath of this tragedy, *The Yonkers Herald* declared, in an editorial: "The terrible accident . . . might or might not have been avoided had there been two trolleymen on the car, a conductor as well as a motorman."[11] The solution, according to the editor of the *Herald*, was "to put an end to the one man trolley cars."[12] The City of Yonkers took a different approach, however. In the aftermath of the tragedy, the corporation counsel petitioned the New York State Public Service Commission to require safety devices on one man trolleys.

Important though it was, as a hot button issue making public transit safer for riders paled in comparison to the myriad problems residents faced as their city and nation plunged even deeper into the economic abyss. As the situation worsened, one of the city's most prominent citizens, Samuel Untermyer, decided it was time for a new approach. When Untermyer went public with his plan in September 1931, he contended that 15,138 Yonkers residents were without jobs. This represented a sea change from the year before. With winter approaching, Untermyer feared that the city would have to come up with more money to relieve the suffering of the unemployed. Although more than $200,000 had been raised through donations, many of them from public employees, he expressed doubt, in a letter to Mayor John Fogarty, that these people would continue giving. While praising the police officers, teachers, firemen, and other average citizens for their generosity, Untermyer leveled criticism at the city's industrial elite, stating that the contributions from industrialists had been "pitiful," thus convincing him that "this method of raising funds is not just and that a more equitable method of distribution of the burden can be effected through taxation."[13]

What Untermyer had in mind was a $1,500,000 unemployment relief bond issue by the City of Yonkers. Convinced that voters would approve this, he called for a referendum on the matter. According to

Untermyer, who made this suggestion at a gathering of representatives from civic and relief groups held at Greystone, this was the only way to effect "an equitable distribution of the burden upon the people who can best bear it but who will not voluntarily do so."[14]

Considering that the Untermyer family had been battling with the city over Greystone's high tax bill only a decade before, this was an intriguing proposal, but it didn't garner the kind of support Samuel Untermyer expected, so he found other ways to help unemployed Yonkers residents. In May 1932, he made his estate available for a garden party to raise funds for unemployed architects. There could not have been a more beautiful venue for this event because Greystone's grounds were at their best in the spring. Visitors were able to enjoy the long row of cypress trees and the Greek gardens "in which have been reproduced the glory that was Greece," according to *Country Life Magazine*.[15] There were also formal terraces and beautiful flowers throughout the estate and a spectacular view of the Hudson River and the Palisades. Upon arriving at Greystone, guests were greeted by Samuel Untermyer himself and Mrs. Cass Gilbert, wife of one of the country's most celebrated architects. Mrs. Gilbert was the chairman of the executive committee of the women's division of the Architects' Emergency Committee, the group sponsoring the fundraiser. The afternoon's events, which Mrs. Gilbert supervised, included treats for both the eyes and ears. The celebrated Isadora Duncan dancers performed and the Symphony Ensemble played in the Greek garden.

Although funds raised at functions such as the one held at Greystone helped relieve the suffering of the unemployed, it was apparent that much more in the way of government aid was needed. Yet, local government was unable to render large-scale assistance because it was hard pressed to meet its regular obligations. One of the biggest items in municipal budgets was salaries, and by 1932 citizens throughout Westchester County were calling for wage reductions for local and county employees. The Yonkers Citizens' Budget Commission was formed that year and sought a state charter to legitimize its efforts to reduce both taxes and the cost of local government. The Crestwood Citizens' Association was also active in this regard. In September 1932 it issued a report stating that the cost of operating the mayor's office had jumped 144 percent since 1927. Attributing this increase to salaries, the association decried the fact that salaries for public employees in Yonkers had increased by a larger percentage than the taxpayers' income had decreased. Objecting to recent city bond issues, the association went on record stating that assessed valuations should be reduced in order to prevent future bond issues that would increase the tax burden.

Mayor Joseph H. Loehr took issue with the assertions and recommendations of the Crestwood Citizens' Association. He pointed out that the alleged 144 percent increase cited by the association had resulted from the shifting of numerous items formerly charged to other departments of city government to the office of the mayor. He also insisted that bond issues had been minimal and that spending for all categories of city services had remained at the levels of the previous year with the exception of welfare expenditures necessitated by the Depression. Mayor Loehr's explanation failed to satisfy his critics. By late September, the Yonkers Citizens' Budget Commission paid a visit to city hall to demand a wage cut for municipal employees. Before the year was over, the Yonkers Real Estate Board was petitioning the city for a 10 percent cut in the salaries of city employees. This time the mayor got the message. He trimmed the city's 1933 budget by more than a million dollars and asked that municipal employees earning in excess of $6,000 refund 12.5 percent of their salaries.

Given the very real problems facing their city, it's not surprising that Yonkers residents longed for the good old days when life was more predictable. Thus, you cannot blame them for being nostalgic on the 250th anniversary of Philipse Manor Hall in the late autumn of 1932. Besides being a tangible reminder of the community's greatness in the colonial period and subsequently, this grand historic site, with its newly refurbished Daughters of the American Revolution hall, on the second floor, was testimony to the fact that a historic site, which had once been neglected, had "been rescued, time after time, from destruction or defamation."[16]

Hope Springs Eternal

If the Manor Hall could rise phoenix-like from the ashes, so, too, could Yonkers triumph over its economic problems. With the recent election of New York Governor Franklin D. Roosevelt as president of the United States, things were looking up. He would not be inaugurated until the following March, but already there was a renewed spirit of optimism. During the rather lengthy interval between the election and the inauguration, Yonkers entertained someone who was almost as well known as Franklin D. Roosevelt. It was England's poet laureate, John Masefield, who forty years earlier had worked at Alexander Smith and Sons. As part of a nationwide lecture tour, he spoke at Gorton High School where "a spellbound audience . . . sat back in their chairs and surrendered themselves completely to his magic."[17] Masefield regaled his listeners with the story of his early days as a seaman when he "cared nothing for literature"; in Yonkers, however, he "fell in love with Chaucer and Shakespeare at

William Palmer East's bookstore."[18] He used his discretionary income to buy books and devoted his spare time to reading and writing verse. Prior to his evening lecture at Gorton, Masefield, who was provided with a police escort, visited the Maple Street house where he had lived and the carpet mill, where he chatted with his old boss and former co-workers. While being driven around the city, Masefield observed the many changes that had taken place since he had lived there. He concluded that Yonkers had "grown beyond all recognition."[19] Yet, it was "still attractive."[20] Describing the city of yesteryear, Masefield said: "The country here was very beautiful when I lived here. There were quite deep woods, quite a primeval forest all around."[21]

A little more than a month after Masefield's visit, president-elect Franklin D. Roosevelt put in not one but two appearances in Yonkers. On both occasions he was en route from his estate in Hyde Park to his New York City residence. During one trip through Yonkers *The Herald Statesman* reported that "thousands of people" thronged the streets.[22] The crowd caught "a momentary glimpse of the car that held the next president."[23] Instead of being disappointed, the crowd "thrilled to the spectacle" of Roosevelt's auto as it went by.[24] Some Yonkers residents actually got to see F.D.R. Schoolchildren waving American flags lined Riverdale Avenue, where they were able to get a look at the president-elect who "nodded, waved and smiled almost continually."[25]

The enthusiasm with which they greeted F.D.R. was a clear indication of the high hopes Yonkers residents had for the new administration, which would soon take office. F.D.R. did not disappoint them. Coming out of the so-called First Hundred Days of Roosevelt's New Deal was a veritable blizzard of legislation designed to jump-start an economy that had sustained yet another blow resulting from a run on banks by depositors who had lost faith in the country's financial institutions. One of Roosevelt's first acts as president was to declare a bank holiday, which meant closing the banks. Following an investigation of each institution, those that were deemed sound were permitted to reopen. In early April, the Yonkers National Bank, an institution entrusted with the accounts of Sing Sing prison and the City of Yonkers, had the distinction of being the first bank in the country "managed by a conservator" to reopen under a federal plan that called for depositors to acquire preferred stock.[26] Other Yonkers financial institutions were still struggling, however. In August, Samuel Untermyer came to the rescue of the First National Bank and Trust Company by offering to put up $100,000 of the $800,000 required to reorganize the bank through the purchase of shares in the institution.

Getting the banks up and running was but one, albeit a very important, goal of the new Democratic administration. Another was the stimulation of business through the N.R.A., or National Recovery Administration, which established codes of fair competition. Speaking before an audience at the Jewish Community Center in Yonkers in September 1933, Samuel Untermyer, who termed Franklin Roosevelt a "genius" and a "superman," held out high hopes for the N.R.A.[27] In Untermyer's opinion, the success of the National Recovery Administration would signal the start of the "greatest social and economic revolution" in peacetime.[28] It would also "confound and destroy" communism.[29] At the same time, the N.R.A. would end the "forced, ruinous competition" resulting from federal antitrust laws.[30]

Taking issue with Henry Ford, who had refused to sign the N.R.A. code, Untermyer declared that he believed Ford would "find he is again mistaken, just as he was some years ago when his great fortune and world-wide business were actively engaged in the contemptible disservice of sowing the seeds of anti-Semitism."[31] Ford's *Dearborn Independent* newspaper had published anti-Semitic articles in order "to put his losing publishing venture . . . since happily extinguished, on a paying basis."[32] Denouncing Hitler, Untermeyer declared that the boycott of German products "will result in the downfall of the Nazi regime."[33] Sadly, neither this prediction nor Untermyer's optimism about the N.R.A. were borne out. The N.R.A. was declared unconstitutional by the U.S. Supreme Court, but while it lasted it gave Americans reason to hope. N.R.A. parades were held all over the country, including Yonkers, where ten thousand marchers wended their way through the business district in November 1933. The parade also included floats created by leading industries to demonstrate their support for the N.R.A.

A month before the N.R.A. parade, Yonkers residents were treated to a different sort of public spectacle: an Indian powwow. More than three hundred Senecas, Onondagas, Cherokees, Iroquois, and Shinnecocks gathered at the Woman's Institute for a meeting of the Universal Indian Alliance of America. Among the assembled delegates were several chiefs, one of whom, Lewis Smith, Chief White Moon, of Brooklyn presided. Another chief, Wilfred Spear, of Yonkers, a Cherokee known as Chief Sunflower, handled the arrangements for the business meeting and the subsequent powwow held at Nodine Field. There, the Indians performed dances, demonstrated Native People's games, and conducted ceremonies around a campfire. Eye-catching though they were, the colorful attire and activities of the Indians failed to divert public attention from the fact that the Great Depression held Yonkers firmly in its grip.

Although they surely didn't need another reminder of how serious things were, Yonkers residents' worst fears were confirmed when the city stopped paying its workers. In an attempt to maintain its credit rating Yonkers had chosen to repay creditors, even though this meant that municipal employees had to periodically forgo paychecks, beginning in the spring of 1933. Police and firemen's associations provided loans to the city to permit partial payment of wages, but by the fall Yonkers was on the verge of default. With less than 60 percent of the sums owed for real estate taxes coming in, the city found itself in the position of having to use all of this revenue for bond and interest payments. There was nothing left to pay municipal employees. Seeking a way out of this dilemma, Mayor Joseph F. Loehr put together a brain trust composed of academicians, financiers, and nationally recognized experts on the problems of municipalities. The result was a new fiscal plan allowing the city to discharge its county and state indebtedness in installments, but this entailed painful budget cuts and the prospect of layoffs.

Hitting Bottom and Bottoms Up

The situation being what it was, is it any wonder that some Yonkers residents tried to forget the city's troubles, at least temporarily, by raising a glass or two? The repeal of the Prohibition amendment in 1933 meant that alcohol was, once again, perfectly legal. Before that happened, though, besides dealing with the economic catastrophe gripping the nation, in the early 1930s Yonkers had to grapple with lawlessness associated with Prohibition. Bootlegging, rumrunning, and shooting incidents did not make headlines to the extent they had in the Roaring Twenties but they did occur. Nineteen-thirty was an especially active year. In March, $170,000 worth of liquor was seized on a sand barge tied up to a Yonkers pier. A half-dozen trucks were needed to cart the alcohol to New York City for disposal in a special sewer system built for this purpose. Additional raids in 1930 uncovered a major beer bottling plant on John Street and a liquor brokerage business operating out of a Riverdale Avenue garage and a South Broadway commercial building. During raids on these premises in November 1930, police arrested six people, one of them a woman, and confiscated numerous documents, breaking up what was believed "to be one of the largest and best organized liquor rings ever found operating in the Eastern part of the country."[34] Only a limited quantity of alcohol was uncovered, however, because the ring operating in Yonkers took "orders for delivery of any quantity of several grades and brands of champagne, scotch or rye whisky, malt or ale" and soon after it arrived, it was delivered to customers throughout the New York area.[35]

Before the year was over, authorities uncovered quite literally, right beneath their feet, the elaborate system of hoses that, throughout the 1920s, had been delivering beer from the State Cereal and Beverage Company, in which Dutch Schultz had a controlling interest, to distribution points. Public works employees cleaning a sewer discovered a "500 foot hose emptying mash."[36] This was followed by an anonymous letter to Mayor John J. Fogarty informing him of a subterranean beer network connected to the municipal sewer system. Through this incredible maze flowed real beer, not the near beer the company serving as a front for Underhill's Brewery had been licensed to manufacture. By 1936, Underhill's Brewery was back in full operation, producing nearly a quarter of a million kegs of beer.

In the mid-1930s, some Yonkers residents were presumably crying in their beer, this despite the fact that, according to the City Planning Commission, "Yonkers has fared proportionately better than the rest of the county."[37] This was small comfort because the commission also noted that "Yonkers industry like retail and wholesale trade has suffered heavily from the depression."[38] With considerably less revenue coming into the city and indebtedness of $10 million, the time had come to implement the recommendations of the Municipal Consultant Service of the National Municipal League. After studying the situation in Yonkers, the service recommended the appointment of a budget director, the phasing out of some city departments, and drastic cuts in expenditures. Only in this way could Yonkers attain the goal of absorbing its municipal debt within five years. A more effective way of collecting taxes was also needed as was a 15 percent reduction in the salaries of municipal workers. The city's one thousand teachers were the first to be hit by the wage reduction. To add insult to injury, they were expected to go without pay entirely for the month of December, when Yonkers planned to close the schools to save money on coal and electricity, as well as salaries. The city ultimately rescinded its decision to shut the schools for December, but that was not enough to assuage the citizenry.

So great was dissatisfaction with the decisions of Yonkers officials that The Council of Yonkers Civic Associations held a mass meeting at the Saunders Trade School to demand that the 1934 budget be revised and the tax rate lowered. The upshot of this gathering was a call for a tax strike, but even those property owners who withheld their taxes paid them to avoid an 8 percent penalty. With new revenue in hand, the city resumed compensating its employees, some of whom had not received salaries for five months. Yonkers was also able to pay $100,000 to Westchester County in arrears on state and county taxes, thereby reducing its unpaid balance to $60,000. Praising Yonkers in an article titled "Tax Skies Clearing for Westchester," *The New York Times* stated: "Yonkers presented the worst problem . . . but it was solved with the utmost cooperation on the part of the city's administration."[39] The Municipal Consultant Service of the National Municipal League, whose recommendations had helped bring this about, was very pleased. The director of the service pointed out, in August 1934, that the previous December the city was up to four months in arrears in salary, as well as interest and principal payments, but by adopting the recommendations of the league its progress "has been astonishing."[40]

With its finances in better shape, Yonkers, which according to *American City* magazine was waging "a successful struggle against apparently insurmountable financial difficulties," was able to borrow $3 million from a syndicate of New York City banks.[41] Things were definitely looking up, but not everyone was convinced Yonkers was out of the woods. Consequently, an old idea, which didn't fly in the past, was resurrected, namely annexation to New York City. Soon after this surfaced, Mayor Joseph F. Loehr issued a denunciation saying he was content "to leave things as they are," adding: "I think that Yonkers should be a unit by itself."[42] This time, the idea for making Yonkers the sixth borough of New York City originated with a New York City legislator who was convinced that real estate values in both the city and Yonkers would increase as a result of annexation. The Yonkers Common Council echoed Mayor Loehr's sentiments, issuing a strongly worded statement calling the proposal "an arrogant assumption."[43] New York City's mayor Fiorello H. La Guardia wasn't exactly thrilled by the prospect either. When queried about the matter, he replied that he had "enough headaches" without adding another borough.[44]

Yonkers, too, had enough headaches and not all of them were attributable to the Great Depression, the effects of which were somewhat mitigated by New Deal public works jobs. In the same year that the city was making a valiant, and ultimately successful, effort to get its finances on an even keel, it had to deal with a horrific explosion. The blast occurred directly in front of Proctor's Theatre at South Broadway and Prospect Street where electrical transformers were being installed in the basement of the theater. According to *The Herald Statesman* the blast "rocked the entire center of the city."[45] A former Yonkers comptroller, who witnessed the explosion, said: "Flames were crackling ominously from the lower windows. The heat was terrific. The entire façade was blackened and charred."[46]

The Proctor's building quite literally shook and the windows of stores in the area shattered, sending glass missiles flying everywhere. Bundles of clothing on the roof of a laundry wagon passing the theater were ignited and the terrified horse pulling the wagon galloped away. Meanwhile, passersby were knocked off their feet. One of them, a girl, her clothing on fire, landed in the gutter. Another girl was hurled into the eight-foot-long, ten-foot-wide crater created by the blast. Eyewitnesses saw her teetering on the edge of the hole but before anyone could reach her, she fell in. Patrick Whalen, a motorcycle policeman, jumped in immediately thereafter. He was followed by Michael Gruber, a taxicab driver. Almost as soon as both men descended into the crater, a second explosion occurred. Eyewitnesses described flames of thirty-five to forty feet rising from the sidewalk. The explosion transported the trapped girl to the top of one of the transformers, some distance away from the men trying to rescue her. At this point, two Yonkers police officers, who had been assigned to traffic duty several blocks away, rushed to the scene and were able to reach into the hole and grab the girl's clothing. They then dragged her out of the crater. The nine-year-old girl survived. While she lay stretched out on what was left of the sidewalk in front of the theater, before being transported to St. John's Riverside Hospital, the Fire Department arrived.

Firemen immediately put on gas masks and went down into the crater, where they made a gruesome discovery. The brave policeman and taxi driver had been incinerated, either by the 13,000 volt power line supplying the transformers or by the second explosion. All that remained were officer Whalen's shield and Gruber's leather wallet. An electrician working at the site was also killed. Between 100 and 150 people employed in offices in the five-story building above the theater all got out safely, however. Although some of them made their escape via an interior staircase, others used the elevators, which, amazingly, kept functioning.

In the aftermath of the tragedy, the Yonkers Electric Light and Power Company contended that the New York State Public Service Commission bore responsibility because it had acceded to the demands of not only Proctor's but the Loew's and Strand theaters for high-tension power, which would afford them considerable savings on their electrical bills. The power company insisted that this was unsafe but was forced to acquiesce as the result of a Public Service Commission ruling. On the day of the explosion, Yonkers Electric Light and Power Company personnel were at the theater to supervise the work. When a power company supervisor saw smoke coming from the newly installed transformers the minute the power was turned on, he had one of his men call headquarters to have everything shut down, but before the order could be executed the first explosion occurred. The Westchester County medical examiner ruled that the power company was partially to blame for what had happened. They were "negligent when they were about to test the transformers not to protect pedestrians . . . by roping off and guarding the roof of the transformer vault when the company considered it necessary to order their own men and others who might be in the vault to leave when the current was turned on at the sub-station."[47] The medical examiner also blamed the Public Service Commission for permitting the installation of high-tension power and Proctor's for putting the transformers "at the very entrance of the theater and not far from the auditorium and also for having the electrical equipment placed in a vault that was not constructed as to provide for the safety of the general public."[48] Although there was surely enough blame to go around, no charges of criminal neglect were filed. "The explosion," the medical examiner concluded, "was the result of a series of poor judgments and negligence but I cannot find any party or parties whom I would be justified in holding criminally responsible."[49]

Building for the Future

As 1934, the year that had witnessed both tragedy and triumph—the latter symbolized by a year-end surplus of nearly $142,000 in the city treasury—drew to an end, Yonkers had a new symbol of hope: a model home. In keeping with the Federal Housing Administration's efforts to promote "modernizing and erecting small dwellings," a few days before Christmas 1934, the Yonkers Better Housing Committee of the F.H.A. broke ground for the model home of 1935.[50] Intended to be part of the Yonkers Chamber of Commerce Own-Your-Own-Home Exposition scheduled for the following spring, the six-room house with "concrete masonry type of construction" featured fireproofing, ample closet space, and air conditioning, then an almost unheard of luxury.[51] Located not far from Central Park Avenue, on a rise of land on Cumberland Drive, the house had a generously proportioned living room, a semicircular dining area, kitchen, and powder room on the first floor. Three bedrooms, a bath, and a dressing room were located on the second floor. Balconies, casement windows, and a garage were additional features. In April 1935, the city staged an official ceremony to mark the opening of the model home. The regional director of the Federal Housing Administration was on hand, as was Mayor Loehr. Everyone in attendance admired the white stuccoed exterior, the over-mantel mirror running the full width of the living room, and the silver and white wallpaper in the master bedroom.

Lovely though it was, the model home paled in comparison with Greystone, which opened its gates to the public in May 1935 to benefit the Westchester County Children's Association. Visitors to the Untermyer estate were treated to a display of magnificent tulips stretching over several acres of the Greek gardens, and that wasn't all. Different varieties of orchids, tropical plants, and beautiful flowers were on view in the greenhouses. Capping off a perfect afternoon, visitors were served tea on the terrace overlooking the Hudson. Surrounded by such incredible beauty, while gazing at the Palisades in the distance, it wasn't difficult to forget the problems facing Yonkers and the nation in the mid-thirties. Samuel Untermyer, however, was unable to simply retreat to his grand estate and shut out the world. A little more than a year after the children's charity event at Greystone, *The New York Times* published an article titled "Untermyer, at 78, Gloomy on Future."[52] Based upon a lengthy interview, the piece quoted Untermyer on a variety of topics, including the challenges facing youth. According to Untermyer: "There is not the same opportunity for young men today."[53] In his view, finding jobs for youth was one of the biggest challenges.

Untermyer also expressed concern over the "monstrous expenses of government," which were causing business people to be risk averse when it came to making capital investments.[54] More pessimistic than optimistic, he declared that the nation's problems "are becoming more difficult."[55] Untermyer's pessimism was attributable, in part, to the persecution of Jews in Nazi Germany. On this subject, he said that it was unbelievable that Jews were being "persecuted by a supposedly cultured people."[56] When asked about the likelihood of war in Europe, Untermyer replied that war would not break out in Europe "until Germany is ready for war," but he was quick to point out that given the destruction caused by war, "its contemplation seems unbelievable."[57]

Unbelievable or not, war in Europe was only three years away. Once under way, World War II proved very beneficial for the American economy. Even before the United States entered the conflict, supplying the European Allies with all manner of items needed for the war effort was the catalyst that got us out of the Depression once and for all. In the interim, the economy, both nationally and locally, sputtered. Unemployment remained high despite New Deal programs, but now and again there were hopeful economic signs. Yonkers tax receipts were up in 1935, and the city continued repaying its debts. In 1936, Yonkers received almost half of the total Works Progress Administration appropriation for the entire state, excluding

New York City. This money was used for various park and playground projects. From 1933 through 1937 the W.P.A., together with New York State, also funded the Yonkers Collegiate Center, which provided college courses for hundreds of students. The program was supervised by the College of the City of New York and credits were awarded by that institution. Recent high school graduates, who could not otherwise have afforded college, were able to amass transfer credits. At the same time, they were kept occupied during a period when jobs were scarce. Prior to the onset of the Great Depression, the city's youth, even those lacking high school diplomas, were able to find jobs in factories or refineries, but all of that had changed.

Some mainstays of the Yonkers economy, for example, Spreckels Federal Sugar Refining Company, had shut their doors for good during the 1930s, and others slashed their work forces. Employees lucky enough to remain on the payroll, even with reduced hourly wages or a shortened work week, or both, were grateful to have jobs, but by 1936 some of them were convinced that the way to safeguard those jobs was to unionize. Employers thought otherwise. Alexander Smith and Sons, where "a pedometer used by . . . the general superintendent showed that mill superintendents covered on an average . . . ten miles a day," went to court in an effort to restrain the Regional Labor Board from hearing complaints filed by three weavers the company had dismissed.[58] The regional board had been created by the National Labor Relations Act, which affirmed workers' rights to bargain collectively through labor organizations. The discharged men insisted they had been fired for assisting the United Textile Workers of America in its efforts to unionize the plant but the company argued that the men had been dismissed for incompetence. Thanks to Supreme Court rulings upholding the National Labor Relations Act, the men were reinstated.

In 1937, the United Textile Workers Union launched a full-scale campaign to unionize the carpet works. The union's national president appeared at a rally in Yonkers and threatened to shut down the company if management interfered with unionization efforts. The gathering, attended by three hundred people, was to have been held in the auditorium of the Polish Community Center but was moved to the Odd Fellows Building when the officers of the community center had second thoughts. Rally organizers suspected that Alexander Smith and Sons officials had been behind the change of venue and persuaded those present in the Odd Fellows Building to pass a resolution stating that "the act of closing [the Polish Community Center] is indicative to us of great subversive influence and the domination that the Alexander Smith Company has over the lives and liberties of the working people of Yonkers."[59] In a conciliatory gesture, the union president held out hope that the process of organizing carpet company workers would not necessitate strikes, but at the same time he insisted: "They're not going to stop us from organizing and if they attempt to we'll stop their production."[60] He went on to say: "It is perfectly legitimate to organize, it is recognized by the U.S. Government and we intend to prosecute it with all the ability at our command," and that's exactly what they did.[61]

Four months after the big rally, 96 percent of more than five thousand workers eligible to vote stepped into a tent erected on Orchard Street and took part in a federally supervised election to choose a collective bargaining agency. The vote was very close but the Textile Workers' Organizing Committee of the Committee for Industrial Organization defeated the Independent Smith Workers' Union, an in-house organization. The day after the election, the company issued a public statement declaring that it would be "governed by the decision reached in the election and trusts that its relations with its employees will continue in a peaceful, fair and friendly way."[62] The union representative who had directed the campaign to organize Smith workers heralded "the dawn of a new day."[63] Given the size of Alexander Smith, he said, industry employees all over the nation "had their eyes turned on this election and will rejoice with the Smith workers in coming through with flying colors for the C.I.O."[64] To celebrate this historic moment, more than a hundred people paraded from union headquarters on Walnut Street, through Getty Square, to the Polish Community Center where a big rally took place. Workers celebrated into the evening as they contemplated a brighter future. Their celebration turned out to be premature, because in 1938 Alexander Smith and Sons imposed a 7 percent wage reduction "and attempted to reinstate the old company union as the bargaining agent for the employees," but in 1939, "the National Labor Relations Board intervened . . . and held another referendum . . . this time the C.I.O. won a clearcut victory, outpolling the company union by 1,209 votes."[65]

Unionized or not, industry was welcome in Yonkers. Not long after the first C.I.O. victory at Alexander Smith and Sons, in an editorial titled "New and Bigger Yonkers Industries," *The Herald Statesman* positively oozed enthusiasm for the successful efforts of the Yonkers Chamber of Commerce in bringing the Progressive Sports Wear company and the Jerome Knitting Mills to the city.[66] Both were expected to open soon and together they would provide employment for hundreds of people. After devoting several paragraphs to new firms lured to Yonkers by the very active Chamber of Commerce, the editorial turned to existing industries, stating that both Alexander Smith and Otis were employing more workers and that the Habirshaw division of the Phelps Dodge Copper Products Corporation was erecting "a new riverfront structure which will provide at least 300 to 350 excellent jobs."[67]

Turning to other companies, this very lengthy editorial noted that Joseph Love, Inc., the biggest manufacturer of children's wear not only in the U.S. but worldwide, announced that it was adding between 150 and 200 employees; this represented "a sudden and unheralded gain of thirty-three per cent."[68] Other companies, including the Yonkers Electric Light and Power Company, were increasing the wages of current employees. The editorial writer concluded that this would impact "the city's life generally."[69]

She Wears Short Shorts!

Things were definitely looking up—way up! Even the death rate was down in the "Queen City of the Hudson." Of the eighty largest cities in the United States, Yonkers had the second lowest death rate. Maybe exercise had something to do with that. Men employed on federally funded public works projects were certainly getting lots of exercise on the job. So, too, were the female college graduates hired by the Yonkers Public Library, thanks to a state grant. One of them recalled that a "professional task" assigned to her and another librarian was cleaning the covers of the three-thousand-volume Young Adult collection.[70] Getting the job done was not easy, because they had to carry buckets of water several flights from the basement of the library. The head of their department "thought the janitor didn't clean the books well enough."[71]

For Yonkers residents who didn't get enough exercise at work and for those left jobless by the national economic catastrophe, there were many ways to stay in shape. One could get out for a stroll, an impromptu game of softball or basketball in city parks or a swim at the county's popular Tibbetts Brook Park. The trail along the Croton Aqueduct attracted many people as well. Some of them, however, incurred the wrath of residents living nearby. Dismayed by the scanty attire of female hikers, they complained to Alderman William Slater, who agreed to launch an investigation. Accompanied by a photographer equipped with a movie camera, the alderman took up a position at McLean Avenue and the aqueduct. Before long, he spotted five scantily clad young women wearing "brief shorts and bandana handkerchiefs, known as 'halters,' draped and knotted about their shoulders."[72] Alderman Slater alerted a police officer who issued summonses to the girls, all of whom were from New York City.

Reporting on the incident the next day, *The Herald Statesman* in a front page article declared: "War against semi-nudists who parade Yonkers each Sunday broke out amid a barrage of police summonses and the clicking of motion picture cameras on the McLean Avenue battlefront yesterday."[73] The article proceeded to quote Alderman Slater, who voiced objections to more than the attire of the New Yorkers who were invading Yonkers. According to the alderman, they "sing, shout and use bad language, pick flowers from private gardens and eat luncheon on taxpayers' lawns."[74] During court proceedings the following day, Slater reiterated his concerns about nonresidents who frequented Tibbetts Brook Park on Sundays disturbing "the peace of residents."[75] City judge Martin Fay dismissed the charges against the young women, informing them that the only thing that was expected of them was that they "dress the way the women in Yonkers dress when upon our public streets."[76] That should have been the end of the matter but it wasn't, because the ever-vigilant alderman was determined to enforce a local ordinance governing attire on city streets. In the opinion of some Yonkers residents this was going too far. Florence Parsons, executive secretary of the Woman's Institute, stated:

> Alderman Slater is several years behind the times. If he had any experience he would know that when girls get to the country they let their hair down and take out the pins. Going with bare legs is just part of this informal behavior. . . . Girls in shorts to me are no more offensive than 200-pound men nearly nude, sprawling on the beaches. Moderation is the answer, moderation for everybody.[77]

Although William Slater's anti-shorts crusade did not enjoy universal support, the management of the Yonkers-Alpine ferry concluded that the alderman meant business. For that reason, they created a dressing room and a check room at the Yonkers terminal. Girls headed for Palisades Interstate Park could leave their skirts at the ferry and according to the terminal manager, hike "in their briefer outfits and pick up their modesty again on the return trip."[78] This arrangement proved workable, but female visitors to Tibbetts Brook Park continued to stroll through Yonkers in shorts and halters and the police "did nothing."[79] Alderman Slater reacted by circulating a petition in the Ninth Ward to require the police to enforce the law governing public attire. At the same time, he issued a statement denouncing what some of his constituents were calling the "shorts parade."[80] In Slater's opinion the scanty attire of young women lowered morals, and he vowed that something would be done "to prevent the wearing of improper costumes in the future."[81] Within days, a new ordinance was enacted. It declared: "No person over the age of 16 years shall be permitted to appear in bathing costume or in any other than customary street attire upon any public street or thoroughfare in the city of Yonkers."[82] Violators were subject to fines of up to $150 and a maximum of thirty days in jail.

Some creative women from New York City strolled along the Croton Aqueduct to the Yonkers border in shorts, quickly donned skirts to cross McLean Avenue, and once back on the aqueduct, which is the property of New York City, pared down to their shorts. Yonkers officials were not pleased. In 1936, in anticipation of a deluge of visitors from the city, they posted a warning sign on the aqueduct. A notice was also put up on Central Park Avenue. Alderman Slater wanted more than signs, however. At the start of the 1936 season he accompanied police officers to the aqueduct, where he viewed New Yorkers doing the on and off skirts routine as they crossed McLean Avenue. According to *The New York Times,* the hikers reacted with "derisive salutes" to Slater and the policemen.[83] Slater was positively livid. Since many hikers typically headed to Tibbetts Brook Park he tried to persuade Westchester County to ban anyone who did not reside in the county. "We object to having a Coney Island in a good residential section," he said, adding that hundreds of hikers were descending upon the park.[84] Banning New Yorkers from county parks would not occur for several decades, but Slater was successful in getting the Yonkers Police Department to beef up its anti-shorts patrol. With tongue in cheek, *The New York Times* observed that ten police officers were required for the anti-shorts patrol because seeing women in brief attire could be "too dazzling for one policeman."[85] Within weeks, the "shorts squad" was reduced to four officers. By September it was down to one.

Early the following year, the Yonkers anti-shorts ordinance was upheld by a county judge who denied the appeals of two New York City reporters convicted of violating the ordinance the previous summer after they "asked to be arrested so they could conduct a test case."[86] The New York State Court of Appeals, however, reversed the county justice's ruling on the grounds that the Yonkers ordinance governing attire was too vague. Referring to the colorful, abbreviated costumes worn by the reporters, the chief justice of the Court of Appeals declared: "The Constitution still leaves some opportunity for people to be foolish, if they so desire."[87] Reflecting the views of the seven-judge panel that reviewed the case, the chief justice noted that the ordinance had to be revised to "describe the costume or lack of which is prohibited."[88] For the next two months, Yonkers officials worked on a new law while simultaneously attempting to persuade the Westchester County Park Commission to wall off Tibbetts Brook Park by erecting a fence, with only one opening, at Yonkers Avenue, on the north side of the park. This barrier would make it more difficult for New York City residents approaching the park from the other direction to actually gain admittance. Yonkers representatives on the Westchester County Board of Supervisors, the county's legislative body, argued that city people were entering Tibbetts in record numbers and were "more obnoxious than ever before."[89] One supervisor said that New Yorkers were also invading private property near the park. Another irate supervisor complained that visitors from the city were "displaying themselves in the most ungodly and indecent manner."[90]

By late July 1937, the sort of attire that the supervisors found so objectionable was about to become a thing of the past, because Yonkers had a brand new anti-shorts law. Its author was none other than Alderman William E. Slater. Crusading harder than ever, Slater persuaded his colleagues on the common council to enact a measure that imposed fines of up to $150 and a maximum of thirty days in jail for wearing anything that "indecently exposes or reveals any part" of the person thus attired."[91] The ordinance did not expressly forbid the wearing of shorts but it put police officers in the difficult position of having to determine whether a person's attire was too revealing. The police chief resisted posting a big detail on the aqueduct to nab scantily dressed New Yorkers, because, as he put it: "We've got to protect the rest of the city, too."[92] Five years later, the ordinance fell by the wayside. In 1942, when Mayor Benjamin F. Barnes, a physician who subscribed to the idea that sun exposure had health benefits, sought repeal of the ordinance, even William Slater, by then out of office, did not protest.

Running, Rowing, and Shaking

During the years that the anti-shorts law had been in effect, accomplished athletes who participated in the Yonkers Marathon were exempt. No one objected to the idea of short shorts on male athletes, whether adults or the eleven to fifteen-year-olds taking part in the Yonkers School Boys' Race, a sort of junior version of the city's popular marathon. These contests, which began during the first decade of the twentieth century, were open to elementary and junior high school students. In the mid and late 1930s the race "began and ended in Glen Park (now Memorial Field). The contestants started on the west side of the park, spread out over the outfield of Diamond #1, and finished on the track in front of the grandstand. The route covered just less than two miles."[93] In the late thirties and early forties, this popular race attracted upward of two hundred runners each year. Some participants went on to lead Gorton High School to regional track championships. One Yonkers resident, Eulace Peacock, inducted into the Yonkers Sports Hall of Fame, was known as the fastest person in the world because, before settling in Yonkers later in life, he beat Jesse Owens, the running star of the 1936 Olympics. Had it not been for an injury sustained while he was competing for Temple University, Peacock would have been in the Olympics.

Interested though they were in just how fast two-legged beings, whether candidates for the Olympics or schoolboys, could travel, in the 1930s Yonkers residents were also attracted to a different type of racing, the sort occurring at the Empire City Racetrack. The Butler family continued to own and manage the track even after the death, in 1934, of James Butler. To make it easier for patrons to reach the track, the Butlers provided free buses from the New York Central Railroad's Harlem Division station in Mount Vernon and from the Jerome Avenue subway stop in the Bronx. In the mid-thirties, racing fans had several opportunities to watch Seabiscuit, the horse whose story was recounted, first in a book, and then in a popular movie, released in 2003. Making his debut at Empire City in October 1935, Seabiscuit won the Ardsley Handicap. The following fall he took the Scarsdale Handicap one week, but the next week he came in third in the Yorktown Handicap. In the summer of 1937, Seabiscuit won the Butler Handicap and the Yonkers Handicap. The latter victory "extended his winning streak to six victories in succession. . . . The next year Seabiscuit went on to win the famous match against War Admiral . . . at the Pimlico Track in Baltimore."[94]

Although the action at Empire City was exciting, for Yonkers residents who preferred to be participants rather than cheering spectators the healthful outdoor activity of canoeing was a popular pastime, not only because it built strong bodies but because it helped divert attention from the Depression. Lots of people got out on the river occasionally, but some, such as the members of the Yonkers Canoe Club, founded in 1886, made the Hudson their second home. "During its years of supremacy, the Yonkers Canoe Club was national champion from 1937–1940," and beginning in 1936 club members competed in the Olympics.[95] The club also made a big splash in *Life* magazine. Taking to the waters in a canoe was such a popular leisure time activity that *Life* published a major article on canoe safety. The beautifully illustrated piece featured "members of the U.S. champion Yonkers Canoe Club."[96]

For those less athletically inclined, a trip on the Yonkers-Alpine ferry was one way to get out on the water and enjoy some music at the same time. To lure riders during the Depression, the ferry company employed a two-man band, consisting of an accordionist and a violinist, to provide operatic arias and ballads, but the traveling public tuned out! The company got the message and substituted swing. The livelier music, introduced in 1937, mirrored the more upbeat attitude of Yonkers residents at that point, but before the Great Depression ended there would be some missed beats, economically speaking, and tremors as well. On a July evening in 1937 there was a different kind of shock. In the middle of the night, the third earthquake (the others having occurred in 1927 and 1935) affecting the New York metropolitan area, coastal Connecticut, and Long Island awakened residents of Yonkers. Not knowing whether the rattling of windows and swaying of china and pictures was the result of an explosion, resident grabbed phones and called the police department and the *Herald Statesman* office. The director of the Harvard University seismograph station determined that an earthquake had indeed occurred. He explained that it had resulted from "continuing correction of a depression caused by an ice cap 25,000 years ago."[97]

New Neighbors

Fast forward tens of thousands of years and there might as well have been an Arctic-size glacier in Yonkers when the celebrated African American religious leader Father Divine purchased a twenty-five room house, complete with twelve baths, on Lowerre Summit, on the fringe of Park Hill. Through the years Yonkers residents were glad to have such famous African Americans as Ella Fitzgerald and W. C. Handy as residents, but it was a different story with Father Divine. He was given a very chilly reception by "residents filled with consternation" at the prospect of the long-vacant house becoming one of Father Divine's "Heavens."[98] Divine had set up homes called "Heavens" for his followers in Harlem and elsewhere. The purchase of the home at 357 Park Hill Avenue, supposedly made by Brother Devout, a white follower of Father Divine, caught residents of the Park Hill enclave off guard. Soon, however, there was speculation that homeowners would attempt to convince the city that Father Divine's latest "Heaven" was actually a rooming house, something the zoning laws specifically prohibited. *The Herald Statesman* quoted one Park Hill resident, a former president of the Yonkers Board of Education, whose home was the closest to "Heaven," as saying: "As long as they are good neighbors, their presence does not bother me a bit," but this seemed to have been a minority opinion.[99]

When Father Divine's followers began moving into the new "Heaven," Park Hill "property owners watched with growing alarm . . . the advent of Father Divine and his disciples."[100] Not long thereafter, a burning cross, the symbol of the Ku Klux Klan, lit up the neighborhood. Father Divine and his "Angels" were unfazed. They proceeded to renovate the mansion and to mark its dedication the following spring, they planned a gigantic parade commencing at the city line and wending its way through New Main Street, Nepperhan Avenue, and Waverly Street to the new "Heaven." Despite the fanfare surrounding the Yonkers "Heaven," the home did not endure. Some residents of the area "could not recall any members of Divine's Heaven still living in the community by the 1950s."[101] Yet individuals residing only two blocks away from "Heaven" reported "Angels" dwelling there in the fifties and working as housecleaners in the area.

The mansion acquired by Father Divine wasn't the only large residence in the news at the tail end of the Depression. Greystone, the Untermyer estate, grabbed headlines in August 1939 when eighty-two-year-old Samuel Untermyer announced that he would offer the estate to the city of Yonkers. Seated on the rear veranda, with his nurse not far away, the ailing Untermyer pointed out to a journalist from *The Herald Statesman* that "Yonkers is a city of 150,000, and can you imagine a city of that size without a large city park? . . . I would like to see Greystone become a public park."[102] Untermyer went on to tell the journalist about how he had collected the statuary gracing the estate and that he intended to offer all of it and the Greek amphitheater, valued at $1,500,000, to the city. Yonkers would also receive "3,000 feet along the Hudson River to build what it desires so the people may enjoy themselves."[103] The mansion, minus its magnificent art work and furnishings, would also go to the city to use "as Yonkers saw fit."[104] All that Untermyer asked was that the city keep up the grounds with their ever-changing seasonal displays of flowers, including fifty thousand chrysanthemums. Untermyer estimated that it would cost the city $75,000 a year to maintain the grounds and while he said that he "would like to endow the park," he indicated that he could not "do that now."[105]

No one wants to "look a gift horse in the mouth," as the old saying goes, but city officials were wary. Untermyer expected they would be, and for that reason he put forth the idea of donating the property to Westchester County should Yonkers refuse the gift. While the city and county deliberated, before both rejected Untermyer's offer, life at

Greystone went on as usual. In keeping with tradition, the gates of the magnificent estate were thrown open, from 10 a.m. to 5 p.m. for an entire week in October, to allow the public to view an incredible display of 3,500,000 chrysanthemums, including a seven and a half foot high, nine foot long replica of the Cathedral of Notre Dame fashioned from mums. This incredible example of floral art was headed for the New York Flower Show following Greystone's open gardens week. Incredible as Notre Dame was, some visitors to the estate were positively charmed by the sundial, measuring thirty-six feet in diameter, and fashioned of 350,000 pansies. People who ventured into the greenhouses saw more than flowers; they learned about a novel experiment, which consisted of infusing melons with different types of wines and liqueurs. Samples of the fruit were not distributed, however.

Less than six months after Greystone's open grounds week, the man who had so generously shared his estate with the public passed away at his winter home in Palm Springs, California. His body was brought back to Greystone by train, with the last leg of the journey on the Twentieth Century Limited. The casket was removed from the train at Croton-on-Hudson and, accompanied by a number of automobiles and a police escort, was transported to Greystone where a funeral took place the following day. In attendance were hundreds of people, including New York governor Herbert H. Lehman, former governor Alfred E. Smith, and Yonkers mayor John J. Condon. According to *The New York Times*: "The coffin, blanketed with orchids and Easter lilies from the Untermyer greenhouses, rested before a flower-banked altar beneath a stained-glass window at the west end of the main hall."[106]

Within days of Untermyer's interment in the family mausoleum in Woodlawn Cemetery, next to his beloved wife, who had died in 1924, the world learned that he had bequeathed Greystone to New York State, "absolutely and in perpetuity, as and for a public park and gardens, to be known as Samuel Untermyer Park and Gardens."[107] Under the terms of the will, the state was given six months to accept the bequest. With the legislature about to adjourn, Governor Lehman held a conference almost immediately and learned from legislators and other state officials that the cost of maintaining the estate would be too great a burden. The state, therefore, turned down the offer, leaving Untermyer's executors in a quandary because the will did not make any provision for the disposition of the property in the event New York State refused to accept it. While trying to decide what to do with Greystone, the Untermyer family continued to maintain the grounds and welcome the general public to the beautiful gardens every Tuesday in spring and summer. Although there was no entry fee for grounds visits, the family imposed a fifty cent charge, with the money going to charity, for public access to the house during a three-day period preceding an auction of furnishings and artwork, including paintings by Rubens and Gainsborough. In addition to selling the contents of the mansion, the Untermyer heirs established a philanthropic corporation to administer the estate as a public park. The property thus became tax exempt, much to the dismay of Yonkers officials. The Untermyers and the city went back and forth in court until 1944, when the New York State Supreme Court ruled that the property was taxable. In 1945 the Appellate Division of the New York State Supreme Court upheld the ruling.

Lending a Helping Hand

Keeping property on the tax rolls was a priority for Yonkers because even after the Depression decade of the thirties ended, the city's assessed valuation dropped. This was attributable in part to reductions in assessments of waterfront commercial property, a move intended to bring in new industries. Another factor in the drop in valuations was the city's acquisition of properties on which tax liens had been placed. With banks divesting themselves of foreclosed properties for which they had provided mortgages, there were numerous undervalued homes and commercial sites. Real estate bargains abounded, but not every transaction was a distress sale. Some homes commanded good prices and when a particularly beautiful residence changed hands, the newspapers were quick to report it. In announcing the purchase, in 1941, of Chateau Fleur de Lys, the Shonnard Terrace mansion of the late president of the American Bankers Association, by Vera Fokine, wife of Michael Fokine, the world-famous ballet master, *The New York Times* included a picture of the stone mansion, with the Hudson in the background. That some people could afford to buy spectacular waterview homes in the "Queen City of the Hudson" was a very positive development, but many Yonkers residents were still struggling to keep a roof over their heads and put food on the table. In an effort to aid those citizens for whom the Depression lingered into the forties, Yonkers became part of the federal government's food stamp program in 1940. Inclusion in the program enabled residents certified for eligibility to obtain orange stamps to be used for normal food purchases at participating local stores and blue stamps entitling them to free surplus commodities. The estimate of those needing this type of help was nearly twenty-one thousand.

With a population that had jumped by almost eight thousand in the previous decade, to approximately 142,000 in 1940, Yonkers was attempting to help more of its citizens by providing not only food but adequate housing. The Yonkers Municipal Housing Authority had been established in 1935 to address the issue of substandard housing in blighted areas, but three years went by before it received a promise of federal money. With funding in the offing, the city obtained a loan from the United States Housing Authority to construct Mulford Gardens, a complex of seventeen three-story, completely fireproof buildings housing 552 families and costing upward of $3 million. The price tag for the landscaping alone was $200,000. The eleven-acre site, with a commanding view of the Hudson River, featured eighteen playgrounds and a number of wading pools for children. A half-dozen indoor recreation spaces ideal for dancing, Ping-Pong, and other activities were included in the complex as well. For the new residents of Mulford Gardens, all of this was a far cry from the substandard dwellings where they had previously lived. Eligibility for one of the new apartments, which rented for from $22 to $26.50 a month, including utilities, was based upon the condition of a family's housing at the time application to Mulford Gardens was made. Living in a cold water flat, a place with windowless bedrooms, or an apartment lacking a private bathroom constituted eligibility.

At a dedication ceremony held in July 1940, Mayor John J. Condon described Mulford Gardens as "an asset for Yonkers," noting that the new housing provided families with "modern conveniences at low cost."[108] Another speaker, Frank L. Palmer, of the United States Housing Authority, was effusive in his praise for the new project. "The opening of Mulford Gardens is a symbol of the American way of living," he said.[109] Given the success of Mulford Gardens, the Yonkers Municipal Housing Authority began formulating plans for similar projects. Siting the new housing posed challenges, however. In 1942, several hundred residents of the Cottage Place area petitioned the common council to reject that location for public housing but the council refused to entertain the objections of the petitioners. A year later, the city revealed that it had acquired options on more than two dozen properties in the vicinity of Irving Place for a public housing project.

When the Kennedys (Yes, *the* Kennedys) Rode the Yonkers Bus

Whether it arose from deep-seated racism or emanated from the belief that local government did not belong in the business of erecting multifamily dwellings for the economically disadvantaged, opposition to public housing was a manifestation of class divisions. Those divisions existed not only within communities but within regions, with some municipalities being generally regarded, at least by outsiders, as working-class, while others were seen as upscale enclaves of the professional and business classes. In an effort to keep a certain distance from their working-class neighbors, affluent municipalities that shared borders with less well-to-do communities were, shall we say, not very receptive to what they perceived as intrusions by those outsiders living just across the municipal boundary line. In 1940, the long-standing class differentiation between Yonkers and the Village of Bronxville, which in years past had prompted Yonkers residents living in enclaves near the Bronxville border to seek annexation to the village, surfaced in the form of the great bus battle. The origins of the confrontation went back to 1938, when the New York, Boston and Westchester Railway, which had served interior portions of the county, ceased operating. Commuters were then forced to travel to the nearest station on the New York Central's Harlem or Putnam divisions or the New Haven Railroad. To serve these residents, the Yonkers Bus Company created an eleven-mile-long line between Yonkers and New Rochelle. Almost immediately there were howls of indignation from residents of Bronxville, notwithstanding the fact that some inhabitants of the village actually used the line. The attorney for the Yonkers Bus Company pointed out that the estates passed by the bus route included the home of Joseph P. Kennedy, ambassador to Great Britain, and "members of the Kennedy family and many village officials often had used the buses."[110]

Be that as it may, after waging a two-year legal battle to prevent buses from traversing the village, Bronxville obtained a court order prohibiting buses from using its streets. This meant that the Yonkers Bus Company route, which began at Larkin Plaza, could go no farther than the New York Central station on the western edge of the Village of Bronxville. Getting to the Bronxville station involved using a mere 1,100 feet of Bronxville roadways, something the village was willing to permit. What it would not allow was buses lumbering along a one-mile stretch of Pondfield Road, through a residential area, and that was the missing link in the Yonkers Bus Company's route from Larkin Plaza to the New Rochelle Railroad Station. None too happy with the court ruling, New Rochelle appealed to the Public Service Commission. Before the commission could intervene, however, Bronxville, exercising the authority granted the village by the Court of Appeals, served notice on the bus company, on a wintry day in December 1940, to suspend operations immediately and the village mayor, Colonel Frederick L. Devereux, really did mean immediately. Counsel for the Yonkers Bus Company reacted by pointing out that it would "not be humane to stop service at once" leaving people standing out in the cold, whereupon the mayor relented and allowed the buses to keep running until midnight![111] The attorney for the bus company then fired off another salvo declaring that in the past year the line had transported seven hundred thousand people. In the month of November alone, 65,076 had used the bus and of these 8,500 traveled only "within the village limits."[112] This was not enough to convert the thousand Bronxville residents who turned out for a public hearing on the question of whether to restore the bus line. Within days of the February 1941 hearing, at which speakers complained about the noise and traffic generated by the buses and the fact that they "marred the appearance of residential streets," the village board voted against the restoration of service.[113]

Three months later, they did a complete about-face! This occurred for several reasons, one of which was the fact that 53 percent of families responding to a questionnaire distributed by the village indicated that they wanted to see bus service restored. Then there was the near defeat of two members of the village board by pro-bus candidates in village elections. Finally, there was the issue of fuel conservation. Although the United States would not enter World War II for another seven months, "buses were now needed because the United States might soon come to rationing gasoline and prohibiting the use of pleasure cars on week-ends," according to a village board member who had been one of the most vigorous bus opponents before reversing himself.[114] "You win some; you lose some," as the old saying goes, and so it was with mass transit. The controversial bus was back, but the Getty Square Branch of the Putnam Division of the New York Central Railroad was discontinued in 1943. This 3.1 mile line ran from downtown Yonkers to the Van Cortlandt Park junction of the Putnam Division. For a year after the last trip, made by twelve riders, Yonkers waged a legal battle to have service reinstated, but this initiative was unsuccessful, as was an earlier attempt, in 1942, by Yonkers mayor Benjamin F. Barnes to have the line acquired by New York City for an extension of the subway from Van Cortlandt Park to Yonkers.

Compared with mass transit, roadways seemed to pose fewer problems for Yonkers. In 1940, the widening, from four to six lanes, of the southern part of the Saw Mill River Parkway between Yonkers Avenue and the Henry Hudson Parkway was completed, as was the link between the Saw Mill River Parkway and the Cross County Parkway. The parkways helped speed cars through Yonkers, but what about autos that tarried in the increasingly crowded business district? An article written by T. T. McCrosky, Yonkers planning director, and published in *American City* magazine in 1938, made a case for meters. According to McCrosky, 1,113 cars parked in the downtown area on any given business day but "216 cars, or 19 per cent, remain longer than the 60 minutes allowed. Yet these violators monopolized more available parking time than the 897 cars whose drivers obeyed the law."[115] In 1940, the city came up with a partial solution to that problem by installing parking meters. As the years went on, parking, especially in downtown Yonkers, became one of many challenges confronting city government in a municipality where just the act of governing was, at times, a major challenge in itself.

Governing Yonkers

During the Depression and beyond, Yonkers was grappling with funda-mental issues of municipal governance, most notably the city manager form of government. The concept of professional management for Yonkers had been advanced in 1925 but was rejected. It resurfaced in 1936, largely because of the efforts of a very committed Yonkers resident, Mrs. Harry T. Welty, who served as chair of the Bryn Mawr-Nepperhan League of Women Voters. Edith P. Welty, "a tennis-playing grandmother," was a most unlikely person to become involved in politics, but after accepting a neigh-bor's invitation to accompany her to a League of Women Voters' meeting, Mrs. Welty became part of a group researching the city manager form of government, a topic the L.W.V. was planning to debate at an upcoming meeting.[116] Approaching this the way she had tackled assignments during her college days, she plunged right in, making repeated trips to the New York Public Library, where she devoured everything she could find on city management. The careful notes she compiled were used to instruct the women preparing for the debate, but Edith Welty didn't stop there. Her research had convinced her of the value of this form of government, and she embarked upon a crusade to bring it to Yonkers. At first, she spoke exclusively to women's organizations, attempting to convince her listeners that the time had come to reform municipal government. Her fame spread quickly, and before long a group of Yonkers businessmen approached her about joining forces with them to campaign for a referendum establishing the city manager form of government.

The next step was the formation of the Committee of One Hundred, a group of citizens who circulated a petition to demand a referendum on the city manager form of government. Committee members were quick to point out that Yonkers was governed under the Second Class Cities Law, which accorded the mayor the majority of votes on the board of estimate. With a city manager plan, Yonkers residents would elect seven councilmen and they, in turn, would choose a city manager. The person elected chairman of the city council would assume the ceremonial duties of mayor. Joining the Committee of One Hundred was the sixteen-member Council of Yonkers Civic Associations, which had a combined membership of three thousand citizens. The three thousand–strong Committee of City Employees, however, opposed the city manager form of government. In 1936, when the referendum was held, opponents carried the day, but supporters charged that election irregularities had occurred. They alleged that poll watchers from the Committee of One Hundred had been banned from some districts and that people who did not sign the register were permitted to vote. Despite proponents' objections, the results of the referendum stood.

To prevent the matter from coming up again, opponents of the city manager concept supported a bill introduced in the state legislature to require 50 percent of the voters in cities having a population of at least fifty thousand, rather than the 10 percent required up until that time, to affix their signatures to a petition before a referendum could be scheduled. Both Democratic and Republican Party officials in Yonkers steadfastly denied that they had been behind the bill. Even without more stringent requirements for holding referenda, the city manager concept went down to defeat again in 1937. The very next year, however, it was approved in a close vote. In 1939, the new system was implemented, a process that entailed electing common council members "by the proportional representation system on paper ballots without party emblems. . . . The Council would elect a mayor from their members and appoint a city manager."[117] Despite some political shenanigans involving an obscure candidate, Elizabeth Weldy, whose name was similar enough to Edith Welty's to confuse voters, Mrs. Welty won a seat on the common council, thus becoming "the first woman member of a City Council in Yonkers history."[118] This achievement was only one extraordinary aspect of a political contest considered "the most important election in the history of Yonkers" because it revolved around the issue of "a business man's government versus machine politics."[119] Interestingly, the Committee of One Hundred "endorsed no individual candidates," but "its members were well pleased" with the outcome of the election.[120] To make sure everything was on the up and up "extraordinary precautions were taken by official agencies to guard against any such recurrence of mischief as attended the voting on the city manager referendum last year."[121]

When it was all over, *The Herald Statesman* observed that despite the negativity of those opposed to proportional representation, "Yonkers voters—nearly 60,000 of them—showed that they 'knew what it was all about.'"[122] Although pleased that the election had gone smoothly, a week later *The Herald Statesman* issued a forceful reminder to the new council, reminding its members that voter approval of a new charter in 1938 proved that they desired "a new order that would end the abuses of the past."[123] Going forward, what was needed was a businesslike approach to government and constant attention to the city's expenditures.

The new city manager chosen by the common council was Raymond J. Whitney, the fiscally conservative village manager of Mamaroneck. Whitney got off to a flying start by ordering city employees to put in a full day's work. He also removed a half-dozen water coolers from city hall, citing the excessive $2.50 per month charge for each device as the reason for his action. Whitney was prepared to tackle far more important issues, including the investigation of political and financial matters during the preceding decade. The Yonkers City Manager League pressed for the inquiry after the New York State Department of Audit and Control found certain discrepancies in the management of the city's finances. A league petition requesting a full state investigation of city administrations prior to the implementation of the city manager form of government was sent to Governor Herbert H. Lehman. Citing the need for very tight supervision of municipal finances throughout the state, the petition blamed a quarter-century of major expenditure plus the absence of "real estate supervision" for a decline in real estate values that had hampered economic expansion and created enormous hardships for low-income residents of Yonkers.[124] The governor did not accede to the league's demand for a state investigation. Citing the fact that the state legislature had not conferred this power upon him, he recommended pursuing the matter with the Westchester district attorney. The end result was a grand jury investigation that produced seventeen thousand pages of testimony, but none of this went anywhere. The league requested the governor "to supersede the DA but again he refused to act, and that ended the matter."[125]

Nine months into the city manager form of government, its biggest supporter, Edith Welty, was becoming disillusioned because, in her view, Yonkers government was still plagued by "plenty of politics."[126] The problem, as Mrs. Welty saw it, was that Democratic holdovers from the previous administration were still administering city departments. The city manager type of government would thus remain ineffective as long as Yonkers had "a machine-controlled Council."[127] By the summer of 1941, the Yonkers City Manager League, while still endorsing this form of government, was calling upon voters to elect council members who would promise to remove City Manager Whitney. Some voters immediately embraced the idea because they had been alienated by Whitney's cost-cutting measures. These included a "roll-your-own" ashcan proposal which would have required residents to place their refuse at curbside and then remove the empty garbage cans after the trash had been collected. A far more important issue was what the Yonkers City Manager League characterized as Whitney's subservience "to unscrupulous political pressure and to the machine members of the Common Council."[128] Although candidates endorsed by the Yonkers City Manager League won the majority of seats on the common council in the 1941 election, removing the city manager proved difficult. Charges relating to Whitney's administration of the city and handling of contracts were filed by the Yonkers City Manager League but they were dismissed by the common council for lack of sufficient evidence. The council left the door open, however, by indicating that it would allow new, well-documented charges to be filed.

In the midst of the battle to oust Whitney, Governor Herbert H. Lehman called upon two city officials to strictly enforce laws prohibiting gambling. The men given this charge were the city manager and Dr. Benjamin F. Barnes, a physician who had been chosen mayor by the common council, despite the fact that Edith Welty had obtained more votes in the 1941 election and had expected to become mayor. As a council member Mrs. Welty sponsored a resolution calling for an investigation of gambling in the city, but her fellow council members refused to act. Within weeks, however, after a councilman resigned, his replacement came out swinging against not only gambling but City Manager Whitney. Declaring that the city had been "held up to public shame and ridicule" by Whitney's failure to eliminate gambling, Thomas B. Sheridan, the new member of the council, put forth a resolution calling for the removal of the city manager.[129] The council responded by voting to suspend Whitney, a preliminary step in the removal process. Whitney then demanded a hearing to answer the charges about gambling, his failure to censure the police for breaking into a home without a warrant, his sale of what he claimed were obsolete inefficient street lights, and the purchase of defective parking meters. No sooner had the hearing gotten under way than the common council reversed itself and dropped all of the charges. No explanation was offered for the about-face. Within days, Whitney's reinstatement appeared to be a moot point because he resigned, ostensibly to take a position with the federal government, but that wasn't the end of the matter! Almost before the ink was dry on the letter of resignation, he rescinded his resignation! But enough was enough. The common council decided to return the retraction document, letting the resignation stand. The council then proceeded to elect former mayor William A. Walsh as city manager and director of public safety.

Walsh immediately tackled the gambling issue by removing the chief of detectives and reassigning several dozen members of the police force. He also banned Bingo at churches. These measures, combined with raids, tidied up the city so much that less than a year later a Westchester County grand jury concluded that organized gambling was nonexistent in Yonkers and the city was indeed enforcing the laws prohibiting gambling. So far so good, but two years later, following a revelation about a floating dice game in which a player lost almost $12,000, City Manager Walsh shook up the Police Department. This turned out to be Walsh's last hurrah, because a majority of the members of the city council, including Mrs. Welty, succeeded in ousting him. Ironically, his successor, City Controller Robert Craig Montgomery, was removed after less than a year in office following allegations of inadequate garbage collection and snow removal. He was succeeded by Norman Henderson, the city engineer. When the next election rolled around in November 1945, League of City Managers candidates were triumphant but before leaving office, lame-duck council members removed Henderson as city manager and appointed Morris L. Rosenwasser, who promptly made a series of political appointments that so infuriated Edith Welty that she declared: "This is the lowest piece of political chicanery I have ever heard of."[130]

Perhaps Welty regretted that she was still involved in Yonkers government. Back in 1942 she had withdrawn from the New York State Senate race to help defeat a referendum, endorsed by the city committees of both major parties, to abolish proportional representation and reinstate the old ward system for choosing members of the common council. Voters rejected the referendum two to one. A year later, three Yonkers League of City Managers candidates, including Mrs. Welty, were elected to the council. Soon thereafter the council decided that henceforth the council member who received the greatest number of votes in the election would automatically become mayor. This time Welty was not the frontrunner, but her chance would come eventually in the postwar period.

"Mutiny" on the *Batory*

The political drama surrounding Welty's mayoral ambitions and the revolving door in the city manager's office caused consternation among the good people of Yonkers, but it was tempered by the realization that some things transcended local politics, especially in wartime. Even before the United States entered World War II, Yonkers was touched by the conflict. Germany's invasion of Poland in 1939 was a blow to Poles all over the world, including the large Polish community in Yonkers. The city's Polish population grew a bit at the start of the war when the *Batory*, a vessel owned by the Polish Gdynia-America Line, was detained in the Hudson off Yonkers by the United States government. As U.S. Customs officials monitored the ship to make sure it did not violate the American Neutrality Act by taking on contraband, wild rumors circulated among the increasingly uneasy crew. The tales, spread by word of mouth among the approximately three hundred sailors, were unfounded, but the majority of the crew became convinced that their ship was going to be put at the disposal of the British Admiralty, which would use it to transport munitions from Canada to England. Lending credibility to this rumor was the fact that after the *Batory* had landed her 642 passengers, more than half of them Americans, at the Polish line's Hoboken, New Jersey, pier, it was cleared for Canada. Nervous sailors were terrified that they would be pressed into service traversing a North Atlantic filled with German submarines.

Rather than transport munitions, some of the crew were ready to mutiny, and since their ship was just off Yonkers, the city's police department had to intervene. Two police captains went aboard the vessel, where they discovered that 150 crew members had taken over the engine room in an attempt to prevent the *Batory* from getting under way. These mutineers in the making were disconsolate because their much-beloved captain, Eustacy Borkowski, a decorated war hero and linguist fluent in seventeen languages, had been ordered by the Polish Consulate General to relinquish command. The police ordered the recalcitrant crew to go ashore. If they refused, they would be forcibly removed by a huge phalanx of Yonkers police officers. Two-thirds of the ship's crew, including twenty of the ship's thirty female stewardesses, disembarked. The remaining crew members were permitted to stay aboard to operate the vessel. The baggage of all those who went ashore was carefully inspected by U.S. Customs officials to ensure that no contraband was being brought into Yonkers.

The first stop for a tearful Captain Borkowski was the Yonkers Canoe Club, where he took pen in hand and wrote: "With best wishes, thanks and appreciation for the kindness tendered to my officers and crew during my stay in Yonkers stream. Long life, good old America."[131] The captain's sentiments were echoed by crew members who, when questioned by U.S. officials about the near-mutiny, offered all sorts of explanations ranging from two months' back pay owed by the shipping line to their reluctance to go to Canada, "preferring to remain in Yonkers, where they had met numerous members of the city's friendly Polish-American colony."[132] Some crew members said that, until the situation in their homeland was clarified, they wanted "to remain off friendly Yonkers."[133] Although Captain Borkowski proceeded to New York, most of the sailors, including young boys ranging in age from fourteen to sixteen, headed to the Polish Community Center, a Yonkers institution that was not only the cultural hub of Polish life in Yonkers but testimony to the can-do spirit of the city's Polish immigrants. The Depression notwithstanding, Polish organizations in Yonkers, having purchased stock in a holding corporation that acquired a former New York State Armory, witnessed the transformation of the structure between 1932 and 1938. When the renovated building opened as the Polish Community Center, in the latter year, all debts associated with its purchase and reconstruction had been repaid. It was to this splendid building that the *Batory* crew came, and while the officials of the center tossed out the welcome mat, they had to scramble to provide suitable accommodations. Cots and blankets were supplied by the Salvation Army and center officials arranged for the female crew members to reside with Polish families in Yonkers. Everyone who went ashore stayed behind when the sixteen thousand–ton *Batory*, "the pride of the Polish merchant marine," commanded by a British naval captain, with an English pilot on board, set sail for Canada.[134] According to *The Herald Statesman,* when the ship departed, the Polish flag "waved proudly in the breeze" and crowds gathered on the banks of the Hudson waved amidst a cacophony of whistles and other sounds emanating from boats that had turned out to bid farewell to the *Batory.*[135]

Crew members who stayed in Yonkers continued to enjoy the hospitality of the Polish Community Center, which provided accommodations and meals for those who had nowhere else to go. Within days, however, the number of men staying at the center had dwindled to sixty as crew members found lodgings with Polish families in Yonkers and environs, or employer-provided living quarters. Eighteen people from the *Batory* were hired as servants or cooks in private homes less than a week after leaving the ship. Other food service workers found jobs in bakeries and restaurants. Temporary employment as painters provided badly needed funds for some. Commenting on this *The New York Times* declared: "And there has been a sudden epidemic of house-painting in the Polish areas, so eager are residents to supply jobs for the destitute seamen."[136]

America at War

Although a real bond had been forged between the city's Polish community and the crew of the *Batory,* it would be several years before Americans would fully understand the far-reaching implications of an unprovoked attack by a hostile power. For Poland, the aggressor had been Germany; for the United States, it was Japan, which, on December 7, 1941, launched a surprise attack on Pearl Harbor, Hawaii. A stunned nation reacted with shock and disbelief. On December 8, in a symbolic gesture, one Yonkers resident, Hedda Bahssin, a Russian immigrant who owned an antique and gift shop on North Broadway, assembled every bit of Japanese merchandise in the store. If an item was stamped "made in Japan" Bahssin tore it apart. After he had finished wielding his axe and hammer, he gathered up the broken pieces and put them in his shop window. On top of the pile was a sign stating that the heap was the store's inventory "of Jap goods."[137]

Following the attack on Pearl Harbor, Yonkers and the nation prepared for all-out war. Young men came forward to volunteer for service, and between volunteers and draftees approximately twenty thousand Yonkers residents, some of them women, served in the military, and 532 forfeited their lives. Most died in combat, but some were killed during training or on routine patrol missions. Fourteen months into the war, Ensign Frank Boryszewski, who gave up a prestigious Hayden scholarship at New York University's Washington Square College of Arts and Sciences to join the Naval Air Force, was killed when a Navy patrol bomber crashed into the Pacific off San Diego. He left behind his parents, who resided on Palisade Avenue, and a fiancée, who was also a Yonkers resident. The couple were to have announced their engagement only a month after the tragic accident. Undeterred by the very real possibility that they might never see their loved ones again, Yonkers men stepped forward to serve their country. One fellow was so eager that he secured a birth certificate giving his age as eighteen. With the document in hand he headed to New York City to enlist, and ended up in the Pacific where he was wounded when Japanese dive-bombers strafed the aircraft carrier on which he was serving. Soon thereafter the young sailor's true age, fifteen, was learned and he was honorably discharged and sent home to Yonkers to resume his studies at Longfellow Junior High School in the fall of 1943. Meanwhile, some Yonkers police officers had to grapple with a difficult decision, namely to take a military leave of absence from the force once they received their draft notices or resign from the force, thereby forfeiting seniority and pension credits, and obtain a deferment by taking a job in an essential industry. What made the choice especially difficult was that some local draft boards viewed the positions of policemen and firemen as critical and granted deferrals on a case-by-case basis while others did not. One of the Yonkers boards was confronted with another issue, the willful destruction of some of its records by the board's assistant chief clerk, a young woman in her twenties who was attempting to prevent her fiancé and brother-in-law from being drafted. The woman confessed to the F.B.I. that her love for her fiancé outweighed her "loyalty as a federal employee."[138] By the time this came to light, the clerk and her fiancé had tied the knot. The happy couple didn't get to spend much time together, however, because he was drafted and she was sentenced to sixty days in jail for draft fraud.

Unlike the clerk and her better half, most citizens of Yonkers merely acquiesced when the draft notices arrived. Fiancées, wives, mothers, and sisters shed tears but, like the men to whom they bade farewell, they hoped and prayed that their soldier boys would one day return to Yonkers. Toward the end of the war, a very celebrated native son, General Joseph W. Stilwell, former commander of United States forces in the China-Burma-India theater, paid a visit to the old home town where he had played quarterback on the Yonkers High School football team before going off to West Point. Better known as "Vinegar Joe," the general was the son of Benjamin W. Stilwell, who had been manager of the local lighting company. His brother, Colonel John Stilwell, still lived in Yonkers and it was his home, Ardenwold, on North Broadway, that the general visited "for a few hours" toward the end of 1944.[139]

Civil Defense

A visit from a person as celebrated as "Vinegar Joe" helped relieve the tedium of everyday life in a city preoccupied by war. For many residents, this was a time of all work and no play, with spare time devoted to war-related activities undertaken by the Red Cross, the Salvation Army, local service organizations, and houses of worship. Some residents were auxiliary policemen and firemen, and two thousand citizens served as air raid wardens. The latter figured prominently in test blackouts, the first of which was held on a Sunday evening, between 9 and 9:20 p.m. in March 1942. So unprecedented was this event that *The Yonkers Home News* wrote: "For the first time in perhaps a hundred years or more, Yonkers was without visible street lights at night. . . . In the memory of the oldest citizen this condition never happened before with the possible exception of storms, including the blizzard of 1888."[140] The purpose of the test blackout was to make the city invisible to the enemy by quite literally extinguishing all lights. Not only were homes, factories, including Otis Elevator and the Phelps Dodge Habirshaw plant, which because of their war work were not expected to participate, darkened, but commercial and municipal buildings, shops, and places of entertainment were blacked out. *The Yonkers Home News* noted: "The streets took on a ghost town look in a few minutes, after the sirens, aided by the powerful whistle at the Otis Elevator Company, proclaimed the first blackout underway."[141] As soon as the blackout began, vehicles were required to pull over to the side of the road, even on parkways, and turn off their lights. Regular and auxiliary police erected barricades to prevent cars on the Bronx River, Saw Mill, and Cross County parkways from entering Yonkers during the blackout. Observing the blackout were the county executive and officials from Yonkers and other communities. Yonkers mayor Benjamin F. Barnes was supposed to have flown over the city in an Army airplane from Mitchel Field on Long Island, but the flight was canceled nine hours before the blackout began, giving the mayor time to make other arrangements. He ended up traveling across the Hudson to view his city from the top of the Palisades. Although moonlight provided quite a bit of illumination on the night of the test, soon after the sirens went off the city was almost completely devoid of artificial light. The blackout was deemed a success not only because it was almost 100 percent effective but because no crimes nor even pranks occurred while the lights were out.

Two weeks after the first blackout, county government decided to stage a blackout at an unspecified time on an evening in mid-March. On this occasion, the full complement of civil defense personnel and equipment was mobilized and a plane carrying the chairman of the Westchester County Defense Council took off from the airport in Armonk to monitor compliance. When the county insisted upon having additional blackouts and a daytime air raid test, Yonkers mayor Benjamin F. Barnes invoked his right, under new state legislation, to take charge of his city's defense. He did so because his constituents were becoming increasingly edgy about the county's surprise blackouts. When the sirens went off, people didn't know whether it was the real thing or just another test. As a physician, Mayor Barnes was doubtless aware of the mind-body connection, and he intended to reduce the sort of angst associated with the county's most recent blackout, which lasted a full eighty minutes. Amazingly, some people remained unruffled no matter how dark or noisy defense exercises were. Fans in attendance at the last full week of Empire City's autumn meeting in October 1942 responded calmly to the first air alarm at a New York State racetrack. Nearly eleven thousand people complied with the directions of track staff members and air raid wardens and took refuge beneath the grandstand, which, along with the clubhouse and other facilities, had been refurbished in 1940, the same year that pari-mutuel wagering, permitting fans to place bets in pools and split the winnings, was legalized. During the air raid, horses returned to their paddocks and everything remained quiet until the all clear siren was sounded. Although the air raid drill went well, the Yonkers track was hampered by gasoline shortages as the war dragged on. In 1943, the meager allotment of gas for commercial vehicles used to transport horses caused Empire City to request the transfer of its summer meet to Jamaica Raceway.

By that time, it had become increasingly clear that Mayor Barnes's idea of having the city handle its own defense was feasible. Yonkers, more than many other communities in New York State, was capable of doing this, in part because of the Yonkers Defense Rangers, a unit organized by H. Armour Smith, director of the Hudson River Museum. Mr. Smith's idea was to gather up healthy men of good character who were also good with rifles or shotguns. Generally older than draftees, these men would assist the military in the event of an attack in Yonkers or environs. To prepare for their new role, the Yonkers Defense Rangers underwent training in marksmanship, guerrilla tactics, and judo at the Naval Militia Armory. They were then deputized by Mayor Barnes to supplement the police and auxiliary police in emergencies and in guarding defense plants, reservoirs, and public transit. Despite the mayor's unrelenting support for the Defense Rangers, Governor Herbert H. Lehman insisted that there was no place for armed units in civil defense. This doesn't seem to have troubled Mayor Barnes, because the Defense Rangers were allowed to practice in Trevor Park. They even staged a mock attack on the Hudson River Museum. Wielding unloaded guns they approached the museum's home, the John Bond Trevor Mansion, but failed to capture the building because the museum's director had placed a dummy bomb in the building. The Yonkers Defense Rangers were so committed that when their indoor practice area, the Naval Militia Armory, was no longer available for their use, they traveled all the way to Mahopac for marksmanship practice.

In addition to the Yonkers Defense Rangers, a group of nearly three dozen radio operators was recruited, at the request of Mayor Barnes, to provide communications throughout the city in the event telephone service was disrupted by the enemy. The mayor beefed up the training of auxiliary firemen as well, by having them summoned, by factory whistles and sirens, to two-alarm fires. Leaving nothing to chance, the good doctor also proposed building four bomb shelters in different locations. One of these was to have been a tunnel under Washington Park on South Broadway. In 1943 twenty-eight buildings were designated as air raid shelters. They included the main post office, the Y.M.C.A., the Y.W.C.A., the Jewish Community Center, the Polish Community Center, Sokol Hall, the Hudson River Museum, and various schools, churches, theaters, and a funeral home. Happily, the people of Yonkers, unlike the inhabitants of London, did not have to take refuge in shelters, but residents of the "Queen City of the Hudson" were always mindful of the war being fought on two fronts, each half a world away.

Doing Without

Despite the very genuine and heartfelt patriotism so evident in Yonkers during World War II, the victory of the United States and her allies over the dark forces of totalitarianism could not be taken for granted. The factors that would determine the outcome of the war were numerous and varied. The military might of the Allies was first and foremost, but seemingly small things such as salvage drives were part of the victory equation as well. In the autumn of 1942, the Yonkers War Salvage Committee launched a drive to collect one hundred pounds of scrap metal for every resident of Yonkers. The goal was 14,200,000 pounds in all. Money raised from the sale of the collected metal was earmarked for the Yonkers War and Community Chest, which provided assistance to those serving in the military and to the citizens of nations affected by the war. Yonkers also had wartime fundraising campaigns for the American Red Cross.

To signify just how serious it was about salvaging metal for the war effort, the common council passed a law, sponsored by Edith Welty, mandating the saving and flattening of tin cans for collection. Violators could be slapped with a ten-dollar fine or a ten-day jail sentence. Sometimes Yonkers residents went a bit overboard in contributing scrap and salvaged material. During a rubber roundup, mats that had lined the marble corridors of city hall were carted off. Then it dawned on Mayor Barnes, who was also director of civilian protection, that citizens strolling through the building on rainy days might go flying on wet marble. The mats, which the mayor said were not pure rubber, were hastily recovered and returned to city hall.

Something else that wasn't exactly pure were counterfeit gas ration coupons. Following a chase through the streets of Yonkers in the spring of 1943, a driver was apprehended by agents of the Secret Service, the Office of Price Administration, and the Westchester County Sheriff's Office. The authorities found coupons for nearly three thousand gallons of gasoline in the suspect's car. With gasoline in limited supply, motorists were curtailing any unnecessary driving during the war, with the result that the Yonkers-Alpine ferry was forced to make up what it had lost in volume by increasing the price for transporting vehicles across the river.

The ferry company pledged to reduce fares once the war was over. For the duration of the conflict, Hudson River Day Line's excursion boats bypassed Yonkers because the City of Yonkers had leased the pier at the foot of Main Street to a private company that overhauled boats. This didn't faze the residents of Yonkers. Leisure-time pursuits involving travel could await the end of hostilities. What mattered at the moment was winning the war, even if it meant working long hours in the city's defense plants and volunteering in one's spare time. With the Depression still fresh in their minds, residents were happy to have good jobs. Time off was not as alluring as a nice paycheck.

Finding things on which to spend that income could be a little bit challenging, however, because of the wartime shortages. Even after the defeat of Germany and the celebration of V-E or Victory in Europe Day in May 1945, meatless Tuesdays were the norm at Yonkers restaurants. Some residents recall that they "poured cooking grease into coffee cans and brought them to our butcher for the war effort."[142] In an effort to deal with the rationing of meat and other foodstuffs, in 1943 the city enacted an ordinance permitting the raising of chickens in residential areas until six months after the war ended. The Boyce Thompson Institute for Plant Research encouraged self-sufficiency in another food category by holding weekly lectures to provide instructions for planting and cultivating "Victory Gardens" where citizens could grow their own vegetables. These initiatives were important because, as the old saying goes, "every little bit helps." That applied to another area of home front activities as well, namely vigilance.

Just as in the early twenty-first century when electronic signs appeared at bridges and tunnels asking the public to report any suspected terrorist activity, during World War II citizens were encouraged to contact the authorities with tips on people, vehicles, or anything else that seemed unusual. Yonkers police and state and federal agents were grateful for civilian reports of suspicious activity, but even without them they were able to ferret out people likely to do harm to the United States. In the spring of 1942, Federal Bureau of Investigation agents descended upon Yonkers to conduct searches resulting in the arrest of seventeen enemy aliens. The twelve Italians and five Germans taken into custody were transported to Ellis Island to appear before an alien enemy hearing board. They left behind an arsenal of weapons, cameras, radio transmission equipment, and nearly three dozen short-wave radios, all of which were carted away by the F.B.I. Yonkers residents slept more comfortably knowing that dangerous aliens had been prevented from carrying out their nefarious plans, but whenever something untoward occurred, city residents wondered whether enemies in their midst were responsible. Explosions and fires made residents especially anxious.

In December 1942, an explosion occurred in the engine room of a large, ocean-going oil tanker that had been owned by the Aluminum Company of America before being turned over to the United States Shipping Board. The vessel was at the Arthur G. Blair, Inc., shipyard, where it was being refitted. Although the resulting fire was put out very quickly, three men sustained severe burns while two others received less serious injuries. Two weeks later, Yonkers was abuzz with rumors of a suspected chemical warfare attack after the Westchester County health commissioner revealed that three workers at the Habirshaw Cable and Wire Corporation in Yonkers and the Anaconda Wire and Cable Company in Hastings-on-Hudson had died of a liver disease, which health authorities attributed to their contact with chemicals employed to make cable lines impervious to fire and water. Four other workers had contracted the illness, and their prognosis was not good. Approximately five hundred employees of the plants had a different form of the disease. They suffered from skin eruptions, but were expected to fully recover following treatment. Medical scientists investigating the outbreak attributed the victims' cell damage to the amount of chlorine used "in a secret preparation" for waterproofing copper cable, but some wary Yonkers residents speculated about a more sinister explanation.[143] The reaction was similar in July 1943 when a ten-block area in the vicinity of the Otis Elevator Company was rocked by an explosion. A malfunctioning metallurgical baking oven in an Otis processing building had quite literally blown its stack. Since police headquarters was only a block away, officers were on the scene in no time, as were some two thousand curious and frightened citizens. Ambulances careened through the streets to get to what everyone assumed was a major disaster. Firefighters arrived with enough equipment to put out a major blaze but there wasn't even a fire, just an ominous cloud of smoke. A year later, an explosion and fire at Suntex, Inc., which was manufacturing duck and canvas, killed two workers and injured seven others but here, too, the blaze appeared to be accidental, rather than the work of the enemy.

Hands and Hearts at Work

As they headed to their jobs in the city's great industrial plants, factory workers couldn't help but contemplate the possibility of accidents or sabotage, but such thoughts did not dissuade them from showing up on time and toiling away at peak efficiency, ever mindful of the sacrifices

Yonkers residents in uniform were making. Those who had gone overseas occupied a special place in the hearts of those they left behind. The letters that went back and forth between men and women in service and their families and friends back in Yonkers bore testimony to the enduring bond between folks on the home front and the uniformed personnel stationed in faraway places. They were also a reminder that every task performed in a factory or other facility doing war-related work was both vital and noble. Yonkers citizens and their city stood ready to do everything asked of them in the hopes of bringing the war to a speedy and successful conclusion. This included taking the unusual step of transforming what had been public parkland along the Hudson River into a shipyard, which was leased to the United States Shipbuilding Corporation. As had been the case during World War I, longtime Yonkers industries converted to war production turning out a variety of items needed by the military. Refined Sugars "developed a substitute blood plasma which was used by our troops to replace blood which was in short supply. It was called Dextran."[144] The company also produced "Flo Sweet Liquid Sugar." This was "a syrup that was exempt from rationing."[145] One Yonkers company, Otis Elevator, retooled to manufacture all sorts of war materials including "recoil mechanisms for heavy guns, ammunition racks, assemblies for combat aircraft, machine tools, motors and generators."[146] Otis so excelled in the manufacturing of munitions that it was presented with the coveted Army-Navy "E" award for excellence less than a year after Pearl Harbor. As the war progressed, other local companies received similar recognition. Among the recipients were the Phelps Dodge Copper Products Corporation and the Habirshaw Cable and Wire Corporation, a subsidiary of Phelps Dodge.

A brand new Habirshaw factory was erected near the Hudson for a project so secret that even most of the people who worked for the company were unaware of it. The plant produced the pipeline placed under the English Channel to provide fuel for the Allies' D-Day invasion. The idea for a pipeline had been conceived by the British government, and Army engineers put together a plan for manufacturing long lengths of pipe, a task requiring new machinery and facilities. Phelps Dodge was up to the task. At the new Habirshaw facility it produced a forty-mile-long section of the pipe, the largest component of the pipeline. This gigantic section weighed in at 3,300 tons. Other sections of the pipe were made at a General Electric plant in Bridgeport, Connecticut, and at two other plants in New Jersey, and much of what they produced was sent to Yonkers to be put together. The entire undertaking was "one of the most ambitious and imaginative projects of World War II."[147] It was given the name

"Operation Pluto," meaning "Pipe Line Under the Ocean."[148] According to Frank Nevin, an executive at Habirshaw, who was very involved with "Operation Pluto," company officials were concerned about the ability of the ships, which had been specifically designed for the task, to safely transport the heavy pipe sections across the Atlantic. The vessels were actually converted Liberty ships and the coiled pipe they transported "was kept filled with water, under pressure at all times"; this was done to "prevent it from being crushed by its own weight."[149] Amazingly, only 162 days had gone by between the time "Operation Pluto," which "carried with it the fate of the whole Normandy invasion," had commenced and the pipe was sent off.[150]

Speed was of the essence during the war and not just for top secret projects. Research and development for all sorts of products had to be accelerated. At Alexander Smith and Sons Carpet Company, work proceeded feverishly on a new tire retread, a composite of cotton and recycled rubber manufactured on a carpet loom. At the same time, "Smith employees manufactured more than 4.4 million yards of duck and 8.5 million yards of blanket material," according to Rosalie Flynn, who noted:

> Their efforts were recognized by a grateful United States government, which presented Alexander Smith with four Army-Navy "E" (excellence) awards. The first of these presentations, made in November of 1943, was an elaborately staged affair complete with the unfurling of the flag. Smith employees contributed further to the war effort by purchasing more than $4 million worth of war bonds and by salvaging more than 5,000 tons of scrap.[151]

Alexander Smith employees also raised nearly $700,000 for the purchase of two military aircraft. These B-17 Flying Fortresses were named "The Yonkers Flying Carpet" and "The Yonkers Magic Carpet."[152]

Toward the end of the war, in April 1945, the Textile Workers Union, Congress of Industrial Organizations affiliate called for a voluntary demonstration by union members at Alexander Smith to protest the company's alleged failure to deal in good faith with the union. Several thousand workers left their posts and the factory shut down. "Yonkers' first wartime strike" lasted twenty-nine hours and ended when the 3,300 union members, representing the majority of the 5,500 Smith employees, voted to return to work while the union discussed wage increases with company management.[153] Harmony was restored and thousands of employees turned out at Smith Field for a clambake to mark the company's centennial in October 1945.

The one-day strike at Alexander Smith and Sons Carpet Company was the only instance of labor unrest in Yonkers during the war. Indeed, the city was considered a model of a good working relationship between workers and management. *The New York Times* noted in January 1944 that neither strikes nor slowdowns had occurred in Yonkers factories producing war-related items, a record that, industrialists said, "might be equaled elsewhere but not beaten."[154] The paper went on to point out that Yonkers was a "bustling industrial city," producing parts for various types of military equipment.[155] That labor grievances in these various industries had not reached a boiling point was attributable to the fact that many of the fifteen thousand Yonkers residents serving in the military were "relatives largely" of the city's fifteen thousand workers who were toiling away in factories producing items for the military.[156] The workers, therefore, embraced a "sit down and reason together" approach when interacting with management, and this ensured that there were no disruptions in factory production.[157] Yonkers residents in uniform were enlightened about the labor harmony on the home front by *The Yonkers Home News.* The cost of publishing the paper and sending it to all service personnel was underwritten by the Alexander Smith Memorial Foundation. Besides the strong link between factory workers and the men and women in the armed forces, another circumstance fostering harmonious relations between labor and management was the creation of a Westchester labor supply plan. According to the executive secretary of the Yonkers Chamber of Commerce, this initiative, which had entailed the opening of labor control centers in the county's major cities, had enabled workers to find employment close to home with the result that "life in the community was more normal than in some of the other industrial areas."[158] Given the tremendous need for people to fill newly created positions and to replace workers who had gone off to war, women had an unprecedented opportunity to enter the workforce. The Westchester County Federation of Women's Clubs actively encouraged its members to enroll in the aircraft department of the war industries training schools, including the one in Yonkers. Healthy women without dependent children were deemed especially suited for this type of education. So great was the need for workers, however, that mothers of young children were welcomed into the workforce and to accommodate them the federal government funded child care centers. Yonkers had four of them, all located in public schools and staffed by teachers and other trained personnel six days a week year-round.

Publicly funded child care and, to a large extent, employment opportunities for women vanished after the war ended. Returning veterans needed jobs, and female employees were considered expendable. Some women regretted losing that weekly paycheck but no one was sorry the war was over. Indeed, the residents of Yonkers were grateful that the long nightmare had come to an end, and many of them flocked to houses of worship to give thanks. One Yonkers church, St. John's in Getty Square, where many a prayer of thanksgiving was said, had celebrated its 250th anniversary a year before the war ended. Among the 1,200 people attending the anniversary service concluding a weeklong celebration were "members of the congregation, as well as other Protestants, Catholics and Jews."[159] Representatives from civic groups were also present. Earlier in the week the Right Reverend William T. Manning, Episcopal bishop of New York, had addressed worshippers at St. John's telling them that more than ever, there was a "greater need" for religion.[160] The bishop cited the Nazis as evidence that a person "acts out" the beliefs he embraces.[161] In the bishop's view, religious tenets had to become "a powerful influence" in the period following the war.[162] Yonkers residents of all religious persuasions agreed and the following year, they began their march forward into that postwar world, rebuilding their lives around their families, houses of worship, schools, and community organizations. The world war and the Depression that had preceded it had taken their toll but the city's heterogeneous population was imbued with new optimism. Maybe Yonkers would again be the "Queen City of the Hudson."

4

The Remaking of Yonkers

The Postwar Years

Three Hundred and Counting

No sooner had the war ended than Yonkers began a series of celebrations to mark the safe return of its native sons and daughters who had served in the military and to honor the memory of those who had made the ultimate sacrifice for their country. In 1946 there was an additional reason to strike up the band, toss confetti in the air, and, if one were so inclined, raise a glass or two! That year marked the three hundredth anniversary of the founding of Yonkers. The tercentennial celebration began in February with a gala dinner for a thousand people, at the Armory. Befitting the importance of the occasion there were two celebrated speakers: New York governor Thomas E. Dewey and Yonkers native General Joseph W. Stilwell. As the year progressed there were many other events, and to make sure that everyone, both in Yonkers and beyond, including passengers in planes flying over the city, knew it was the Queen City of the Hudson's three hundredth birthday, a whopping three hundred gallons of paint were used to create what may have been the world's longest sign. This message, running a mile along Central Park Avenue, and visible from the air, proclaimed for all the world to see that Yonkers was "Celebrating Its 300th Anniversary."[1] Besides noting the bright yellow tercentennial sign, *The New York Times* pointed out that the celebration featured all sorts of events including a food conference hosted by Secretary of Agriculture Henry Wallace at Boyce Thompson Institute and a "Commuters Day."[2] Such a multifaceted, year-long celebration would have amazed Yonkers's first inhabitants, who would scarcely "believe their eyes" if they were transported to the mid-twentieth century.[3]

The tercentennial celebration was not limited to residents of Yonkers on the Hudson. In the late fall of 1946, nearly a dozen men, women and children from Yonkers, Oklahoma, were given a royal welcome. That the population of their community, which had been founded by George Lowery from Yonkers, New York, had shrunk to sixty-nine, and that the town itself would soon be underwater once a new dam was completed, were minor technicalities. What mattered was the friendship uniting the two communities named Yonkers. As a sign of that bond, after the delegation from Oklahoma, which included a Cherokee Indian girl, had crossed the Hudson on the ferryboat *John J. Walsh,* they were greeted by a fife and drum corps from a Yonkers church. The trailer in which the Oklahomans had traveled halfway across the country displayed signs announcing that it was heading for Yonkers, New York, for "the 300th birthday of the City of Gracious Living."[4] Yonkers, New York's new appellation was viewed skeptically in some quarters. On the eve of the Oklahomans' arrival, *The New York Times* noted that Yonkers was "determined to still the jibes and jeers" that had made it tie with Brooklyn as the butt of jokes.[5]

Poking fun at Yonkers was not so common during the tercentennial because the city put its best foot forward, especially during the last month of the year-long celebration. Photo ops and extensive press coverage proved very beneficial in changing outsiders' perception of the "City of Gracious Living," and Yonkers officials rarely passed up an opportunity to generate favorable publicity. Toward that end, as soon as the Oklahomans disembarked from the ferry, they were whisked away to city hall where they were given a three-foot-high cardboard replica of the key to the city. The visitors then presented a three-foot-high Cherokee headdress to Vice Mayor James A. Sullivan, who was presiding in the absence of the mayor. Sullivan promptly donned the headdress and kept it on for the entire ceremony. Then it was off to Saunders Trade School for a tercentennial birthday party, complete with three-foot cake and more speeches. The next day, the Oklahomans attended Sunday services at the Baptist Church of the Redeemer and St. John's Episcopal Church before setting out to visit Alexander Smith and Sons, Otis Elevator, Habirshaw Wire and Cable, the Hudson River Museum, and Philipse Manor Hall. At the conclusion of this whirlwind tour, the Oklahomans were entertained by Oliver J. Troster, chairman of the Yonkers Tercentennial Commission, at his Franklin Avenue home.

In addition to the publicity garnered from the visit of residents of the soon-to-be-inundated community of Yonkers, Oklahoma, Yonkers, New York, benefited from a unique event marking the conclusion of the tercentennial: a call for world peace. On December 18, which was designated as "Permanent Peace Day" in Yonkers, fifteen thousand letters calling for world peace, and written by children in the city's schools, were sent from the Yonkers post office to heads of state and other movers and shakers all over the world. At Yonkers High School of Commerce a thousand students listened attentively as a speaker from the United Nations, then a new organization meeting in Lake Success, Long Island, discussed the UN's noble mission. City and school officials also spoke, as did the chairman of the tercentennial commission, while Dr. Harold Taylor, president of Sarah Lawrence College, presided at the event. Elsewhere in the building, amateur radio operators were busy sending peace messages in Morse code. Outside the school, several hundred carrier pigeons bearing peace messages attached to their feet were released with the expectation that they would carry their pleas for global harmony to places within a hundred miles of Yonkers.

Two months earlier, the peace theme had been emphasized during the observance of the 175th anniversary of the Asbury Methodist Church. On that occasion, Bishop G. Bromley Oxnan, president of the Federal Council of Churches of Christ in America, made a plea for "a greater understanding of the world."[6] St. Joseph's Church on Ashburton Avenue also celebrated an anniversary, its seventy-fifth, during the city's tercentennial year and St. Joseph's Seminary, Dunwoodie, marked its golden jubilee. Before the decade ended, the first Roman Catholic parish in Yonkers, the Church of the Immaculate Conception, established in 1848, celebrated its centennial.

City Hall

Despite all of the wonderful celebrations in the years immediately following World War II, the favorable publicity they generated was not enough to overcome the bad press the city received because of ongoing problems at city hall. Right in the middle of the tercentennial year, huge headlines proclaimed: "Garbage Men Take 'Holiday' as Union Holds City Ignored Promise to Raise Pay."[7] According to union officials, the pledge to increase the pay of some Department of Public Works employees by $120 a year and add a week to their two weeks of paid vacation had been made by City Manager Robert Craig Montgomery, who termed the whole thing a misunderstanding. Montgomery found himself in the unenviable position of city manager following a sort of chain reaction that began in January 1946 after Edith Welty and her fellow League of City Managers candidates were sworn in as members of the city council. They wasted no time in ousting City Manager Morris Rosenwasser, replacing him with former city manager Norman Henderson, who served as acting city manager for a month. During that time he appointed former city manager Robert Craig Montgomery controller, paving the way for him to be named city manager!

As city manager, it was Montgomery who had to deal with the thorny issues leading to the 1946 work stoppage, which according to *The Herald Statesman* had rendered the citizen a "helpless victim."[8] In an editorial supplementing its front page coverage of the walkout, the paper declared that the so-called holiday taken by six hundred Public Works employees, as directed by their union, was "a rehearsal for a strike."[9] In October, after Montgomery angered Public Works Department employees by refusing to recognize the C.I.O. as their collective bargaining agent and rejecting a demand for dues check-off, which would have made the city responsible for withholding union dues from members' paychecks, a strike seemed imminent. It was averted, however, after a state mediator worked out an agreement calling for a wage increase, contingent upon the city's ability to secure, from the state legislature, authority to broaden its tax base. Since Yonkers had reached its legal ceiling on real estate taxes, state authorization was required to impose additional taxes. As for the dues check-off and other matters put forward by the workers, ongoing discussions were planned to resolve these issues.

Ensuring that Public Works employees were manning garbage trucks instead of picket lines was only one of the post-tercentennial challenges facing the "City of Gracious Living." Another was the negative publicity surrounding the vice mayor who had sported the Cherokee headdress during the city's three hundredth anniversary. Six months after the tercentennial ended, James A. Sullivan resigned from the Common Council only days before a special committee of the council was slated to hear testimony from financiers about large stock purchases and bank deposits Sullivan and his wife had made. Sullivan was suspected of amassing this money by facilitating the activities of an illegal gambling ring operating in the city. In November 1947, he was indicted by a Westchester County grand jury for allegedly forging a business certificate for the Maritime Oil Company of Yonkers. The company rented offices in the Yonkers Labor Temple Building where, instead of trading oil, employees accepted bets on horse races. Calls came into this thriving operation from all over the world for nearly a year and a half, between November 1944 and April 1946, producing more than $6 million in revenue.

In reporting Sullivan's indictment, the press was quick to point out an earlier transgression that had surfaced during the 1945 city council campaign. At that time, Sullivan was accused of plagiarizing a famous letter written by Abraham Lincoln during the Civil War. Sullivan had incorporated Lincoln's wording into letters he sent to Yonkers mothers who had lost sons in World War II. Sullivan passed this off by saying that two great minds think alike, but he was unable to explain away the gambling ring charge. During a month-long trial held in the Westchester County Court in the spring of 1948, jurors were told that the former Democratic minority leader of the county board of supervisors, whose political career had spanned twenty-four of his fifty-five years, had provided the bookmaking operation with phones from the Democratic Club. Then, unable to secure additional lines from the telephone company, Sullivan created the Maritime Oil Company. As a supposedly legitimate business, Maritime was able to obtain extra lines. It took the jury slightly over four hours to determine that Maritime was anything but legitimate and that Sullivan was guilty as charged. Although he could have received a sentence of twenty-seven years, Sullivan was packed off to the county penitentiary in Eastview for only a year.

Meanwhile, back in Yonkers, 1948 was a year of transition in the office of the city manager. Robert Craig Montgomery resigned amidst "reports that the Common Council majority had formal removal proceedings already drafted."[10] Montgomery was succeeded by city controller Thomas V. Kennedy, who probably wondered what he had gotten himself into when reporters asked him whether Yonkers was suing itself. During his tenure as controller Kennedy had initiated thousands of foreclosure proceedings for nonpayment of taxes and fees. City hall, the Yonkers Library, and the Health Center were all on the foreclosure list because of delinquent water and sewer bills. Since the Common Council could enact legislation to simply eliminate these obligations, this was not a big deal. A much greater challenge was increasing the assessed valuation of Yonkers real estate. This was necessary in order to enable the city to generate enough tax revenue to balance its budget, while preventing expenditures from exceeding the 2 percent cap of assessed valuation imposed by the state legislature upon large municipalities. Persuading the state to increase the spending limit to 2.5 percent of assessed valuation was the solution, in the city manager's opinion, but that could not be accomplished quickly enough to balance the budget for 1949. A sales tax would be needed in the meantime. Some members of the Common Council thought this was a bad idea. They favored shifting anticipated revenue to the budget from real estate the city was planning to sell, but Kennedy adamantly refused to do that. In December 1948, he resigned and Yonkers began looking for a new city manager, its seventh in seven years! In the interim, the city controller, John A. Peterson, served as acting city manager.

Garbage Galore

It was on Peterson's watch that the "City of Gracious Living" became the most fragrant community on the Hudson, thanks to a garbage strike that had musical origins. The American Federation of Musicians, an affiliate of the gigantic American Federation of Labor or A.F.L., was picketing the Polish Community Center because it allowed nonunion bands to perform there. Sympathetic to the union musicians, Yonkers sanitation men conveniently overlooked the garbage that was piling up outside the Community Center. After this had gone on for several weeks, Acting City Manager Peterson read the riot act to the C.I.O. local representing the city's Public Works employees. Reminding the union that the Condon–Wadlin Act prohibited strikes by public employees, Peterson dispatched a garbage truck with a three-man crew to deal with the mess in front of the Polish Community Center. The workers refused to obey orders, as did fifteen other sanitation men sent out the following day. All eighteen were suspended. At that point the union held a meeting on the city pier; a strike vote was taken and five hundred Public Works Department employees walked off the job, leaving garbage uncollected and snow unplowed. A day later, in New York State's first test of the Condon–Wadlin Law, the striking workers were fired. The city manager then proceeded to have his assistants scrutinize civil service, unemployment, and welfare lists to find replacements for the dismissed workers. To deal with the immediate emergency posed by the snow, Yonkers received help from the Westchester County Highway Department, the Yonkers Street Railway Company, and local bus companies.

Despite the strike, the union urged workers in charge of water pumping and chlorination to report to their jobs. At the same time, it called for a resolution of the dispute over pay for Sunday work. The acting city manager had contended that the double pay the union was seeking for its workers was appropriate only for genuine emergencies such as major snowstorms but the union insisted that it should be the norm for all Sunday work. With union members picketing city hall and other municipal buildings, the acting city manager declared a state of emergency. The entire police force, including off-duty officers, was deployed to safeguard the city. When two garbage trucks manned by nonunion workers hit the streets, a policeman was on each truck. Confronted by striking Department of Public Works employees when they reached the neighborhoods where they were supposed to pick up garbage, the trucks turned around. A truck bearing a huge emergency sign, however, was able to clear the entrances to the City Hospital for Communicable Diseases and the

Grey Oaks Hospital. To accomplish this a police escort was required. The very next day Acting City Manager Peterson, seemingly unfazed, declared: "We will continue to try to hire men and send out trucks as we get the men."[11] The response from the union was quick and unequivocal. If the city moved equipment with nonunion workers, there would be "war from now on."[12] The union vowed to picket city facilities, according to a spokesman, who said "and I guarantee that if we picket the buildings, they'll get no heat."[13] Those were fighting words, and they were soon translated into action.

With pickets ringing city hall and the building's maintenance staff on strike, heat was turned off and municipal officials contemplated closing all city buildings. What was Yonkers to do? Well, for starters it could appeal to Albany. Thanks to Senator William F. Condon of Yonkers, co-author of the law forbidding strikes by public employees, a conference at the Executive Mansion was hastily arranged. In addition to Condon and New York governor Thomas E. Dewey, Acting City Manager Peterson and Yonkers assemblyman Malcolm Wilson were in attendance. For about an hour the governor heard the men from Yonkers express concern about the repercussions of the work stoppage. These included the strike's impact upon the city's water supply, which had already been affected by two minor water main breaks. If a large main were severed, the resulting low pressure would compromise the city's ability to fight fires. Although Governor Dewey assured the Yonkers delegation that the state would provide personnel to ensure the availability and purity of water in the city, this proved unnecessary because the union exempted pumping and filtering station workers from participating in the strike. If a major water main break occurred, the union was prepared to send additional men to deal with the problem. The union made good on that pledge when a water main on Nepperhan Avenue, in the vicinity of Myrtle Street, burst.

Garbage was another matter. Neither the governor nor the union was ready to help the city deal with the growing mess. Yonkers health commissioner Dr. Ralph Sikes determined that the uncollected garbage was posing a threat to the health of city residents in a variety of ways. It was, for example, contributing to air pollution because some Yonkers residents were burning their garbage. Then there was the fire danger posed by the piling up of flammable refuse in the basements of stores and factories. The Yonkers Academy of Medicine was so concerned about the situation that its board of governors sent telegrams to the Yonkers health commissioner and to the acting city manager indicating their fear of an "impending health hazard due to the accumulation of garbage" and urging that "garbage collection be resumed immediately in the interest of public health regardless of how the labor dispute is settled."[14] With no settlement in the offing, the acting city manager met with two private contractors to discuss their offer to help the city out, for a fee, by providing their own personnel to man Yonkers garbage trucks. No agreement was reached. Instead, Yonkers resorted to legal action by seeking an injunction prohibiting city employees from remaining off the job. The city argued that the strike posed a "grave and serious danger to the health, welfare, safety and convenience of Yonkers citizens."[15]

The New York State Supreme Court agreed, issuing a restraining order prohibiting the striking workers from continuing their walkout. This was not expected to be a quick fix, however, "even though the court order was one of the most sweeping ever issued in this state in connection with a labor dispute," according to *The New York Times*.[16] The court order specifically prohibited the striking workers from congregating "within three blocks of any city building or interfering in any way with the conduct of municipal operations."[17] To union members, this amounted to deprivation of their constitutional rights. The chairman of the Joint A.F.L.-C.I.O. Non-Partisan Committee of Westchester County pointed this out in a telegram to the attorney general of the United States. Declaring the injunction a setback for labor relations, the chairman called for negotiations between Yonkers officials and union representatives. Emmet Burke, a member of the Yonkers Common Council, agreed. He urged the reinstatement, without penalty, of striking workers, the establishment of a grievance board to deal with workers' complaints, and negotiations to resolve the pay issues.

The penalties proved to be an insurmountable obstacle, however, because the Condon–Wadlin Law imposed a mandatory five-year probationary period for striking workers upon their return to their old jobs. Not only did they forfeit tenure but returning workers were not eligible for raises for three years. Mayor Curtiss E. Frank was sympathetic to the plight of the workers but contended that his hands were tied by the law. Yet the mayor was willing to meet with union leaders. Following a closed-door session lasting two and a half hours, an agreement to end the strike was announced. Union members were to be reinstated, with penalties under the Condon–Wadlin Law to be determined at an indefinite time in the future. In the near future, actually within days, negotiations were planned to resolve pay issues and create a grievance board. It would soon be time for Yonkers residents to remove the clothespins from their noses and breathe some fresh air untainted by the fragrance of garbage. The day after the agreement was reached, *The Herald Statesman* reported that garbage trucks "rolled out on collection routes."[18] The *Statesman*, which denounced the eight-day work stoppage as a "misguided and illegal strike," published an editorial, titled "Now Let's Clean Up the Mess Fast!"[19] According to the paper, there was much work to be done, and it wasn't limited to burning the garbage at the Yonkers incinerator. An enormous amount of garbage had to be collected and the water system's filter beds had to be cleaned. Going forward, the paper felt that a lesson could be learned about the strike's impact upon the public, who the paper felt were the "goats in every strike."[20]

In an editorial *The New York Times* predicted that "the real test" of Condon-Wadlin was still to come.[21] As for abolishing or weakening the law, "the place to do it is in the Legislature."[22] The controversy over the penalty provisions of the Condon-Wadlin Law nearly undermined the Yonkers settlement only days after it had been reached. During a closed-door meeting with union representatives in the mayor's reception room at city hall, where, happily, the heat had been turned back on, Mayor Frank refused to say whether the penalties would be invoked. Acting City Manager Peterson, however, was said to be steadfast in his belief that the workers "had forfeited their seniority and pay increase rights."[23] Adamant or not, Peterson would not have to deal with the matter much longer, because former Portsmouth, Ohio, city manager Donald C. Wagner took over as Yonkers city manager the following week, enabling Peterson to devote his full attention to his other position as city controller. Wagner found himself on the hot seat immediately because of his decision to abide by the Condon-Wadlin Law. He did, however, try to assuage union members by saying that the penalties prescribed by the law could be set aside by the legislature and that he would work toward achieving this. A few days later, city workers created a three-man delegation to lobby the legislature, but at the same time they held an emergency meeting at the Strand Theatre and voted to authorize the union to take any action officials deemed necessary. Yonkers residents reached for their clothespins once again, but the strike they feared did not materialize.

Nearly a year went by without major interruptions in municipal services. During that time, City Manager Wagner issued a formal ruling, in January 1950, in which he stated that the 1949 walkout had been a strike but the Common Council proposed an amendment to the Condon-Wadlin Law limiting penalties. In February 1950, Senator Condon presented the amendment to the New York State Legislature. While the legislature considered the amendment, the appellate division of the State Supreme Court ruled that forty-eight clerks, mechanics, and foremen, who had been absent from their jobs during the 1949 strike and were then placed on probation by City Manager Wagner in accordance with the Condon-Wadlin

Law, "had been made idle against their will" because of the action of 450 sanitation men and drivers who did not report for work after eighteen of their colleagues were suspended.[24] This was good news for the forty-eight who were cleared of violating the Condon-Wadlin Law but a setback for the other workers who had to tough it out on probation for another few years. During that time many of them must have surely wondered whether all good things really do come to those who wait.

A Woman's Touch in City Hall

The Common Council member who was named mayor of Yonkers in 1949 probably had similar thoughts because *she* (yes, she!) had almost landed in city hall back in 1941. Oh well, better late than never! Mrs. Welty's big chance came in 1949 when Curtiss E. Frank announced that he would be stepping down as mayor and resigning from a Wall Street law firm to become vice president and general counsel of a major publishing and advertising firm with offices in New York and Chicago. Since he would be spending considerable time in the Midwest, Frank felt duty bound to give up his Yonkers position. Mrs. Welty was selected to fill out the remainder of his term following a recount, in September 1949, of the proportional representation ballots from the 1947 election. Welty had won nearly three hundred more votes than her closest rival in that election, and as soon as the recount had been completed, at the State Armory, she made history by being sworn in as the first female mayor in the city's history. The very next day, in a page one story *The New York Times* reported that Edith Welty viewed her triumph at the polls as a victory for women who had labored "in the interest of good government."[25] The *Times* also noted that as Yonkers would be reverting to voting by wards, she would be "the last Mayor to hold office under the present PR (proportional representation) system."[26] The public relations value of having a woman at the helm of one of the largest cities in New York State was not lost on *The Herald Statesman*. In an editorial, the paper declared that Welty's election was a source of pride not only for her but for "all men and women in the community as well" and it removed the "edge of bitterness" from her loss in the primary for the Republican Party's nomination for council from the Tenth Ward. [27]

Despite the fact that her political career seemed to be waning, Mayor Welty was a media sensation. Her first day on the job was covered by newsreels, radio, and television, making the bread-baking grandmother, who had fought so hard to bring about the city manager form of government, an overnight sensation in many places besides Yonkers. No stranger to controversy, when questioned about the fact that as of December 31 she would be out of government for the first time in a decade, Mrs. Welty, expressing concern that an attempt would be made to eliminate the city manager form of government, said she was planning "to organize, speak, teach, inspire, try to get back city-wide elections so we'll have a chance in 1951."[28] Unwilling to run as an independent, thereby running the risk of splitting the Republican vote—something she did not want to do, as a good Republican—Mayor Welty planned to take some time off. Starting in January, she told a reporter, "I'll be able to arrange my schedule to suit myself."[29] Baking bread was out of the question, however. Speaking about her life before she entered politics, Welty said that she had been "busy with my home, my husband and children" but now that her household consisted only of herself and her husband, she wasn't baking very much.[30] Although she did not run again for public office, Edith Welty played a leadership role in the Yonkers Citizens' Union. In 1951, when the organization came out against holding a referendum on a proposed salary increase for city workers, Welty defended this position on the grounds that a referendum would undermine the power of the city manager.

The position of city manager remained intact, however, and in 1952 attorney Charles L. Curran, a native of Yonkers, became the eighth city manager since 1940. Chosen by the Democrats, who won control of the Common Council in 1951, he succeeded Donald C. Wagner, who resigned to accept a position in Philadelphia. As Democrats and Republicans vied for control of the Common Council for the remainder of the decade, Democrats attempted to prevent the redistricting of the city because they feared loss of some of the traditional Democratic wards. In 1958, redistricting was ordered by the Republican-controlled Common Council. The city also had a Republican mayor, Kristen Kristensen, a Danish immigrant who had arrived in the United States at the age of eighteen. First elected by the Common Council, he was subsequently reelected by popular vote after the city abandoned the practice of choosing as mayor the top vote getter in the election for Common Council. On the state level, in 1958, Yonkers native and multiterm Assemblyman Malcolm Wilson was elected lieutenant governor of New York State.

The Silence of the Looms

In the twenty years since Wilson had won his first term as an assemblyman from Yonkers, his hometown had undergone an economic transformation.

By the time Wilson was elected lieutenant governor, industry, long the foundation of the city's economy, had entered a period of steep decline. The city, nevertheless, still had brilliant people whose ideas spawned successful businesses. Tom Carvel, inventor of the first machine to produce soft ice cream, made Yonkers the headquarters of his ice cream franchise business. Robert Abplanalp, who in 1947 patented the valve system used in aerosol products, bought out his partners and established the Precision Valve Corporation soon thereafter; he then proceeded to establish a global empire from his Yonkers base. Carvel and Abplanalp were following in the footsteps of earlier inventors turned entrepreneurs.

At the beginning of the twentieth century, Leo Hendrik Baekeland, a chemist, invented Bakelite, a synthetic plastic used in products as diverse as airplane parts and kitchen utensils. Dr. Baekeland's General Bakelite Corporation, established in Yonkers in 1910, became part of the Union Carbide Corporation in 1939. A year earlier, another Yonkers inventor, Edwin Howard Armstrong, built a tower and radio station in Alpine, New Jersey, just across the Hudson from his childhood home on Warburton Avenue, where he had begun his radio experiments as a teenager. At Columbia University, where he was a student of Michael Pupin, inventor of communications and medical devices and a Yonkers resident, Armstrong "invented the regenerative-oscillating, or feedback, circuit which greatly increased radio signals . . . and led the way to transatlantic radio telegraphy."[31] In the thirties, Armstrong obtained patents "which were to be the basis for frequency modulation . . . an entirely new system of broadcasting."[32] The latter part of Armstrong's life was consumed by patent infringement suits, which had negative financial and psychological consequences. In 1954, he committed suicide. Ironically, that was the same year that Yonkers was dragged unwittingly into the postindustrial age.

Yet, if a decade earlier anyone had predicted that the city's economy would undergo a major transformation, they would have been laughed out of town, because in the immediate postwar period, problems besetting the local economy were perceived as temporary challenges related to the shift from lucrative military contracts to peacetime production of consumer goods. Thus, when *The Herald Statesman* informed its readers that Otis was reducing the work week to four days for three hundred employees, for what the company termed "an indefinite period," no one seemed overly concerned; referring to "a seasonal cutback in escalator work and over-production," a union official declared that the shortened work week would be temporary, lasting a month or two.[33] Over at Alexander Smith and Sons, the conversion from wartime to peacetime production created some new challenges, but to outsiders, at least, the company seemed to be forging ahead. In 1948, it purchased a seventeen-room home with extensive property that ran from North Broadway to Palisade Avenue. The house was needed to accommodate managerial and sales personnel who spent a portion of their time at the Yonkers mill. Major customers were also provided with rooms, along with meals, and recreational activities.

Keeping big clients happy was a good idea but so, too, was ensuring the satisfaction of workers. At the very time it was putting the finishing touches on its elegant new guesthouse, Alexander Smith and Sons, along with only a handful of other U.S. companies, was singled out for its successful dealings with its workers, in a study done by Princeton University's Labor Relations Section. Maybe that would account for all of those smiling faces at the mill when President Harry S. Truman paid a visit during the 1948 campaign, in which he made a successful bid for a full four-year term of his own against the Republican candidate, New York governor Thomas E. Dewey. As a nonelected president who had taken office upon the death of the hugely popular president and former New York State governor Franklin D. Roosevelt, Truman left no stone unturned in his quest to remain in the White House. His visit to Yonkers was part of a New York area campaign blitz. Truman's reception in the "City of Gracious Living" surely must have warmed his heart, because Yonkers "put on an extraordinary demonstration for a city of its size."[34] According to *The New York Times*: "The visit was unique in many ways. So far as anyone could recall, it was the first time a President had come to Yonkers on an official visit. It was also the first time that a detail of New York City policemen . . . had ever been invited into Yonkers, to supplement the police there."[35] After a stop at Larkin Plaza to speak about the national housing shortage of the postwar period, Truman and his entourage headed to Axminster Street and Nepperhan Avenue. There, outside the gate of Alexander Smith and Sons, the president was greeted by upward of seven thousand people; most of them were carpet workers, but residents of the surrounding area also turned out to hear the president express his support for the working class and declare his opposition to legislation curtailing the rights of unions.

Scarcely six months after Truman was reelected, Alexander Smith and Sons began to sell off multifamily and a few single-family dwellings housing mill workers. Nearly two hundred units were offered for sale, with the current tenants being given the first opportunity to buy the places where they lived. That Alexander Smith was divesting itself of residential real estate did not set off alarm bells because the company was expanding. In 1950 it purchased a 23,000 square foot building four miles north of Yonkers in Ardsley. The former home of the Indiana Steel

Company, the new facility was to become part of the company's research and development division. That same year, there was a change at the helm of Alexander Smith occasioned by the resignation of Frederick B. Klein, for health reasons. Klein died, at age sixty-three, a month later. A Yonkers native who had begun his career at age seventeen as a timekeeper in the company's velvet finishing department, Klein had risen all the way to the top, serving as president of Alexander Smith and Sons for seventeen years, longer than any other CEO, including the founder's son, Warren B. Smith, who had a fifteen-year tenure as president. Klein was succeeded by William F. C. Ewing.

Early in Ewing's tenure, Alexander Smith and Sons was one of the venues selected by the United States government for an in-depth visit by nearly a dozen high-ranking industrial and labor leaders from Japan. Hoping to teach the Japanese a thing or two about how to achieve maximum cooperation between workers and management, Dr. Edward MacDonald of the Institute of International Education, the organization that had arranged the factory visits for the Japanese, chose Alexander Smith and Sons not only because of its high profile in the industry but because of its history of "harmonious and constructive labor relations."[36] Although Alexander Smith and Sons tossed out the welcome mat for the Japanese, some companies questioned the wisdom of the U.S. government's efforts to rebuild the Japanese economy following World War II. Sternwild Mills, for example, which manufactured knitted gloves in Yonkers, was suffering from intense competition from cheap Japanese gloves then flooding the American market thanks to a reduction in the tariff on imported gloves.

Two years later, Alexander Smith and Sons had its own problems, but they were not the result of foreign competition. They originated instead with a demand for higher wages by the Textile Workers Union, C.I.O. When Smith and other carpet manufacturers refused to accede to the union's request, textile workers struck all of the big carpet mills in the eastern United States. With the entire industry depressed, the carpet manufacturers were seeking greater efficiency on the part of workers. At Alexander Smith, where more than four thousand employees walked off the job, the company issued a statement laying everything on the line. It declared that "continued operation of Smith in Yonkers will depend largely on the extent to which inefficient practices can be corrected."[37] Following intense negotiations, an agreement was reached nine weeks later. It included union concessions on shop stewards and downtime, and a ten cent per hour raise for salaried workers, rather than the twenty-five cent increase the union was seeking. Some of the 2,500 Smith employees thronging the Polish Community Center to hear the details of the pact weren't exactly thrilled but the union official who urged them to approve it underscored the fact that the company had "to get back into production to meet its fall commitments," and that it was "in serious difficulty in many respects."[38] To extract the company, at least partially, from that difficulty, within days of the reopening of the mill, Alexander Smith's president, W. F. C. Ewing, announced that the layout of the plant would be reconfigured to make it more efficient. His plan was to concentrate production in the core area of the mill instead of having it spread out over fifty-six acres of floor space. Within a year, some of the buildings that were no longer needed were sold. None of this resulted in increased profitability for the company, however. Sadly, "no matter how much local people relinquished . . . their sacrifices brought no guarantees."[39]

In the first quarter of 1954, Alexander Smith announced that the mill would close for a week. The expectation was that spring sales would soon deplete existing inventory and new orders would permit the resumption of production. Despite a general slump in the carpet industry, the furloughed workers were recalled, but a few months later, in June 1954, when their contract expired, the Alexander Smith workforce, which had dwindled from 7,000 to 2,500 in the previous half-dozen years, went out on strike. Management proposed a revised pay plan calling for increases for many, but not all, employees and the union rejected it. This walkout lacked the drama of previous strikes. There were no big picket lines. Perhaps the workers realized it was a lost cause, because ever since the previous strike, two years before, the possibility of a permanent plant closure had hung like a sword over Smith employees and, in actuality, the entire city. Ten days after the 1954 strike began, everyone's worst fears were confirmed. Alexander Smith, "in shocking disregard" for the city where it had "prospered for most of a century," as a union official put it, was leaving Yonkers for good.[40] The announcement prompted the president of the Yonkers Chamber of Commerce, along with other members of the business community, including the president of the Yonkers First National Bank, to call upon city hall to intervene. Mayor Kristensen and City Manager Charles L. Curran sought an immediate conference with the New York State Department of Commerce.

With the backing of Governor Dewey, Commerce Commissioner Harold Keller offered to make the full facilities of the department available to Alexander Smith. Keller informed the company that the department wanted "to avert an unemployment crisis in Yonkers" and was convinced that access to a huge market in the New York area would enable the company to remain in Yonkers.[41] Alexander Smith was unmoved, because Greenville, Mississippi, had made it an offer it couldn't refuse: a brand new air-conditioned plant, funded by a bond issue, which it would make available to the company at a very favorable rent. This seemed almost too good to be true. The company would swap its outdated Yonkers complex for a modern facility staffed by a nonunion workforce. Alexander Smith plants in Philadelphia and Liberty, South Carolina, would remain open, but for the company Greenville, Mississippi, would provide, in the twentieth century, what Yonkers did in the nineteenth, namely a new beginning. In the meantime, it had to fill remaining orders at the Yonkers plant, which meant rehiring three hundred workers for a period of several months.

On December 1, 1954, the looms fell silent for good. The numerous buildings comprising the mill would not remain empty for long, however. Six months after carpet production ended, an industrial syndicate purchased the core Smith complex, consisting of sixty buildings on thirty-five acres. All of these structures were "of brick and concrete construction and are fully equipped with sprinklers."[42] One of the buildings, a specialized facility "for water softening processes," had cost "more than $1 million."[43] Another plus was the property's potential as a distribution center near the New York State Thruway, then under construction. Also significant was the presence of a large labor pool, consisting in part of former Alexander Smith employees, many of whom were still unemployed or underemployed. The northern part of the Smith property had previously been sold to cigarette manufacturer Benson and Hedges, which then sold it to Artcraft, a greeting card company. Following the sale of the core complex, small and medium-sized companies snapped up space in the various buildings, using some of the square footage for manufacturing. Firms moving into the old mill buildings had the option of buying or leasing, but either way this "was a great step in the industrial development of Yonkers," according to former city manager Thomas V. Kennedy, who was chairman of the Community Committee for Economic Development.[44]

What Goes Up Must Come Down: Otis Elevator

Just as Yonkers was breathing a sigh of relief over the final disposition of the Alexander Smith property and the prospect of having the county's largest industrial center emerge at the site of the old mill, another challenge appeared. Otis Elevator was threatening to leave Yonkers. Like Alexander Smith, Otis had experienced labor problems in the postwar years. In 1951, 1,700 members of the International Union of Electrical Workers, C.I.O., walked off the job. They were seeking a ten cent per hour raise and increased benefits, including additional vacation time. The company termed the work stoppage "unnecessary" and insisted it was willing to negotiate but to draw public attention to the situation of the workers the union instituted "24-hour-a-day picketing at the city's second largest industrial plant."[45] Soon after the strike began, the union established a "kitchen for pickets" at the Veterans of Foreign Wars headquarters and every member was "assigned to strike duties on picket lines, in the kitchen or at the union hall."[46]

The workers made some gains as a result of the strike, which lasted three months, but the work stoppage had taken its toll on the company. Otis's earnings for 1951 were down. The company's annual report noted that the strike, combined with the high cost of labor and raw materials, had affected sales and earnings. Four years later, Otis was still struggling. Once the Korean War ended, military contracts dwindled, forcing the company to let four hundred employees go. To continue operating, Otis needed help, whether a more affordable new facility in an area of the country with less burdensome taxation and lower labor costs, or major concessions from its Yonkers workforce and from the city. In January 1955, Otis CEO Leroy A. Petersen invited city officials and all 2,100 company employees to attend a meeting the following Saturday at the only venue large enough to accommodate a gathering of this size: Brandt's Theatre on South Broadway. The principal "performer" on Brandt's stage that day was Petersen, and his words, which echoed through the vast auditorium, were not intended to generate applause. His message was simple. If the workers and the city did not cooperate in order to effect a reduction in Otis's operating costs, the company would shut the doors of the Yonkers plant and head to the Midwest. Coming as it did soon after Alexander Smith and Sons had announced it was leaving, the possibility that Otis would depart as well was a double blow.

With so much at stake, the city seized the initiative. The mayor and city manager declared almost immediately that they felt that something could be worked out, provided the union cooperated. The city then proceeded to conduct a study of the assessed valuations of all Otis property in Yonkers. At the same time, union leaders and company officials held closed-door meetings to discuss what the company expected of its workers and what the union was willing to concede. The company wanted to eliminate certain bonuses and incentives and, if necessary, move employees from its facilities in New Jersey and New York City to Yonkers. The transferred workers would retain their seniority. Besides union concessions and lower taxes, Otis wanted the city to close portions of several streets near the plant. This was deemed necessary to permit modernization of the company's manufacturing facilities. Since Otis was clearly in the driver's seat, it obtained most of what it wanted. *America, the National Catholic Weekly Review,* had an interesting take on this. It stated: "Though the immediate crisis has been weathered, the problem which brought it on remains. It will remain until somebody finds a way, within the antitrust statutes, of outlawing cut throat competition" from other regions of the country.[47] The problem did not go away, of course, but for the time being it was downplayed because Otis received a new $20 million contract, not for elevators, but for automatic pin-setting machines for bowling alleys. Buoyed by this favorable turn of events, the company expanded, acquiring an additional one hundred thousand square feet of space in the former Alexander Smith complex. The space had been occupied by Benson and Hedges, but when that company merged with Philip Morris it headed south.

Joining Otis in what had been renamed the Westchester County Industrial Center was Joseph A. Kaplan & Sons, Inc., a manufacturer of vinyl film products, which bought two of the old factory buildings. Bassons Industries Corporation, a plastics company displaced by the New York State Thruway from its Bronx home, also moved to the center. Even before it had fully moved in, the company was manufacturing a highly classified item for the U.S. Air Force "in a corner where the wool weavers' looms formerly stood."[48] The company was also planning to mass produce a full-size plastic automobile it had displayed at an exhibition at the New York Coliseum. Another car manufacturer, General Motors, was also represented at the Westchester County Industrial Center. G.M., which had a major automobile assembly plant in North Tarrytown, acquired one of the old mill buildings for a parts warehouse. By the summer of 1956, companies manufacturing a diverse array of products had bought or leased space in the industrial center. These companies turned out furniture, clothing, batteries, pharmaceuticals, cardboard boxes, briefcases, plumbing supplies, and nuts and bolts. From the perspective of real estate agent William J. Sherry, who headed the syndicate that had purchased the property from Alexander Smith, Yonkers "was better off now than before the carpet works shut down. Never again will Yonkers be dependent on one or two big industries. We have gained a wonderful stabilizing force in this city by the diversification of industry."[49]

That was all well and good, but when companies began to look beyond the downtown area for space for new facilities, there was some opposition. In 1957, the Western Electric Company wanted to purchase a twenty-two-acre parcel on Tuckahoe Road for a warehouse and distribution center. Located in northeast Yonkers, near the New York State Thruway and the proposed Sprain Brook Parkway, most of this land was owned by the Hebrew National Orphan Home, which had plans to relocate. Residents of the surrounding area, however, preferred the orphans to Western Electric and according to *The New York Times*, went "on the warpath," raising objections to the proposal through their civic associations.[50] In the end, the homeowners were no match for business groups favoring the project. At a packed meeting attended by five hundred people, the Common Council voted to rezone the property from residential to business. It surely seemed that Yonkers was moving full speed ahead in its efforts to attract new business, even if this meant alienating some of its citizens. This was not surprising. Only two years earlier the city had been characterized by *The New York Times,* in one article in a series devoted to the transformation of Yonkers, as a place whose "future has caught up with it—and is about to engulf it at the supersonic speeds of the twenty-first century."[51] The paper conceded that "Yonkers can, to a great extent, pick the kind of future it will have. . . . And it must pursue its objective vigorously and in intelligent accord with the majority interests of its citizens."[52]

Despite the newspaper's clarion call to action, for many Yonkers residents in the mid-twentieth century the past was closer than the future. Not surprisingly, there was a yearning for the good old days when factories sustained the local economy and a simultaneous desire to see remaining industries and new ones succeed. Toward that end, the Yonkers Chamber of Commerce sponsored a mammoth Salute to Yonkers Industry exhibition in 1957. Intended to dispel "false and misleading information about Yonkers," the exhibit featured fifty items manufactured in Yonkers for sale both at home and abroad.[53] They included Otis's automatic pin-setting device for bowling machines, different types of cable made by the Habirshaw Division of the Phelps Dodge Copper Products Corporation, Gestetner duplicating machines, and valves from Precision Valve Corporation. New York State commissioner of commerce Edward T. Dickinson, a featured speaker at the exhibit, urged Yonkers to "plan big" but not rely upon the proximity of Yonkers to New York City.[54] What Yonkers needed to do in his opinion was to address the challenges of traffic congestion, dilapidated buildings, and "substandard housing."[55] During the week that it graced the auditorium of the John Wanamaker store in the Cross County Shopping Center, the exhibition drew one hundred thousand visitors, and according to the director of the Chamber of Commerce, some of the participating companies received inquiries about ordering their products.

Shop Till You Drop

The Cross County Shopping Center, where the industrial exhibit took place, was the new crown jewel of the city's economy. The center had been in the planning stage since 1947, when the Common Council voted to approve the use of a fifty-four-acre parcel, previously considered for a war memorial, along Central Park Avenue and the Cross County Parkway, for commercial development. In 1948, John Wanamaker announced that it would erect its first suburban store in New York State at Cross County. It was to be a three-story emporium surrounded by the largest parking lot in Westchester County. When the Cross County Shopping Center was dedicated in April 1954, Wanamaker's and Gimbel's, the two anchor stores, along with twenty other stores in the forty-store shopping hub, were not ready to open, but the center was a big hit nonetheless. Chilly temperatures and drizzle kept the crowd at the dedication ceremony down to about five hundred, but those who braved the elements heard Yonkers mayor Kristen Kristensen praise Sol G. Atlas, Cross County's developer, for his "vision, integrity and fortitude."[56] Atlas responded by saying that he attributed his accomplishments to God and "the men who have worked with me."[57] According to Sol Atlas, although there were other retail centers with more land, Cross County's 1,250,000 square feet of space made it the world's largest *suburban* shopping center. Cross County had another distinction as well. The top four floors of the center's tallest building, an eight-story structure fashioned of blue-glazed brick, served as a 125-bed hospital, while professional offices were located on the lower floors.

Despite the unfavorable weather, before the day was over fifteen thousand people had visited the center. Even those who didn't make purchases took home mementos, including flowers, shiny new pennies, and pens donated by merchants. Although many of the first-day visitors were from Yonkers, the center's developer was convinced that people would travel from other areas to enjoy a totally new type of shopping experience. Given the $30 million that had been poured into the center, some of it to blast away fifty thousand cubic yards of rock and haul in one million cubic yards of fill, a lot was riding on the belief that if you build it they will come. The developer's optimism was warranted, for several very sound reasons. First of all, 1,500,000 people lived within ten miles of Cross County. Of that number, 650,000 were among the most affluent people in the United States. In addition to the enormous pool of potential customers with plenty of discretionary income to spend, a second factor ensuring the center's success was its location on major highways, including the New York State Thruway, then under construction. Other elements in the new shopping center's profitability were the mix of stores, the vast array of items offered for sale, and the care that was taken to avoid duplication of merchandise. All of this was bound to attract shoppers. Indeed, so many flocked to Cross County during the week following its dedication that the merchants' association voted in early May to keep the stores open until 9:30 p.m. on Mondays, Thursdays, and Fridays to accommodate the deluge of customers.

Part of the attraction Cross County held for the legions of people who frequented the newly opened center was the fact that something always seemed to be happening there. In June, a ceremony was held to unveil the cornerstone of the Wanamaker's store, then under construction. John R. Wanamaker, vice president of Wanamaker Stores and great-grandson of the chain's founder, and other company officers were on hand for the event. With its two hundred thousand square feet of retail space on three floors, the store would have parking on all three levels because that's what the hilly topography of its location dictated. While work on the new Wanamaker's branch proceeded, other stores, including Wallachs, opened. At the Wallachs dedication, in September 1954, company president John D. Gray pointed with pride to the new outlet's sleek modern décor and its huge windows affording shoppers a view of the mall, which was really a sort of Main Street lined by shops and flanked at either end by the center's two anchor stores. Offering clothing for both men and women on its two floors of retail space, Wallachs featured suburban sportswear, as well as more traditional apparel. Less than a week after Wallachs made its debut, Russeks, which had heretofore been located only in cities, opened its first suburban branch at Cross County. With its Scandinavian-style furniture and muted gray, charcoal, and pink color scheme the store was ultramodern. It was graced by a mural that had a "windswept country look," and some of the merchandise consisted of "sophisticated country fashions."[58]

Sleek modern stores and appealing merchandise drew hordes of shoppers to Cross County during its first six months of operation, and the center's merchants expected their first Christmas season to be a good one. To make sure it would be, they pulled out all the stops, opening what was termed "Christmas City" in late November. Its centerpiece was what purported to be the world's largest Santa Claus, a thirty-five-foot depiction of the great man fashioned of canvas, wood, and steel. Gigantic candles, Christmas trees, and prancing reindeer gracing store roofs also enlivened Cross County. Opening day of "Christmas City" featured an appearance by "Miss Christmas City" and three live Santa Clauses, one of whom alighted from a helicopter. All of this paid off—big time! Between

Thanksgiving and Christmas, Cross County racked up $7 million in sales; since its opening, sales totaled a whopping $30 million. Developer Sol Atlas was tickled pink. He predicted annual sales of $85 million once the department stores opened. To accommodate all of the shoppers who would contribute to that healthy sales figure, Atlas planned to increase the number of parking spaces to six thousand and add two gas stations to the center. One auto that arrived at Cross County in April 1955 was given a V.I.P. parking space atop a revolving platform. This was a spot befitting a gold-plated Cadillac valued at $30,000, a princely sum for a car in the mid-fifties. The Caddy, which even had gold windshield wipers and door handles, was one of 130 domestic and foreign cars on display at the Cross County International Automobile Show. The exhibition attracted nineteen thousand visitors on opening day alone. Although it was a big draw, as a revenue generator the auto show was insignificant compared with the new Wanamaker's, which opened in late April.

With one anchor store open for business and the other nearing completion, Sol Atlas decided it was time to expand, and this time it wasn't more parking spaces. Instead, it was a dozen small stores on the Upper Mall. In June, Atlas said that a travel agency, antiques shop, and other outlets would soon open. Before the summer was over, Gimbel's announced that its first suburban store in the New York area would open right after Labor Day. To whet the public's appetite, the CEO of Gimbel's New York revealed details of the new store. A full three weeks before opening day, he pointed out that the new store would "present in 124 departments on three air-conditioned floors a choice of over 100,000 items."[59] The store would also feature a 250-seat auditorium, which could be used by community organizations. In addition, there would be sewing and needlework classes, and gardening, slipcover, and drapery-making clinics, all of which would be complimentary. How quaint! Viewed from the perspective of the twenty-first century, that might be an understandable reaction, but fifty years ago suburban women had time for these things because they had not yet entered the workforce in large numbers. They also presumably had time for afternoon tea, which, along with lunch and dinner, was served in Gimbel's restaurant. One suspects the restaurant staff may have been a bit overwhelmed on the early September day when the store was dedicated. The minute the doors opened, five thousand people rushed in. Forty minutes later, the store had given out ten thousand free shopping bags! An estimated sixty-five thousand people visited before the close of business, keeping Cross County's parking lots filled to overflowing. They purchased $100,000 worth of merchandise. Not bad for a first day, especially since the store did not open until noon, following the ribbon-cutting ceremony and speeches by local and county officials.

The opening of Gimbel's marked the completion of the Cross County Shopping Center, an event that merited an editorial in *The New York Times*. Describing the Gimbel's building, the *Times* noted that its interior was "cheerful."[60] A stroll along the promenade linking the two department stores was reminiscent "of a world's fair atmosphere."[61]

For the merchants in Getty Square, the city's traditional shopping hub, the prevailing mood was pessimism following the completion of Cross County because they could not compete with "a center created by and for the automobile."[62] The preferred mode of transportation for shopping expeditions was the car, whether the destination was Cross County or S. Klein, which opened a huge three-story store on Central Park Avenue in 1959. Homeowners in the surrounding area had waged a vigorous battle to prevent rezoning of the property from residential to commercial, but the New York City retailing giant, intent upon making a foray into the suburbs, won out. On opening day twenty-five thousand shoppers competed for the three thousand parking spaces surrounding the store.

Where the Rubber Meets the Road

Such a scene would have been hardly imaginable a decade earlier. In the period immediately following World War II, before the federal government poured enormous sums into a new interstate highway system, mass transit held its own against the auto, especially in cities. Besides multiple rail lines linking it with New York City, Yonkers had trolleys tying disparate parts of the city together and extending to nearby communities. By January 1952, however, with its parent corporation, the Third Avenue Transit Company, in bankruptcy, the Yonkers Street Railway Company was on the verge of suspending service. Such a move would have stranded seventy thousand riders who used its Warburton Avenue, Park Avenue, McLean Avenue, Nepera Park, Nepperhan Station, South Broadway, Riverdale Avenue, and Elm Street lines. For that reason, the Public Service Commission took its time when considering the company's request to abandon its lines. Various alternatives were considered. These included the awarding of a bus franchise to one of several operators eager to provide such service, and the complete replacement of the trolley rails and equipment. The latter was not deemed feasible because of its $2.5 million price tag. Even minimal repairs were out of the question as far as the Yonkers Street Railway

Company was concerned. The company's track superintendent informed the Public Service Commission that practically all of the track ties were rotted and, despite frequent patching, the tracks continued to deteriorate. In his view, the continuation of trolley service beyond the spring would pose a genuine threat to the well-being of the public.

None of this seemed to bother a group of Antioch College students who chartered a trolley running between Yonkers and Mount Vernon for a festive get-together, which included a singalong, in late March 1952. This was their last fling before heading to jobs in various parts of the country to earn credits in the college's work-study program. Before the year was over, trolleys were replaced by buses. To mark the transition Mayor Kristensen and members of the Common Council were aboard the very last trolley to emerge from the car barn. Draped in black in recognition of the somberness of the occasion, the trolley traveled a mere three blocks to Getty Square before heading back to the car barn for the last time.

Although some Yonkers residents missed the historic trolleys, like the conversion to dial phones, a process completed in 1951, the transition to buses was initially welcomed by most riders. Over the course of the next few years, however, the popularity of the new form of transportation waned somewhat. To counter the decline in ridership, bus drivers were packed off to charm school—well, sort of! They were trained to flash genuine smiles as they greeted passengers with a hearty "good morning." It's hard to say whether riders were more surprised by the cheery greetings or by the drivers' blue and white beribboned badges proclaiming: "Glad to have you aboard."[63] This short-lived public relations campaign was the brainchild of bus company officials, who conceded that ridership had declined in recent years as more people resorted to "private cars" or merely stayed home to watch television.[64]

To be sure, people were opting to travel by automobile, even if it meant paying tolls on Westchester County parkways. Soon after World War II ended, the county began collecting ten cents per vehicle on these roads, but few drivers complained. In August 1947, on the first day that tolls were collected, a smiling Colonel John Stilwell, brother of World War II hero General Joseph W. Stilwell and a member of the Westchester County Parkway Commission, was the first motorist to pay the new toll on the Saw Mill River Parkway. Besides paying tolls on the parkways, drivers would be required to hand over change to use the New York State Thruway, but that wouldn't happen for another decade. Constructing the Thruway took considerable time, not only because a bridge had to be built to carry the road across the Hudson River at Tarrytown but because of the complex task of aligning the highway's path in a way that would limit its interference with the communities through which it ran. No matter which alignment was chosen, people whose homes and businesses stood in the path of the Thruway would be dislocated. When the new highway's path through Yonkers was announced in 1951, occupants of seventy-four homes and forty-three other structures were put on notice that they would have to move. Property owners along the portion of Central Park Avenue slated for incorporation into the Thruway began organizing to fight the designated alignment, and some adjustments were made. County government officials were pleased with the route that was ultimately chosen because the State Thruway Authority agreed to realign the Cross County Parkway where it intersected with Central Park Avenue. This saved county taxpayers $1.5 million.

Just a stone's throw from the Cross County Parkway, the Thruway was set to pass very close to Yonkers Raceway, and this raised eyebrows. Individuals whose homes and businesses would be sacrificed for the new road speculated about a rumored deal between the raceway and the Thruway Authority. Instead of having the road take an easterly route bringing it right past the track, disgruntled property owners proposed extending it through Tibbetts Brook Park. Since Tibbetts has a ridge, which would have necessitated construction of a tunnel, engineers deemed that route too costly. Running the highway through the park would also have deprived the public of a badly needed recreational venue. *The New York Times* pointed this out in an editorial stating that the decision about the route was based upon traffic, and "there is no disputing that the Yonkers Raceway generates heavy motor vehicle flow."[65] Even after the engineers had weighed in on the different routes, controversy over the alignment bringing the highway close to the racetrack continued, with opponents of this path obtaining help from what appeared to be an unlikely source: the president of Alexander's Department Stores. George Farkas, CEO of Alexander's, which had stores in the Bronx and White Plains, filed suit in the New York State Supreme Court contending that the more westerly route, through Tibbetts Brook Park, would be less costly than the easterly one favored by the Thruway Authority. Selection of the latter path for the road would result in the demolition of more homes and businesses and significant disruptions along Central Park Avenue. The suit also claimed that the easterly route would divide Yonkers into two parts and reduce real estate values. Given the fact that the Cross County Shopping Center, then under construction, would benefit from the easterly route, potentially drawing shoppers away from Mr. Farkas's stores, his decision to champion the cause of the small business people and homeowners, who would be displaced by the route recommended by the Thruway Authority, is understandable. The suit went nowhere, however. It was dismissed and a subsequent appeal failed, thereby allowing the Thruway Authority to commence work on the easterly route through Yonkers.

Work progressed nicely but, as with any major project, there were a few hitches. One involved a woman who refused to move even as construction crews demolished homes surrounding her residence on Fern Terrace. Claiming that the $23,500 the Thruway Authority had offered her for the home where she and her sister resided was not sufficient to enable them to obtain a comparable dwelling, she defied the bulldozers. Legal proceedings forestalled the sisters' eviction, but only for a few weeks. In the end, they were dispossessed and had to accept what the Thruway Authority offered. The next obstacle the authority faced was the cancellation of blasting permits by the inspector of combustibles for the City of Yonkers. A major blast in August 1954 had blown out windows in nine buildings, spewing glass in every direction and injuring one person, who had to be hospitalized. It also precipitated a landslide that shut down a portion of Sprain Road for three days. After the city and the Thruway Authority worked out an agreement permitting the use of the unfinished roadbed of the Thruway paralleling Sprain Road as a detour in the event of future construction-related landslides, the ban on blasting was lifted. Fourteen months later, in December 1955, Governor Averell Harriman traveled from Albany to Westchester to officially open a twenty-eight-mile stretch of the Thruway from Suffern to Yonkers.

The Thruway link between Yonkers and the Bronx was opened in time for Labor Day weekend in 1956. Construction of this portion of the road was behind schedule, and right down to the last moment the Thruway Authority wondered whether the new stretch of roadway would be ready in time. Despite the use of a type of concrete that required just a few days to cure, rather than the usual week to ten days, completion of the project depended upon the arrival of equipment for a new pump house at the Hillview Reservoir. The original stone pump house had to be replaced because it was right in the path of the Thruway. Everyone breathed a sigh of relief when the machinery for the new pump house arrived. Once it was installed and the forty-foot hole left by the removal of its predecessor had been filled, the last section of the New York State Thruway was ready to make its debut; it wasn't a moment too soon judging from the number of cars depicted in photos of the barricaded north and southbound lanes just before the Thruway opened. These pictures graced the front page of The Herald Statesman, along with a headline proclaiming: "Final Link of Thruway Opens to a Labor Day Crowd."[66] Although the road was opened without any fanfare other than the cheers of motorists who lined up to watch a crane lift the barricades that had blocked access to the last piece of the new road, the completion of the long-awaited 427-mile express route to Buffalo was a great achievement. But it had come at a price for, as *The New York Times* noted: "The job in Yonkers, one of the most costly and involved suburban road jobs ever undertaken, runs to $15,416,892."[67]

The New York State Thruway was one of several highway construction projects undertaken in Yonkers in the 1950s. Another consisted of four new lanes and a center island on the Cross County Parkway in Fleetwood. This improvement, completed in 1954, was paralleled by the reconfiguration of three miles of the Bronx River Parkway, including the intersection of that roadway and the Cross County Parkway. In 1955, additional work was done on the Cross County at the spot where the New York State Thruway passes beneath the parkway. By the end of the decade, construction began on the Sprain Brook Parkway, which had been on the drawing board for thirty years. This road had originally been proposed by the Westchester County Park Commission but when the construction work commenced, in 1959, the Sprain was a state project, its right of way having been ceded by Westchester County. Given the fact that Westchester's parkways had become through routes used extensively by nonresidents, thrusting the responsibility for building new roads in the county upon the state seemed logical in the post–World War II period.

Strolling Through the Park

Although parkways were no longer viewed as access roads to the county's splendid parks, something envisioned by the Westchester County Park Commission in the 1920s, they still enabled people to reach waterfront and inland recreational areas created decades earlier. With the end of gasoline rationing and the proliferation of automobiles in the years after World War II, the parks were more popular than ever, and not just with Westchesterites. Residents of the Bronx were flocking to Southern Westchester parks in such numbers that they constituted a veritable invasion. In 1948, the problem was so severe at Tibbetts Brook Park that the Yonkers representative on the county board of supervisors, the predecessor body of the county board of legislators, called for a limitation on nonresident use of the park. In addition to overcrowding at the park, the Yonkers supervisor was concerned about safety. Riots and knife attacks had occurred at Tibbetts, and homeowners in the surrounding area had informed him of unruly behavior by motorists exiting the park. A bottle hurled from a car window had narrowly missed a local resident and more assaults were feared. Despite the pleas of the supervisor and his Yonkers constituents, Westchester County took its time in making Tibbetts off limits to nonresidents. Although a ban on nonresidents was instituted in 1955 at several county golf courses and swimming areas, it wasn't until 1958 that the board of supervisors authorized the Westchester County Park Commission to limit access to Tibbetts. In the meantime, in 1955, the county purchased the private Dunwoodie Golf Club in Yonkers and turned it into a public facility despite the objections of Yonkers officials concerned about removing such a large parcel of land from the city's tax rolls. Dunwoodie opened as a public course, for the exclusive use of Westchester residents, in 1957.

In addition to enjoying county recreational facilities, Yonkers residents had access to an increasing number of municipal parks. Like the county, the city recognized the need to acquire additional open space to meet the needs of its growing population. For that reason, Yonkers approached New York City in 1959 with a proposal to buy or lease part of Van Cortlandt Park, but New York's feisty park commissioner Robert Moses characterized the Yonkers request as "manifestly absurd" and "a preposterous idea."[68]

It was a different story with Untermyer Park. The city was offered the former estate of Samuel Untermyer but wasn't sure whether to accept it, because of the cost of maintaining the estate and the financial implications of removing such a large piece of property from the tax rolls. The latter concern became a moot point when the Untermyer family established Samuel Untermyer Park and Gardens as a charitable corporation, thereby obtaining a tax exemption upheld by the courts. The corporation proved temporary, however, because the Untermyers really wanted to transfer the remainder of their portion of the estate to the public. Since neither the state nor Westchester County was interested, only Yonkers was left. To overcome the city's reluctance to assume responsibility for the estate, an arrangement was worked out in 1946, whereby Yonkers agreed to maintain fifteen acres as the Samuel Untermyer Park and Gardens in return for the right to sell the rest of the property. Once the city took over, the enormity of the task of keeping up the property, particularly the mansion, became apparent. Foxes, hawks, raccoons, and other wild creatures overran the estate and the once-beautiful home fell into a state of disrepair, prompting a visitor to Samuel Untermyer's Greystone in May 1948 to write a letter to the editor of *The New York Times*. Decrying the condition of the estate, he wrote that the front door's glass panes were shattered and in the marble hall "were pools of water; and there was a dank winter smell."[69]

Irwin Untermyer was quick to respond. The letter he fired off to the *Times* declared that the Untermyer family "neither owned nor controlled" the property.[70] Irwin Untermyer made it perfectly clear that responsibility for Greystone rested with Yonkers. Since that responsibility proved too great for the city to handle, the mansion was razed after the home and twenty-four surrounding acres were sold to a developer. The core of the estate where the Samuel Untermyer Park and Gardens were located remained city property. As the years went on, Yonkers divested itself of additional portions of the estate beyond the core. In 1955, the New York Cardiac Home, a convalescent facility for heart patients, opened on North Broadway on acreage that had been part of Greystone. Four years later, plans for the Andrus Pavilion at St. John's Riverside Hospital were announced. Donated by the Surdna Foundation, established by John E. Andrus, the new facility rose on the northern end of the former Untermyer estate.

Off to the Races

As the years went on, Yonkers was able to devote more resources to the portion of the Greystone estate for which it was still responsible. As a result, Yonkers residents flocked to Untermyer Park, especially in spring to enjoy an abundance of floral displays. When statuary and fountain restoration were completed, this beautiful place overlooking the Hudson became a tranquil oasis in a bustling city. For some residents of Yonkers, simply strolling through the park and gazing out at the waterway that had played such an integral part in the city's development was an incomparable recreational experience. Other Yonkers residents who, whether regularly or occasionally, preferred more exciting leisure time activities, however, headed to the eastern part of their vast city to enjoy a day at the races. That they were able to do so was quite remarkable considering that the Yonkers racetrack almost didn't reopen after the war. During the conflict, the Empire City Racing Association, whose home track was Yonkers Raceway, held its meets at Jamaica Raceway on Long Island. Eager to see the action return to Westchester, the county executive and the Westchester County Board of Supervisors joined forces with the Yonkers Common Council in 1947 to petition the association to return to Yonkers. Such a move required the approval of the New York State Racing Commission, but that body was adamantly opposed. Citing the growth in the racing industry, something which both the county and the City of Yonkers eyed from the standpoint of tax revenue, the commission deemed seating, parking, and stable facilities at the Yonkers track so inadequate that patron safety would be an issue should racing resume.

Convinced that the limited acreage comprising the racetrack property precluded upgrades needed for thoroughbred racing, the Empire City Racing Association, in 1949, sold the Yonkers track for $2.4 million to a syndicate whose members had a different vision for the historic track. They planned to bring harness racing to Yonkers. In the meantime, in September 1949, the track played host to the Westchester County Fair. A quarter-century had passed since the last county fair had been held and in that time most of Westchester's remaining farms had disappeared. Nevertheless, at the 1949 fair, farm animals, along with industrial and household products more representative of life in the mid-twentieth century, were displayed. Less than three months after the nine-day fair ended, the New York State Harness Racing Commission granted a license to the Yonkers Trotting Association to hold a meet at the Yonkers racetrack. In January 1950, the former Empire City racetrack was renamed Yonkers Raceway. Over the course of the next few months construction crews reduced the size of the track from a mile to a half-mile, freeing up space for additional parking; stalls were renovated and the grandstand was structurally reinforced. The existing seats were replaced and nearly three hundred private boxes were added, along with new lights. But it was all worth it. On opening night in April 1950, more than twenty-one thousand fans showed up. They wagered almost $700,000 and when they weren't cheering, placing bets, collecting their winnings, or lamenting their losses, they were able to catch a glimpse of the $1.5 million worth of improvements that, in the opinion of a *New York Times* sportswriter, had transformed the "beautifully renovated" Empire City track into the "eye-catching Yonkers Raceway."[71] The fans positively loved the place and they kept on coming back.

Following a strong first season, Yonkers Raceway had a spectacular second year, setting two records for the amount of money wagered on harness racing. On the last night of the 1951 season, more than twenty-five thousand people turned out and bet a recordbreaking $1,524,597. Despite all of the money wagered at the track, very little was finding its way into the city's coffers. Although the owners of the track made good on a promise to donate something to Yonkers, their six-figure contribution, the largest they could legally make, wasn't sufficient. What the city wanted was a tax on the track's income but some New York State legislators questioned the constitutionality of this. In time, Yonkers would secure approval for a tax on racetrack admissions. Giving the city a sizable chunk of money would become part of the cost of doing business for the group acquiring voting control of the Yonkers Raceway Corporation. Having introduced night harness racing at Roosevelt Raceway, these investors knew what they were getting into. From a business standpoint, their new venture proved very beneficial because the Yonkers track was immensely popular. On opening night in April 1953, nearly thirty-one thousand patrons showed up, setting a new national mark for night harness racing. Purses were also increased that year to head off a threatened boycott of the track by horse owners. A possible owners' strike was the least of the raceway's problems, however.

In September 1953, the New York State Harness Racing Commission launched an inquiry of Yonkers Raceway because two track employees were persons of interest in the investigation of the murder of the president of the union that represented hundreds of raceway workers. Within a month, the provisions of the 1907 Moreland Act law allowing the governor to investigate any state agency were invoked. The racing commission was then subjected to scrutiny, as was the entire harness racing industry. No sooner had the investigation been announced than a civic committee was formed to lobby for the permanent closing of Yonkers Raceway. Politically active Yonkers residents from both major parties were among the founders of the committee. Besides being concerned about what they claimed was racketeering at the track, they were disturbed by the number of municipal workers who were moonlighting at the raceway. Six months later, after a series of hearings, the state enacted new legislation requiring the fingerprinting of all track employees, owners, and directors. At the same time, the Yonkers Common Council passed a statute allowing city employees earning less than $5,000 annually to work part-time at the track. Police officers were expressly prohibited from taking jobs at the raceway, however.

Over the course of the next few years, things settled down at Yonkers Raceway. The fans kept coming and the track was garnering favorable press coverage, whether for sizable attendance or, as was the case in 1956, for the first change in a century in the apparel of harness racing drivers: new caps designed to protect the wearer's head in the event of a spill. Made of fiberglass, the caps were light in weight but strong enough to withstand the force of an eight-pound steel ball dropped from a height of five feet. Owners and drivers embraced the new headgear, but they were less accepting of the purses offered at Yonkers Raceway. In 1957, failure to resolve this issue seemed certain to result in a strike. A federal court injunction headed off a cessation of racing at Yonkers for a brief period, but when arbitration proved fruitless horse owners refused to file entries. This aroused the ire of a federal judge who threatened to hold the owners in contempt. Undeterred, owners started to remove their horses from the stables at Yonkers. As a result, the raceway had very limited programs. Attendance dwindled, but it picked up once the owners and raceway officials came to a meeting of the minds.

With the issue of the purses behind them, the owners of Yonkers Raceway decided to invest a whopping $17.5 million in the track in 1958. Improvements included a new multicolored clubhouse costing $9 million, four-tier parking for two thousand cars, and an underground passage to the grandstand for the numerous fans arriving on buses. Since nearly 20 percent of patrons took shuttle buses from the subway to Yonkers Raceway, the new dropoff area was designed to keep them dry in inclement weather and eager to plunk down their money at the betting windows. New windows were added as part of the renovations and to make everything very convenient, fans enjoying a meal in the 1,200-seat Empire Terrace dining room had to take only a few steps to make a bet. Additional dining rooms, a cafeteria, and refreshment bars in various parts of the grandstand ensured that no one would go hungry or thirsty. Despite the fact that it had sacrificed seven acres for the New York State Thruway, Yonkers Raceway was on its way to becoming bigger and better. When the renovations were completed, the track would have four thousand additional seats, bringing the total number to fourteen thousand. Including space for standees, the rebuilt raceway would be able to accommodate forty-two thousand people. The new parking facility, called the Parkadrome, increased to 9,400 the number of vehicles that could be handled.

When the new, improved track made its debut in the summer of 1958, even *The New York Times* was impressed by the renovations. In an enthusiastic article the paper declared that the remodeled raceway was "as posh as an East Side night club."[72] Of special note, in addition to the Parkadrome, were the Vista-Windows, which despite their hefty twenty-eight-ton combined weight were "raised or lowered . . . by push-buttons," and the Good Time Room, located behind the Empire Terrace dining room, where a horseplayer could enjoy a cocktail and view the races on TV at the same time.[73] As for the color scheme, the designer of the facility said that the fusion of colors ensured that you would not be offended "even if you were losing."[74] It's safe to say that the color scheme mattered little to the nearly thirty-one thousand people, including "men in big cars, and sun-tanned women trimmed in fur," who turned out for opening night at what the *Times* characterized as "the Fort Knox of

Westchester County."[75] *The Herald Statesman* was just as effusive. "Raceway Joy Unconfined" was how the paper put it; the article that followed noted that there were 30,998 patrons at "what certainly has to be the world's most lavish merry-go-round, a super structure officially dubbed Yonkers Raceway."[76]

Two weeks after the grand opening, a new attendance record was set when almost forty-one thousand fans showed up. When the numbers for August were tallied, it was clear that the remodeled raceway was a big hit. A total of $52.4 million had been wagered, with the $12.5 million bet from August 11 through August 16 setting a world record. More than a quarter of a million people had visited the track during August, and that too was a record for harness racing. Yonkers Raceway was definitely the place to be even if you weren't from Yonkers. In September 1958, raceway officials played host to a delegation of visiting Russians touring selected American cities. One member of the group placed a two-dollar bet, picked up his winnings, which totaled a little over twenty dollars, and announced that he wasn't going to try his luck again. That same month, the track welcomed several hundred United Nations delegates. These distinguished visitors and their wives were wined and dined in addition to seeing the races. Before the year ended, the Westchester County Board of Supervisors also sought a little special treatment. Citing challenges associated with the presence of the track in Westchester, the board proposed a 15 percent county tax on raceway admissions. The county didn't get what it asked for, but in 1959 it did secure the approval of the New York State Legislature for a 5 percent tax on racetrack admissions. The new tax did little to discourage fans. As the decade of the fifties came to an end, the refurbished Yonkers Raceway was a magnet attracting people from Yonkers and beyond, including New York City residents who took the Yonkers Raceway subway special, an express train that began at Grand Central and made only one stop, at Eighty-Sixth Street, before depositing passengers at Woodlawn, where a bus was waiting to take them directly to the track. What more could anyone want?

Cruisin' Down the River

The answer to that question depended, of course, upon the individual. Some people preferred to spend their leisure time in a more peaceful setting. For boat owners, the majestic Hudson River was the ideal place to find tranquility. Whether one had a canoe or a good-sized powerboat, getting out on the water was an absolute delight from late spring through autumn. For those who didn't have boats, a ride on the Hudson River Day Line was a great way to enjoy the water. Soon after World War II ended, Yonkers had visions of Day Line steamers and other vessels tying up at the city pier, which had been leased for the duration of the conflict to a shipyard doing defense work. After the pier had reverted to its prewar function, the city entered into an agreement with the Wilson Line to operate excursion steamboats between Yonkers and Rockaway Beach.

In addition to steamboats and private pleasure craft, the Yonkers-Alpine ferry was a familiar sight on the Hudson in the late forties. A *Herald Statesman* headline declaring "Ferry Adds Vessel on Alpine Run" testified to the popularity of the crossing from Yonkers in 1947.[77] In 1950, the ferry had its best year since the opening of the George Washington Bridge in 1931, but this didn't last long, because the completion of the Tappan Zee Bridge in 1955 caused a significant reduction in the number of vehicles using the ferry. The ferry company lowered fares to lure customers back, but to no avail. In October 1956, its board of directors announced that service would end right after Thanksgiving, but the boats kept running into December while the State of New York considered various options, including Port Authority acquisition of the ferry. Since it was precluded from undertaking projects that were not self-supporting, the Port Authority bowed out. Ferry service ended on December 27, 1956. Another big change on the Hudson was the passage, in 1959, of a bill requiring commercial vessels sailing up the Hudson from Yonkers to use licensed river pilots. Captains had the option of refusing to take pilots aboard but they still had to pay pilotage fees, and since lack of a licensed pilot affected vessels' insurance, the new state law had the effect of placing pilots with at least two years' experience on every ship heading from Yonkers to Troy. A piloting requirement was already in effect from New York Harbor to Yonkers.

A private vessel not covered by the new piloting requirement carried a very special person from New York City to Yonkers in September 1959. The distinguished visitor, who cruised upriver on Laurance Rockefeller's yacht, was Princess Beatrix of the Netherlands. Disembarking in Yonkers, the princess was greeted by Boy Scouts, some in Indian attire and others dressed in the sort of clothing Henry Hudson's sailors were believed to have worn. Following a ceremonial dance by one of the scouts, the princess was presented with an eagle claw necklace.

Another festive occasion with a Hudson River connection involved a celebrity better known to Americans than the heir presumptive to the Dutch throne. It was Bill (Bojangles) Robinson, who spent a milestone birthday on the Hudson, just off Yonkers, on an excursion boat that had just been christened *Bojangles*. As he sliced into a cake big enough to feed the three hundred guests on board to celebrate his seventieth birthday, the famous dancer declared: "All I can say is that I'm 70 and I feel like 20."[78]

Sadly, the celebrity guest of honor at another mid-twentieth-century birthday party could not say the same. Although 150 guests were entertained at a dinner party at his Chester Drive home in Yonkers to mark his eighty-third birthday, in 1956, the "Father of the Blues," composer William Christopher Handy, better known as W. C. Handy, had suffered a stroke and lost his vision. Yet he continued to compose, dictating arrangements "for new and old music, mostly sacred."[79] He also kept up with what was going on in Washington. A lifelong Republican, he was pleased to tell a reporter that he had recently met President Eisenhower. Commenting on *Brown v. the Board of Education of Topeka, Kansas,* the landmark 1954 case on school desegregation, Handy declared that challenges relating to desegregation would be "ironed out."[80] Ironically, the city on the Hudson where this native of Alabama had chosen to live would figure in another landmark desegregation case decades later. Although it would not be evident for some time, the foundation of that case was being laid in the postwar years when the city's growing African American community became concentrated in the western part of Yonkers. Some inhabitants of this area enjoyed the sort of water views for which purchasers of new condominiums paid considerable sums in the early twenty-first century, when upscale residential buildings were erected overlooking the river. Fifty years earlier, pricey dwellings on and near the river seemed inconceivable.

Backyards and Barbecues

Nineteenth-century reformer and Westchester resident Horace Greeley may have said "Go West, young man!" but in the post–World War II era, the east was the real frontier for Yonkers. It was here that suburban homes, complete with the requisite barbecue-equipped backyards, rose on once-vacant land, and apartment complexes were built to meet a housing shortage that grew more acute as returning veterans started or added to their families. So great was the demand for housing that Yonkers actually considered the possibility of using the stables and trainers' quarters at the Empire City racetrack to house veterans. The track's water and electrical lines were deemed sufficient, and since the complex was not being used for racing at the time, the idea of having temporary living quarters there did not seem absurd. Nothing came of the proposal, however. Instead, new prefabricated housing sprouted in various parts of the city. In 1946, manufactured dwellings for a hundred veterans and their families went up on the McLean Avenue baseball park. The federal government provided the prefab units and Yonkers contributed such infrastructure elements as sewers, water mains, roads, and sidewalks. The apartments varied in size, ranging from one to three bedrooms. In contrast with these prefab dwellings, which were intended to be temporary and were slated for removal when the housing emergency ended, the Crestwood Lake Apartments on Central Park Avenue and Roxbury Drive East were permanent. The demand for housing was so enormous that nearly three hundred apartments in the complex, which had huge living rooms and its own twenty-five acre lake for the exclusive use of residents, were rented before the first units were finished in 1951. Of course, it probably didn't hurt that Wanamaker's, which was then setting its sights on Cross County, furnished the two model apartments. Rent, including gas and electric, for a three and one-half-room unit was $92.50 per month, and $114.50 for a four and one-half-room apartment.

The year that Crestwood Lake made its debut, Yonkers had the biggest per capita growth in home construction in the entire state. An impressive 2,500 units had been completed or were nearing completion and 1,500 additional units were about to leap from the drawing board to the construction phase. Building was already well under way at the Hearth-Stone development on Fort Hill Avenue, where three-bedroom, two-bath Cape Cod–style homes were priced at $14,850. Two-bedroom homes in the development cost $11,900 and three-bedroom ranch-style homes $12,700. All of the homes had cellars and came complete with appliances. Yonkers was not only leading in new construction but it was pioneering in cooperative conversions. In 1951, the 135-unit Brooklands complex, composed of three six-story buildings, with luxury apartments ranging in size from three to eight rooms, some with fireplaces, became a cooperative. Situated on the western edge of Bronxville, with its parklike setting Brooklands seemed removed from Kimball and Palmer Avenues just outside the complex. Closer to Palmer Avenue, where that road intersected with Kimball, a highrise building with an underground garage went up in the fifties. Several miles away at Kimball and Midland Avenues two apartment houses, with a combined total of four hundred units, were erected before the close of the decade. Elsewhere, more than five hundred apartment units sprouted on the site of the former Grassy Sprain golf course in an area called "Bronxville West."[81] During the same period, several hundred split-level homes rose on a hill overlooking the Grassy Sprain Reservoir and the Sprain Lake golf course. The topography of the site, "one of the last large areas in Yonkers available for mass housing," had caused two developers to throw up their hands, but the third persevered.[82] Undaunted by the need to blast eight thousand cubic yards of rock, he succeeded in building homes perfectly suited for the site: split-levels ranging in price from $18,990 to $22,990.

New suburban homes and apartments weren't the only kind of housing emerging in postwar Yonkers. In 1946, the Julia Dyckman Andrus Memorial, Inc., announced plans to convert the twenty-four-room mansion of the late John E. Andrus into a home for children. A decade later, following the merger of the Gustave Hartman Home for Children in Far Rockaway, Queens, and the Hebrew National Orphan Home in Yonkers, Hartman residents moved to the Tuckahoe Road estate, where the Hebrew Home was located. In 1959, the Leake and Watts Children's Home made a commitment to remain in its Hawthorne Avenue location. To accommodate an additional fifty children, renovation of existing facilities and the addition of new cottages were planned at the facility, which, at the time, housed four hundred. Providing housing for children in need was praiseworthy, but there were many adults who lacked a decent place to live. To remedy this situation, government got involved.

Less than a year after World War II ended the Yonkers Municipal Housing Authority was moving ahead with plans to build subsidized housing between Hawthorne and Riverdale Avenues. Erection of a proposed complex, known as Cottage Place Gardens, required the demolition of existing buildings in the area. The process of evicting families residing in them took longer than expected because of the challenge of finding housing for those displaced. Yonkers, nevertheless, persevered and in 1951, when it played host to sixty municipal planners from all over the county, a major stop on the tour conducted for the planners was the site of the proposed Cottage Place project. The group also visited the site of a proposed 415-unit public housing complex at Palisade Avenue and Garden Street. At the same time that it was taking steps to meet the housing needs of low-income residents, Yonkers was providing opportunities for middle-class families. In 1956, the New York State Housing Commission provided a mortgage for the construction of a cooperative development on a vacant parcel extending from Hawthorne Avenue to Buena Vista Avenue adjacent to Sunset Park. As the fifties drew to a close, the city was disappointed to learn that the Federal Housing and Home Finance Administration would provide only limited funding for slum clearance at South Broadway and Prospect Street, but Yonkers, hoping to obtain state aid, was determined to forge ahead.

School Days

New housing, whether subsidized or market rate, had significant implications for the city's public schools. This was apparent as early as 1950,
when the Yonkers Board of Education leased space in one of the twenty
buildings in the new Bryn Mawr Ridge apartments. Children in kindergarten through third grade were able to attend classes onsite in the
527 family complex. Between 1950 and 1951, enrollment in the city's
public schools increased by 650 students. By the mid-fifties overcrowding
had become a serious problem. In 1954, nearly four thousand students
were in classes with thirty-five or more and approximately a thousand
pupils were in classes of forty or more. At the time, Yonkers was spending
$207 per pupil annually for instruction, the lowest outlay in the county.
Expenditures for books, supplies, and building maintenance were also
below those of other communities. Teachers' salaries were considerably
lower than those of other districts as well. Given the seriousness of this
situation, a group of citizens formed the Emergency Committee for
Improving Yonkers Public Schools and petitioned the State Education
Department to launch an investigation. The Yonkers Board of Education
insisted that the city's school system met minimum standards set by
the state but the emergency committee disputed this and blamed the
Common Council for not providing adequate funding for the schools.
Following several hearings in Albany, Dr. Lewis A. Wilson, commissioner
of education, concluded that the real issue was the method of financing
the schools. He characterized the state-imposed limitation of 2 percent
on the amount the city could raise real estate taxes, a figure based on the
five-year assessed value of real estate, as "a real problem."[83] Nevertheless,
Yonkers had the "right to impose other taxes as other communities have
done."[84] As for the full state investigation of the city's schools requested
by the emergency committee, the commissioner indicated that the state
did not have the funds for this. He did, however, direct the Yonkers
corporation counsel to answer the committee's charges.

Within a month, Corporation Counsel J. Raymond Hannon
responded in a memorandum stating that the school system was "being
properly and efficiently managed."[85] Addressing specific complaints made
by the emergency committee, he denied that capable teachers were leaving because of "heavy pupil loads and overcrowded conditions."[86] He
also disputed the charges that replacements were not being appointed for
teachers who departed and that there was widespread dissatisfaction among
teachers. Denouncing the corporation counsel's findings, the emergency
committee once again pressed for a state investigation. This time the state

education commissioner ordered the Yonkers Board of Education to submit, by January 1, 1956, "sufficient evidence of an adequate program, both in respect to its education offerings and its building needs."[87] Failure to comply, Yonkers was warned, would mean the loss of state aid. Ten days later, Yonkers authorized the issuance of $5 million in bonds for school renovations and for the completion of Southeast Yonkers Junior-Senior High School on Kneeland Avenue. Not everyone applauded increased spending for the schools. The Yonkers Council of Civic and Taxpayers Associations fired off a letter to Governor Averell Harriman stating that the commissioner of education had no right to require Yonkers to appropriate additional sums for its schools. With almost six hundred new students in the city's public schools, for a grand total of nearly twenty thousand in 1955, per-pupil spending in Yonkers, which had risen to $301, was still the lowest in Westchester. City Manager Charles L. Curran included $700,000 in additional funding for education in the proposed budget for 1956. This was less than half of what the board of education had requested and, in the board's view, as stated in its report to the new commissioner of education, Dr. James E. Allen Jr., who succeeded Dr. Wilson upon his retirement, it was simply inadequate.

After reviewing the report forwarded from Yonkers, Commissioner Allen proposed an amendment to the New York State Constitution to permit Yonkers and four other large cities to sever the ties between their schools and municipal government. Approval of such an amendment by voters in each of the municipalities would have enabled school districts to impose their own taxes. In the meantime, Commissioner Allen, conceding that some improvements had been made, decided that Yonkers would receive its full allotment of state aid but there was a string attached to the $2.5 million award. Yonkers was required to have a complete survey of its schools done by an outside agency. *The Herald Statesman*'s assessment of this was summed up in an editorial titled "We Get Our State Aid for Schools but City Is Left in Dunce Corner."[88] After conceding that the increased number of students in the Yonkers schools might require additional spending for education, the paper pointed out that since other municipalities in New York State were experiencing the same thing, it was wrong to make Yonkers "a lone scapegoat."[89]

Many residents of Yonkers agreed with the newspaper's perspective on the schools controversy. As unacceptable as Commissioner Allen's actions were, however, the city had to proceed with the survey he ordered; Yonkers and the state split the $50,000 cost of this investigation. While the schools study progressed, the Common Council approved a 1957 budget containing a $1.3 million increase in education spending. This enabled the board of education to improve maintenance and increase the starting salary for new teachers by $800.

The eagerly anticipated survey of the Yonkers schools was revealed in stages beginning in June 1957. Since the previous October, approximately a hundred experts from the state education department, supplemented by forty consultants, had scrutinized the city's educational system. More than a thousand Yonkers residents also participated in different phases of the study. In its report, the survey group recommended the adoption of a master plan aimed at "improving relations between the Yonkers schools system and the community."[90] The report characterized the city as "a community divided within itself" and proceeded to enumerate factors standing in the way of improving the schools.[91] They included a reluctance of many residents to identify themselves with the city and "a physical, social and political schism" within Yonkers.[92] A month later, the final four reports of the seven-part survey were issued. They pointed to deficiencies in class size, noting that "classes of thirty-nine and forty were not uncommon."[93] School maintenance was also an issue. Declaring that many school buildings were "in critical condition" because of inadequate funding, the consultants also found fault with school libraries "starved for books, staff, space and equipment."[94] Yonkers was urged to address all of these issues plus improve mathematics and science education and reorganize the school system's administrative staff to bring about greater efficiency and better communication with the residents of Yonkers. This was a tall order and a very expensive one. For that reason, the survey group recommended that the board of education get behind a plan for a county sales tax to raise money for education.

In the meantime, the common council had to bite the bullet and include additional funding for the schools in the 1958 city budget. When the new school year began in September 1958, things were looking up. A hundred teachers had been added to the staff; half of them filled newly created positions while the others replaced educators who had left. Initially, this was interpreted as a good sign. Maybe those overcrowded classrooms would finally become a thing of the past. At least that's what some parents hoped. Reductions in class size were one thing, but if an entire school simply had too many students, which was the case at Roosevelt High School, the board of education felt that there was only one remedy: double sessions. Although this was intended to be a temporary measure until the fall of 1959 when Walt Whitman Junior High School was expected to open, parents of a half-dozen students at Roosevelt nevertheless objected to the double sessions. Claiming that they were expressing the views of four hundred Roosevelt parents, they tried to enlist the aid of State

Education Commissioner Allen in reversing the school board's decision. Following a hearing in Albany at which the parents and Yonkers school officials presented arguments, the commissioner ruled in favor of the double sessions.

As the decade of the fifties neared an end, the total number of students in the city's public schools exceeded twenty-five thousand, and the board of education continued to struggle with less than optimal budgets. This caused some citizens to wonder about the future of the "Queen City of the Hudson" while pondering the observations made by Harrison Salisbury in the mid-fifties when the severity of the challenges facing the public schools had become readily apparent. The celebrated journalist noted: "Past neglect rather than disinterest lies more at the heart of the schools problem. Economic shifts can be treated as opportunities. . . . Community differences can be utilized as the channel for generating closer relations rather than for encouraging fratricidal feuds."[95] This was good advice but, as the citizens of Yonkers would soon discover, implementing it would not be easy in a city where geographic, political, and racial divisions were beginning to resemble seismic fault lines.

Andrew Carnegie donated $50,000 to build this beautiful library in 1901. Designed by local architects Edwin Quick and H. Lansing Quick, it opened to the public in 1904. The building was demolished in 1982. (All photographs courtesy of Yonkers Historical Society; Mary Hoar, Executive Illustrations Editor, Marianne Winstanley, Assistant Illustrations Editor.)

Founded in 1889, the Corinthian Yacht Club is located at 771 Warburton Avenue.

The foot of Main Street in the early 20th century.

Glenview Mansion was built by John Bond Trevor on a bluff overlooking the Hudson River. It was designed by architect Charles Clinton and completed in 1877. It now is the home of the Hudson River Museum.

Greystone was built by John Waring shortly after the Civil War. Also the home of Samuel Tilden and Samuel Untermyer, the house was demolished in 1948.

This entrance to the Greystone estate was on North Broadway.

Funded by William F. Cochran, the Hollywood Inn was recognized as a model and inspiration for recreational centers all over the world.

Yonkers docks in the early 20th century.

The Lake at Park Hill was one of the many attractions of this planned community.

Monroe's Clothing Store was in the heart of Getty Square in the early 20th century.

An aerial view of west Yonkers in the early 20th century.

An early 20th century photograph of Alexander Smith and Sons Carpet Company and the surrounding area.

Trolley 404 rounding Nepperhan Avenue near Roberts Avenue.

Union Place near Warburton Avenue.

Yonkers City Pier was built on two levels in 1901 to accommodate 400-passenger Hudson River Dayliners. Passengers could embark and disembark to and from both levels of the pier.

The Park Hill Train Station was part of the Getty Square spur of the Putnam Line.

One of Yonkers's largest and most popular restaurants, the Park Hill Inn, closed in 1918 for a combination of reasons: Gasless Sundays, enforcement of the Saturday midnight closing, and Prohibition.

Mining tycoon and financier William Boyce Thompson built Alder Manor in 1912, designed by Carrere and Hastings. The Thompson family lived in it until the mid–20th century.

In 1920 William Boyce Thompson established an institute for plant research across the street from his home on North Broadway because he wanted to be personally involved.

The Flagg Building was erected in 1845 at the corner of New Main Street and Palisade Avenue and demolished in 1915.

The Gazette Building at 59-61 Main Street.

The Yonkers City Pier and waterfront as seen from an excursion boat.

Part of the way through the process of tearing down old wooden buildings in preparation for "fluming" the Nepperhan (Saw Mill) River.

Dock Street in preparation for "fluming" the Nepperhan (Saw Mill) River.

Larkin Plaza in the 1920s after the Nepperhan (Saw Mill) River has been encased.

Started in 1886, the Yonkers Canoe Club at Glenwood was the home of several Olympic medal winners.

The terminal of the Getty Square spur of the Putnam Line was at 20 South Broadway.

The Warburton Building at 45 Warburton Avenue was built in 1876 by Benjamin Washburn. The building, immediately next to Philipse Manor Hall and home to the Warburton Theater, was torn down in the 1970s for the Otis expansion.

The Bryn Mawr Station on the Putnam Line.

The Getty House and Getty Square in the early 1920s.

The Hamilton Theater at 9 Main Street circa 1920. The theater was built in 1913 and demolished in 1927.

South Broadway near the McLean Avenue junction in the 1920s. Part of this area would become Lincoln Park.

Labeled the "Wheeler Block," the building was built over the underground flume that carried the Nepperhan (Saw Mill) River. Owner and architect Charles Wheeler actually built three separate buildings, one for each of his two children and himself.

The "Sugar House," one of Yonkers's dominant industries along the bank of the
Hudson River.

The Yonkers trolleys were part of the Third Avenue Railway System. Pictured is
Car 49 on the Broadway trolley line.

Larkin Plaza in the late 1950s.

Sherwood House, a restored pre-Revolutionary tenant farm house, was acquired by the Yonkers Historical Society in 1955. It also was the home of John Ingersoll, the first doctor in Yonkers.

William Lawrence built Westlands as his home in 1917; it now serves as the administration building for Sarah Lawrence College.

One of the first buses of the Yonkers Street Railway Company.

St. Joseph's Seminary, built on part of the historic Valentine property.

Ohab Zedek was the first permanent synagogue in Westchester; it was founded in 1887 by Adolph Klein.

St. John's Episcopal Church in Getty Square.

An aerial view of Getty Square in the late 1950s.

Shopping on South Broadway in the late 1950s.

An aerial view of the Alexander Smith and Sons Carpet Company.

An Urban/Suburban Metropolis

Yonkers in the Sixties and Seventies

The British Are Coming! The British Are Coming!

As every confirmed shopaholic knows, when the going gets tough, the tough go shopping, and that's exactly what a British company did in 1960. Dollar Land Holdings, Ltd., purchased the Cross County Shopping Center from its developer, Sol G. Atlas, who had built other successful shopping centers and, according to the press, was eager to embark upon new ventures in construction. When Cross County changed hands, its seventy-six stores were attracting customers from far and wide, and Gimbel's was about to add another floor to its massive department store. By the mid-sixties, retail competition in Yonkers was heating up. In 1965, Alexander's Department Stores, Inc., announced that it would build a large store on Central Park Avenue, adjacent to the Cross County Shopping Center. Legal battles over ownership of street rights and title to the property caused Alexander's to abandon this location in favor of a more northerly spot on Central Park Avenue, the former S. Klein store, where Alexander's opened in 1977. In the meantime, a different sort of iconic New York City establishment, Nathan's Famous, which had its origins as a Coney Island hot dog stand, purchased the Adventurers Inn on Central Park Avenue in 1964 and began luring hungry customers. Practically everybody loves a good hot dog. Like apple pie, the humble frankfurter is, after all, an American tradition. So, too, is the shopping center, and, as such, it is warmly embraced, unless developers plunk it down in an area deemed unsuitable.

Such was the case in Yonkers in 1973 when the Taubman Company proposed building the largest shopping center in Westchester County on land in northwest Yonkers owned by the Boyce Thompson Institute. At the time, the world-renowned center for plant research was in the process of moving to Cornell University, in part because of increased pollution, which made the cultivation of various plant species more difficult in Yonkers. In the early sixties, the Boyce Thompson property was one of several Westchester County sites considered for a State University of New York campus, but commercial development of the property held far greater appeal for the Yonkers City Council because of the tax revenue it would funnel into municipal coffers. For that reason, the council was willing to consider a zoning change to permit the erection of a shopping center on the Boyce Thompson property. Before the city council could take up this matter, however, opposition forces in nearby Hastings-on-Hudson, as well as in Yonkers, began organizing to fight the proposal. With 160 smaller stores and several major department stores, including Ohrbach's, Macy's, and Abraham & Straus, and an unnamed fourth retailer with whom negotiations were proceeding when the plan was announced, the center was envisioned as a shopping mecca. The addition of movie theaters, an ice-skating rink, restaurants, office buildings, banks, and a medical center later on would transform the center into a mixed-use development. Yonkers mayor Alfred B. DelBello, who was running for county executive at the time, joined the opposition. He cited the impact the proposed center would have on the surrounding residential area and the dampening effect it might have on plans for the redevelopment of Getty Square. In July 1973, the city council rejected the Taubman Company's rezoning request. Although the former Boyce Thompson property did not become a destination for shopaholics, a site on Tuckahoe Road became a national distribution center for the upscale retailer Saks Fifth Avenue. A former Western Electric facility, the sprawling single-story building, close to both the New York State Thruway and the Sprain Brook Parkway, served thirty Saks stores all over the United States. In addition to the obvious tax benefits of the distribution center, the fact that Saks had chosen Yonkers over sites in New York City and New Jersey was taken as a very positive sign in a city attempting to strengthen its economy in a period of industrial decline.

The Times They Are A-Changin'

Although it was apparent by the early 1960s that Yonkers was no longer an industrial powerhouse, the city did have some very substantial factories. In the sixties, the Polychrome Corporation expanded by commissioning a

Yonkers architect to design a new building facing the Hudson River. Part factory, where aluminum plates and stencils were made for the printing industry, and part office building, the new facility, constructed of insulated concrete blocks with an exposed steel frame, had phenomenal views of the waterway at its doorstep. Elsewhere in Yonkers, the Habirshaw Division of Phelps Dodge Copper Products Corporation, which had four plants, was beset by labor problems. When negotiations for a new contract broke down in the late fall of 1963, a thousand electrical workers struck Habirshaw. For the first two weeks of the walkout, everything was peaceful. As the strike entered its third week, *The Herald Statesman* ran a front page story titled "Striking Workers Gather Outside Habirshaw Plant" and reported that strikers had started to back up the picket lines at all four plants.[1] Their presence was felt the very next day. During a demonstration outside one of the Yonkers facilities, a striker sprawled out in the middle of the street and when police attempted to remove him from the road, a melee, involving approximately two hundred workers and fifty police officers, broke out. Although no serious injuries resulted, several men were arrested.

In the mid-sixties, another major Yonkers company was in transition. Otis Elevator, the city's largest employer, announced in 1965 that it was preparing to move a substantial portion of its production to a plant in Indiana. Only a year earlier, Otis had sold three buildings at Lake Avenue and Saw Mill River Road when it ceased manufacturing pinball machines. Some of the space was quickly absorbed by Clairol and another subsidiary of the Bristol-Myers Company but this did not allay the fears of Yonkers officials that Otis would go the way of Alexander Smith and Sons. That Otis was willing to offer the 550 employees it was planning to lay off in Yonkers jobs in its Bloomington, Indiana, plant was a nice gesture, but this would do nothing for the sinking fortunes of the city Otis had called home for more than a century. State Senator Royden A. Letsen called upon the governor to intervene, while Mayor John E. Flynn appointed a committee to examine the consequences of the Otis downsizing. In 1967, there was a new concern: a strike against Otis plants in Yonkers and Harrison, New Jersey, by members of the International Union of Electrical, Radio and Machine Workers following the breakdown of contract negotiations, but fortunately this did not prove to be an insurmountable obstacle to resolving the downsizing matter. It took a few years but the city convinced Otis to remain a major presence in Yonkers.

In 1972, the company signed an agreement with the city for the acquisition of land needed to construct a state-of-the-art facility where it could fill the increasing number of orders for its high-speed elevators. As part of its plans for the redevelopment of its historic downtown, Yonkers, with the help of the federal and state governments, acquired the property Otis needed, razed everything on the various parcels and then transferred the vacant land to Otis. In 1973, when the company's Yonkers expansion plan was announced, *The Herald Statesman* noted that "by 1980 Otis expects to employ some 2,000 people at the new facility."[2] This represented an increase of six hundred workers over the 1973 staff. Trouble was, though, that 1980 was a long way off, and in the meantime a stagnant U.S. economy caused orders for elevators to drop. This resulted in layoffs at Otis in 1973. The company, nevertheless, proceeded with its expansion plans, breaking ground for a larger plant on a dismal, rainy day in 1974. Two years later, when the new facility was dedicated, both the weather and the economy were decidedly better. With New York governor Hugh Carey and dozens of other government officials in attendance, there was lots of speechmaking. Ralph P. Weller, the chairman of the board of United Technologies Corporation, Otis's parent company, declared that the new plant "will be part of a *new* Yonkers."[3] Having begun his career at Otis while still a student some three decades earlier, Weller was familiar with every aspect of the company's operations and he proudly declared that the Yonkers factory produced "the best high-speed elevator equipment in the world. Yonkers has employees with skills that can't be duplicated."[4] Yonkers mayor Angelo Martinelli, whose company, *Gazette Press,* was forced to relocate because of the Otis expansion, was equally enthusiastic, declaring: "Otis' commitment will be a catalyst for many more industries in Yonkers. Yonkers is on the way back."[5] Like most Yonkers residents, the editor of *The Herald Statesman* could not have been more delighted. He noted in an editorial that Otis's expansion represented collaboration between the company "and the city that gave it birth 123 years ago."[6]

On the day of the dedication, visitors had an opportunity to admire more than bricks and mortar. During a tour that preceded the speeches, they caught a glimpse of a gigantic gearless device similar to what had been installed in the World Trade Center and a newly completed elevator that was about to be shipped to a South African gold mine. Surprised to see a gigantic valve for an offshore oil rig during their stroll through the 243,000 square foot facility, the tour group was enlightened about the special orders Otis filled during periods when a downturn in construction activity reduced the demand for elevators.

For another Yonkers industry, the Loral Corporation, economic slumps were not an issue. Its electronic systems division, at Central Park Avenue and the New York State Thruway, was producing radar jamming and submarine tracking devices and other items used by the U.S. military.

The company provided equipment for F-15 fighter jets, including those sold to foreign nations. Loral also manufactured electronic warfare systems for British and Belgian military aircraft. All told, between 1972 and 1978 Loral experienced a whopping fourfold increase in its business. Despite parking problems and runaway dogs from an animal shelter in the vicinity of its super-secure Yonkers plant, as the decade of the seventies neared an end, the company was confident that the city would address these issues. In fact, Loral was so bullish on Yonkers that, in 1979, it approached New York State about leasing an eighty-six-acre site occupied for nearly a decade by Ridge Hill, an in-patient drug treatment center. This was an offer the state couldn't refuse; Loral obtained a ninety-nine-year lease and began making plans for a low-rise three hundred thousand square foot building.

Urban Renewal (Urban *renewal?*)

Like Otis's decision to stay in Yonkers, Loral's expansion plans warmed the hearts of city officials. The commitment these companies made to Yonkers engendered hope that the long-awaited revitalization politicians and citizens alike had been hoping for was finally occurring. For the better part of two decades, Yonkers, like many other American municipalities, had been attempting to remake itself, with help from the federal and state governments. In reviewing the history of urban renewal in the fourth-largest city in the State of New York, one is struck by the fact that, when the effort got under way in the sixties, this objective seemed attainable. Early in that decade, New York State made good on a promise to give the city a little more than $300,000 for the Jefferson-Riverdale urban renewal project, which was planned for an eleven-acre site near city hall, but in handing over the check, the New York State Division of Housing and Community Renewal warned Yonkers that future grants would be dependent upon the city's ability to relocate families displaced by urban renewal projects. Yonkers officials got the message and began to scramble to find suitable housing. The end result was that the city was able to obtain additional funding; this money was used for Phillipse Towers, the name given the complex of three middle-income buildings, which began to rise on the Jefferson-Riverdale site in 1963.

As Westchester County's first urban renewal project, Phillipse Towers became an object of scrutiny. Government officials, as well as the usual "sidewalk superintendents" who make a habit of strolling by construction sites to monitor a job's progress, took a keen interest in every aspect of the complex, including the playgrounds, garage, swimming pool, and apartment balconies affording a view of the Hudson. Of interest as well was the fact that people already residing in Yonkers were given priority for renting apartments at Phillipse Towers. In 1964, as the complex neared completion, *The New York Times* published a major article titled "Yonkers Works to End Industrial Blight and Revitalize Decaying Areas."[7] The piece, which was accompanied by four illustrations of historic and contemporary scenes, characterized Yonkers as "a prosperous city, but like many other urban communities in the United States it is suffering today from vehicular and pedestrian traffic congestion, inadequate off-street parking, obsolete structures and a generally shabby appearance."[8] The city's ambitious urban renewal program was designed to address these problems. What city officials contemplated was nothing less than a complete transformation of the Getty Square area, which in the prewar period had been "a regional shopping hub serving communities throughout lower Westchester," but now needed revitalization.[9]

What a difference a year makes! In the spring of 1965, *The Herald Statesman* positively oozed enthusiasm in an editorial extolling recently planted red geraniums gracing tubs in the downtown business district. The paper proclaimed: "Geraniums Light Up Getty Square Inspiring Other Beautification" before proceeding to describe a more realistic vision for the downtown area.[10] The *Statesman* noted that Yonkers had filed a revised plan for "a much less ambitious" urban renewal project.[11] This scaled-back version for the Riverview Project, slated for a six-block area behind Phillipse Towers, was prepared at the request of the federal government, which deemed the city's original plan too costly. Despite the note of caution sounded by the federal government, in 1973 the city embarked upon an ambitious program to transform the Getty Square area into a series of auto-free shopping malls occupying five downtown streets converging on the square. With cars tucked away in multilevel parking garages, pedestrians would be free to roam as far as the Hudson. In addition to the malls, city officials envisioned a new police headquarters, library, and civic center, all designed by the firm of noted architect I. M. Pei. Way to go, Yonkers! At least, that's what some residents thought. Others may have been a wee bit disappointed, however, because, unlike an earlier plan, this one did not include an enclosed shopping mall, with major department stores and smaller stores, on Chicken Island. It was omitted because city officials had concluded that Getty Square was not likely to become a regional shopping center. The big stores were at Cross County or along Central Park Avenue and Getty Square just wasn't in the running to attract the kind of anchor stores malls needed. Thus, instead of morphing into a regional center rivaling those in the eastern part of the city, the square would become "a busy, attractive, financially rewarding community, retail and government center"; according to the city's department of development the resources in Getty Square were "at least as impressive as those which led to creation of successful downtown shopping districts in San Francisco, Montreal, Washington, Milwaukee, and other cities."[12] The press dutifully reported that henceforth Getty Square would become a unique community shopping center, having "the flavor of a European town square."[13]

Commenting on the latest proposal for Getty Square, *The Herald Statesman,* while reserving judgment, probably shocked some of its readers by using a four-letter word in an editorial dealing with Getty Square merchants' reactions to the redevelopment plan. The paper urged the Getty Square Merchants' Association and the Chamber of Commerce "to present a unified approach to what the hell is to be done with Getty Square."[14]

The merchants took heed, and responded so quickly that within two months the newspaper was able to report that "Getty Square merchants, and landlords, long known for their resistance to change, are now willing to get the ball rolling."[15] The timing certainly seemed right, because the city council had just voted unanimously (yes, unanimously!) to approve plans for the I. M. Pei complex, which was being called the City Center. Yonkers mayor Alfred B. DelBello termed this "the largest single commitment to the Square the city has ever made."[16] Two years later, at a time when a number of big cities in the state were grappling with a fiscal crisis, Yonkers scaled back plans for what was to have been the centerpiece of the city's renewal efforts. Instead of a complete package composed of a new municipal building, police headquarters, library and seven hundred–car garage, all linked with one another and costing a grand total of $24 million, only the garage, intended to alleviate parking woes, which were a constant source of complaint by merchants and their customers, got the go-ahead. As for the municipal building, that would have to wait, and if, at some point in the future, it made it off the drawing board, it would be considerably smaller than what had been envisioned by I. M. Pei. The end result would be a government complex of municipal, county, state, and federal offices, with each of these levels of government helping fund the project.

In an effort to breathe life into the retail sector of the downtown economy, the city, in 1976, revived the idea of luring major department stores to a redeveloped Getty Square, and toward that end signed a contract with Ginsburg-Taubman Associates giving the development company a year to sign up national retailers. If successful, the firm would become the sole developer of an indoor shopping mall containing more than a million square feet of space. Although Jerome V. Ginsburg had tried and failed a few years earlier to entice major stores to open branches in downtown Yonkers, he was confident that the completion of arterial roads capable of funneling shoppers into the heart of the historic district would sway major retailers. Getting them to commit to Yonkers, however, would take time. A year simply wasn't long enough according to Ginsburg-Taubman. Despite reluctance on the part of some city officials, the developers were granted an extension until 1979 to lure big stores.

In the meantime, on a spring day in 1978, the city began building, with federal funds, a plaza and colonnade that *The New York Times* declared "may have more than the intended cosmetic effect."[17] Unlike the temporary colonnade that had greeted Theodore Roosevelt and the visiting firemen oh so long ago, this structure was supposed to be permanent. Its columns, pedestrian area, and fountain were intended to be a visible symbol of the city's "commitment to Getty Square."[18] Most of the remarks at the groundbreaking ceremony focused on the future, but one speaker provided a somewhat different perspective. Noting that the past often colored the outlook on the future in Yonkers, *The New York Times* informed its readers that Richard Cronin, president of the Yonkers Chamber of Commerce, spoke "of a hope for a return of the days of 'Hello, Dolly!'"[19] According to the paper: "He was thinking of Horace Vandergelder, the Yonkers merchant and his prosperous general store, of course."[20] In the long-running Broadway musical set in the 1890s, actress Carol Channing played the role of a matchmaker who arrived in Yonkers to help the merchant find the perfect wife. She identified ideal mates for employees and relatives of the bachelor store owner while she herself went after the well-to-do merchant.

Hello, Dolly! made some residents of the "Queen City of the Hudson" yearn for the good old days, but that was just wishful thinking. So, too, was the belief that Yonkers could transform its historic business district into a major regional center, this despite the fact that Ginsburg-Taubman Associates expressed confidence that it could be done, provided the city extended its contract with the firm for a minimum of two years beyond its 1979 expiration and withheld city approval for large commercial projects in areas outside Getty Square. Downtown merchants and many citizens of Yonkers were opposed to the extension; they wanted a quick fix for two decades of decline. Instead of large-scale development along the lines of what Taubman, with a local partner, had undertaken in Stamford, Connecticut, they felt Yonkers should opt for something more modest that would take the form of neighborhood retail development. What the Yonkers Chamber of Commerce envisioned was a Getty Square dotted with stores that "would meet the needs of the people who live in the area of the Square, rather than planning a development that must attract customers from the Cross County Shopping Center and Central Park Avenue shopping area."[21] In April 1979, the city challenged the developers to either commit to the original concept of a regional mall containing more than a million square feet of space or get behind a neighborhood shopping area of two hundred thousand square feet. Since Yonkers was forfeiting an estimated $650,000 in tax revenue for every year Getty Square redevelopment remained on hold, time was clearly of the essence here.

In the end, the "Queen City of the Hudson's" historic downtown was not reshaped by Ginsburg-Taubman. Yet, the old saying about one door closing and another opening certainly seemed applicable to Yonkers in 1979. The idea of Getty Square as a regional shopping center was no longer feasible but there was an exciting new vision for the city's neglected waterfront. S/E Asset Development, together with the Morelite Construction Company, unveiled plans for a hotel, convention center, restaurants, a new recreation pier, restoration of the pier used by the Hudson River Day Line, and refurbishing of the former trolley barn. Best of all, the developers were willing to put up a substantial amount of money for these projects. Since previous development plans dating back to the early seventies had gone nowhere, there was cautious optimism about the latest proposal.

Playing Politics

The revitalization of downtown Yonkers, including the waterfront, was one of a number of key issues the city's leaders had to address in the sixties and seventies. There were times, however, when politics got in the way, preventing speedy resolution of problems. In Yonkers, politics was not a polite parlor game. Rather, it was, figuratively speaking, more reminiscent of the televised wrestling matches so popular in the mid-twentieth century, but instead of coming to blows, those who played the game of politics in Yonkers hurled verbal salvos at one another. Still, there was a "rock'em, sock'em" quality to politics in the "Queen City of the Hudson." Hey, maybe it was something in the water! Just kidding, but, actually, one can't help thinking of Yonkers politicos quaffing something stronger than water, for example the robust beverage that once poured forth from Underhill's Brewery. No sissy tea in bone china cups for these guys and the occasional woman who ventured into city politics! Actually, no matter what one's preferred beverage was, even if it happened to be good old H_2O from the Hillview Reservoir, those who entered the political fray in Yonkers had to have thick skin to survive, especially when they had to respond to the question: "Is Yonkers wicked?"

This query arose in connection with a State Investigation Commission inquiry into illegal gambling in Westchester County in 1963. The commission was especially interested in Yonkers because the city was said to be a bookmaking mecca. Thomas A. Brogan, the chairman of the Democratic Committee, who was "reputedly the most powerful political figure in this city of 200,000," disagreed.[22] According to him, Yonkers was "one of the cleanest cities of its size."[23] Alice Allen, a Republican council member, said: "I wouldn't know a bookie if I fell over one."[24] Mayor John E. (Chippie) Flynn, a Republican, who would go on to an illustrious career in the New York State Legislature, serving as a state senator from 1967 through 1986, said that he had been informed about places where illegal betting was occurring but, he declared: "I honestly can't say where they are."[25] As far as Flynn was concerned, City Manager Charles L. Curran should have been responding to the allegations. Curran did respond following eleven days of hearings, during which Carl A. Vergari, chief counsel to the State Investigation Commission, estimated the total revenue from illegal gambling in Yonkers to be a whopping $10 million annually. Vergari also insinuated that the police were turning a blind eye to what was going on. City Manager Curran disagreed. After reviewing the voluminous transcript of the hearings, he concluded that there was insufficient evidence to warrant charges. As far as he was concerned, most police officers and the Yonkers public safety commissioner were honest people. Be that as it may, Yonkers complied with the State Investigation Commission's recommendation to rotate officers in and out of the detective division in order to create greater efficiency in the police department. The police department was also required to revise its reporting system. In 1963, the department actually investigated 54 percent more cases than what appeared in official reports, but the reports themselves were deficient because of the peculiar way of categorizing certain crimes. A number of burglaries were listed under missing dogs and the disappearance of concrete benches, each weighing three hundred pounds, appeared as missing objects.

In addition to new faces in the detective division and a revised system for reporting police investigations, there was a big change in city hall. Mayor Flynn, who was elected to the New York State Senate in 1966, resigned his post in Yonkers, and Governor Nelson A. Rockefeller appointed Dr. James F. X. O'Rourke to serve the remainder of Flynn's mayoral term. Within months of taking office, Mayor O'Rourke found himself in the midst of a controversy involving City Manager Frederick

J. Adler, who in 1965 succeeded William Walsh Jr., city manager since the retirement of Charles L. Curran in 1963. Adler was dismissed after being charged with inefficient management, which had resulted in a budget deficit and new taxes. As a parting shot, Adler fired five city employees, including the corporation counsel. They were quickly reinstated by his successor, Acting City Manager Merrill A. Portman, chairman of the board of assessors. Two months later Elder Gunter, a deputy assistant secretary in the U.S. Department of Housing and Urban Development, was appointed city manager. In less than a year he was gone, driven from Yonkers, in part, by the daunting challenge posed by the city's nearly $12 million budget gap. Mr. Gunter may have felt fortunate to have vacated his position before Yonkers made headlines for a private carting arrangement that allegedly cost taxpayers $1 million a year. Once again, the State Investigation Commission descended upon Yonkers to search for suspected corruption in the city's government. During two weeks of hearings in 1969, the commission sought evidence to substantiate suspicions that city officials had permitted private carting firms to use the Yonkers incinerator while municipal garbage trucks were diverted to other locations to dump their refuse. Alfred B. DelBello, who had been elected mayor that November, defeating the incumbent Dr. James F. X. O'Rourke to become not only the first Democratic mayor of Yonkers in thirty-two years but, at age thirty-five, the youngest mayor in Yonkers history, said that upon taking office he would recommend the appointment of a special counsel to initiate legal action aimed at recouping money lost due to the garbage arrangement. In an editorial titled "Yonkers: Another Newark?" *The New York Times* compared Yonkers with the troubled city across the river in New Jersey. Referring to the recent State Investigation Commission hearings, the *Times* pointed out that the Westchester County district attorney had launched a grand jury investigation and that Alfred DelBello would be sworn in as mayor on New Year's Day; DelBello, in the opinion of the paper, had "a reputation for energy and honesty. He will need all of that and more as he undertakes his staggering responsibilities."[26]

Since DelBello was the first Democratic mayor in more than three decades, his election was a sign that the citizens of Yonkers desired a change. DelBello was prepared to give the voters what they wanted and, in the process, put Yonkers on the map. In his first month in office the new mayor played host to the mayors of the six largest cities in New York State. Yonkers was the first stop on a series of tours designed to acquaint the mayors with the common challenges confronting their municipalities. *The Herald Statesman* published a lengthy article, titled "Mayors See Us At Our Worst," detailing how Yonkers greeted New York City's mayor,

John Lindsay, along with the mayors of Buffalo, Rochester, Syracuse, and Albany.[27] According to the paper, Mayor DelBello, who conducted a narrated tour for his visiting colleagues, included run-down portions of Yonkers because he felt "they're the most interesting."[28] During the tour, DelBello pointed out that Yonkers lacked funding to complete projects that had been begun.

By the end of his first year in office, DelBello had taken steps to address matters the State Investigation Commission had enumerated in a report labeling Yonkers a city "riddled with corruption."[29] Gone were the days when private carters received preferential treatment at the Yonkers incinerator, and that was only the beginning. The city's purchasing practices were revised and party patronage gave way to the appointment of professionals. Since many of the new hires were not Yonkers residents, there was a hue and a cry but DelBello stuck to his guns. The mayor's choice for city manager was Seymour Scher, city manager of Rochester, who held a doctorate in political science from the University of Chicago. Appointed to the Yonkers post in 1971, Scher was the first professional manager, with big city experience, in two decades. Only time would tell whether Mayor DelBello's emphasis upon professionalism and reform would be the antidote to the corruption he sought to eliminate. As for citizen reaction to all of this, given the fact that Yonkers mayors served for only two years, DelBello didn't have to wait long to learn how his constituents felt about the new broom sweeping every nook and cranny of city hall clean as a whistle. On the way to the 1971 election, however, something untoward occurred. The mayor's campaign office on Yonkers Avenue was riddled with bullets late one night. Although DelBello concluded that someone was probably trying to send him a message about getting out of the race, he didn't back down. DelBello stayed in the race and was reelected by a margin of more than eight thousand votes. Fellow Democrats running for the city council did not fare as well, however. The Democrats lost two of the eight seats on the council, with the result that the body was evenly divided between Republicans and Democrats.

Shortly after the election and before the new council took office, the existing city council, which had been battling with the city manager over the restructuring of the police department, attempted to thwart Scher's efforts to dismiss the public safety commissioner. Viewing the council's stance as a vote of no confidence in his own leadership, Dr. Scher handed in his resignation. The timing could not have been worse. A teachers' strike, discussed later in this chapter, was under way, and the city's other unions were working under old contracts that had to be renegotiated. Complicating the unsettled labor situation was the fact that Yonkers anticipated a $3 million budget deficit for the next fiscal year. In the end, the city manager did not resign, at least not right away, because the city council did an about-face and passed a vote of confidence expressing its support for him. Only in Yonkers! That the city council and the city manager patched things up was a welcome sign in a municipality where the negatives seemed to outweigh the positives.

Soon after Alfred DelBello was sworn in for his second term, the police staged a job action to express their dissatisfaction with contract negotiations, which had proceeded slowly before coming to a complete halt. Although the contract matter was resolved, other issues surfaced in 1972, among them a city council resolution calling for abolition of the city manager form of government and its replacement by a strong mayor. To many people in Yonkers government, Seymour Scher was too forceful. His successful efforts to eliminate patronage had rubbed politicians of both parties the wrong way. Thus, it came as no surprise that he was "considerably more popular with the electorate at large than he has been among the professional politicians."[30] Average citizens were pleased with Scher's reorganization of the police department and his insistence upon competitive bidding for city contracts. Thanks to Scher, Yonkers had a balanced budget for the first time in a decade, in part because of job cuts. Seymour Scher remained city manager until the end of the DelBello administration. Having announced that he would not run for a third term as mayor of Yonkers, DelBello was chosen as the Democratic candidate for county executive. His election, in 1973, was historic because it was the first time a Democrat was elected to the position.

Mayor Martinelli

Meanwhile, back in Yonkers that fall Angelo Martinelli, a successful businessman and the Republican candidate for mayor, defeated his Democratic opponent, John R. Morrissey. Commenting on the transition from the DelBello administration to that of Mayor Martinelli, *The Herald Statesman,* referring to the new positions assumed by both men, noted that the mayor's position was "perhaps even more exciting than DelBello's," because the mayor "has the opportunity to preside over two elements vital to the city's future—the redevelopment of Getty Square and the development of the Hudson River Waterfront."[31]

As things turned out, Mayor Martinelli also had the "opportunity" to preside over a fiscal crisis of enormous proportions. The specter of default, with all of its terrifying implications, seemed light years away, however, at the mayor's gala inauguration on a chilly New Year's Day in 1974. Since the United States was in the midst of an energy crisis at the time, the new mayor decided to have an outdoor ceremony in order to conserve both heat and electricity. Despite the on and off rain and temperatures hovering in the thirties, more than five hundred people turned out for the event. The swearing-in ceremony, for both the mayor and the city council, was conducted by a Yonkers native son, Malcolm Wilson, who had succeeded Nelson Rockefeller as governor of New York State in December 1973 when Rockefeller resigned "to devote his efforts to a commission he organized on Critical Choices for America."[32] Rockefeller was appointed to serve as Gerald Ford's vice president the following year.

If the inauguration was any indication Mayor Martinelli's first term got off to a great start, but after a year in office, he was deflecting criticism about all sorts of things. His opponents were pointing accusing fingers at stalled urban renewal efforts, a big leap in unemployment, and juvenile delinquency so severe that the city was seriously thinking about imposing a curfew on young residents. One bright spot, however, was the Nepperhan arterial highway, but according to *The New York Times,* which characterized the new road as a lifeline, "the lifeline itself may not assure recovery."[33] The city's topography could be overcome by new roads linking the east side with the west but the racial and economic barriers were something else. One year into his first term, Mayor Martinelli surely had his work cut out for him. Although the *Times* contended that Martinelli dominated the city council, it noted that council members were "elected from wards and whose primary interests are most often local rather than citywide"; the paper went on to say: "Council sessions often flare into shouting matches and last until well past midnight."[34] Toward the end of the lengthy article it devoted to Mayor Martinelli's first year in office, *The New York Times* mentioned the city's potentially serious fiscal situation. In the next few years, it would allocate lots of space to the crisis that brought the city to the edge of insolvency.

Yonkers was not alone in grappling with enormous financial woes. Indeed, to a certain extent the city's problems were overshadowed by those of its big neighbor to the south. When Yonkers had difficulty selling bond anticipation notes in the fall of 1975, City Manager J. Emmet Casey placed part of the blame on the fact that investors perceived New York and Yonkers as being in the same boat in terms of risk. Of course the fact that Moody's Investors Service reduced Yonkers's rating from A to B-AA didn't help. Moody's criticized the city's management practices, including the fact that, for a number of years, Yonkers had not converted short-term obligations to longer-term bonds. Another no-no was rolling over expenses from one fiscal year to the next and moving some expenses from the operating to the capital budget, which enabled the city to pay for these items by borrowing. Of course, one can only do this for so long. Eventually the piper must be paid. Yonkers found this out the hard way. The city simply did not have the money to repay $21.8 million in short-term notes due on November 14, 1975. With bankruptcy just around the corner, Yonkers looked to New York State for help. While the legislature considered various remedies, *The New York Times* published an article criticizing Mayor Martinelli for failing to deliver on his promises. After noting that the mayor had "promised a bright future" for his city while he was campaigning, the paper was quick to point out that "few of his promises have materialized. . . . Bank officials have asked the city why they should assist a municipality that faces default and yet refuses to raise its own taxes."[35]

As things turned out, Yonkers did have to increase its sales tax and raise property taxes to the legal limit as part of an agreement with New York State. The deal also required a pay freeze for city employees and elimination of a $6 million budget deficit within a year. This was part of the price Yonkers paid for the state legislature to come to its rescue by providing $10 million. Banks would supply $15 million, but via a circuitous route. Concerned about a direct loan to Yonkers, the banks agreed to purchase $15 million of the State Insurance Fund's securities, and the State Insurance Fund then turned around and provided this sum, as a loan, to Yonkers. Before Yonkers could grab onto the big life preserver the state was willing to toss it, the city was required to accept a financial control board, an oversight group similar to the one created for New York City. The Yonkers board was composed of Mayor Martinelli, the city manager, New York State comptroller Arthur Levitt, Secretary of State Mario Cuomo, and three citizens appointed by Governor Hugh Carey and approved by the state senate. This was tough medicine to swallow but the Yonkers City Council, in a rare show of unanimity, approved the legislative package by a vote of 13 to 0. Yet, according to *The Herald Statesman,* "the City Council appears to have lost the most power" as a result of the new state oversight, which was expected to last for at least three years.[36] Nevertheless, the paper was cautiously optimistic about the city's ability to emerge from the financial morass, provided its citizens were upbeat. "One advantage Yonkers can maintain now and during the months to come as the city wrestles to overcome its financial problems is a positive attitude," declared the paper.[37]

Unions representing city workers were anything but cheerful. There were threats of suits against the city because the wage freeze would preclude the granting of previously negotiated increments. In addition, there was opposition to drastic cuts in the capital budget. Gone were funds for the design and planning phase of the new police headquarters; so, too, the purchase of police cars, erection of new fire stations, and refurbishing of existing ones were all shelved. School renovation projects were going to be undertaken on a decelerated timetable to save money but, as part of the commitment to revitalize downtown Yonkers, the city center and municipal parking garage were going forward. Despite all of the cuts, the city was still experiencing major problems. In December 1975, as municipal unions staged a rally to protest the wage freeze, the city once again found itself in the predicament of not having the funds to repay noteholders. As before, the banks were unwilling to take a chance on Yonkers until New York State purchased the bulk of the more than $12 million in tax anticipation notes the city needed to sell, to cover notes due in both December and January plus pay normal municipal expenses. Once the state agreed to take nearly $9 million in one-year bond antici- pation notes, local banks bought $3.5 million. Thus, with "Default Again Averted," as the headline in *The Herald Statesman* proclaimed, Yonkers could breathe a little easier, at least for a while, and city workers, whose paychecks banks waited briefly before cashing until they verified the city's balance for every check, could finally get their money on time.[38]

City Managers: Here Today, Gone Tomorrow

No sooner had the latest episode in the ongoing saga of the fiscal cri- sis concluded than Yonkers faced a perennial problem, namely booting out a city manager who didn't want to go. Aside from the fact that the new city council, to be sworn in on New Year's Day, would have a Democratic majority and might want to choose a new city manager to replace J. Emmet Casey, appointed by Republican mayor Martinelli, there was a growing rift between the mayor and the city manager. Indeed, Martinelli asked Casey to step down supposedly because, before seeking state help with the city's financial problems, Casey met with bankers and as part of his open government philosophy, toward the end of October he allowed reporters to sit in on a meeting, "revealing the city's risk of default and jeopardizing the election of the Mayor."[39] Martinelli went on to win reelection but his margin of victory was less than he expected. In mid-December, Mayor Martinelli joined forces with Dominick Iannacone, a city council member who, beginning in January, would be the leader of the new Democratic majority on the council. Together they co-sponsored a resolution asserting that Casey's deficiencies as an administrator had led to a "substantial budget deficit and debt."[40] Casey was accused of failing to comply with "stringent fiscal restraints mandated by the City Council."[41] To many Yonkers residents and some members of the city council, these were trumped-up charges, but Casey was nonetheless suspended. His deputy, Vincent Castaldo, was appointed acting city manager. Almost immediately he found himself in hot water for failing to consult the mayor and city council, in a timely fashion, about the specifics of a proposal enumerating all sorts of unpopular ways of complying with a budget reduction mandated by the state. Branch libraries and a number of public schools would be closed, school crossing guards would be eliminated, and the city would no longer fund the Hudson River Museum nor any public celebrations. Most drastic of all, fully one-fourth of city workers would be cut from the payroll.

In the midst of the mayor's squabble with the acting city manager, some members of the city council, concerned that the politicization of the budget crisis was detrimental to Yonkers, put forward a resolution calling for the removal of Mayor Martinelli and Councilman Iannacone from the financial control review board. The resolution was defeated by one vote. Commenting on all of this in an editorial, *The New York Times* declared: "The day of reckoning has been long in coming in Yonkers."[42] From the paper's perspective, Yonkers politics had accelerated the arrival of that day. Singling out the city council, the paper said the city's legislative body was mired in "ward-oriented squabbles" that detracted from its real work.[43] The mayor came in for criticism as well. He was accused of "usurpation of powers" that belonged to the city manager.[44] The only remedy, at this point, was compliance with the directives of the Yonkers Emergency Financial Control Board.

When the Yonkers Emergency Financial Control Board held a closed meeting at Yonkers City Hall two days after Christmas, Mayor Martinelli and Councilman Iannacone called for revisions in the planned cuts, but they were outvoted by state comptroller Levitt and Secretary of State Mario Cuomo. Ultimately the mayor and councilman voted for the plan, which required closing the Yonkers jail, three branch libraries, seven schools, three fire stations, and the Hudson River Museum; city services were also cut. Amazingly, the person who had to oversee this mammoth municipal downsizing was none other than J. Emmet Casey. Following his suspension, Casey had demanded a public hearing, to which he was entitled, and word got around that he was planning to use this forum to play the blame game on a grand scale, accusing the mayor of bringing the city down financially by interfering in the budgetary process and the general administration of the city. To avoid this, or, to use the words of Councilman Iannacone, "to stem any further polarization of our community," Casey was reappointed, by a vote of the city council, which passed a resolution withdrawing the charges that had resulted in Casey's suspension.[45] Mayor Martinelli, who felt that a public hearing would have provided "the public with the facts and truth," cast a negative vote on the reinstatement of Casey and the retraction of the charges against him.[46] After all of this, Casey resumed his post for only a month before resigning, and in a sort of instant replay Vincent Castaldo was chosen by the city council to serve as Yonkers City Manager.

The Deepening Financial Crisis

Although Castaldo would have to deal with the city's ongoing financial problems, during his brief second stint as city manager Casey had to grapple with a rollback of municipal salaries to the level of June 30, 1975. Reducing teachers' salaries was a real conundrum because the State Supreme Court had ruled, the previous September, that the board of education could not change the pay scale included in the teachers' current contract even if the city council did not provide the money to enable the board to fulfill its contractual obligation to the teachers. What could the council do? That was the key question at a city council meeting attended by five hundred citizens. Amidst boos, shouts, and some cheers, the members of the council voted to request the state legislature to authorize a rollback in municipal salaries, including those of teachers. The council also initiated the process leading to the imposition of a 1 percent income tax on everyone who worked in Yonkers. Requiring municipal workers, whose wages had been rolled back, to pay an additional tax on their reduced salaries was perceived as adding insult to injury. By itself, the rollback, combined with state ordered cuts resulting in the dismissal of additional workers, was difficult to accept, and workers' displeasure was evidenced by calling in sick and refusing to do anything not specifically required by their job descriptions. When sanitation men refused to operate equipment they claimed was unsafe, the garbage began piling up. As long as snow camouflaged the accumulating mess, there weren't too many complaints, but after twelve days without garbage pickup, Mayor Martinelli, citing the threat to public health, threatened to fire the sanitation workers unless they performed their duties.

Dealing with recalcitrant city workers was one thing. Figuring out how to meet the next deadline for repaying short-term notes was another.

Yonkers missed a Friday midnight deadline in February 1976 and was technically in default, but officials, including J. Emmet Casey, who was quite literally on his way out of government, rolled up their sleeves and called officers of banks, some of whom were enjoying a winter weekend on the ski slopes. In the end, a few banks purchased one-year notes and a number of state agencies galloped to the rescue by purchasing most of the city's obligations. The fact that local banks were willing to commit was viewed as an especially good sign. During a news conference, Mayor Martinelli pointed out that the involvement of local banks was significant. "We now have the largest participation by banks. It's more than ever," he noted.[47] *The Herald Statesman* was not overly impressed. In an editorial, the paper warned that while the city had avoided default, funding operating expenses remained a major challenge. Moreover, New York State had to borrow funds to assist Yonkers, which "means both the state and the city will be paying interest on the same money. All this invites more serious questions about the continuing crisis."[48]

New York State was not only asking those questions but attempting to answer them. The state comptroller's office was looking into long-term financing for Yonkers through the sale of fifteen and twenty-year bonds. Whether any big purchasers were willing to make that sort of commitment to a city that had narrowly avoided bankruptcy multiple times remained to be seen. Large banks were helping both New York City and New York State and were wary of getting involved with municipalities such as Yonkers. Yet, State Comptroller Arthur Levitt urged Yonkers to turn to the banks for help in meeting a rapidly approaching mid-March deadline for repaying short-term notes and renewing bond anticipation notes. In a sense, Levitt was reading the riot act to Yonkers and other municipalities that had relied on the state to bail them out. Given the magnitude of the problems facing not only New York City and Yonkers but Buffalo, Rochester, and Syracuse as well, the New York State Legislature appropriated funds for those cities. The money was included in the state budget for the year beginning April 1, 1977, but the cities were permitted to access it for their fiscal years beginning July 1, 1976. Things were looking up—at last.

In October 1976, City Manager Castaldo stepped before the microphones to announce that an investment syndicate had agreed to purchase nearly $84 million in short and long-term city bonds, some stretching out for twenty years, at interest rates lower than expected. This seeming miracle occurred because the city council, though not overly enthusiastic about the idea, had requested and secured passage of state legislation requiring that a percentage of the city's tax revenue be set aside annually to ensure repayment of securities. City Manager Castaldo was positively jubilant about the bond sale. "The Little Apple has pulled out," he declared; speaking with reporters in his city hall office, Castaldo said: "It's a good day, a very good day. We're the Little Apple, right next to the Big Apple, but we pulled ourselves out in seven months."[49] Within days of the big announcement about the bond sale, Yonkers was buzzing about a distinguished visitor who would soon arrive in the city: President Gerald Ford, who came to town in mid-October to sign new revenue-sharing legislation extending this federal program to 1980. The bond sale notwithstanding, Yonkers really needed the money, as did other communities that benefited from the legislation. How the money was used raised some red flags, however. The Yonkers chapter of the National Association for the Advancement of Colored People claimed that the city was using revenue-sharing funds to pay the salaries of its mostly white police and fire departments and hence was not abiding by the antidiscrimination provisions of the law.

By the spring of 1977, Yonkers was looking forward to having a balanced budget by June 30. If all went well, the supervision of its finances by the emergency financial control board would end six months later, as stipulated in the legislation creating the board, but there was one catch. Yonkers was awaiting a judicial ruling on its appeal of a State Supreme Court decision negating the dismissal of 350 teachers at the height of the fiscal crisis. If Yonkers lost on appeal it would not only have to offer the teachers jobs but give them back pay amounting to as much as $5 million. State Comptroller Arthur Levitt determined that should this occur, the city would have to charge the back pay to its current budget, making it impossible for Yonkers to avoid continuing scrutiny of its every financial move. In mid-June the city lost the appeal, but the state comptroller's office softened its stance and permitted Yonkers to issue bonds to raise the money needed to meet its court-ordered obligations to the dismissed teachers.

Besides the issue relating to the teachers, Yonkers was grappling with a very unhappy police force in the spring of 1977. Dissatisfied with the increments recommended by an arbitrator, officers by the droves staged a sick-out. At the onset of the "blue flu" police were nowhere to be seen, but lieutenants and sergeants "recovered" and provided minimal security for the fourth-largest city in the state. After four days everyone was back thanks to a former Yonkers mayor, State Senator John E. Flynn, who convinced the police union that passage by the state legislature of a state aid bill for municipalities was virtually assured. When the walkout ended, "the apprehension that filled Yonkers . . . receded . . . as patrol cars returned to the city's streets."[50] To everyone's dismay, it resurfaced less than two weeks later when State Comptroller Levitt refused to allow the city to balance its budget by using aid included in the Municipal Overburden Bill then awaiting passage. The city council had no choice but to approve a budget that omitted the expected state aid, but since raises for the police force were predicated upon the receipt of the state funds, officers were disheartened. When contract negotiations between the city and the Yonkers Patrolmen's Benevolent Association broke down in early July, the president of the P.B.A. accused city officials of "bad-faith bargaining" and called for the intervention of a state arbitrator.[51] Once the police contract issue was resolved things were again looking up in Yonkers. In August, the city was able to sell short-term notes to the Bank of New York. From one perspective, this was a very positive development, but given all that Yonkers had been through in the past few years, some citizens wondered whether their city was truly out of the woods.

The Game of Politics, Yonkers Style

The city's problems, both actual and potential, were the subject of con-siderable debate during the 1977 mayoral contest. Foreshadowing the election was an attempt, spearheaded by Mayor Martinelli, to end the city manager form of government. The mayor's Democratic opponents, however, mustered enough support to defeat a 1976 referendum calling for the replacement of the city manager system by a strong mayor. In the 1977 mayoral election the Democrats nominated Dominick Iannacone, the majority leader of the city council. Iannacone was also the candidate of the newly created City Manager Party. Martinelli received the endorsement of the Republican and Conservative Parties. Running against both men was Randy Guilette, a twenty-two-year-old social worker nominated by the Liberal Party. In a sort of primer of Yonkers politics for uninitiated readers, *The New York Times* explained that central to the mayoral race was City Manager Vincent Castaldo "and whether voters support or oppose his conduct of city government."[52] Providing background on the type of government Yonkers had, the paper said that "the majority party in the council governs along with the city manager," with the mayor being pri-marily a ceremonial figure.[53] Getting down to specifics, the *Times* pointed out that the mayor and city manager had been at odds for two years and that the mayor "maintains the dispute is the result of his attempt to be 'an independent voice and ombudsman' for Yonkers residents. He terms Mr. Iannacone a 'rubber stamp' for Mr. Castaldo."[54] The paper went on to quote the mayor, who was quick to add: "I haven't opposed Mr. Castaldo on everything, but only when I think he is wrong."[55] The mayor also indicated that should the Republicans and Conservatives win a majority of the thirteen seats on the city council, and hence be in a position to choose a city manager, this would not "necessarily" mean that Castaldo would be replaced as city manager.[56]

The fate of Mr. Castaldo was, nevertheless, a major issue in the campaign, along with the ongoing fiscal crisis, the police walkout earlier in the year, and a lengthy teachers' strike, discussed in a subsequent section of this chapter. In the midst of the campaign there was a grand jury investigation of charges that Mr. Iannacone had used the career center of the Yonkers schools and some of its students to print his campaign literature. The Democrats created some unfavorable publicity for Mayor Martinelli by spreading the word that his printing firm produced tip sheets for horse races. There was nothing illegal about this, but the Iannacone camp was quick to point that this sort of betting information could be used for illegal gambling. None of this hurt the incumbent. He emerged victorious in the November election, as did the Republican Party, which gained a majority of seats on the city council.

Before the new council members took office, the existing council planned to vote a 50 percent pay increase for council members and the mayor. Not so fast, was the reaction of hundreds of citizens who converged on city hall for a public hearing on the proposed raises. With the police walkout and teachers' strike still fresh in their minds and ongoing concern about the city's fiscal situation, residents who packed the council chambers sent a very clear message to their elected representatives. The result was that the salary increase was shelved. Something that couldn't be shelved, however, was the ticklish matter of whether to retain or replace City Manager Castaldo. In January 1978, once the Republican majority had assumed control of the city council, speculation about Castaldo's likely departure was rampant. Castaldo himself, however, was not about to leave quietly. "I will be City Manager as long as I wish," he told a reporter soon after the start of the new year, but he qualified this by saying that he would remain in his position until the city council withdrew its support.[57] The reporter wondered whether Castaldo, who held a position that was supposed to be apolitical, was being confrontational. Providing a little background on the city manager's approach, the reporter pointed out that Castaldo could be perceived as "a hometown kid playing a scrappy and aggressive game on his home court."[58] At the end of January Castaldo's supporters were not cheering but Republicans in city government were, because the city manager resigned. He did not leave quietly, however. Rather, he pointed an accusing finger at his opponents, claiming that his ability to administer the city had been hampered by the Republicans on the city council.

Succeeding Vincent Castaldo was Pat Ravo, deputy city manager. A native of New Jersey who had come to Yonkers as parks commissioner in 1974, Ravo declared at the time of his appointment as city manager that he was a career public official and as such refrained from taking sides politically. He then proceeded to set a new tone at city hall by quite literally opening the door that separated the city manager's office from the mayor's office. Although the bolt that had long barred the occupants of the two offices from entering each other's space was removed, new barriers were being erected by the city council. A month after Ravo took over as city manager, the council adopted new rules depriving the mayor and the majority leader of the right to set agendas for meetings; the mayor was also deprived of his power to appoint committee members. They would be chosen by a new rules committee. In addition, the mayor was denied the right to call special meetings, and he would no longer be a voting member of committees. Since the only power a ceremonial mayor has under a city manager form of government resides in his role as presiding officer of the city council, this was a major blow to Mayor Martinelli, especially as some Republican members of the council joined with Democrats to enact the new rules. Authorship of the rules was attributed to Nicholas V. Longo, a Republican councilman whose opponent in the previous fall's election had garnered the support of Martinelli, thereby leading to a primary fight for the nomination. The city council's new rules represented a major change in the way the business of government was conducted in Yonkers. The same could be said for City Manager Ravo's consolidation of twenty-eight separate agencies of city government. In the spring of 1978, Ravo proposed having them subsumed by seven super-agencies, each with a commissioner reporting directly to the city manager.

A *New* Day Dawning?

Besides making government more efficient, the city moved ahead with a public relations campaign to tidy up its image. Yonkers hoped that a series of advertisements in national magazines, highlighting its proximity to New York City and favorable business climate as evidenced by "the recent move by Saks Fifth Avenue to establish a warehouse here," as well as the proposed Getty Square redevelopment, would lure new business.[59] As far as Pat Ravo was concerned, Yonkers needed all of the new business it could get because once again, to achieve a balanced budget, major surgery in the form of massive dismissals of city workers and a 13 percent increase in taxes seemed likely unless the lobbying efforts of the city's representatives in the state legislature were successful. What Yonkers really wanted was a no-strings-attached grant of the sort New York City had obtained from Albany. This would have been especially welcome in view of a recent judicial ruling denying Yonkers and other New York State cities the right to raise taxes above the constitutional limit for certain budgetary items. Instead of direct aid, however, Yonkers received an offer that, despite the protests of the city council, it couldn't refuse. The state was willing to provide a $10,000,000 loan, to be repaid within four years. In the end, the city council relented but as Assemblyman Thomas McInerney, who had helped guide the loan measure through the legislature, said, the loan provided to Yonkers was "just buying it some time."[60] In all fairness, there was an upside to this. Had the money not been forthcoming, the projected layoffs might have led to mass protests and job actions by city workers. The resulting reduction in city services would have spawned growing dissatisfaction on the part of the electorate. As it was, dozens of white collar workers at Yonkers City Hall called in sick for several days in July 1978 to protest projected layoffs after Comptroller Levitt refused to approve the city's budget. He did so because the city council, in order to repay the state loan enabling Yonkers to avoid layoffs, had voted to increase the utility tax without seeking legislative and gubernatorial approval of the home-rule measure required for the increase. The matter was resolved and the new budget was approved by the comptroller. In the meantime, Yonkers operated under the funding limits in the previous year's budget.

Although future job cuts and their consequences were by no means ruled out, Yonkers had bought itself some breathing space and the city had balanced its budget. Consequently, as stipulated in the terms of the agreement establishing the Yonkers Emergency Financial Control Board three years earlier, the city was able to regain control of its finances. Going forward, for the next twenty years the New York State comptroller would still evaluate the city's estimates of revenues and expenditures and set aside funds needed to pay interest and part of the principal on money Yonkers had borrowed. However, the minute scrutiny of the city's finances exercised by the emergency financial control board ended when the board officially disbanded on December 31, 1978. A month earlier, when board members took a vote on the formal dissolution of their body, State Comptroller Arthur Levitt declared: "Through our action today the board is released of its responsibility in the affairs of the fair city of Yonkers."[61] Surely this was cause for celebration, but not everyone was ecstatic. Mayor Martinelli, who earlier that month had lost the election for a congressional seat from the Twenty-Third District to Peter Peyser, wasn't so sure. A fiscal conservative, Martinelli, whose role as a member of the emergency financial control board was seen as augmenting his power as mayor, declared, as the board was on its way out, that it had provided a "stable feeling and confidence."[62] Confidence began to disappear in some quarters, however, literally within hours after the board held its final meeting at Yonkers City Hall. That very day, City Manager Pat Ravo conducted a budget briefing for the city council to discuss finances for the next fiscal year. Ravo laid everything out, telling the councilmen that Yonkers would have to, once again, reduce services unless the city could generate more revenue. Ravo's suggestion for coming up with more money was to impose a citywide income tax. Howls of protest went up, and not just from the councilmen. Mayor Martinelli was opposed to the very idea of an income tax because of the chilling effect it would have on the city's efforts to attract more business.

While the debate over the income tax dragged on, the city's elected officials had a new challenge. Stalled contract talks with the firefighters' union resulted in a one-hour walkout by firefighters in March 1979. A month later, after the firefighters obtained a new contract, sanitation workers resorted to a slowdown when the city's negotiations with their union came to a halt. When both sides agreed to the intervention of a state mediator, sanitation workers made quick work disposing of the fragrant mess created by one thousand tons of garbage decorating sidewalks all over the city. Before the month ended, the sanitation workers had a new contract. Since Yonkers teachers had obtained a new contract in November 1978, that left only the Patrolmen's Benevolent Association and the Civil Service Employees Association, and negotiations with those organizations were proceeding. In addition to the labor harmony Yonkers was enjoying in the spring of 1979, there was the added bonus of a projected revenue surplus as the fiscal year neared its end. To ensure that the city would continue to be financially stable, however, the budget adopted by the city council for the fiscal year beginning July 1, 1979, contained a property tax hike of a little over 5 percent.

Concern about the tax increase was voiced by some voters during the 1979 election campaign but more significant, from the standpoint of Mayor Martinelli, who was making a bid for a fourth term, was the tendency of his opponent, Councilman Gerald E. Loehr, to emphasize problems relating to the Yonkers Community Development Agency. An audit of the agency by the state comptroller's office turned up recordkeeping and accounting problems. Loehr was able to make political capital of this because the mayor was a member of the agency's board, but there was another aspect as well. Herman Keith, program manager of the agency, and a number of other minorities employed by the agency were dismissed the summer before the mayoral election. At the time, a spokesman for Mayor Martinelli said that the mayor "had no control" over the agency and that the dismissals had resulted from a decision by the United States Department of Housing and Urban Development concerning the percentage of federal funding that could be used for agency salaries.[63] Mr. Keith, who was president of the Yonkers branch of the National Association for the Advancement of Colored People, viewed the dismissals as political retribution because of his role as an advocate for minorities. The ongoing controversy over the dismissals was a factor in the outcome of the mayoral election. Although the vote was close, Loehr defeated Martinelli. With a new mayor and a city council composed of seven Republicans and six Democrats, some close observers of Yonkers politics heralded the dawn of a new era characterized by increased harmony at city hall. Even the greatest optimists among them, however, conceded that many challenges lay ahead. One of them was improving the city's schools.

Reading, Writing, 'Rithmetic + Rallying and Protesting

Public education in Yonkers had figured in the city's fiscal crisis, and for the remainder of the twentieth century it would preoccupy political and civic leaders. Just as the city's three-year brush with bankruptcy had captured the attention of the national media, so, too, would the controversy over desegregation, which will be covered in subsequent chapters of this volume. To understand how the school system came to play such a major role in the city's history during the second half of the twentieth century, a journey through time back to the 1960s is warranted. As the decade began, teachers' salaries were the lowest in Westchester and workloads had increased because of a longer school day, additional meetings, and monitoring duties. In 1964, when contract negotiations between the Yonkers Teachers Association and the city's board of education came to a halt, teachers fulfilled their classroom obligations but refused to do anything else. The matter was resolved, but for the remainder of the decade there was a certain level of discontent among the professional staff. In 1969, the Yonkers Federation of Teachers, the teachers' collective bargaining organization, called for a strike over a proposed contract offering salaries for both new and experienced teachers that were below those of other Westchester school districts. At the time, a Yonkers teacher with a Master's degree and twenty-five years in the classroom was earning $14,200 whereas the average for county educators with comparable experience was $17,000. What the Yonkers Federation of Teachers wanted was a contract that narrowed that gap, but as in most negotiations, neither side obtained everything it wanted. There was, however, a partial resolution, and things reverted to normal in the city's public schools, at least for a while.

Although the teachers were satisfied, at least temporarily, as the decade of the sixties drew to a close, students were becoming increasingly restless. In April 1969, African American students staged sit-ins at the city's six high schools. At Yonkers High School, protesting students were amenable to the idea of gathering in the school auditorium for a special assembly called by the principal to present their concerns. At an afternoon meeting at Gorton High School, students discussed a wide variety of issues, including "housing, narcotics, Urban Renewal," as well as recently announced federal cutbacks in spending for health, education, and welfare but, according to *The Herald Statesman,* "no written list of demands was presented by the students."[64] The following day, however, several hundred African American high school students staged a five-hour demonstration at city hall to voice concerns about education and housing. Their protest got off to a rousing start because it coincided with a performance, outside city hall, by a band composed of visiting police officers from Switzerland. Whether the band played on or not mattered little to the protesters, several of whom were injured in scuffles. At that point, some of the students retreated to the city council chambers where they barricaded themselves. Following a meeting with Yonkers officials, they departed peacefully, having made known their desire for better housing, additional minority teachers and guidance counselors, and greater sensitivity to the needs of African American students. Similar demands relating to the schools had been put forward a year earlier, when four hundred students walked out of five city schools. Singing "We Shall Overcome," they marched to board of education headquarters where they met with the superintendent of schools to voice concerns about school segregation. In the ensuing year, not much had changed from their perspective; thus, in the spring of 1969, the students seemed more determined than ever to press their demands. As a follow-up to the city hall demonstration, a hundred students at Longfellow Junior High School staged a sit-in in the school's assembly hall, but a clergyman, who acceded to school officials' request to speak to the students, convinced them to end their sit-in.

Meanwhile, elsewhere in Yonkers, at Sarah Lawrence College, which had become coeducational only a year before, five young men joined dozens of their female classmates in a sit-in at the administration building to protest a tuition increase. According to *The Herald Statesman,* the vast majority of students "responded unfavorably to the sit-in, and classes have continued normally."[65] Two months later, African American students at Sarah Lawrence staged a sit-in to demand that the school's Institute for Community Studies forgo future studies of minorities in nearby communities in favor of taking concrete action to help residents of such areas. In the 1970s, Sarah Lawrence College itself needed help in the form of a State Supreme Court ruling to enable it to build new dormitories. The Yonkers Zoning Board of Appeals had contended that the new buildings did not conform to the city's master plan. The matter was resolved, and the town/gown controversy faded from the headlines. In the meantime, public education became big news once again.

Starting in December 1971, there was considerable press coverage of the imminent expiration of the Yonkers public school teachers' contract. Absent a new contract, the Yonkers Federation of Teachers called for a strike to coincide with the reopening of the schools following the Christmas break. Once again, salaries were an issue because the board of education had refused to accept a state fact finder's recommendation regarding the percentage increase teachers deserved. Class size was another sticking point. Although limited by the contract that was set to expire, the proposed contract gave the city's new superintendent of schools, Dr. Robert F. Alioto, leeway to exceed the limits. Whether salary increments or hiring enough teachers to keep class sizes down, it was all a matter of money, and the timing could not have been worse. The Yonkers property tax rate had reached the limit permitted under the New York State Constitution and the city was scrambling to economize. Provisional workers had been dismissed and the board of education was threatening to eliminate 170 teaching positions when the schools reopened unless the Yonkers Federation of Teachers made some concessions, including postponing teachers' raises. The city's educators didn't exactly warm to this idea, and many of them wondered why Yonkers did not attempt to secure state approval to exclude from its debt limit the cost of pensions and Social Security. The answer, of course, is that such a move would have necessitated raising property taxes, something common council members hoping to be reelected were reluctant to do. Money was really the heart of the matter, as *The New York Times* pointed out. Describing the first day of the post-Christmas strike, the paper noted that Yonkers had "never been able to overcome the legacy of school problems, many of them stemming from inadequate funds."[66]

Several days into the strike, Yonkers obtained an injunction against the striking teachers. If they refused to return to work, the city planned to initiate contempt proceedings. The Yonkers Federation of Teachers would not budge, however, and they called in reinforcements in the person of Albert Shanker, president of the New York City United Federation of Teachers, who had led a protracted strike in the city's schools in 1968. Shanker joined Walter Tice, president of the Yonkers Federation of Teachers, and the heads of the Yonkers Patrolmen's Benevolent Association, the Firefighters Association, and the Civil Service Employees Association on the steps of the Yonkers City Hall in a show of solidarity. The rally was held and run by the United Public Employees of Yonkers in support of the teachers and in opposition to the city's bad faith bargaining with other unions. The other unions realized that the teachers were, in effect, doing the negotiating for all of the city unions. What the teachers won, all the unions would receive, and the city would be confronted with an even bigger budget deficit. That was the city's problem, not theirs, as far as the teachers who crowded the city hall parking lot were concerned. As they watched the perfect photo op on the steps of the grand building, they shouted, "Alioto must go" and "Tice is nice."[67] Two days later, 1,500 Civil Service employees showed up at a rally at Brandt's Theater. The objective of this massive gathering was twofold: to support the striking teachers and to send a message that city workers would present a united front in seeking new contracts. Less than a week later, following marathon negotiations, the teachers had a new contract. Their wage increases were not as large as the state fact finder had recommended but they were considerably in excess of what the board of education had originally offered. On the issue of class size, there had been a compromise permitting the superintendent to increase the limits on an experimental basis. So eager were the teachers to get back into their classrooms after the ten-day strike that they showed up for an early morning ratification vote. It was completed around 9 a.m., and the teachers were in their rooms conducting classes an hour later.

For the next few years, things were looking up on the educational front. A threatened strike in 1974 was headed off when teachers ratified a three-year contract giving them a 15 percent salary increment over the life of the agreement and inflation adjustments in the second and third years. One year into the contract, the New York State Appellate Division upheld a State Supreme Court ruling mandating that the Yonkers Board of Education abide by its contract with the city's teachers, even if the common council did not provide adequate funding. Simultaneous with this ruling was a decision by the public employees relations board that the board of education, and not the common council, was "the appropriate legislative body to approve additional funds" for Yonkers public schools.[68] That was all well and good, but like other cities in the state of New York, Yonkers was experiencing an unprecedented fiscal crisis in the mid-1970s. The city simply didn't have the money to meet all of its obligations. Something had to give. The only way the board of education could fulfill its obligations under the teachers' contract was to lay off more than a hundred professional staff members, but as the city's financial crisis deepened, additional cuts were needed. In 1976, a particularly bleak year, the board of education was planning to terminate 175 teachers. This was in addition to the "30 school administrators, 290 teachers and 350 education system employees" terminated since the previous summer.[69] With nearly one-third of the school system's professional and support staff gone, the board of education made the difficult decision to close seven public schools in the summer of 1976. In March, when the announcement of the planned closings was made, there was an immediate outcry. Parents staged demonstrations at board meetings, and the board relented. Three of the schools would be functioning in the fall but as two of them were "all-white schools on the East Side," African American and Hispanic parents objected.[70] For them, this was an all or nothing situation. Either all seven of the schools should be open or all should remain shuttered.

The board's decision to proceed with selective school closings galvanized the city's minorities. In the mid-seventies, although whites constituted 85 percent of the population, African Americans 8 percent, and Hispanics 7 percent, the composition of the school population was 18 percent African American and 11 percent Hispanic. Providing an alternative to the public schools were more than twenty parochial schools attended largely by white children whose parents could afford to pay tuition. To some, these schools underscored what *The New York Times* termed the "2 Faces of Yonkers."[71] Describing heated meetings on the school closings, the paper referred to Yonkers as "increasingly divided between a western half of urban decay, residential redevelopment and unfulfilled commercial promise and an eastern half of quiet, residential communities that prefer neighborhood identification to the name Yonkers."[72] Divided or not, all of Yonkers was affected by a State Supreme Court decision upholding a ruling requiring the board of education to rehire and provide back pay for 350 teachers dismissed as a result of the city's fiscal crisis. A sizable number of those educators were brought back to fill positions left vacant by attrition, but the pay issue remained a sticking point.

As if this weren't a big enough hurdle to overcome at a time when the city was still trying to get its financial house in order, Yonkers teachers took to the picket lines in September 1977. Nearly six months earlier, the board of education notified teachers in their April 1977 contract proposal that salaries would be reduced by 20 percent to their 1975 level and many provisions of previous contracts would be eliminated. In September teachers were protesting the fact that they had not received an increment stipulated in their last contract and that the one-year contract extension proposed by the board of education contained no provision for a raise. Other issues were job security, seniority, and arbitration of grievances. In an effort to get the new school year off to a proper start, the board of education obtained a temporary restraining order against the striking teachers, but they ignored it. According to *The Herald Statesman*, the board negotiator contended that the teachers' union "wanted the strike and round-the-clock talks to wear us down—but they're in for a surprise."[73] In an editorial, the paper termed the teachers' continued absence from the schools an "illegal strike" and called upon both sides to recognize the fact that "the city cannot afford a contract it cannot fund."[74] The strike dragged on for an entire month, ending in early October with the ratification of a new two-year contract calling for a total wage increase of a little over 13 percent and the preservation of seniority for teachers transferred to other schools and/or positions within the district. Although they faced fines under the provisions of the Taylor Law, prohibiting strikes by public employees, the teachers were elated, but their joy was short-lived. To enable Yonkers to close a budget gap, as required by the state body overseeing the city's finances during the fiscal crisis of the mid-seventies, the new two-year contract had to be renegotiated, with the result that the total average increment was reduced to a bit over 9 percent and the contract became a one-year agreement. Taking a cue from the teachers, nonteaching employees of the Yonkers school district staged a four-day walkout in the spring of 1978 before agreeing to a new one-year contract.

As divisive as contract negotiations could be, they paled in comparison with the uproar that resulted in 1978, when the board of education revealed a proposal for busing. A component of a plan to reorganize the schools at a time when enrollment was declining, in part because of a lower birth rate, the board of education hoped to save money by closing several middle and elementary schools and busing students to schools that had spare capacity. Since children from the west side of the city would be bused to schools on the predominantly white east side of Yonkers and vice versa, desegregation would be a byproduct. This did not go over well in white neighborhoods, where parents staged a day-long boycott that kept two thousand students out of school in the spring of 1978. Their protest notwithstanding, the board of education seemed determined to implement busing by the target date of 1979.

Home Sweet Home?

Integrating the city's schools, whether by busing or other means, would have been a less pressing issue had housing patterns in Yonkers been different, but in the sixties and seventies, as in the immediate post–World War II period, white families gravitated toward the east side while minorities took up residence on the west side. This pattern persisted even after housing for the middle class became a feature of the city's urban renewal efforts in the seventies. A decade earlier, private developers erected multifamily housing for the middle class, but these new complexes were distant, geographically, economically, and socially, from the subsidized housing on the west side of the city. At the very start of the 1960s the Tudor Woods Apartments, featuring a swimming pool and roller and ice skating rinks, opened in what had been the estate section of North Yonkers. Set on twenty-one acres, the complex had 150 rental units, in two buildings. In the mid-sixties, The Gateway, a hundred-unit garden apartment complex on North Broadway and Gateway Road, lured tenants with antique-looking brick, a swimming pool, and a choice of single level or split-level units. Gateway Park, off Gateway Road, on part of the old Untermyer estate, began offering condominium apartments for sale in 1966. Five years later, Futura, a twenty-story, 110-unit luxury rental building, became the "first systems-built highrise apartment in the U.S."[75] Its modular components were erected, using French equipment, in a Bronx factory that employed minority workers who were provided with intensive training in construction technology.

Although state-of-the-art apartments could be very appealing, many people seeking new residences yearned for a single-family home. An African American family offering $36,000 for a house on the fringes of Crestwood in 1964 thought they had realized the goal of home ownership until the owner of the dwelling turned around and sold it to a white buyer for $34,500. Invoking a New York State law of 1945 prohibiting discrimination in housing, the state attorney general intervened to obtain an injunction preventing the homeowner from selling the house until the state commission for human rights ruled on the discrimination complaint made by the African American purchaser. This set a precedent, because it was the first time that the state had obtained an injunction in a housing discrimination case. In another case, also in 1964, the state commission for human rights directed the owners of an apartment building on McLean Avenue to make units available "without regard to race, color, creed or national origin" after a prospective African American tenant filed a discrimination complaint.[76] Five years later, the New York State Division of

Human Rights, acting on the complaint of a woman who had been denied an equal opportunity to rent an apartment on South Broadway, required the building's owners to notify the Yonkers Fair Housing Committee of vacancies for a two-year period during which the committee would have the right of first refusal. The owners were also directed to supply a list containing the names of everyone seeking apartments; for people who did not move into apartments, the building's owners had to document why the prospective tenant chose not to or why the owners had refused to rent to them. This ruling was upheld by the appellate division in 1970. Two years later, a grand jury indicted a Yonkers man for refusing to rent an apartment in his six-family house to an African American family.

Despite the aggressive action taken to end housing discrimination in Yonkers, it not only persisted but took on a frightening new form as the decade of the seventies neared an end. In the summer of 1979, almost immediately after Thomas Porter, an African American executive with the IBM corporation, moved his family into a $100,000 home in Crestwood, an explosion and fire destroyed the house. The conflagration occurred in the wee hours of the morning while the unsuspecting family, exhausted from the previous day's move, slept. Mrs. Porter, two daughters, and a niece and nephew were injured as they fled the house; they all required treatment at Lawrence Hospital in Bronxville. Mrs. Porter, a registered nurse, had first- and second-degree burns on her arms and face. While concerned for the welfare of the Porters, residents of the neighborhood were not totally shocked by what had happened. Some told of past attacks on not only African Americans but Catholics and Jews who had moved into the area. An African American resident recounted stories of attempts to burn his home down shortly after he and his wife moved in and incidents involving dead animals intentionally deposited on his lawn and eggs hurled at his vehicle. The attack on the Porter residence seemed to be part of a pattern. *The Herald Statesman* agreed. Denouncing this and similar attacks elsewhere, the paper referred to "the long road to tolerance that we still must travel."[77]

The views expressed by the newspaper notwithstanding, the Yonkers Police Department did not jump to the conclusion that the attack on the Porter residence was racially motivated. Deputy Police Commissioner Charles Connolly declared that "it would be imprudent" to confine the investigation to racial motivation while omitting other motives.[78] City Manager Pat Ravo said something similar, noting that categorizing the attack as racially motivated would "cloud this city's reputation as well as that of Colonial Heights."[79] There was some speculation that the Porters weren't the intended targets of the arson attack. Instead, the person or persons responsible for torching the home may have been out to get a Bronxville contractor who had previously owned the house. An attorney for the Porters, however, filed a complaint claiming that "possible violations of a federal statute outlawing discrimination in housing" had occurred and at that point the Federal Bureau of Investigation became involved in the case.[80] The IBM Corporation offered a $25,000 reward for information resulting in the arrest and conviction of the arsonist or arsonists. In another arson case, also in 1979, a reward was offered for information about the person or persons responsible for setting a fire that killed an eighty-seven-year-old resident of Nepperhan Avenue. The city and the firefighter's association, along with the son of the deceased woman, put up the money for the fund in hopes of catching the so-called "Nepperhan Valley arsonist." Puzzled authorities, however, were quick to admit that more than one person may have been responsible for setting forty fires in the Nepperhan Valley.

Although arson can be an extreme and potentially deadly form of protest, during the 1970s when the Yonkers police were attempting to solve arson crimes, other sorts of protests were occurring in the city. When residents of Colonial Heights learned in 1976 that a group home for the developmentally disabled was planned for their community, thirty people turned out for a meeting to voice their concerns. In contrast with the opposition that arose to the placement of group homes in neighborhood settings, not only in Yonkers but elsewhere, following passage, in 1975, of legislation calling for the deinstitutionalization of the developmentally disabled, expansion of existing institutions proved more acceptable. In the early sixties, the Leake and Watts Children's Home, situated on a large campus overlooking the Hudson, erected four cottages to house some of its young residents, many of whom were emotionally disturbed. A pilot project involving three cottages a decade earlier had been the first of its kind, and Leake and Watts, which celebrated its 130th anniversary in 1961, wished to extend it.

At the very time Leake and Watts was expanding, a problem that would eventually overwhelm some Yonkers youths was just beginning to surface: drugs. In 1960, an old bakery truck transporting twenty-four pounds of pure heroin, worth $5 million, from a Manhattan pier where the drugs had been smuggled in on board an Italian steamship, was stopped as it exited the New York State Thruway at the Cross County Shopping Center. By the mid-sixties Yonkers authorities put the number of young people, of both sexes, who were using drugs at almost one thousand. Of this number, more than one hundred were addicts from middle-class families, many of them residing in the northwest part of the city. Untermyer Park was said to be a favorite gathering place of young drug users. The magnitude of the problem was so great that the Yonkers Police Department, in 1964, not only launched an investigation, which involved reaching out to New York State Police, but Mayor John E. Flynn appointed a committee to study the problem. Another approach was taken by Christ the King Church, whose pastor was so alarmed by the revelations of narcotics use in northwest Yonkers that he implored churchgoers to join him in a black fast, a practice that had fallen into disuse in Western Christianity. For twelve hours, beginning at 6 a.m., parishioners were to abstain from all food and liquids, including water, while praying for the young addicts of Yonkers. Six months later the common council voted to create the positions of narcotics coordinator and chemist to deal with the drug problem and to implement an educational program recommended by the study group established the previous year.

These were positive steps, but the drug problem throughout Westchester County was so enormous that New York State's narcotics addiction control commission decided to open a residential treatment center in the county in 1967. The site the commission selected was the Seventh-day Adventists' Bates Memorial Hospital on Sprain Ridge, the property the Loral Corporation would eventually acquire. When the drug treatment site was proposed for this large parcel, residents of such nearby communities as Runyon Heights, Valley View, Homefield, Homecrest, Gateway Woods, and Fawn Ridge perceived the facility as a direct threat to the well-being of their families and the value of their homes. Some of them descended upon city hall to voice their objections, but their shouts and picket signs were for naught. Yet, when construction crews arrived, in February 1967, to retrofit Bates, residents of the surrounding area used their automobiles to block the entrance. They also deposited a six-foot black coffin, bearing a sign saying "Yonkers died of Malcolmitis," in the center of the road leading up to the hospital.[81] Yonkers resident and lieutenant governor Malcolm Wilson, who supported the idea of placing a treatment center on the Bates property, came in for more criticism the following day when a larger demonstration took place. Representatives from neighborhood associations throughout the city showed up to help shut down the principal access route to the site of the treatment center. As they stood defiantly on a bridge across the New York State Thruway, some of the two hundred protesters positioned themselves outside the entrance to the Bates property. Besides cars, they used baby carriages and pet dogs on leashes to make the point that they did not want this facility in their area.

Among those picketing the site was Alfred B. DelBello, then a member of the common council, who objected to the fact that Yonkers would lose nearly a million dollars a year in taxes by having a tax-exempt facility on the Bates site rather than the retirement community the Seventh-day Adventists had originally hoped to build on the property. More important than the tax consequences, as far as many residents of the area were concerned, was the danger they felt addicts posed to the surrounding community. For that reason, the protesters kept up their blockade for a week, and at one point two of them were arrested following a scuffle with police. The state temporarily suspended work on the new facility, which was going to be known as the Ridge Hill Rehabilitation Center, but almost immediately construction resumed and the center opened in the spring of 1967. Not long thereafter, residents of the surrounding Sprain Ridge area were able to say "I told you so," after a half dozen male patients escaped. Like it or not, Yonkers had to adjust to having a residential treatment center within its borders for nearly a decade until the state decided to phase out the facility. During the period that the center functioned, life in the surrounding area went on and real estate values in the Sprain Ridge vicinity did not hit rock bottom as some alarmists had predicted. The treatment center notwithstanding, this part of Yonkers had much to recommend itself, including a brand-new road, the Sprain Brook Parkway.

Strengthening the Infrastructure

In the planning stage since the 1920s, the Sprain Brook Parkway did not materialize until after World War II, when it was built, in stages, by the East Hudson Parkway Authority, with state funding. Two days before Christmas in 1963, the section from Tuckahoe Road to Jackson Avenue was opened. It linked up with a more southerly portion, completed in 1961, extending down to the Cross County Parkway. In the 1970s, work got under way to modernize the Cross County Parkway, southern Westchester's major east-west route. The outmoded six-mile long parkway was used by fifty thousand cars a day in the early seventies, whereas the Hutchinson River Parkway, fifteen miles in length, accommodated thirty-seven thousand cars daily. Several sections of the Cross County were rebuilt by the mid-seventies, but the most challenging task, reconstructing the portion between the New York State Thruway and the Saw Mill River Parkway, began in 1975. Government officials, who gathered alongside the parkway at the start of this phase, agreed that it wasn't a minute too soon because in the previous three years alone there had been dozens of accidents, including several resulting in fatalities, on this stretch of antiquated roadway.

In addition to dealing with dangerous roads, motorists had to contend with a gasoline shortage caused by an oil embargo instituted in 1973 by the oil-producing nations of the Middle East. Gasoline rationing led to long lines at stations that were able to obtain only a fraction of their usual supply. Tempers flared. Horns honked. Fights broke out and motorists fumed even after lines became shorter thanks to a mandate requiring people with odd numbered license plates to queue up for gas on specific days and those with even numbered plates to line up on other days. All of this was enough to persuade some people to take mass transit, this despite the fact that only a few years earlier, when the public service commission held hearings in Yonkers on service on the Penn Central's Hudson and Harlem divisions, commuters voiced complaints about old equipment, disgruntled railroad employees, and chronically late trains. In fact, most of the people who testified arrived late for the evening hearing because of train delays! Although the Penn Central was a major source of irritation to its riders, Amtrak was viewed more favorably, so much so that in 1979 the City of Yonkers was doing its utmost to persuade the long distance railroad to make Yonkers a stop on the line linking New York City with upstate. It took almost a decade but Yonkers did become an Amtrak stop, to the delight of residents heading north. They could now avoid traveling either to Manhattan or to Croton-on-Hudson to board the train, and for quite some distance they could enjoy a scenic river view.

In Yonkers itself, however, some residents felt that the waterfront had become less appealing because of the erection of a Westchester County sewage treatment plant. *The Herald Statesman* put it this way: "There is nothing glamorous, certainly, in a sewage treatment plant."[82] Yet, the paper noted, the facility played an important role in keeping the metropolitan area healthy. Indeed, the new facility, which opened in 1961, following seven years of construction and a shakedown period of one year, was deemed essential by the interstate sanitation commission, a body established by a tri-state compact to regulate water quality in New York, Connecticut, and New Jersey. As part of the effort to alleviate pollution of the Hudson, the antiquated North Yonkers and South Yonkers sewage treatment plants were also updated and functioned as components of the new system. All of this capacity was needed because half of Westchester County's sewage flowed into the Hudson. According to *The Herald Statesman,* the new plant was "modern, effective and built for expansion" to accommodate an estimated population of a half-million people by 1980.[83]

In recognition of the fact that a growing population generates not only more sewage but additional garbage, Yonkers wanted to create a dump on an embankment between Warburton Avenue and the New York Central railroad tracks. The city intended to eventually create a park atop the compacted garbage, but the very idea of dumping refuse so close to the Hudson River infuriated conservationists from as far away as Staten Island. They turned out to voice their objections at a hearing held by New York State's Hudson River Valley Commission in 1967. In the end, the commission approved the dump, but it insisted that Yonkers comply with its recommendations, which included the building of a retaining wall to prevent garbage from sliding down onto the railroad tracks. The city was also required to come up with a comprehensive plan for dealing with solid waste in the future. Ultimately, it was Westchester County that came up with a solution by constructing a garbage-to-energy plant in Peekskill. The county had originally contemplated building two plants, and an Austin Avenue site in Yonkers was considered for the southern Westchester plant. The city offered the land in the belief that the county would erect a bridge that would provide access to not only the proposed plant but to a corporate park or some other type of development Yonkers hoped would materialize in the immediate vicinity. Yonkers had to set aside this dream for the time being, but its dealings with the county on the solid waste issue were a reminder that even a municipality as large as Yonkers was impacted by other governmental entities, whether the county or the gigantic metropolis to its south. In 1966, the interconnectedness of Yonkers and New York City became apparent when New York announced plans for a gigantic new water tunnel linking the Hillview Reservoir in Yonkers with Queens. Plagued by construction delays, Water Tunnel No. 3, which was intended to supplement two tunnels completed in the first half of the twentieth century and permit the temporary closure of each of the older tunnels for inspection and repair, was still a work in progress at the end of the century.

Taking a Break

The importance of New York City's third water tunnel was undeniable, but when the good people of Yonkers thought of H_2O, the refreshing liquid pouring out of the tap wasn't the only thing that came to mind. Besides the life-sustaining property of water, there was also a recreational component; in the summer months, the mere mention of the word *water* conjured up images of splashing around in a pool or at the beach or enjoying a leisurely boat ride on the Hudson. In the summer of 1967, Yonkers residents eager to get out on the water could enjoy a day trip to Rockaway Beach on the Sound Steamship Company's *Bay Belle*. Three years later, they were able to enjoy free concerts performed by the American Waterways Wind Orchestra on barges moored south of the Hudson River Museum.

Throughout the sixties and seventies, the museum hosted a series of innovative exhibitions, including one in 1961 featuring paintings that highlighted the ideals expressed in the U.S. Constitution and the Declaration of Independence. The museum was so well attended that the John Bond Trevor mansion, built in 1876 and home of the museum since 1924, was no longer adequate. In 1966 the city came to the rescue, approving a forty thousand–square-foot addition containing the Andrus planetarium, galleries, a lecture hall, and a branch of the Yonkers Public Library. Meanwhile, on the east side of the city, Westchester County's largest library, the Sprain Brook Branch of the Yonkers Public Library, was dedicated in 1962. Later renamed for Grinton I. Will, longtime director of the Yonkers Public Library, the new branch attracted ten thousand visitors on its very first day. According to *The Herald Statesman*: "Crowds flowed through the children's room, where tea, punch, and cookies were served. In the adult section, some rested and chatted in the various reading areas furnished with upholstered furniture."[84]

Through the years, various types of lectures and performances were held in the library's large auditorium, but for residents interested in, shall we say, something "jazzier" there was the Westchester Dinner Theatre, at the Westchester Town House, a large motel on Tuckahoe Road. The theatre/restaurant, which could accommodate hundreds of patrons for an evening of dining and entertainment, opened in 1962 with a production of the musical *Can-Can*. Some Yonkers clergymen and members of the city council objected to the so-called "burlesque" form of entertainment at the dinner theatre and at watering holes near the Yonkers Raceway but most people were unruffled by these shows. In addition to dinner theatre, Yonkers had legitimate theatre, beginning in 1964 when the Strand, on South Broadway, was transformed from a movie theatre into the Yonkers Playhouse. At the time it was the only venue of its type in the county regularly offering live stage productions. That movie theatres were closing was not surprising, given the popularity of television, but there was another reason people stayed away from at least one movie house, the Park Hill Theatre. On a June evening in 1961, three tear gas bombs exploded about fifteen minutes apart. When the first device went off, in the orchestra, moviegoers hastened toward the exits. More than a dozen people were injured, none seriously. Fortunately, before the second and third bombs, which had been affixed with tape to the underside of balcony seats, exploded, sending more foul-smelling smoke through the theatre, the building had been emptied of patrons.

Anyone who had been in the Park Hill Theatre the night the tear gas bombs exploded readily grasped the meaning of the term "a breath of fresh air." When it came to recreation, some people preferred outdoor activities to theatregoing or anything else in a confined indoor space. Golf was the favorite sport of many fresh air enthusiasts, and in 1963 St. Andrew's, America's first golf club, celebrated its seventy-fifth anniversary with "a simple yet strangely moving ceremony" in which the first golf match in the United States was restaged on North Broadway and Shonnard Place, where the original game had taken place.[85] The group of friends who had played the original game in 1888 were known as the "Apple Tree Gang" because of the beverage they sipped to quench their thirst during rounds, although some people contend that the men hung small flasks, along with their coats, from the branches of the apple tree. Since the game began and ended by the tree this was reputedly the first "nineteenth hole." Jugs of apple juice were hung for the reenactment and the modern-day golfers stopped periodically to take a swig before continuing with the game. Another highlight of the St. Andrew's anniversary festivities was the rededication, in the presence of city officials, of a plaque on the site of the first green of the original golf course. The Yonkers Historical Society, which had been established in 1952 to preserve documents, artifacts, and buildings illustrative of the proud history of the "Queen City of the Hudson," sponsored the St. Andrew's celebration. Costumed society volunteers, known as Ladies of the Manor, who served as guides at the society's Sherwood House museum, were in charge of refreshments for the golf club commemorative event and society president Frank L. Walton, who owned the site of the original St. Andrew's first hole, announced that he had transferred the property, actually one square yard of earth, where the first hole had been located to the society "to be maintained in perpetuity."[86]

In addition to being celebrated as the birthplace of the sport of golf in the United States, Yonkers was famous for its marathon. On the eve of the 1978 run, which *The New York Times* characterized as "one of the country's most prestigious and difficult marathons," the paper noted that the race was "expected to attract about 800 runners from around the country."[87] Entrants came from as far away as California and Florida, and they included fifty women. A year later, as part of the preparations for the forty-third marathon, Yonkers officials launched a public relations campaign aimed at improving the city's image. Runners were presented with T-shirts bearing the slogan "I Believe in Yonkers," and days before marathon participants assembled at the Lake Avenue starting line, some local residents were sporting the eye-catching blue shirts with the rainbow logo in shades of yellow, red, and orange. This was all to the good as far as the city's director of public relations was concerned because the idea was to get "people to see the other side of Yonkers."[88] Another feature of the campaign was a disco record ending with the upbeat refrain:

> Believing in Yonkers means building for the future
> To keep it a great place to live, work and play.[89]

Horsing Around

Playing, of course, meant different things to different people. For some, running a marathon was play, but for others it was a day at the races; and it wasn't just men who were flocking to Yonkers Raceway. In 1960, the track held an experimental Ladies Night, which featured discounted admissions for women and a woman driver racing against her male counterparts. A year later, Yonkers Raceway was garnering publicity for a different reason, namely its plan to acquire a controlling interest in Roosevelt Raceway. The biggest trotting tracks in the United States, Yonkers and Roosevelt had previously had interlocking directorates. Since a New York State investigating commission had objected to this, the idea of one track purchasing control of the other was also unacceptable, and the plan was dropped. Within months, another deal involving the sale of a one-third interest in Yonkers Raceway to the Zeckendorf real estate interests was also shelved. That Yonkers Raceway was attractive to investors was not surprising, however, because in 1961 it had the biggest attendance record and betting handle of any harness track in New York State.

Duplicating this success in 1962 proved difficult because of several unexpected developments. One was a work slowdown by off-duty Yonkers police officers demanding an increase in the hourly pay they received for providing traffic control. Cars inching along toward the raceway, bumper to bumper, their drivers fuming, were bad enough but in May 1962 something far more ominous occurred. Unruly fans, reacting to a big drop in the odds on a pacer in the eighth race, began booing; soon, beer cans and racing programs were being thrown about indiscriminately. Raceway officials, nevertheless, decided against canceling the ninth race. Just before that race began, shouts were heard, and some fans rushed forward and demolished a steel mesh fence separating the public from the racetrack's wooden rail. Nearly all of the men responsible for this vandalism were quickly subdued by the track's security force but one got away, running onto the track, where he received a sharp blow to the head when the starting gate opened. Within seconds lots of people ran onto the track, demolishing more of the mesh fence and part of the wooden rail. Meanwhile, some of the wooden seats in the grandstand were set afire. The destruction didn't end there. Someone hurled a brick at the huge window of the track's restaurant, and soon rioters were inside wreaking havoc. To bring the situation under control, the Yonkers Police Department called for backup from New York City.

Despite the riot, racing resumed the next day. The previous night's damage was repaired and to ensure that order would be maintained, the track's normal security force, consisting of eighty uniformed Pinkerton guards, grew to 120. This paid off, because except for a bit of shouting in the grandstand, things were otherwise quiet, but that wasn't the end of the riot story because the New York State Harness Racing Commission penalized the raceway, two drivers, and an owner for the race that provoked the riot. Citing the fact that the owner of the winning horse had a partial ownership interest in the horse that came in second and that the driver for the second horse wasn't really making an effort to move ahead, the commission imposed sixty-day suspensions on both drivers and the owner. Although the commission found that only about one hundred people, out of a crowd of more than thirty thousand, had taken part in the rioting, it criticized Yonkers Raceway for not maintaining order at the track.

As the decade of the sixties progressed, the track had to deal with issues that were every bit as challenging as ensuring the safety of raceway patrons. In 1963, a virus outbreak among horses stabled at Yonkers manifested itself in equine coughing and temperatures as high as 105 degrees. Horses at tracks up and down the East Coast exhibited symptoms, but the disease ran its course and things got back to normal. That same year, to make sure it would remain competitive with other sporting venues, Yonkers Raceway introduced a form of wagering known as the twin double. It was an instant hit with race fans. More innovations followed. In the spring of 1964 a new mezzanine made its debut. New mutuel machines, betting windows, concession stands, including one offering Kosher hot dogs, plus all-season climate control, were part of this major improvement. The fans could not have been happier. In terms of attendance and money wagered, the summer meet that year was the best ever in the entire history of the sport. Winter meets weren't bad either. Nearly forty thousand people were in attendance for the start of the season in February 1965. Equally impressive was the fact that ten thousand more fans tried to get into the track but had to be turned away. Instead of seeing Cold Front win the Snowball Stakes, disappointed racegoers crawled along Central Park Avenue in a seemingly endless traffic jam.

With the raceway doing incredibly well, pari-mutuel workers felt that a wage increase was in order, and when they didn't get what they wanted they struck, shutting down the track for several days in the spring of 1965. The short duration of the work stoppage was attributable to the intervention of the New York State Mediation Board and the state harness racing commission. Every night the track remained closed the state lost significant revenue and was thus very anxious to see the strike settled. Although the pari-mutuel workers didn't get everything they wanted, they settled for a two dollar a night increase in pay, over the course of two years. In 1968 another strike by pari-mutuel workers closed Yonkers Raceway for more than a week. Like the previous work stoppage, it ended following the intervention of the state.

Strikes and bad weather, whether snow or heavy rain, took their toll on Yonkers Raceway for several years in the mid and late sixties but the 1970s got off to a phenomenal start. The first session that year concluded with record setting nightly averages and total bets for a harness racing meeting. There was so much activity at Yonkers that at one point, the track needed a temporary infusion of cash. A call went out to the New York Racing Association, which arranged for Aqueduct Raceway to send two cash-laden helicopters. Following a fifteen-minute trip from the Long Island track, they landed behind the Yonkers tote board. Fearful that the choppers would disturb the horses, raceway officials postponed the post parade. On the last racing night of 1970, a horse collapsed and died in the midst of a race. That unfortunate occurrence notwithstanding, when all the figures were in, the track set new annual records for both average and total bets. In 1971 Off Track Betting was instituted, but only after Yonkers Raceway pari-mutuel clerks threatened to strike unless they received job guarantees. No sooner had the OTB issue been resolved than fans, protesting a low exacta payoff, hurled garbage cans, newspapers, and programs, some of which they had ignited, onto the track. The quick arrival of Yonkers police cars brought an end to the disturbance.

Toward the end of 1971, there was a changing of the guard at Yonkers Raceway. Although Stanley Tannanbaum remained president, with the recent deaths of his two brothers, each of whom had, in turn, been president of Yonkers Raceway, the Tannanbaum family sold the raceway to a group headed by John Rooney of Pennsylvania. Rooney was president of the William Penn Racing Association, which owned Liberty Bell Park, a Philadelphia racetrack. To increase attendance the new owners tried various promotions, including a night of nostalgia, featuring a Dixieland band and a parade of historic sulkies, and Ladies' Night, which was dropped after the New York State Division of Human Rights, acting on complaints from men who resented having to pay a $2.25 admission fee while women were charged only $.75, announced it was considering legal action against the raceway. Even if Ladies' Night had worked, the opening of the Meadowlands racetrack in New Jersey in 1976 and competition from Off Track Betting would have continued to cut into Yonkers Raceway's attendance figures. Unusual betting patterns at OTB facilities sparked an investigation leading to the indictment of more than two dozen harness drivers for collusion with gamblers to fix superfecta races at Yonkers Raceway and Roosevelt Raceway. Adding insult to injury, in 1977, three nights of Yonkers Raceway receipts were carted off by two masked men who hid in the Hudson Valley National Bank on Grassy Sprain Road overnight and surprised two bank employees early the next morning. Despite the myriad challenges facing the raceway in the seventies, as the decade neared an end *The New York Times* published an article titled "Yonkers Hits the Wire and Finishes in Money."[90] The paper noted that the raceway had "defied predictions" regarding several visions for redevelopment.[91] Fortunately, talk of residential development, a gigantic parking lot and even a dog track was just that: talk. Referring to Tim Rooney, president of the raceway, the paper said that he was "happy over thin rays of hope."[92] Despite competition from the Meadowlands, "the big gamblers have not deserted the Westchester County track."[93]

The Russians are Coming!

Although favorable odds and a great location near New York City and within easy reach of the northern suburbs were key factors in attracting patronage, a lesser known international component lured race fans. In addition to hosting United Nations delegates, Yonkers Raceway, back in 1963, welcomed horses from the Soviet Union. With the approval of the State Department, raceway officials conducted talks with Russian officials and arranged for two Russian mares to be transported by a rather circuitous route from Moscow to Berlin, to Amsterdam, to London, and from there, on Pan American Airlines, to New York, for the Transoceanic Trot, an event limited to foreign horses. During their first race at Yonkers, the Russian horses were eliminated after locking wheels. They didn't fare much better in the United Nations Consolation Trot. Nevertheless, Yonkers Raceway was eager to maintain a relationship with the Russians and for that reason presented the Soviet government with a brood mare. The Russians reciprocated by extending invitations to two American trotters to compete in the Soviet Union.

In 1965, a Russian woman had the distinction of being the first driver from her country to win a race in America. A few days before the race, the thirty-year-old female driver and other members of the Russian harness racing delegation, who had traveled to the United States for Yonkers Raceway's international trotting series, were treated to a baseball game at Yankee Stadium. Prior to the game, the female driver headed to one of the top hair salons in Manhattan for the works, including a cut, set, facial, and eyebrows. Yonkers Raceway had every intention of picking up the bill for all of this, but the salon insisted that the services were on the house. The popular female driver was back in the United States the following year, but she and other members of the Soviet delegation did not have a smooth trip because, after flying from Moscow to East Berlin, they were denied entry into West Berlin for several days. This was, after all, the era of the Cold War and authorities in Western countries were suspicious of persons from Communist nations. The same could be said of Communist countries when citizens of capitalist nations landed in their midst.

The Tragic Case of Hugh Redmond

In the early years of the Cold War, 1951 to be precise, Yonkers native Hugh Francis Redmond Jr. was arrested in Shanghai. A graduate of Roosevelt High School, Redmond went on to Manhattan College but left to join the Army during World War II. He served as a paratrooper in Europe, earning numerous commendations, including the Purple Heart. Severe wounds led to his discharge from service in 1945. The following year he went to mainland China, ostensibly as a representative of an import–export company but he was believed to be working for the Central Intelligence Agency, gathering and transmitting information about Communist activity on the Chinese mainland. Three years later, following a civil war between Chinese Communists and anticommunist Nationalists, the Communists triumphed, creating the People's Republic of China. Redmond remained in China for another two years, marrying a Russian-born pianist. Summoned home, he was preparing to depart from Shanghai on an American ship but was arrested shortly before he was to have boarded the vessel. Redmond's bride was permitted to sail to the United States, where she lived with her husband's parents for a time. She eventually divorced Redmond. In his 1998 book *China Spy,* which is based upon interviews conducted, for the most part, in the 1980s, Maury Allen asserted: "It would be years later before the Redmond Family became aware of the most crushing blow of all. A CIA agent told a friend of Redmond's that Lena had been a double agent. She was working for the Communists as well as for us. No one knew it at the time, but Lena Petrov Redmond had betrayed Hugh Redmond."[94] Some Yonkers residents who participated in a community effort to secure Redmond's freedom did not subscribe to the theory that Redmond was betrayed by his wife. What seems likely, however, is that someone provided Chinese authorities with enough information to charge Redmond with espionage.

Following a trial, Redmond was convicted and sentenced to life in prison. All the while, he insisted that he was an innocent American businessman. After spending five years in jail, Redmond was allowed to communicate with his family by mail, but it would be another few years before his mother was permitted to make the first of three trips to visit him. In Yonkers, various community groups raised funds to assist Mrs. Redmond and an organization called The Committee to Free Hugh Redmond, composed of more than two dozen local groups, was established. Since the People's Republic of China released other foreign prisoners, provided they signed documents admitting they had engaged in espionage and acknowledging their willingness to apologize to the Chinese, Yonkers veterans who had journeyed to Washington, D.C., to meet with C.I.A. Director Allen Dulles were hopeful that Redmond would be freed. Redmond, however, did not sign the incriminating document that was required as the price for his release, and he died in a Shanghai prison in 1970. Chinese authorities claimed he committed suicide, but his family and friends back in Yonkers doubted that. Redmond's cremated remains were returned by the Red Cross and were buried in Oakland Cemetery. Describing the funeral, which was all the more poignant because the cortege passed by the nursing home where Hugh Redmond's mother Ruth, who had suffered three strokes, was residing, *The Herald Statesman* observed that people turned out to view the funeral procession of a person who forfeited his life rather than betray the United States or, in the words of a member of the Redmond Committee, "was an innocent victim of 'man's inhumanity to man.'"[95]

The paper went on to quote Sol Friedman, the Yonkers attorney who had been chairman of the Redmond Committee, "which for years had sought in vain the Yonkers man's freedom."[96] Friedman eulogized Redmond, saying that the ashes of Hugh Redmond were being buried but "no one can ever bury the indomitable spirit and courage of the man. . . . Never once could the Chinese government exact a confession or an admission of guilt."[97]

Unspeakable Crimes

Losing a famous native son, whether under mysterious circumstances, as was the case with Hugh Redmond, or as a result of natural causes, such as the heart failure and leukemia that, in 1973, claimed the life of drummer Gene Krupa, who resided on Ritchie Drive, is always sad. Although grief is sometimes tempered if the passing is not completely unexpected, when the end comes suddenly, grief is overwhelming, as evidenced by the reaction to the loss of a dozen lives, most of them very young, in a fire that had been deliberately set at the Jewish Community Center in 1965. The children were on the fourth floor for music lessons when smoke engulfed the room. Some of the youngsters headed for the windows and were plucked from the building and carried down fire department ladders. Two passersby bravely entered the structure and guided people on the lower floors to safety. Nine children and three adults perished in the fire. In an article titled "Shocked Jewish Leaders Call It Yonkers' Worst Tragedy Ever" *The Herald Statesman* recounted the story of one victim, Lucille Sacks, who managed to get her daughter out of the burning building and then went back in to rescue other children, only to lose her life.[98] In the immediate aftermath of the fire, Yonkers officials determined that a delay in turning in a fire alarm had made the difference between life and death for the unfortunate victims. There was also some question about whether fire drills had been conducted at the center, but as the facility was not technically speaking a school, such drills were not required. Plastic panels recently installed in the balcony of the building's auditorium were also being eyed as possibly contributing to the rapid spread of the fire and the toxicity of the smoke.

As fire officials struggled to find the cause of the blaze, there was an enormous outpouring of grief throughout Yonkers by people of all faiths. Although owned by the Jewish Federation of Yonkers, the center was non-denominational and its programs were open to all. In the aftermath of the fire, some residents and shop owners dismantled their Christmas displays and various local organizations joined forces to raise money to rebuild the center. The *Herald Statesman* summed up the feelings of Yonkers's citizens in an editorial titled "Combination of Tragedy and Horror Mystically Unites In Mourning Entire Yonkers Community."[99] The paper proceeded to raise serious questions about whether a cigarette could have started the fire and whether sprinklers and fire escapes should be required in all public buildings. A key question posed by the paper was whether there was "a prospect of a similar tragedy in some other building" in the city.[100]

These were all valid questions that needed to be answered, but the responses were slow in coming. In the days following the fire, two teenage boys employed at the center under the federal government's Youth Corps program were questioned. One of the boys, Thomas Alfred Ruppert, confessed to setting the fire to Yonkers detectives and to Zvi Almog, the director of the Jewish Community Center. Nevertheless, Ruppert was released at the direction of the Westchester County district attorney for unspecified reasons. Some people were puzzled by this, just as they were mystified by allegations that fire dispatchers had not taken seriously phone calls reporting that the center was on fire and that firefighters had not ascended rescue ladders quickly enough nor directed sufficient water at the burning building when they first arrived on the scene. An investigation by the Yonkers police, under the direction of the Westchester County district attorney's office, found no evidence for these charges.

A month after the tragic fire, an arrest warrant was issued for Thomas Alfred Ruppert, who Yonkers detectives believed had set the blaze. It was while he was still a student at Yonkers High School that Ruppert had found employment through the federal government's Youth Corps, an antipoverty program. He was assigned to the Jewish Community Center, where he performed a variety of tasks, many of them intended to keep the building tidy. Ironically, after his release following the supposedly coerced confession in December, Ruppert was one of the workers who helped remove debris from the Community Center. After that he seemed to have disappeared, thereby causing Yonkers police to send out a bulletin to police departments all over the East Coast. This proved unnecessary because Ruppert was still in Westchester, in the custody of the Westchester County Family Court for violating probation in an earlier case. According to press accounts, Ruppert had been in trouble as a preteen and had been previously suspected of arson. Committed to Westchester County's Grasslands Hospital for psychiatric evaluation, Ruppert remained there for nearly three weeks despite attempts by William M. Kunstler, his Legal Aid attorney, to secure his release on grounds that authorities had violated the youth's civil rights. Kunstler claimed that Ruppert had not been represented by an attorney during multiple interrogations and that Yonkers and Westchester County officials had taken advantage of his "limited mentality and emotional immaturity."[101] Upon his release from Grasslands, Ruppert was incarcerated in the Yonkers jail. Soon thereafter, his mother died of cancer, leaving his father, a diaper delivery truck driver, to care for seven of the family's eight children who resided with him in Yonkers public housing.

A few months later, a Westchester County grand jury indicted Ruppert. Before his trial began, as a result of the 1966 U.S. Supreme

Court ruling in the Miranda case, Ruppert's confession to the Yonkers police was ruled inadmissible, this despite the fact that it had been made the year before the imposition of the Miranda Rule requiring police to inform suspects of their rights. The confession Ruppert made to the executive director of the Jewish Community Center was admissible, however. The center official testified at Ruppert's trial and following a day and a half of deliberation, a Westchester County jury found the defendant guilty of first-degree murder and first-degree arson. At his sentencing to life in prison, in June 1967, Ruppert told the court: "All I can say is I am innocent."[102] In 1970, New York State's highest court reversed the conviction and ordered a new trial because it found that the executive director of the Jewish Community Center had cooperated so closely with the Yonkers police that he had really been an agent of the police and thus his testimony had been tainted. A retrial was avoided after the state court of appeals dismissed the case and ordered Ruppert released.

Subsequent court proceedings brought by the families of fire victims resulted, in 1972, in a judgment against the center, its architect, and the manufacturer of the plastic panels that had contributed to the spread of the fire. Although the center steadfastly insisted that the fire had resulted from arson, a jury concluded that it and the other defendants were culpable for actions that had allowed the fire to spread. Following this trial, the Jewish Community Center fire faded from the headlines until 1984, when newspapers reported that Thomas Ruppert, who had been working at a warehouse in New Jersey, had died of liver disease. He was thirty-five years old.

The guilt or innocence of Thomas Ruppert remained a topic of ongoing debate even after his death, but there was no debate about the culpability of David Berkowitz, the infamous "Son of Sam." Although there had been a sensational murder case in the fifties involving a twenty-four-year-old Yonkers woman who taught in the Bronx and whose body was found in a wooded area near Jackson Avenue, press coverage was limited compared with the "Son of Sam" case. When the thirty-one-year-old coffee salesman who had murdered the teacher died in the electric chair at Sing Sing, *The New York Times* merely mentioned the execution. In the summer of 1976, newspapers devoted more space to dart gun attacks on women in various parts of Westchester, including Yonkers, where several women were struck. A year later, press coverage of crime intensified because of the fatal shootings of six young people and the wounding of seven others in a series of random attacks in different parts of New York City. When a detailed sketch of the suspect, in what was sometimes referred to as the "Lover's Lane" killings, was released in the summer of 1977, the New York City police received nearly two thousand calls.

Among the people who contacted New York detectives was a resident of the Yonkers apartment building where David Berkowitz, a twenty-four-year-old postal worker, lived. The neighbor had received threatening letters and thought that David Berkowitz might be responsible for them, as well as for the shooting spree. He also suspected Berkowitz may have set the fire that flared up outside the door to his apartment. Another Yonkers resident, Sam Carr, a businessman who lived not far from the Pine Street building where Berkowitz resided, was also suspicious. He was beginning to realize that he just might be the "Sam" Berkowitz had referred to in hand-printed letters found near some of the crime scenes. Carr suspected Berkowitz was the person who had firebombed his home, sent him threatening letters complaining about his dog, and shot and injured the dog. Two Yonkers Community Patrol Unit police officers investigated these incidents and concluded that David Berkowitz was the Son of Sam. They informed the New York City Police Department task force investigating the Son of Sam attacks of their suspicions. Sam Carr had done so as well.

At the time, a New York City detective was investigating a traffic summons issued to David Berkowitz in the area where a recent Son of Sam killing had occurred. The detective called Yonkers police headquarters and asked that the Yonkers police investigate Berkowitz. Interestingly, the Yonkers Police Department dispatcher who received the call was Sam Carr's daughter. She provided the New York City detective with information about both her father's suspicions and those of the community patrol officers. The end result was that New York City and Yonkers detectives went to Berkowitz's address and found his vehicle, which contained a partially concealed rifle. Surveillance was set up, and late on an August night in 1977 when Berkowitz tried to get into his car, he was apprehended. Initially taken to the Yonkers Detective Division, a smiling Berkowitz was questioned before being transferred to Manhattan for processing. There Berkowitz, who was described as "a loner, a quiet man who kept to himself," again smiled for reporters as he was led into the building.[103] During his arraignment, Berkowitz said Sam was a Yonkers neighbor, "who really is a man who lived 6,000 years ago," and who communicated through a dog.[104] According to Berkowitz, it was Sam who told him to kill.

In recognition of the collaborative effort that resulted in Berkowitz's apprehension, Ms. Carr, nine members of the Yonkers Police Department, the sheriff of Westchester County, and a deputy sheriff, who, as a resident of Berkowitz's building, had reported his suspicions about his neighbor to the New York police, were honored, along with nearly two hundred members of the New York City police force by New York Mayor Abraham Beame at an awards ceremony. The two Yonkers officers most closely associated with the case were also promoted. The city's police department, nevertheless, was sued by the family of the last person slain by Berkowitz and by an individual seriously injured in the same attack. The plaintiffs alleged that the Yonkers police had enough information months earlier to link Berkowitz with the shooting spree that had been ongoing, at that point, for the better part of a year.

Berkowitz admitted shooting thirteen people, killing six of them, and was sentenced to life imprisonment. Through the years his old apartment has had a number of different residents, but they, as well as other inhabitants of the Pine Street building where David Berkowitz lived, have avoided publicity. With the release of Spike Lee's film *Summer of Sam,* in 1999, the building once again became a tourist attraction but, happily, most of the curious visitors simply drove or walked by without tarrying.

A Song in My Heart

Although parts of the Spike Lee movie were filmed in Yonkers, a movie that some city residents felt should have been made in their community, *Hello, Dolly!,* was filmed elsewhere. Based on the enormously popular Broadway play, the 1969 film starred Barbra Streisand. Like the play, the film featured delightful music and had a happy ending. Less felicitous, though, was 20th Century Fox's choice of Garrison, in Putnam County, rather than Yonkers, for on location filming. At a spot near the Garrison railroad station, the Yonkers of the 1890s was recreated. In 1978, practically all of the made-for-television film *Sooner or Later* was filmed in Yonkers but in the actual movie, the name of the community was never mentioned. A few years earlier, in 1975, however, lots of publicity was generated for Yonkers when Tawny Elaine Godin, a native of the city, was crowned Miss America. At the time, nineteen-year-old Miss Godin, a graduate of Roosevelt High School, was a linguistics major at Skidmore College, where she earned straight As. Besides praising her academic record, the hometown paper noted the "beauty, personality and poise" she would bring to "the demanding job" of being Miss America during the upcoming bicentennial year when the nation would celebrate the two hundredth anniversary of its founding.[105] At the pageant in Atlantic City, another of her attributes was highlighted. An accomplished pianist, she played one of her own compositions during the talent portion of the pageant.

At five feet, ten and a half inches tall, Tawny Godin was the tallest Miss America and only the second winner from the State of New York. As the first Yonkers woman to be crowned Miss America, she was given the red carpet treatment when she returned to her hometown for official appearances. Since her visit coincided with the campaign season, *The New York Times* couldn't resist saying that her whirlwind tour of the city resembled "an election rally for Yonkers politicians."[106] In addition to a stop at Getty Square to receive a key to the city, there was an appearance, complete with speeches and proclamations, at Cross County Shopping Center. When this portion of the day's activities concluded, "the Miss America party," which included Tawny Godin's mother, Mayor Martinelli, and other members of the city government, "roared off with a siren-blowing, light-flashing police escort"; their destination was the Yonkers Public Library branch at the Hudson River Museum, where Miss America viewed a photographic exhibition "showing feminist progress."[107]

Had Tawny Godin returned to the museum/library complex a few years later and entered the modern portion of the museum itself, she would have been treated to a delightful, partially tongue-in-cheek program on UFOs. Using a sophisticated machine donated to the museum's Andrus Planetarium by the Surdna Foundation, the museum staff created a thought-provoking show that explored the possibility of life on other planets. Whether any beings from distant galaxies had actually visited Planet Earth was another matter, however. Despite the fact that the Andrus Planetarium received frequent calls about UFOs in the skies above Yonkers and environs, the curator of the Hudson River Museum pointed out that what people were seeing were planets that were visible to the naked eye. According to the curator, the man who insisted he saw a UFO hovering above Tuckahoe Road had really witnessed Venus. Try telling that, though, to those who believed in little green space aliens who travel to our neck of the woods in otherworldly, intergalactic craft! Yet, maybe at some point in the future, contact will be made with worlds beyond our own. Right now, that may seem improbable, but who knows what the future will bring.

For the Yonkers Historical Society, the future may be a time of limitless wealth. That's what society president and city historian Frank L. Walton had in mind when he announced, in 1965, that two bank accounts, one in the amount of fifty dollars, and the other for one hundred dollars, had been opened for the society. Through the miracle of compound interest, the first of the accounts would grow to $300 billion. Needless to say, it would take some time, until the year 5565 to be exact, because the money was to remain on deposit "for 3,600 years to mark the initial settlement of the Manhattes Indians."[108] According to Mr. Walton, "that makes Yonkers, as an inhabited spot, older than Paris or Rome."[109] As for the hundred-dollar gift, to mark the 1756 "wedding of Frederick Philipse and Elizabeth Rutger," that was to remain on deposit until the year 2174, when it would be worth $10 billion.[110] If the Yonkers Historical Society is not around when these milestones are reached, the accumulated billions can be used for museums, schools, and hospitals in Yonkers. Let's hope someone remembers where the bankbooks are!

To be sure, there was something whimsical and facetious about the small monetary gifts that were expected to grow into gigantic sums. At the time they were made, untold riches in the distant future seemed about as likely as a UFO landing in the parking lot at the Cross County Shopping Center. Something else that seemed improbable in the mid-sixties when Frank Walton was opening those bank accounts was the fiscal crisis that nearly shattered the city a decade later. With outside help, Yonkers survived, and by the end of the 1970s, the city appeared to be overcoming the negative publicity associated with near bankruptcy, a faltering urban renewal program, and the Son of Sam. A return to the glory days when Yonkers was the "Queen City of the Hudson" and the "City of Gracious Living" was perhaps too much to hope for, at least in the near future, but it was reasonable to expect that the decade ahead would be a more tranquil time.

6

A City in Transition

Challenges and Opportunities in the Decade of the Eighties

Not Again!

As the 1980s dawned, few residents of Yonkers could envision the new challenges their community would face in the not-too-distant future because the decade started off well, especially on the economic front. Longtime Yonkers companies were not only staying put but some were expanding. The Excelsior Transparent Bag Corporation, which had built a thirty thousand square foot plant in Yonkers in 1951, acquired additional space in the early eighties to meet the demands of such major customers as Lipton Tea, American Greeting Cards, Nabisco, and ShopRite supermarkets. Originally located on Nepperhan Avenue, Excelsior had moved to a site overlooking the Hudson River in the 1970s. At that time Yonkers was actively encouraging industrial development at the water's edge. As orders for its packaging materials increased, Excelsior, with loans from the New York State Job Development Authority and a bank, expanded its facilities, just opposite the former Alpine ferry dock, in the early eighties. Another company perched at the river's edge, Refined Syrups and Sugars, wasn't contemplating expansion as the 1980s got under way. It merely wanted to stay in business, but to do so it had to dredge the deep-water berth where ships delivering raw sugar tied up. This wasn't going to be easy, because PCBs had been found in samples taken from mud in the vicinity of the plant and the Environmental Protection Agency was reluctant to okay a permit to dump contaminated material in the Atlantic Ocean. In the end, Refined Syrups obtained the long-sought permit, but only

223

after congressional intervention. The uphill fight the company waged to secure the permit, however, was a reminder that doing business in Yonkers wasn't always easy.

Eager to convey a new, positive message about their fair city, Yonkers officials launched a "Yonkers Means Business" advertising blitz in the spring of 1982. The ads touted the city's comparatively low rents for commercial space, its pool of skilled workers, and its location on the Hudson River and major highways. A key supporter of this new campaign, Martin Berger, president of the Robert Martin Company, which was then Westchester's major developer, felt that businesses considering a move to Yonkers were impressed by the ease with which executives could gain access to city officials. Mr. Berger knew whereof he spoke because he was in the process of luring firms to his South Westchester Executive Park on the former Boyce Thompson property in the northern part of the city. In the spring of 1982, companies were also attracted to the portion of the Alexander Smith and Sons mills that was in the process of being marketed, as cooperatives, to manufacturing companies.

Although these developments were all positive, they could not offset the departure of Otis Elevator. This mainstay of the city's industrial sector had been a fixture on the local scene for 130 years, but in the summer of 1982, following a round of layoffs, rumors of the company's departure began to circulate. At the beginning of December, Otis ended the speculation with an announcement by its parent company, United Technologies Corporation, that the Yonkers plant would be permanently closed the following year. The company's rationale for abandoning the plant was that orders for the gearless elevators manufactured there had declined. Elevators with electronic controls constituted the new technology, and the Yonkers facility was deemed unsuitable for this type of manufacturing. Upon learning of United Technologies' decision to pull out of the city, Mayor Angelo Martinelli accused the company, which had acquired Otis in 1975, of breaking faith with Yonkers. The mayor was referring to the fact that United Technologies had benefited from Otis's acquisition, for a mere $600,000, of a site that had cost $14 million of taxpayers' money to purchase and prepare for the new plant Otis had erected in the 1970s. The mayor wasn't the only one who was fuming.

On a frigid December day, approximately 150 Otis employees gathered outside the plant and marched around, chanting: "Otis stays or UTC pays."[1] In his remarks to the assembled protesters, the president of the union representing Otis workers stated that after acquiring the elevator company in a hostile takeover in 1976, United Technologies "promised us 500 jobs" but instead moved work elsewhere, reducing the total number of employees from 1,400 to fewer than four hundred.[2] Soon after addressing the crowd, the union president joined Mayor Martinelli and four busloads of protesters for a trip to United Technologies' Hartford, Connecticut, headquarters for another demonstration, but before leaving Yonkers, the mayor declared war on UTC, vowing to sue the company "to get our money back."[3] Turning up the rhetoric, the mayor declared: "We want to make U.T.C. a bad household word. We want to make U.T.C. known as the company that raped Yonkers."[4] In Martinelli's opinion, "If a company buys the assets of a company, we say they should also buy their moral commitments."[5] None of this swayed United Technologies' CEO. He assumed full responsibility for the decision to close the Yonkers plant and insisted that there was nothing wrong with this. Absent a formal, written promise by Otis to keep the Yonkers plant functioning, in return for the site acquisition and clearance spearheaded by the Yonkers Development Agency, city officials wondered whether unjust enrichment would constitute grounds for a lawsuit against United Technologies. In March 1983, Mayor Martinelli headed to Washington, D.C., to seek support for the lawsuit from A.F.L.-C.I.O. leadership. Two unions representing employees of the Otis facility had already signed on to assist the city. With Mayor Martinelli contending that "this is a very significant test case with nationwide implications," the goal was to not only recoup the $14 million expended to purchase and clear the site of Otis's 1970s expansion but to "protect the investment of people's tax money and make a company think twice about doing something like this."[6]

While Yonkers was considering taking legal action against UTC, the company was actively marketing space in the Otis complex. Only a month after the plant closure was announced, the Proctor Paint and Varnish Company leased one of the nine buildings comprising the plant. The space taken by Proctor was located in one of Otis's original buildings, an area that had not benefited from the infusion of the $14 million. Despite its battle with Otis over this funding, Yonkers actually facilitated Proctor's move to the Otis plant because the company would have relocated had it not been able to obtain suitable space for expansion within the city. Proctor's decision to remain in Yonkers was good news. Yet, city officials wondered whether the rest of the vast Otis complex would attract new businesses. They didn't have to wait too long for an answer, because in 1984 the Port Authority of New York and New Jersey agreed to purchase the Otis site and, following renovations, rent it to industrial companies. This bold move, financed in part by New York State's portion of toll revenues from the Hudson River crossings, reflected "the state's commitment to rebuilding the economic base of the city of Yonkers," according to Governor Mario Cuomo.[7] Alfred B. DelBello, a former Yonkers mayor who was lieutenant governor of New York State at the time, declared that job creation at the former Otis site was "a critical element in our effort to return the site to its full potential as a revenue and job-producing resource" that would benefit Yonkers and the Hudson Valley.[8] The Port Authority, which was then developing industrial parks in the South Bronx and Elizabeth, New Jersey, envisioned the creation of nearly three thousand jobs at the Yonkers Industrial Park. Some of those positions would entail building state-of-the-art air-conditioned cars for the Trans-Hudson rail line and refurbishing older rolling stock. Contracts for this work were awarded to Kawasaki Heavy Industries of Kobe, Japan, which leased space in one of the Otis buildings, as well as outdoor areas to be used for a test track and storage of equipment.

Six months after Kawasaki was in full operation in Yonkers, manufacturing subway cars for the New York City transit system, as well as for Trans-Hudson, *The New York Times* noted that "many officials regard the Yonkers plant as a cross-cultural experiment that has arrived in the right place at the right time. Eventually, they hope, the plant will be making cars for railroad and subway systems around the world."[9] At the time, the plant had enough work to keep its employees busy for three years, including one hundred low-income Yonkers residents who were being trained by Kawasaki as required by the company's agreement with the city. To ensure that the plant would keep on humming well into the future, Yonkers officials journeyed halfway around the world in 1988 in an effort to convince Taiwanese officials to award a contract worth a whopping one billion dollars to the Yonkers plant. In return for that very nice piece of change, Taiwan's capital city, Taipei, would get eight hundred spanking new cars for its subway system, which was then under construction. Given the size of the contract and the fact that successful fulfillment would make the lucky company that landed it a prime candidate for similar jobs in other countries, Kawasaki was not the only firm competing to build subway cars for Taipei. Other Japanese companies, as well as European and Canadian firms, were wooing Taipei, as was an American consortium that included General Electric. Yonkers, nevertheless, thought it had an edge over the other bidders because its plant was building railroad cars from the ground up, not just putting them together. Assemblyman Terence Zaleski, a member of the Yonkers delegation meeting with Taiwanese officials, felt that the Taiwanese "were very impressed that, with us, they would be dealing with a manufacturer of rail cars rather than a dealer, or broker."[10] Summing up the trip, the assemblyman declared that it had "put us on the map, where previously we were an unknown quantity."[11]

Yonkers was definitely on the map in 1989 when Kawasaki won the coveted contract to build the Taiwanese subway cars. Soon thereafter, a congressional subcommittee launched an inquiry aimed at determining whether the contract had gone to a company that was largely American. Provided at least half of the parts incorporated into the finished products were made in the United States, the company was considered American. The contract ultimately survived the congressional investigation, but in 1993 a German company underbid the Yonkers plant to build several hundred additional cars for the Taipei subway. Local, state, and federal officials cried foul, accusing the successful bidder, which was subcontracting work to a South African company, of receiving a subsidy from the South African government. The Yonkers company was, in turn, accused of being nothing more than a front for a Japanese conglomerate.

In the context of the Taipei subway contract, too close an association with Japan was a negative, but in the 1980s this sort of relationship was a real boon for a six-year-old Yonkers telecommunications company that became the first non-Japanese firm to secure the right to market its connectivity systems in Japan. V Brand Systems Inc. manufactured telephone systems permitting simultaneous access to dozens of lines, just the sort of thing needed by securities and commodities traders. In fact, V Brand's telephone system was selected for installation in Tokyo's financial district. This was quite a coup, because the Japanese city had one of the biggest financial centers on the planet. V Brand wasn't the only Yonkers company making a successful foray into international markets in the eighties. The Loral Corporation was another. In 1986, Loral received the Governor's Award for Achievement in Export. Chosen because of its outstanding success in stimulating exports from New York State, Loral's foreign sales jumped by a whopping 42 percent in the mid-eighties. In an interview with *The New York Times,* Edward Borrazzo, president of Loral International Inc., the export component of the Loral Corporation, said that he expected the company's international business to "increase at a rate of about 10 per cent a year."[12] "The potential is there," he declared, adding: "We already have a presence, either through direct export or representatives in 15 companies, and we expect to expand and open new offices in the Far East shortly."[13] As if to foretell the future, the *Times* pointed out that "Mr. Borrazzo acknowledged that interest in buying Loral systems increased after every act of terrorism."[14] The Loral executive was, of course, referring to terrorist incidents abroad. That the United States would be targeted and that the deadliest of the September 11, 2001, attacks would occur in lower Manhattan, a relatively short distance from Yonkers, was unthinkable in the mid-1980s. At that time, businesses considering

A City in Transition • 227

relocating to Yonkers and developers contemplating major projects viewed proximity to Manhattan as a distinct advantage. Martin S. Berger, president of the Robert Martin Company, which was in the process of building the South Westchester Executive Park, asserted that "this location in Yonkers is geographically advantageous in every respect."[15] Pointing out that the new executive park, where seven buildings had been completed, was only ten minutes from the Bronx and a half hour from midtown Manhattan, Mr. Berger declared: "Yonkers is a tremendous bet for economic vitality in the next decade. It has all the ingredients—transportation, labor."[16] These were precisely the things that attracted former aerospace engineer Dr. Bernard Glassman, who had a PhD degree in applied mathematics from the University of California, when he was seeking a location for a bakery that would further the work of the Buddhist community he headed.

Now and Zen

The opening of Greyston Bakery in 1982 in an industrial area not far from the Hudson River took some Yonkers residents by surprise. They wondered why someone would be pouring money into an old lasagna factory on Woodworth Avenue, and there was also concern that the new enterprise would concentrate on turning out converts rather than cookies. Yet, from the very beginning, founder Bernard Glassman, who had become interested in Zen in the late fifties and had become a Buddhist monk in 1970, proclaimed that his goal was to teach "meditation-in-action" or the "work-practice" of Zen Buddhism.[17] Zen spirituality was very much in evidence at Greyston, especially during its start-up phase, among the staff of nearly three dozen monks and students, a handful of whom had been trained at a bakery operated by a Zen community in San Francisco. Before long, however, people of many different religious faiths were working at the Greyston bakery and were not subjected to proselytizing. Some employees, as well as outsiders including Roman Catholic, Jewish, and Muslim clergy, attended lectures given by Greyston's founder, as abbot of the Zen Community of New York, and meditated with him. Non-Buddhists viewed their experiences at Greyston as complements to their own religious beliefs.

Buddhists and non-Buddhists alike were attracted by the social mission of Greyston, namely to provide job training and positions for hundreds of Yonkers residents. A pilot program, funded in part by a performance grant from the Yonkers Private Industry Council, and aided by donations from Zaro's Bread Baskets, a major bakery in the New York area at the time, Japan's Takaki Baking Company, and Chemical Bank, enabled Greyston to demonstrate that unskilled people, including the homeless, could be transformed into successful workers. According to Bernard Glassman: "We felt that breaking the cycle of homelessness wasn't just a matter of providing temporary or even permanent housing if there wasn't a means of supporting that home or that life style."[18]

As part of its efforts to achieve these goals, Greyston provided very intensive training, which included months of classroom and lab work. The hands-on component consisted of rotations, lasting several weeks, through various stations. Throughout the process, trainees were provided with extensive support, which included counseling and, for mothers of young children, day care funded by the Westchester County Department of Social Services and the Yonkers Private Industry Council. Help with parenting skills was also available.

Although the thorough instruction provided by the Greyston Bakery program was designed to qualify its trainees for positions in other bakeries, restaurants, and hotels, some graduates not only landed jobs at the Greyston Bakery, but thanks to Bernard Glassman they found new homes as well at the Greyston Family Inn apartments. This burned-out shell of a building was completely rehabilitated by Greyston Builders, a minority-managed company. To purchase the building, the Zen Community of New York sold its Riverdale mansion in the late eighties. Another component of Bernard Glassman's grand plan was the Greyston Network, which provided all sorts of assistance ranging from day care to financial counseling. Before long, Greyston became as famous, at least in philanthropic circles, for its multipronged approach to alleviating the problems of the poor as it was for its baked goods. Yet, even the delectable goodies turned out during two eight-hour shifts per day at the Yonkers bakery were making a difference. Greyston donated part of the income from the sale of its Rainforest Crunch cookies to the effort to save the South American rain forest.

Equally as famous as the Rainforest cookies were the brownies the Greyston Bakery supplied to Ben & Jerry's for incorporation into their ice cream and the incredible mousses, cakes, and artistic tarts ordered by upscale restaurants, such as Windows on the World at the World Trade Center, and tony stores. Among Greyston's customers were Neiman Marcus, Bloomingdale's, Godiva Chocolatier, and Dean and deLuca. Not bad for a little place that originally marketed its products at the tiny Greyston Café in Riverdale, where the headquarters of the Zen Community of New York was located.

A New Day Dawning?

With Zen and the art of baking providing an antidote to homelessness, nothing seemed impossible in the Yonkers of the late 1980s, especially after one square mile in the southwestern part of the city was designated a New York State economic development zone in 1988. Created in 1986 by the state legislature to assist communities whose economies needed a boost, the program enabled municipalities receiving the coveted designation to utilize tax breaks and other incentives to lure developers. In the late eighties, when Yonkers became part of the program, the area included in the city's new development zone really needed help. Located in the zone were the Alexander Smith and Sons complex, Otis Elevator's buildings, the Getty Square business district, and empty parcels on the once-bustling Hudson River waterfront. Developers willing to commit to property in the zone would pay absolutely nothing in real estate taxes for the first seven years, with taxes increasing gradually after that until the tenth year, when the full amount would kick in. Discounted utilities for five years sweetened the deal as did refunds for both local and state taxes on any building materials. And that wasn't all. Investment tax credits and credits for wages paid employees holding the new jobs that were created were also part of the deal.

Almost immediately, the city was eyeing empty space at the Alexander Smith and Sons complex for an incubator where new businesses could be launched and nourished. During a tour of the state development zone for Vincent Tese, New York State director of economic development, Dean J. Grandin Jr., the city's planning director, pointed out that initially such companies employed only a few people but once they grew, jobs were created for dozens of people. The tour also included the Ashburton Urban Renewal Area where the city hoped to see light industry and the waterfront, which already had some thriving businesses, including a company that manufactured theatrical lighting. The Lockwood Lumber Company was rising in the same area. When the tour reached Getty Square, the Yonkers planning director pointed out that the city was "reviewing everything, including changing the zoning ordinances."[19] He also said that the colonnades "will go once we've decided on a new design for the area."[20]

Within months, a headline in *The New York Times* proclaimed: "Yonkers Razes a Blighted Parthenon."[21] The *Times* article began with the observation that when the colonnades were erected, they "held out all the hope of a heart transplant for Getty Square."[22] But instead of breathing new economic life into the area, the colonnades, which were akin to "plunking the Parthenon down, in, well, Yonkers," failed to attract shoppers.[23] It was clearly time for the colonnades, which were erected with $800,000 in federal community development funds, to go and no one quibbled over the $95,000 the city had to spend to get rid of them. With a junior high band playing in the background, on an October day in 1988, Mayor Nicholas Wasicsko grabbed a sledgehammer and, with gusto, took a swing at one of the columns. Then he declared that the city was now eliminating "this embarrassment."[24] The mayor described the colonnades as "a gimmick" rather than a cure for the city's economic decline.[25] Referring to the colonnades as "this monstrosity," he asserted that they had contributed to the decline of the area.[26] Proposing a novel way to dispose of this failed experiment, the Mayor suggested using some of the demolition debris to make what he called "Colonn-Aid" paperweights.[27]

It was clearly time for Yonkers to move forward, and attracting new businesses like Consumers Union was one way to do so. The highly respected independent testing laboratory and publisher of *Consumer Reports* magazine moved from Mount Vernon to Yonkers, to what had formerly been the headquarters of the Gestetner business machines corporation. This was a win-win situation for the city and the company because, according to Consumers Union's executive director, the new building was "a larger, better-functioning facility."[28]

Charge It, Please

Consumers Union's arrival in Yonkers, coupled with its expansion a few years later, was a welcome addition to the "Queen City of the Hudson's" economic base. It was a real achievement for a municipality valiantly striving to replace the industries that had once been engines of growth. As part of that effort, Yonkers, in the last decades of the twentieth century, endeavored, through its industrial development agency, to provide funding for all sorts of new businesses. In 1985, for example, the city put together a package of loans and grants for a developer who proposed erecting a large supermarket in an underserved area a few blocks from city hall. On the east side of the city, a thriving retail area for decades, new businesses could be launched more readily and often without government assistance. Such was the case when Stern's replaced Gimbel's as one of the anchor stores at the Cross County Shopping Center. Ironically, the Yonkers store was the single most profitable outlet in Gimbel's eastern division but Allied Stores Corporation, which acquired the department store chain in the mid-eighties, decided to divest itself of Gimbel's. Upon taking over, the new owners announced that the building would be shut down for nearly six months for top to bottom remodeling, before reopening as Stern's.

Besides being able to say "Charge it, please!" at the new anchor store at the Cross County Shopping Center, shoppers could give their plastic a workout at the Cross County Square Mall, which opened in 1987. Occupying the site where Alexander's had planned to build a store years earlier, the new shopping center was adjacent to the Cross County Shopping Center. Building in this location was not easy, because tons of rock had to be removed, but Bernard Rosenshein, developer of the Cross County Square Mall, was undaunted. He was also convinced that this new retailing venue, which included Crazy Eddie, an electronics store, Lens Crafters, Kids R Us, and Channel Home Center, would not compete with the adjacent Cross County Shopping Center. As far as the city was concerned, the more the merrier, because the new two-story mall was expected to contribute at least a million dollars a year in tax revenue to Yonkers. Ringing cash registers were music to the ears of city officials, as were the real estate taxes paid by retailers and the local income taxes paid by store employees, but Yonkers residents were not always favorably inclined toward new stores, especially those which, if built, would be a little too close to home. Such was the case with the Wilmorite mall proposed, in the eighties, for Nepperhan Avenue and Executive Boulevard. Although some city officials were impressed by the projected multimillion dollar tax revenue Yonkers would derive from the new project and the estimated thousand-plus jobs it would create, residents of Hastings-on-Hudson, Ardsley, Dobbs Ferry, and Greenburgh were concerned about the resulting traffic congestion. Their fears were laid to rest when Consumers Union acquired the property.

All Aboard!

Although some retailing initiatives failed to materialize, the city was decidedly pro-business, even going so far as to attempt to revive freight service between the Bronx and Ardsley on the Putnam Line. Nearly a year after the last freight train had made its way through Yonkers, the city began working with Westchester County and the New York State Urban Development Corporation to study the feasibility of reopening the line. The results of the study were disappointing. There just weren't enough businesses that were interested in using the line. Previous customers had switched over to trucks and indicated that they weren't likely to embrace rail service again. Thus, the idea of reviving the "Old Put"—as it was affectionately called—was derailed!

Yonkers had better luck with the garage and maintenance facility for county buses. A building that had once been part of Phelps Dodge Cable and Wire Company's sizable industrial operation in Yonkers was transformed inside and out. Part of the old brick façade was replaced by eyecatching blue and white siding, and the dingy interior was reconfigured for bus parking, washing, repairs, and offices, all with cheerful lighting. The new facility, which opened in 1982, was built by a company affiliated with Liberty Lines, which operated the public bus system for Westchester County. Financing for the project was facilitated by the county and once completed the building was leased by Westchester County and run by Liberty Lines.

Another form of mass transit, ferries, failed to attract financing, however. In 1984, with the governor of New Jersey calling for the Port Authority to restore ferry service on the Hudson to relieve congestion in tunnels and on bridges, Yonkers mayor Angelo Martinelli insisted that restoration of ferry service between Yonkers and Alpine, New Jersey, should be examined in a proposed feasibility study. The ferry idea went nowhere, but in 1985 as the New York Metropolitan Transportation Council examined ways of relieving congestion, the concept of a new Hudson River bridge was proposed. Where to put it was the problem, however. Riverfront communities in Westchester wanted no part of this, with one exception: Yonkers. Just as he was open to the idea of ferry service, Mayor Martinelli was willing for a bridge to make landfall in the "Queen City of the Hudson." Viewed from one perspective, an architecturally distinctive bridge would have added some pizzazz to the city's waterfront, maybe even jumpstarting the long-awaited revitalization.

The Mighty Hudson

Throughout the 1980s, however, the worthy goal of reclaiming the Hudson River shoreline was obscured by controversy over the sewage treatment plant in southwest Yonkers. In operation since 1929, the plant, which was enlarged over the years, had been upgraded in 1978 to a secondary treatment facility where state-of-the-art technology subjected the waste from 60 percent of Westchester County to processes that served to better protect the adjacent Hudson River. The sewage residue, known as sludge, was then placed on barges and taken to ocean dumping sites. When federal legislation known as the Clean Water Act mandated the phasing out of ocean dumping, Westchester County had to find a new way to dispose of its sludge. From the standpoint of county officials the logical solution was to enlarge the Yonkers sewage treatment facility once again by erecting a dewatering plant to transform the sludge into small, odorless chunks suitable for incineration at the county's yet-to-be-built solid waste plant in Peekskill. Residents of the Ludlow Park area where the sewage treatment plant was located were furious. Their councilman, Peter A. Chema, was quick to point out that when the original plant had been built, "they said there would be no smell, no problems," but this proved untrue for according to Chema: "On some days you can't even walk through there."[29] Commenting specifically on the proposed dewatering plant, he said that the new facility slated for the parking lot of the sewage treatment plant was "just another example of the county using southwest Yonkers as a dumping ground for its unwanted projects."[30] The Ludlow Park Homeowners Association wasn't going to stand for it this time, though. It sued both Westchester County and the Environmental Protection Agency, the federal entity that had approved construction of the dewatering plant in the neighborhood.

Besides grappling with the issue of how to dispose of sludge, Westchester County had to deal with the challenge posed by the sheer volume of sewage entering its treatment plants, some of it the result of illegal hookups. The county's aging facilities were reaching or exceeding capacity. Even with upgrades, the Yonkers plant was designed to process a maximum of ninety-two million gallons per day; by the late 1980s when it was handling the sewage of approximately 65 percent of the county's population, 115 million gallons per day were flowing through the plant. This set off an alarm bell at the New York State Department of Environmental Conservation, and in 1988 the agency imposed a six-month moratorium on new sewer extensions flowing into the Yonkers plant. This resulted in a virtual cessation of new residential and commercial construction in communities as far north as Bedford. Despite howls from developers, the moratorium was extended.

Given the obvious need for a sewage treatment plant and the fact that the facility, albeit on a smaller scale, had been a fixture on the river since the 1920s, it is not surprising that the coastal management document published by the city's department of planning in 1980 noted that "the waterfront deserves a plan which balances the continued need for industrial development and the need for the public to have access to the Hudson River for recreation as well as housing and commercial activities."[31] A most enjoyable way of accessing the river was to board the *Clearwater*, a reproduction of a nineteenth-century sloop that became reality thanks to the promotional and fundraising efforts of folk singer Pete Seeger and other volunteers of the nonprofit Hudson River Sloop

Clearwater Inc. For environmentalism the sloop was a "flagship" because of its pioneering role in educating the public, especially children, about the need for environmental awareness, beginning in the 1970s when it became a familiar sight on the Hudson.[32] A decade later, with help from Pete Seeger and the members of Ferry Sloops, a nonprofit organization spun off by Clearwater, Inc., the *Sojourner Truth* was launched in Yonkers, where volunteers had worked on it for three years. Named for a nineteenth-century slave who was an advocate of abolitionism and women's rights, the sloop's mission was to provide environmental education.

Reproductions of sailing vessels wouldn't have been the only new boats on the river if the developer selected by the city to undertake Phase 1A of a waterfront revitalization plan in the early eighties had been able to implement his vision, which included a new ferry to Alpine, a restaurant on a city pier, commercial space in a former power generating plant, and, a bit inland, a shopping mall in a trolley barn. By 1987, part of the Phase 1A revitalization was moving forward at the old power plant, but instead of offices the space was being converted into the Scrimshaw House condominiums. At Pierpointe on the Hudson, a marina, stores, restaurant, health club, boardwalk, and two thousand condominiums in high-rise buildings were part of a revised plan. Scenic Hudson, Inc., and Clearwater, Inc. voiced concerns about the visual impact of the proposed thirty-five-story towers and the potential for reduced public access to the water. Both groups felt it would set a bad precedent, thus opening the door to rapid, urban-style development throughout the Hudson Valley. Pierpointe's implications for the racial composition of southwest Yonkers proved to be the most significant local issue. In 1988, when, as the result of a landmark judicial case (discussed later in this chapter), the city had agreed to build low-income housing in white neighborhoods on the east side of Yonkers, Herman Keith, a member of the Westchester County Board of Legislators and a former president of the Yonkers chapter of the National Association for the Advancement of Colored People, observed that Pierpointe, which was likely to attract mostly white buyers, would "resegregate the west side as we move to integrate the east side."[33] Fearing that the influx of upward of four thousand new, mainly Caucasian, residents would cause the area to forfeit its minority representation on the Yonkers City Council and the county board of legislators, Keith endorsed the idea of a scaled-down project. The Yonkers Chamber of Commerce, on the other hand, thought that Pierpointe was just fine, as proposed. Chamber president Thomas J. Caramadre declared that the project would energize an area "that once was a bleak eyesore."[34] According to Mr. Caramadre, the project would lead to job creation and tax revenues of "$5 million annually."[35] It would take a while before any benefits would be realized, however, because, in the midst of a recession, with its attendant impact upon the real estate market, Pierponte's developers fell behind in interest payments and the bank that had provided the construction loan for the first phase of the project foreclosed.

Down Time

Although the city's waterfront redevelopment appeared stalled, other projects proceeded. Westchester County built tennis courts and a new playground in Tibbetts Brook Park in the eighties. The county also rebuilt the Dunwoodie Golf Course in the 1980s. Elsewhere in Yonkers, another recreational venue was created to educate the public about the county's agrarian heritage. This was the work of the Greater Westchester County and Exposition Corporation, whose CEO Timothy J. Rooney, president of Yonkers Raceway, revived the Westchester County Fair in 1981. Rooney had fond memories of the country fairs he had attended as a boy in western Pennsylvania and wanted to provide an opportunity for Westchester residents, especially children, to experience something similar. Since the last such event in the county had taken place three decades earlier, it was safe to assume that the parents of those youngsters were unfamiliar with both country fairs and the agrarian economy responsible for spawning them. As part of his effort to educate visitors about agriculture, Timothy Rooney installed livestock exhibits in the raceway's paddock area and he enlisted 4-H clubs in northern Westchester and elsewhere to create displays. The clubhouse served as the fair's exhibition hall; horticultural specimens and products of area businesses were on view there throughout the nine-day fair. Dominating the track's infield was a midway featuring rides and games, and both day and night there was entertainment. With so much to enjoy, it's not surprising that two hundred thousand people showed up.

This surely must have warmed the heart of Timothy Rooney, because only a year earlier the fate of Yonkers Raceway was in doubt. A threatened strike over the issue of wage parity for clerks selling and cashing pari-mutuel tickets, plus competition from the Meadowlands racetrack, clouded the future of the raceway. A resolution of the pay dispute and the introduction of Sunday racing gave the Yonkers track a new lease on life. But other problems soon surfaced. Members of the Standardized Owners Association boycotted the track in 1982 because of the lack of minimum purses at Yonkers. Two years later, the raceway was sued by the federal government for discriminating against minorities, including women, in the hiring and recruitment process. At the same time, it was facing increased competition not only from the Meadowlands but from nonequestrian forms of gambling at Atlantic City casinos. Even Lotto, the popular New York State lottery, was suspected of diverting betting money from the track. Should Off Track Betting come to Westchester County, that would be the final blow. Since the raceway, with nearly seven hundred workers, was the second-largest employer in Yonkers, neither the city nor Westchester County, both of which received tax revenue from the track, wanted to see it close. Closed-circuit televised simulcasts of races at Aqueduct on which Yonkers patrons could place bets helped but another strike by pari-mutuel clerks in the mid-eighties closed the track for a time.

Local Politics: Déjà vu and "Yonkitis"

Ensuring the continued survival of the Yonkers Raceway was a real challenge, but it was only one of many problems the city had to grapple with in the eighties. Mayor Gerald Loehr, who was inaugurated in January 1980, was well aware of those issues. The grandson of former Yonkers mayor Joseph Loehr, whose administration had begun in 1932, Gerald Loehr admitted a half-century later when he followed in his grandfather's political footsteps that things would "get tougher before they got better," but he was undaunted, declaring: "Yonkers can be great again."[36] For the city to rebound, however, what was needed was bipartisanship, but that was hard to come by in Yonkers. The reporter who covered Gerald Loehr's inauguration observed that "the ward system remains firmly entrenched and City Managers, technically more powerful than the 'ceremonial' mayors, seem to come and go with ease."[37] A few months after Loehr succeeded Angelo Martinelli, whom he defeated in the previous November's election, City Manager Pat T. Ravo was on the way out. A federal audit had uncovered questionable practices in the use of funds awarded to the Yonkers Community Development Agency, which Ravo chaired, and while denying that he had personally done anything wrong, Ravo resigned as city manager. He was succeeded by Yonkers corporation counsel Eugene Fox, who was appointed acting city manager. The revolving door in the city manager's office had turned once again, for the sixth time since 1974!

Was this any way to run the government of the fourth-largest city in the State of New York? Some citizens of Yonkers thought not, preferring instead a strong mayor, and this is precisely what a committee appointed by the city's charter revision commission recommended in 1980, after studying the issue for two years. In view of voters' rejection of a previous referendum calling for the replacement of the city manager form of government with a system in which mayors would have more power, floating the idea a second time would not be easy. Of course, given the frequency with which city managers were twirling around in the revolving door, even some opponents of the strong mayor concept were willing to at least consider it. One wonders whether Acting City Manager Eugene Fox was himself ready to endorse the idea. Like some of his predecessors, who had experienced health problems during their tenure, Fox called in sick a month after being appointed acting city manager. Veteran city hall staffers joked, only half facetiously, it would seem, that Fox had a bad case of "Yonkitis," brought on by a slowdown by sanitation workers in response to a new city budget that necessitated layoffs. There was another not-so-little problem as well: a strike threat by firefighters. Fortunately, Acting City Manager Fox made a quick recovery and the issues with the city's unions were resolved, if only temporarily.

Soon after the November 1980 election, in which a strong mayor referendum went down to defeat again, Fox was no longer acting. The city council voted to make his appointment permanent. Within months, the city manager was dealing with labor unrest once again. This time firefighters not only threatened to strike; they actually did so, in April 1981, over wages and a demand for a shorter week, something the police had already negotiated. With a projected budget deficit of $6 million for the fiscal year ending in June 1981, the city simply could not accede to union demands, especially since there was no guarantee that the additional state aid Yonkers representatives in Albany were seeking would be forthcoming. What could the city do? Well, aside from having the mayor don jeans and a casual jacket in the middle of the night before picking up a fire hose to help douse a blaze in southwest Yonkers, something Gerald Loehr actually did, the city sent an SOS requesting Governor Hugh Carey to dispatch the National Guard to the "Queen City of the Hudson." Albany sent a team of fact finders instead, and Yonkers continued to rely on neighboring communities to put out its blazes. While state officials tried to assess the situation, a bomb threat forced the evacuation of the Holiday Inn on Tuckahoe Road where negotiations were taking place between the city and representatives of not only the firefighters but superior police officers, holding such ranks as captain, and sanitation workers, who had joined the firefighters in striking the city.

The fragrance of garbage permeating the spring air could be tolerated, at least for a while, but the fire emergency could not. With plumes of smoke ascending from the rubble of still smoldering buildings and fire companies from neighboring communities growing reluctant to risk encounters with their picketing Yonkers counterparts, the city kept on pressing Governor Carey to send in the National Guard. Should he have done so, the National Guard would not have actually fought fires; its role would have been to escort visiting firefighters to Yonkers blazes. The nature of the Guard's duties notwithstanding, its presence in the state's fourth largest municipality would have sent a signal that Yonkers was truly unraveling. Appearances do count and images of armed, uniformed guardsmen would have been picked up by the media and broadcast nationally and maybe even globally, discouraging potential investors and developers. The way around this was to go the judicial route, which is what Yonkers did. The city obtained a restraining order against the unions; strikers abandoned picket lines and went back to work with the understanding that their differences with the city would be resolved by arbitration. Within weeks, the workers were awarded some of the fringe benefits they had demanded and the unions agreed to certain givebacks such as the performance, for a few hours each week, of duties not specifically included in their job descriptions. But could Yonkers afford the new contracts? The fiscal year that would soon end was the first since the fiscal crisis of the seventies that saw the city in the red, and the deficit projected for the fiscal year beginning July 1 was even larger. It seemed like "déjà vu" because without a major infusion of state aid, layoffs and cuts in municipal services would be unavoidable.

Until the precise amount of assistance from Albany was known, the Yonkers budget was delayed. County executive and former Yonkers mayor Alfred B. DelBello offered to help by renting cells in the Yonkers jail, contributing to the purchase of the Austin Avenue industrial site, and providing a quarter of a million dollars for the Hudson River Museum, but in return the Austin Avenue land would have been transferred to the county, which would have also assumed ownership of the museum. The city council rejected Westchester's offer in early August, and along with it a revised budget. Soon thereafter, the council approved a balanced budget, which reflected the elimination of major capital expenditures. Layoffs of municipal workers were deferred for several months and the hope was that a combination of aid from both New York State and the county would make them unnecessary. Andrew P. O'Rourke, chairman of the county board of legislators and a Yonkers resident, put forth a plan to assist Yonkers without taking title to any of the city's real estate, with the exception of the jail, which O'Rourke recommended the county purchase outright to alleviate overcrowding in the county's correctional facility.

While Yonkers and county officials considered this proposal, the city awaited the state comptroller's verdict on the 1981–82 municipal budget.

Yonkers was required, by law, to submit its budget to the comptroller, who had to certify that the budget was fiscally sound. Absent that certification by the August 15, 1981, deadline the city would have been technically bankrupt. Fortunately, this was avoided. Moreover, Yonkers benefited from adoption by the New York State Legislature of a package to aid cities. Ironically, in October, when the city was awarded $6.4 million from the state, auditors doing the final accounting for the previous fiscal year announced that the city had a million dollar surplus. That should have been good news for incumbent mayor Gerald Loehr, who was running for reelection against his old rival, former mayor Angelo Martinelli, but Yonkers being Yonkers, winning reelection wasn't easy, as Martinelli had learned two years before when he lost by fewer than a thousand votes. This time it was a different story. Martinelli won.

Familiar Face, Familiar Problems

Having a familiar face back in city hall may have been comforting, but following his inauguration, the once and current mayor had to grapple with challenges that were all too familiar. Within days of being sworn in, he took a stab at the city's ongoing financial woes by dismissing provisional employees and asking all department heads to resign. Soon after the election, Martinelli had launched a search for a new city manager, and a month after the inauguration the city council voted to appoint Dr. Sal J. Prezioso, director of the graduate program in public administration at Pace University, to the position. In reporting the appointment of "a courtly, white-haired university administrator," whose resume included extensive experience in government, as administrator of Long Branch, New Jersey, commissioner of parks and recreation of New York State, and chief executive officer of Westchester County, *The New York Times* observed that Dr. Prezioso would be required to obtain aid totaling at least $14 million from New York State and Westchester County to close a gap in the 1983–84 budget, and that he would need the approval of "a City Council whose members frequently appear motivated more by ward politics than city needs."[38]

Given all of these challenges, the reporter couldn't help but wonder why Dr. Prezioso was willing to take the Yonkers position. The new city manager's response was: "A friend of mine said, 'You need psychiatric treatment,'" but, with a smile on his face, he added: "I know I'm not going into a bed of roses. I don't know all the nuts and bolts, but I'm optimistic enough to believe I can make a substantial contribution."[39] He was also a realist, and that's why he demanded a contract, a first for a Yonkers city manager, which coincided with the terms of the mayor and city council.

Dr. Prezioso had scarcely settled into his new position when a building that was a mere stone's throw from his city hall office became a cause celebre. It was the grand old Carnegie Public Library, the gift of industrialist Andrew Carnegie in 1903. Although Yonkers, in the 1960s, had transferred the building to New York State, which planned to demolish it because it stood in the way of an arterial road plan for the downtown area, the city continued to use the building as a library for a number of years before moving its downtown library to the Howland's Department Store building. The Carnegie Library was then set for demolition. A committee to save the library was formed, but its efforts were unsuccessful. Sacrificing the old in order to make way for the new, in this case a road system that would make the downtown area more accessible and hence more desirable from the standpoint of development, represented progress to some and a setback to others. Above all, it was a reminder that nothing came easy in Yonkers. The city seemed to be engaged in a perpetual balancing act, especially at budget time. As the deadline for the 1982–83 budget approached, City Manager Prezioso was confident that Yonkers would receive additional state aid, but a promise made is not a promise fulfilled. Thus, the proposed budget included an increase in property taxes, new taxes on previously exempt waterfront property, and a reduction in library funding. State aid was forthcoming but it was contingent upon Yonkers receiving a little over a million dollars for transferring the Austin Avenue property to the county. Once this deal was in place, the state kicked in an additional $2.5 million. Amazingly, the new budget was the first in seven years to be approved by the city council by the July 1 deadline.

With the budget in place, Yonkers officials may have hoped for smooth sailing, but they were preoccupied by a major issue, the ward system. In a municipality where council members, elected by voters in each of a dozen wards, were long suspected of putting their constituents' needs before those of the city as a whole, the leadership of both the Republican and Democratic parties, as well as the League of Women Voters, thought it was time for a change. Therefore, Proposition 1 appeared on the ballot in 1982. It called for reducing the number of wards to four, which would be renamed city council districts, each of which would cover the same areas as the four county legislative districts, with four council members chosen by each district, two elected by all Yonkers voters, and the one receiving the most votes becoming vice mayor. Proposed by the charter revision commission, a body that included representatives of the major political parties, as well as business and civic leaders, the proposition was wholeheartedly endorsed by Mayor Martinelli. To the consternation of those who opposed tinkering with the way Yonkers representatives had been elected for a century, the proposition passed, but that wasn't the end of the matter because the New York Civil Liberties Union filed suit on behalf of three minority residents and the Black and Hispanic Political Club of Yonkers. Contending that the new system would make the election of a minority council member almost impossible, the suit claimed it was unconstitutional and a clear violation of the Federal Voting Rights Act. The suit led to a negotiated agreement calling for a return to the old system of twelve wards, under which one ward's large minority population would ensure the election of a minority member to the city council. This was to be a temporary measure until a referendum could be held on a proposal for a city council composed of seven members.

In addition to dealing with the issue of minority representation on the city council, Yonkers continued to face fiscal challenges. As work began on the 1983–84 budget, a financial storm cloud every bit as menacing as the one that had hovered over Yonkers in the mid-seventies appeared on the horizon. With a projected budget deficit of approximately $25 million for the fiscal year beginning July 1, massive layoffs and new taxes, including an income tax surcharge, seemed likely. This was not the sort of thing that would make the mayor and city council endearing to voters in an election year. Although the mayor was willing to bite the bullet and support new taxes, the council refused to approve budgets containing such levies. Still without a budget six weeks beyond the deadline, Yonkers was confronted with the very real possibility that New York State would step in. The state comptroller had been empowered to do so by legislation enacted during the fiscal crisis of the seventies to protect holders of the city's bonds. The adoption of a budget by the city council, forty-eight hours before a state-imposed deadline, avoided intervention, but it was a close call. Following the vote to approve the budget, Mayor Martinelli was quick to declare: "We'll have troubles up and down the line with this budget."[40] And it would be Martnelli who would have to deal with those problems because he was reelected in November. During the campaign he managed to convince a sufficient number of voters that a proposed surcharge on the New York State income taxes paid by residents of the city would be the key to funding the school system. Although some seasoned political observers thought that Martinelli's pro-tax stance would cost him the election, he came out ahead of his opponents in a four-way race. Elated though he was over his election, Martinelli was saddened by the decision of City Manager Prezioso to leave Yonkers.

Prezioso was departing in early 1984, but former mayor Alfred DelBello, now the lieutenant governor of New York State, was returning to Yonkers. Governor Mario Cuomo had appointed DelBello to chair a panel reviewing the city's budget with an eye toward proposing remedies for the latest projected deficit. Of special concern was funding for the city's public schools because the board of education was considering shutting down schools for nearly a month as a way of dealing with lack of money. Compounding the schools' very real financial problems was the prospect of a multimillion-dollar suit by the mother of a student who, after being permitted to join a high school football team without the required physical exam, died during a game. Also on the education front, the landmark suit linking school and housing segregation (covered later in this chapter) was pending.

Assisting the mayor and city council in working through some of these issues was a new city manager, Rodney H. Irwin, who had been the administrator of Mahwah, New Jersey. Although Irwin wasn't supposed to take over officially until February, he journeyed to the Albany office of Lieutenant Governor DelBello a month earlier for a meeting at which Nicholas DeSantis, who had been serving as acting city manager since Sal Prezioso's departure, delivered some very bad news. The city's projected deficit for the remainder of the current fiscal year and the following year could be as high as $71 million! Even the lieutenant governor seemed to be taken aback by this figure. Something had to be done. Getting help from the state was sort of taken for granted but the city was urged to not only find some money on its own but to come up with ways of resolving its financial problems, long-term. This would not be easy. Recent auctions of properties on which taxes had not been paid brought in some revenue but the city had to refund $7 million to the Cross County Shopping Center after it successfully challenged its assessment. Yonkers also stood to lose another $7 million because of an adverse court ruling on what was called the "Yonkers Plan," a system involving sales and property taxes, in which Westchester County shared revenue with municipalities. The way this worked was that Yonkers and the other cities in Westchester were permitted to keep county sales tax revenues while county government collected a like amount in property taxes in the cities. Since this was a way around the 2 percent limit on municipal property taxes, a State Supreme Court judge concluded that the "Yonkers Plan" violated the New York State Constitution. Although the judge was willing to allow the arrangement to remain in place for the duration of the fiscal year, beleaguered Yonkers had to find a new source of revenue.

To Yonkers residents both inside and outside of government, it seemed that nothing was going right for the "Queen City of the Hudson." But then, like a knight in shining armor, State Senator John E. Flynn galloped to the rescue in February with a proposal for ten measures, most of which would have required approval by the state legislature as well as by the city council. These measures included increased property taxes, removal of the cap on state revenue sharing, and changing formulas for state aid to education. Mayor Martinelli urged the city council to consider the entire proposal immediately, but that did not happen. Moreover, Lieutenant Governor DelBello indicated that some of the measures posed constitutional or other problems. Within weeks, he issued an ultimatum demanding that Yonkers put forth a plan to get its fiscal house in order. As a former mayor of the fourth-largest city in the State of New York, DelBello certainly knew that this was easier said than done. In the final analysis, help from the state was the only way out of the fiscal morass, at least in the short run. But, as before, it came with strings attached. With the city expected to quite literally run out of money in two months, Governor Mario Cuomo, in March 1984, offered Yonkers an infusion of cash provided the city agreed to financial oversight. The city council, however, had to pass a home rule request for state legislation authorizing the arrangement proposed by the governor. Mayor Martinelli favored this but the city council was slow to act. *The New York Times* found this inexplicable. In an editorial, the paper noted: "Yonkers has lurched from crisis to crisis long enough. Its chance for fully independent action has expired."[41]

The city council wasn't about to cave in, however; nor was the state. The end result was that the cash-starved Yonkers public schools would have to close at the end of April. In an attempt to prevent this, the board of education sued the city. Arguing in State Supreme Court that curtailing the school year by forty days would violate state law and result in a loss of state aid, the Board demanded $12.5 million from the city to keep the schools open. The city offered to transfer $1.5 million to the schools but Dr. Joan M. Raymond, superintendent of schools since 1979, was quick to point out that this was only enough to keep classes in session for a few days. Although spring break was extended for three days, the remainder of the school year was salvaged, despite the fact that the board of education lost its suit against the city. What saved the day was the willingness, albeit reluctant, of the city council to finally accept state oversight of its finances by a control board chaired by Lieutenant Governor DelBello. The board would have sweeping power over budgets, contracts, and salaries of municipal employees for a minimum period of three years, after which it would be dissolved if the city repaid the $9.5 million loan advanced by the state and provided other evidence of fiscal responsibility.

As the city labored to get its financial house in order, it grappled with another recurring issue, namely the concept of a strong mayor form of government. For the fourth time in a dozen years, a proposition calling for the elimination of the position of city manager appeared on the ballot in November 1984 and once again it went down to defeat, but by fewer than four hundred votes. No less contentious than the battles over a strong mayor form of government were actual mayoral elections, and 1985 was no exception.

That year, incumbent mayor Angelo Martinelli and his Democratic opponent Bernice Spreckman, a member of the city council, duked it out verbally. Although Mrs. Spreckman came out swinging on the fiscal issue, blaming the incumbent mayor, he was quick to point an accusing finger at the Democratic majority on the city council. Voters evidently believed Martinelli, because they reelected him, thus ensuring continuity in the office of the mayor as the city worked to address its fiscal problems and other ongoing challenges. There was also a new issue that landed Yonkers on the front page of newspapers nationwide.

The Tylenol Mystery

A month after Angelo Martinelli was inaugurated, a twenty-three-year-old Peekskill woman died while spending the weekend with her boyfriend, a former college classmate, and his parents at their Yonkers home. Since she wasn't feeling well, the young woman took two Extra-Strength Tylenol capsules on Saturday evening. When she did not join the family for breakfast on Sunday morning, her boyfriend went to check on her and found her lifeless body. The cause of death was cyanide poisoning. One of the pills she had taken was laced with the substance, as were three others contained in a bottle of Tylenol that had been purchased at the A&P supermarket in Bronxville. Five years earlier, Tylenol tainted with cyanide had caused the deaths of seven people in the Midwest.

Following the death of the Westchester woman, Tylenol was pulled from store shelves and the public was warned not to use the nonprescription drug. A thorough investigation of the Johnson & Johnson pharmaceutical company's subsidiary where the Tylenol that killed the Westchester woman had been manufactured ruled out the plant as the source of the cyanide. As Yonkers police moved forward with a homicide investigation, U.S. Food and Drug Administration chemists discovered cyanide in capsules contained in a bottle seized from the Woolworth's store in Bronxville, a mere block and a half from the A&P. That wasn't the only bottle of poisoned pills in Westchester. Chemists analyzing Tylenol capsules in a bottle taken from an A&P in the Northern Westchester community of Shrub Oak discovered a trace amount of a substance that could have been either cyanide or a cleanser. How these poisons were getting into triple-sealed bottles of Tylenol was a real mystery, but Johnson & Johnson, which suspended the manufacturing of Tylenol capsules, indicated that the product was tamper resistant, not tamper proof. A skilled person could alter the contents of a tamper-resistant bottle and the unsuspecting public had no way of knowing that the over the counter drug they were about to consume could be deadly.

Unwilling to rule out the possibility that such an individual might be a disgruntled employee, the F.B.I. announced that employee data and other records pertaining to the Midwest deaths would be reviewed in an attempt to solve the Yonkers case. Meanwhile, in Yonkers the police made a valiant effort to gather evidence. Focusing special attention on the Bronxville A&P, they interviewed store employees, delivery people, and shoppers. In the midst of the investigation, Bronxville police arrested a young man who wrote a letter making a false claim that he had been responsible for the death in Yonkers and demanding $2 million to cease tampering with Tylenol. The suspect was already known to police because of a recent credit card fraud charge. In addition to the man seeking the big payoff to refrain from doing something he hadn't actually been doing, threats to poison other drugs in capsule form emanated from unknown sources. Less than two months after the death of the Westchester woman, however, the trail was growing cold. Three months later it was colder still, but Johnson & Johnson had made a full recovery. By the summer of 1986 sales of the new caplet form of the drug were within four percentage points of total Tylenol sales prior to the tampering. The pharmaceutical giant was batting a thousand but, sadly, none of the agencies investigating the tampering case got to first base. Nearly a quarter-century later, the case remained unsolved.

Politics as Usual?

There's no way of knowing whether members of the Yonkers municipal government were reaching for the new, more tamper-resistant Tylenol caplets to alleviate headaches brought on by political wrangling, but there was a time in the autumn of 1986 when the mayor and city council were able to leave the Tylenol in the medicine cabinet. Amazingly, peace and harmony prevailed at city hall as the mayor and city council united to appoint Nicholas DeSantis city manager, the third in two years! For once, members of the city government saw eye to eye because, as commissioner of fiscal services and budget, DeSantis was not only an expert on municipal finances but he had saved Yonkers millions by refinancing part of the city's outstanding debt at lower interest rates. Within six months of becoming city manager, DeSantis presented a proposed budget for the fiscal year beginning in July 1987. Although he was confident that Yonkers was working its way out of its financial problems, DeSantis recommended retaining the income tax surcharge that had been enacted in 1984 and increasing property taxes. In August 1987, DeSantis presented a four-year fiscal plan. Any hopes Nicholas DeSantis may have had of sticking around long enough to implement a four-year plan were abandoned, however, following the 1987 mayoral election in which incumbent Angelo Martinelli was defeated by Nicholas C. Wasicsko, a twenty-something one-term member of the city council. DeSantis resigned as city manager soon after an election that would set Yonkers on a new course, and although no one recognized it at the time, the key factor in Wasicsko's victory, the landmark desegregation case linking schools and housing, would prove to be his undoing.

Background of the Case

When Angelo Martinelli turned over the keys to the mayor's office to Nicholas Wasicsko on inauguration day 1988, the landmark desegregation case linking schools and housing was officially in its eighth year, but it had begun taking shape earlier, in 1975, when Winston Ross, director of the Westchester Community Opportunity Program, filed a segregation complaint with the Yonkers School Board. Years before, while a student in the city's public schools, Mr. Ross, along with the majority of African American students, was unable to gain admission to an academic high school. As a result he lacked the prerequisites for acceptance at a four-year college and therefore enrolled in a community college before going on to earn undergraduate and graduate degrees at top universities. In the absence of any progress on the complaint he filed in 1975, Winston Ross decided to pursue a different strategy, resulting, in 1978, in the Yonkers chapter of the National Association for the Advancement of Colored People filing a complaint with the Justice Department and the United States Department of Health Education and Welfare. The Justice Department reacted to the complaint in June 1980, a year when "19 out of 25 elementary schools were either over 80% white or 80% minority" and "almost one-half of the elementary schools' minority enrollment . . . attended five schools in West Yonkers."[42] The Justice Department accused the City of Yonkers, its board of education, and the Yonkers Community Development Agency of engaging in an illegal pattern of racial segregation in the public schools and of contributing to racial imbalance in the schools by erecting most of the city's subsidized housing west of the Saw Mill River. The city and its school district were given a month to indicate their willingness to negotiate with the Justice Department to correct these problems. If they failed to comply, a federal lawsuit aimed at effecting total desegregation would be filed. Immediately after the Justice Department's intentions were revealed, *The Herald Statesman* sent two reporters out to different parts of the city to gauge public reaction. The resulting article noted that "as with most black and white residents interviewed," the major concern was busing of students.[43] According to the paper, the majority of white residents opposed busing and indicated they would choose private schools for their children or leave Yonkers, while "black residents are generally split on the issue."[44] In 1978, Yonkers schools superintendent Dr. Joseph P. Robitaille had proposed a reorganization plan, which, by changing district boundaries, would have led to busing from one side of the city to the other but the board of education did not approve the plan.

In the wake of the 1980 accusations by the Justice Department, busing came to the forefront again, but before busing or any other remedies for school segregation could be implemented, Yonkers had to come up with a plan acceptable to the Justice Department. What Yonkers wanted was a voluntary plan that would not involve federal intervention. Toward that end the city filed a motion in Federal District Court in the fall of 1980 but Judge Leonard B. Sand denied the motion. Since three Midwestern cities that were also accused of school segregation by the Justice Department entered into agreements with the department to implement desegregation plans, Yonkers was viewed as obstructionist. The end result was that on the last day of November 1980 the United States Justice Department filed suit in Federal District Court in New York City charging Yonkers with having deliberately and illegally segregated public schools and housing. The case broke legal ground because it was the first federal action that linked housing and school discrimination. Considering how long the case would drag on, it is interesting to note that when the suit was filed the Justice Department asked the court to order Yonkers to "develop and implement a comprehensive plan to integrate housing throughout the city by next September."[45] Talk about optimism! In all fairness, however, an attempt was made to move things along. After Judge Sand ordered the Yonkers school district and the federal government to negotiate an out of court settlement, the school district came up with a plan to address the issue of racial imbalance in Yonkers high schools by creating magnet schools, but this would have involved busing. In a unanimous vote, the board of education rejected the proposal in March 1981.

Interestingly, the council's stand on busing mirrored the views of Ronald Reagan, who had been sworn into office as president of the United States only two months earlier. During Reagan's first year in office, the Justice Department did a partial about-face on school desegregation plans in several cities, declining to support even voluntary busing. In July 1981, Robert J. D'Agostino, deputy assistant attorney general in the Civil Rights Division of the Justice Department, recommended that the case against Yonkers be dropped. Terming the case "the end result of a mind-set in the educational area and one of the opening shots in a new attempt to remake America through coerced residential integration," D'Agostino, in a memorandum to William Bradford Reynolds, head of the Civil Rights Division, included comments that were viewed as racist.[46] He declared, for example, that "Blacks because of their family, cultural and economic background are more disruptive in the classroom on the average."[47] The memo caused an uproar in the Civil Rights Division. Of the division's 175 attorneys, one hundred signed a petition expressing dismay. Had the memo and the controversy it engendered remained within the Justice Department, there might have been no further repercussions. It was a different story after *The Washington Post* obtained a copy and then published it for all the world to see. At that point the Reagan administration found itself in the position of choosing whether to abandon desegregation cases initiated during the administration of President Jimmy Carter or pursue them. When the Reagan Justice Department opted to go down the latter path, the fate of Yonkers was sealed.

Yonkers on Trial

By the end of the year, the Justice Department sought an injunction in Federal District Court in Manhattan requiring Yonkers to eliminate all vestiges of segregation in its schools by September 1982. When the city failed to comply, the Justice Department's case against Yonkers went to trial. According to Dr. Joseph Pastore, who in 1986 would become the court-appointed monitor for the schools portion of the case, although the case was "essentially about insuring one's legal right to an equitable, non-discriminatory public education, *U.S. v. Yonkers* naturally reaches to the rights and obligations of living in a communal setting."[48] From Dr. Pastore's perspective, "*U.S. v. Yonkers* seems as much about morality as legality. Inherent in the moral challenge is the need to weigh one's right to individual liberty with an obligation to assure the common good."[49] At the start of the proceedings in Federal District Court in Manhattan, in August 1983, Judge Leonard Sand noted that for everyone present there had to be "some sense of regret and frustration that this moment has arrived."[50] Reflecting upon the events leading up to the start of the non-jury trial, the judge said that he had counseled people on both sides of the issue that "an early consensual resolution would be vastly preferential to any disposition from this court."[51] Michael Sussman, an attorney for the National Association for the Advancement of Colored People, which had been allowed to join the suit as a plaintiff, observed that the Justice Department and the City of Yonkers "must share equally in the blame."[52] To get beyond blame and achieve the goal of consensual resolution, Judge Sand ordered Yonkers city and school officials and representatives of the Justice Department to meet with a court-appointed mediator to work out their differences. The negotiations proceeded, but so too did the city's problems.

Facing a budget shortfall, the board of education voted in December 1983 to extend the Christmas vacation by a month. During that time, school personnel, including teachers, would not be paid. If that amounted to a lump of coal in the stockings hung by the fire with care, an announcement by the court-appointed mediator that both sides were close to reaching an agreement in the desegregation case was the most welcome of holiday gifts. As things turned out, however, reopening the schools on schedule after the Christmas vacation ended up being the real gift. Once the city council agreed to seek the $12 million needed to keep the schools open, the board of education reversed its decision to keep the schools shuttered in January. Although it was business as usual in the city's classrooms after the vacation ended, winter interscholastic sports were suspended by order of the New York State Department of Education. In view of the death of the football player whose heart disease should have precluded his participation in sports, the state wanted to make sure that the Yonkers Board of Education corrected deficiencies in the operation of its athletic programs before allowing sports to resume. Happily for the city's public school students, the suspension was reversed within days after the school district compiled medical records for student athletes and launched a search for a full-time athletic director.

In the grand scheme of things, complying with the state's very legitimate demand that Yonkers ensure the safety of student athletes was relatively quick and easy; satisfying the federal government in the matter of the segregation suit was anything but. A tentative agreement between the Justice Department and the Yonkers School Board in December 1983 called for student transfers, closing certain schools, reopening schools already closed, and the creation of a magnet school, but the city council rejected the plan. Clearly, this was one step backward but not long thereafter, in February 1984, the city appeared to be taking two giant steps forward when an accord was reached with the National Association for the Advancement of Colored People and the United States Department of Housing and Urban Development. H.U.D. had become involved in the suit as a result of the city's insistence that the agency had approved all of the sites chosen for public housing and hence was ultimately responsible for the housing pattern in Yonkers. The agreement hammered out with the assistance of the court-appointed mediator called for the city to build two hundred units of public housing in predominantly white areas. If Yonkers failed to recommend sites for the new construction within sixty days, the city stood to lose millions in direct federal aid and urban development grants. In informing its readers of the details of the agreement, *The Herald Statesman* observed: "The issue of public housing in East Yonkers for years has met with community opposition," and according to the paper, Emmet Burke, head of the municipal housing authority, "does not expect things to be different this time around."[53]

The Decision

Within the sixty-day period for site selection, there was news on the education front. With the assistance of the court-appointed mediator, a plan calling for the redrawing of school district lines, the creation of magnet schools, and the closing of some schools was devised. The plan's hefty $18.5 million estimated cost proved to be the stumbling block, however. Although the board of education approved it at a heated meeting attended by eight hundred concerned citizens, the city council refused to finance it. Hopes for a voluntary agreement having been all but abandoned, the trial, which had been recessed to permit the mediation process to go forward, resumed. A seemingly endless parade of witnesses, many of them present and former Yonkers officials, were questioned, and in November 1985 Judge Sand issued his ruling. In the introduction to his six-hundred-page decision, he noted that "the primary issue in this case is whether the City of Yonkers and the Yonkers Board of Education intentionally segregated its housing and schools, since it is clear that by all relevant standards Yonkers and its public school system are, in fact, racially segregated."[54] The judge's conclusion, as stated in his ruling, was that "city and school officials in Yonkers had 'illegally and intentionally' segregated the city's public schools and public housing along racial lines."[55] According to Judge Sand:

> Whether direct or indirect, the City's housing practices, the mayoral appointment of board members and other City involvement in school affairs are more than adequate evidence of the City's intentional perpetuation and exacerbation of racial segregation in Yonkers public schools. We therefore hold that the City is liable for the racial segregation of Yonkers public schools.[56]

In the aftermath of Judge Sand's ruling, *The New York Times* observed that the outcome of the case would "echo through the country."[57] The paper went on to praise President Ronald Reagan for pursuing cases initiated by his predecessor, adding that the Reagan administration "will deserve considerably more credit if it now pushes for an effective remedy, including, if necessary, court-ordered busing."[58]

Although busing was one way of addressing the problem of school segregation, Judge Sand's ruling did not impose specific remedies. Instead, the judge held a hearing on December 18. At that time he ordered the city and its school board to submit, by the following February, a plan for desegregating the schools and housing. It wasn't going to be easy to comply with the judge's mandate. Shortly before the mid-December hearing, two sites the city had proposed for housing were rejected by the Department of Housing and Urban Development, but shocked city officials only learned of it during the hearing. The rationale for the rejection was not immediately provided by H.U.D. but an attorney for the N.A.A.C.P. indicated that the sites, which were the former Yonkers Motor Inn near Yonkers Raceway and a location on Tuckahoe Road, were located on the outskirts of neighborhoods and hence would not result in integration of the nearby neighborhoods. While the city grappled with the issue of site selection for housing, Dr. Joan Raymond, whose contract as superintendent of schools had been renewed in December, worked on a plan for desegregating the schools. Her proposal called for reducing the number of schools from thirty-four to thirty-one, some of them in new buildings, the redrawing of district lines, and the addition of five magnet schools to the two already functioning. The price tag for implementing the plan over a five-year period was an estimated $37 million. The day before the deadline for submitting the plan to Judge Sand, the Yonkers School Board unanimously approved Dr. Raymond's recommendations. The N.A.A.C.P.'s reaction to the plan came in March and it was negative. Although magnet schools were acceptable to the organization, the time required to establish them and to accomplish the other goals set forth in the plan was simply too long. There was also the issue of decontaminating and reopening the asbestos-laden Whitman Middle School in the northeastern part of the city. Both the N.A.A.C.P. and the Justice Department opposed this. As a result, the school board voted to reject a negotiated settlement. The ball was now back in Judge Sand's court, literally and figuratively.

As both sides waited for the judge to unveil his own plan for deseg-regating the schools, a one-day boycott of the schools was organized by parents who feared that a court-mandated plan would include busing and the closing of neighborhood schools. Reporting on the boycott, *The Herald Statesman* observed that whether in schools with a majority of minority or white students, fully half of the pupils were absent. "Those who helped publicize the boycott . . . hailed it as a successful statement of protest that united white and minority parents."[59] Less than a week after the boycott, Judge Sand issued a ruling requiring Yonkers to begin integrating the schools by the following September; at the same time he put forth a plan that was similar to the one proposed by the school board. There would be greater emphasis on magnet schools and additional redrawing of district lines. Fearing that the latter requirement would lead to busing, many residents called for an appeal, as did Dr. Raymond. "If the plan stands as it is now, I could not embrace or successfully implement it," she said.[60] In her view, there just wasn't enough time to get things in place for September. Conceding this point, the judge modified his plan. Although all of the junior and senior high schools would have to be integrated during the first year of the plan's implementation, only half of the elementary schools would have to be integrated in that time. Additional redrawing of district lines was also postponed for a year; if magnet schools achieved the desired integration goal by that time, further amending of district lines would not be necessary. During the first year of the plan, children would go to one of three schools, whether neighborhood or magnet, on a list submitted by their parents; in year two, parents would also choose three schools but one had to be "where the child's attendance will further the goals of desegregation."[61] In an editorial, *The New York Times* said the modified court plan had the potential to "be a model for desegregation without mandatory busing."[62] The paper went on to point out that the city council still had to approve the plan, and it recommended that the people of Yonkers and their elected leaders take everyone's interest into account and "meet Judge Sand as he has met them."[63]

The Appeal

Despite the willingness of some city officials to do just that, the city council voted ten to three, in June, to appeal Judge Sand's ruling that Yonkers had intentionally segregated its schools and housing. According to Minority Leader Nicholas Longo, "We were not given a choice" because of lack of money, "not even a promise of money from the state or federal governments"; nevertheless, Mayor Martinelli and councilmen Harry Oxman and Joseph Burgess, who voted against the appeal, feared that "the vote could result in even harsher school and housing orders."[64] Reporting on the vote to appeal, *The New York Times* quoted Mayor Martinelli, who termed the decision "a sad thing"; as the mayor saw it, Yonkers was forfeiting an opportunity to have an excellent school system "which other communities would have been very jealous of."[65] *The Herald Statesman* concurred. In an editorial, the paper urged the city council to "reconsider its vote to appeal and join in the building of a new Yonkers. The alternative . . . should be unacceptable to everyone," declared the *Statesman.*[66]

Despite the city council's action, the board of education announced that it would continue its efforts to implement the school desegregation plan. This resulted in anti-integration protests, involving several hundred people, outside district headquarters and the homes of board members. Nevertheless, the board's decision proved essential because Judge Sand denied a request for a stay to delay implementation until a verdict was rendered in the appeals case. To ensure that Yonkers did not lag in desegregating its schools, the judge then proceeded to appoint Dr. Joseph Pastore, provost of Pace University, to monitor the situation. By July 1986, when most students had registered for the fall term, statistical data indicated that the majority of students would be enrolled in integrated schools. This was good news as far as the superintendent of schools was concerned, but Dr. Raymond would not remain in Yonkers to oversee implementation of the desegregation plan. Having accepted a position as superintendent of schools in Houston, Texas, she left Yonkers just prior to the start of the new school year. Donald Batista, a longtime teacher and administrator in the Yonkers schools, was appointed to succeed her. Toward the end of August, as Dr. Raymond was preparing to leave, both the Second Circuit

Court of Appeals and the United States Supreme Court rejected a stay in implementing both school and housing desegregation in Yonkers.

In December, as school integration moved forward, the Justice Department sought a contempt ruling against Yonkers for failing to address the housing integration issue. Within a month Judge Sand ordered Yonkers to hire a housing specialist to assist with site selection and the determination of how many units of low-income dwellings would be erected. Architect and city planner Oscar Newman was appointed to the new position by Judge Sand. In March 1987, after the Walt Whitman school and School No. 4 had been designated as suitable sites, Judge Sand ordered Yonkers to rezone these parcels to permit the construction of subsidized housing. A month later, at a meeting attended by approximately one thousand people, the city council voted, nine to four, "to have middle-class neighborhoods in east and north Yonkers also take in the city's minorities."[67] Although the Department of Housing and Urban Development, which was going to fund the construction of the initial two hundred units of housing as a quid pro quo for being removed as a defendant in the case, had reservations about the semidetached two-family houses Oscar Newman favored, the city council went along with Newman's recommendation.

Approving sites for the new housing, ensuring that they were controlled by the city and that the requisite zoning was in place, was easier said than done, however. When the city failed to get everything lined up for the first two hundred units out of a possible total of six hundred, with the final number to be determined by the court, Judge Sand threatened to hold Yonkers in contempt and impose massive fines on the city. The judge relented when the city council voted, in July, to approve the construction of two hundred units on eight sites, including school property and parks, in the eastern part of Yonkers. Taking actual possession of the sites would not be easy. The board of education wasn't about to abandon its plans to utilize the Walt Whitman School for administrative offices, and a faction within the N.A.A.C.P. had reservations about low-income housing in white areas, as well as busing minority students to schools outside their neighborhoods. By August, the school board, which only two months earlier had been taking bows for the relative smoothness that had characterized the first year of integration involving 25,000 students and school personnel, was reevaluating its plans for Walt Whitman. In September, the board of education filed suit against New York State seeking to have the state pay part of the cost of integrating the Yonkers schools. In the suit, the Yonkers School Board argued that the state's reduction of funding and its antibusing legislation had prevented the city from integrating its schools.

This latest litigation, along with the ongoing housing saga, weighed heavily on the minds of Yonkers voters as they entered the polling places to cast their ballots for mayor in an election pitting Councilman Nicholas Wasicsko against incumbent mayor Angelo Martinelli. Some voters, who had supported Martinelli throughout the entire time he had served as mayor, found it inexplicable that he would advocate settling the lawsuit. During the campaign, the incumbent told voters "We're talking about 200 units—if it happens. It's not going to kill us."[68] As someone who in his own words "played to the crowd" during his first three terms as mayor, Martinelli reversed course midstream; the soul searching that followed his defeat in 1979 made him decide that in the future, should he be reelected, he would sacrifice popularity to do the right thing.[69] And so he did, voting against a city council resolution to appeal Judge Sand's desegregation ruling because the council failed to provide support for a plan "that would have laid the groundwork for a local solution to the judge's order."[70] Councilman Nicholas Wasicsko, on the other hand, voted to appeal, and the rest, as they say, is history. Basking in his defeat of the longtime incumbent, the mayor-elect declared, almost immediately after the election, that he was "looking forward to forming a community advisory group representing all the elements in Yonkers."[71] Wasicsko said he would turn to this body for guidance on the desegregation suit.

The mayor-elect needed all the advice he could get, because within weeks of his election Yonkers was informed, in no uncertain terms, by Judge Sand that it had to designate sites for two hundred units of low-income housing and that until it did, the city was prohibited from providing assistance for any commercial and residential development. Four major projects were affected, namely, Austin Avenue and the Wilmorite Shopping Mall in northwest Yonkers, both still in the planning stage, and Pierpointe and the Southwest Yonkers Executive Park, both of which were partially completed. As far as the judge was concerned, a municipality willing to offer incentives to developers was able to assist with housing for minority residents, and toward that end Judge Sand ordered the Yonkers Board of Education to release three sites for new housing. Commenting on these developments in an editorial, *The New York Times* characterized the order affecting development as "a creative answer" and urged support.[72] As for the appeal, the paper cautioned that it would be costly and warned that it was clear that Judge Sand had "raised the stakes too high to risk continuing the fight."[73]

Before the month of November was over, Judge Sand raised the stakes even higher. Since the Westchester County Board of Legislators had voted against ceding county property to the city for use as one of the housing sites, the judge authorized Oscar Newman to identify private property that could be used for housing. Newman was given ten days to come up with a list of sites, and the city then had two weeks to comment on their suitability. City employees, some of whom, according to Mr. Newman, had thwarted his previous efforts to obtain files on private property, would be held in contempt of court if they did not cooperate with the housing expert. With the full force of the court behind him, Oscar Newman quickly identified nine sites, one of which was owned by St. Joseph's Seminary and another by the Lincoln Park Jewish Center. Attorneys for the city informed Judge Sand that the seminary site would "intrude upon the serenity of the college's grounds" and they argued that the judge's directive to Yonkers to purchase property for public housing was unconstitutional.[74] In the past the U.S. Department of Housing and Urban Development had provided the land for public housing. Requiring the city to assume this burden would fly in the face of court rulings limiting federal judges to remedies having "the least adverse effect upon state and local functions."[75]

Opponents of the housing order were buoyed by the city's latest legal initiative, but within days discouragement engulfed them because of yet another legal action: a ruling by a federal appeals court upholding a lower court ruling requiring Yonkers to desegregate its schools and erect subsidized housing. After quoting Judge Sand's conclusion that "the extreme concentration of subsidized housing that exists in Southwest Yonkers today is the result of a pattern and practice of racial discrimination by city officials, pursued in response to constituent pressures to select or support only sites that would preserve existing patterns of racial segregation and to reject or oppose sites that would threaten existing patterns of segregation," the appeals court "found that the city's segregative housing practices had been a contributing cause of the racial segregation of the schools."[76] The appeals court attributed the board of education's failure to promote integration, at least partially, to "the will of the city and the white community members who opposed desegregation."[77] The appeals court had spoken, and some citizens of Yonkers thought that should have been the end of the legal wrangling over the desegregation order, but given the strength of the opposition, both on the city council and among the electorate, there was immediate talk of an appeal to the U.S. Supreme Court. With three days left in his term of office, Mayor

Angelo Martinelli appeared to be a lone voice crying in the wilderness when he expressed the hope that "the City Council understands the severity of the situation."[78] Martinelli raised the specter of fines imposed by Judge Sand. If that were to happen, the mayor said, "I hope he levies them against the individuals, rather than against the city. You have to hit these guys in their own pocketbooks."[79]

1988: The City's *Annus Terribilis*

The outgoing mayor's observation proved to be very prescient, but months would go by before Yonkers was actually slapped with fines. In the meantime, the new men in city hall, Mayor Nicholas Wasicsko and Neil J. DeLuca, a former youth services director for the city who was appointed city manager, juggled the ordinary problems facing a municipality the size of Yonkers while pondering the extraordinary challenges posed by the desegregation case. By late January 1988 it appeared that they would not have to ruminate about this much longer because, faced with a contempt order and the imminent imposition of fines, the city agreed to the use of seven sites, four of them schools, and three privately owned parcels, for the first two hundred units of housing. In return, Judge Sand lifted the ban on private development. Although this seemed to be a win–win situation all around, some members of the city council, which voted five to one, with one member absent, to approve the agreement, had received death threats. The day the vote was taken council members were forced to endure boisterous opposition from citizens opposed to the agreement but the councilmen persevered, because to have done otherwise would have been tantamount to bankrupting their city in less than a month. A week later, at a public meeting at Saunders Technical School, with sixty police officers present to keep the peace, the council, in a five to two vote, passed a resolution committing the city to proceed with building the housing, designating one additional site, and, at the same time, abandoning the appeal to the Supreme Court. Of the approximately eight hundred people in attendance, all of whom had to pass through metal detectors, fifty approached the microphone to lambaste councilmen for reneging on their campaign promises to oppose the desegregation order. The new mayor, in office not even a month, was literally drowned out each time he attempted to address the crowd. Councilmen Peter Chema and Henry Spallone, who voted against the resolution, on the other hand, were the heroes of the evening. As a portent of things to come, Spallone received a standing ovation.

In the months ahead, "Hank" Spallone, a former New York City detective, continued to call for an appeal of the housing order. This resonated with many citizens and was viewed by the council, which was having increasing difficulty governing a divided city, as a way of enabling opponents of the housing order to be heard in the federal halls of justice. For that reason the city petitioned Judge Sand to release Yonkers from its pledge not to appeal to the Supreme Court. The judge rejected the city's request, but Yonkers wasn't going to take no for an answer. When John Cardinal O'Connor, the Roman Catholic Archbishop of New York, asserted that he had only agreed to sell the seminary site to the city because he had been informed that it would otherwise be acquired through condemnation, Yonkers, citing "mistaken impressions over the seminary site," proceeded to request Judge Sand to nullify the consent decree.[80] The judge labeled this a "transparent ploy" aimed at reinstating the city's right to appeal or a way "to avoid responsibility for the housing remedy."[81] The question of an appeal became a moot point in June when the U.S. Supreme Court refused to hear the city's appeal of the 1985 ruling finding Yonkers culpable of promoting segregation in its schools and housing.

Two days after the U.S. Supreme Court issued its ruling, Judge Sand met in his chambers with fifty residents of the "Queen City of the Hudson." The judge told the visitors from Yonkers that "the courts have had their say."[82] Responding to those who felt that they were being held accountable for the actions of previous governmental administrations, Judge Sand pointed out that the issue was not the intentions of former officials but "whether government action" had been responsible for discrimination.[83] Most of the people present in the judge's chamber accepted this explanation, but unswerving opponents of the housing order, including some who had staged demonstrations outside the judge's homes in Manhattan and Pound Ridge, voiced their objections to his 1985 ruling. On the evening before the gathering in Judge Sand's chambers, nearly one hundred opponents of the housing plan attempted to disrupt a Yonkers City Council meeting by shouting at council members; other opponents beeped horns and blew whistles outside. This demonstration prompted *The Herald Statesman* to question, in an editorial, why the protesters couldn't "put the issue behind them."[84] The paper proceeded to observe that the housing opponents who said that they would be "satisfied" with just getting to the Supreme Court "whatever the outcome" had to abide by what they said and the city council had to exercise leadership.[85]

The city council, however, was not about to act in the face of growing opposition to the housing plan, mainly from white residents of the east side and northwest Yonkers. Some members of the black community also opposed the housing plan because it would reduce black political power in the minority ward created in southwest Yonkers by redistricting. With some constituents, both black and white, advocating enhancing existing public housing, the council passed a moratorium on the construction of all new public housing. The judge then requested the city council to pass a motion reaffirming its agreement to build public housing in white neighborhoods, but instead of doing so, at the end of June the council voted, five to one, to not only refuse the request but to stop condemnation proceedings for the St. Joseph's Seminary site. The judge saw red! He imposed a deadline by which the council had to approve a long-term plan for eight hundred units of subsidized housing, with all new housing in east and northwest Yonkers subject to the requirement that 20 percent of the units in any development had to be reserved for low-income residents. If the city council failed to vote for the plan, Yonkers would be fined $100 for the first day of noncompliance and the fine would double each day thereafter. In a little over three weeks the fines would eat up the entire municipal budget. Individual councilmen refusing to support the plan would be fined $500 a day; failure to acquiesce by an August 10 deadline imposed by the judge would result in imprisonment. Clearly the time for posturing had come to an end. At least that's what the city's young mayor thought. Nicholas Wasicsko was quick to point out that Judge Sand possessed "power to carry out what he's threatened, and the city can't afford it, either financially or in terms of our image. I don't want the national media feasting on the spectacle of a Yonkers thumbing its nose at a Federal judge."[86]

The Showdown

Not surprisingly, the meeting at which the crucial vote was taken turned out to be quite a spectacle. Describing the event, which attracted representatives of print and broadcast media, *The Herald Statesman* reported that some three hundred people descended upon city hall. Amidst chants of "No justice, no peace," they proceeded to block "streets, pasted bumper stickers to their foreheads, blew whistles and shouted threats"; instead of defying this determined crowd, the council "defied the judge."[87] The vote was four to three. Castigating the defiant council members, whose actions prompted Judge Sand to declare the city and the councilmen in contempt, *The New York Times,* in an editorial, said that they "make no apologies for defying the law. But in doing so, they condemn Yonkers to a form of municipal suicide."[88]

The *Herald Statesman* weighed in with an editorial titled "Four Who said 'No' Should be Removed"; singling out Edward Fagan Jr., who had kept his cards close to his chest by refusing to state his position prior to the vote, the paper said that he could have been heroic but, instead, "he failed."[89] The *Statesman* castigated the other council members who voted no, pointing out that "lawlessness knows no party lines."[90]

What needed to be done, in the opinion of the *Statesman's* editor, was for the emergency financial control board to assume control over Yonkers, replacing city officials who had "run amok."[91] And that wasn't all! As far as the paper was concerned Governor Cuomo had the power to remove the councilmen and should do so rather than allowing them to "play martyr."[92]

It wasn't that simple, because the four councilmen and the city appealed the contempt ruling and despite Judge Sand's insistence that Governor Cuomo remove the dissenting councilmen, the governor said he would take no action until the appeals had been exhausted. The governor also urged the city's young mayor to seek a political solution by either persuading one of the councilmen to change his vote or, in the event of Edward Fagan's rumored resignation, appointing someone who would support the housing plan. That wasn't good enough, as *The New York Times* stated in a scathing editorial titled "Governor Nobody-Asked-Me."[93] With Judge Sand having characterized Yonkers as a "national symbol of defiance to civil rights," the *Times* said it was incumbent upon the governor "to feel a special obligation to extinguish flames of hatred spreading from the Yonkers case."[94]

With Moody's Investors Service suspending the city's bond rating and the emergency financial control board planning to lower the ax on Yonkers, help from the governor would have been viewed in some quarters as a positive thing. Perhaps to test the waters, Cuomo did propose a compromise plan calling for more housing units in small-scale developments scattered over a wider area of the city, but he really steered clear of the Yonkers dilemma until after an appeals court panel ruled on appeals filed by the city and the councilmen. As they argued before the appeals court panel, a key point made by attorneys for the council members was that as elected representatives, they had a constitutional right to vote in accordance with their consciences and with the views of the constituents they represented. Responding to this argument, Judge J. O. Newman, one of three justices to hear the appeals, questioned a person's "right to do something that violates the law of the land."[95] Nevertheless, with Judge Newman dissenting, the appeals court panel temporarily suspended the fines against the city and the four council members and at the same time stayed Judge Sand's very real threat to imprison the councilmen. This provided everyone with a breathing space of eight days until the full U.S. Court of Appeals for the Second Circuit heard the appeal of the contempt ruling.

A few hours before the temporary suspension of fines and jail sentences was announced, New York Secretary of State Gail S. Shaffer, chairperson of the emergency financial control board, presided at a meeting in Yonkers City Hall. Both literally and figuratively, the humidity-laden air on that August day made conditions in the room where the control board met almost unbearable. Nevertheless, the board went about its business, terminating all discretionary spending and instituting a wage and hiring freeze in Yonkers. Worse things were in the offing. Issuing a warning to the citizens of Yonkers about the loss of vital municipal services, Ms. Shaffer asked if they could "reasonably accept these consequences which loom as a direct result of your City Council's refusal to uphold the law?"[96] Calling upon the people of Yonkers to take a stand, Ms. Shaffer said: "You have a responsibility to yourself and to your city's future to express your reasoned concern to the four people you elected who have brought you to this precipice today."[97]

If that failed, the emergency financial control board was considering bringing criminal charges against the four councilmen, though at least one board member told *The Herald Statesman*: "There is no way we can make the City Council do anything."[98] Nor for that matter could the control board be forced to do anything. Indeed, its members refused to comment publicly on whether they thought the housing plan was a good thing for Yonkers. African American leaders attributed the board's failure to take a position to its unwillingness to alienate white voters. The same was said of Mario Cuomo, even after he went to Yonkers to meet with N.A.A.C.P. leaders. In the aftermath of the meeting, the governor called upon local leaders to resolve the problem.

Less than a week later, as a city council meeting stretched on interminably into the wee hours of the morning of August 16, a crowd of approximately eighty people opposed to the housing desegregation plan staged a noisy demonstration outside city hall. A placard carried by one protester declared "Don't Get Mad. Get a New Governor"; periodically, the crowd shouted: "The heat's on Mario," but the governor wasn't the only elected official on the receiving end of their jibes.[99] "Don't get mad—get a new Mayor," was another frequent refrain rising from the angry crowd.[100] Inside the building, Mayor Nicholas Wasicsko saw any hopes he had for a reversal of the council's stance on the housing plan dashed as the council voted four to three against the housing plan by rejecting an amendment to the city's zoning ordinance that would have provided density bonuses and other assistance to developers creating the eight hundred additional housing units required by the court. The city's planning department had actually recommended that the council reject the amendment to the zoning ordinance because it would have abrogated some of the city's powers relating to such things as the size and height of multifamily buildings in single-family neighborhoods. The outcome of the vote greatly pleased the majority of people who had addressed the council earlier in the meeting. Standing at a microphone, under the hot glare of television cameras, most of the speakers expressed their opposition to housing desegregation; the few who supported compliance with the court order were drowned out and told to move to the Bronx!

On August 26, although a federal appeals court affirmed a lower court's finding of contempt against both the city and the councilmen and limited the fines against the city to $1 million per day, the fines were suspended in order to permit the city to appeal to the U.S. Supreme Court. But what if the high court ruled against Yonkers? That was the question uppermost on the minds of members of nearly twenty groups comprising a new umbrella organization called COMPLY (Committee of Organizations Meeting to Preserve Law in Yonkers). Prior to the formation of the new body, which included unions, the Yonkers Federation of Teachers, which was a unit of the A.F.L.-C.I.O., and homeowners' associations, an organization named CANOPY (Citizens and Neighbors Organized to Protect Yonkers) had been pushing for compliance, even going so far as to file a $100 million lawsuit charging the four councilmen with wasting tax dollars by putting the city in a position where it was obligated to pay crushing fines. Although another group, the Save Yonkers Federation, which was opposed to the housing plan, supported the councilmen, those favoring compliance appeared to be in the ascendancy at the end of August when COMPLY announced its intention to pressure the council to abandon its opposition to housing desegregation.

At the same time, Governor Cuomo moved from the sidelines to center stage with his announcement that he would remove the four councilmen unless the U.S. Supreme Court agreed to hear their appeal of the contempt ruling. "If there is no further stay, then we will enforce the law," Cuomo declared.[101] He explained that he was taking this position because it enabled him to warn the councilmen that if they did not comply, "we'll hit you with everything."[102] "Not so fast!" would have been the logical response of the councilmen following a Supreme Court ruling continuing the stay of the councilmen's fines to give them ninety days to request the court to review their cases. The city was not so lucky. The

Supreme Court refused to stay a contempt ruling against the city, and the very next day Judge Sand ordered Yonkers to resume paying the fines. Although a portion of the fines was earmarked for the public schools and for repayment of municipal bonds, the remainder would go to the United States Treasury and with the fines doubling daily, within a week the once proud "Queen City of the Hudson," where every expenditure over $1 now had to be approved by the emergency financial control board, would be forking over a million dollars a day! No one, including Judge Sand, wanted to see this happen. In fact, the judge came up with a novel solution, namely to establish a commission to execute the housing plan, thereby depoliticizing the issue by removing it from the city council. The four councilmen didn't like the idea nor did the U.S. Justice Department, which questioned whether a commission would violate the separation of the legislative and judicial branches of government. At this point the only solution was to persuade the council to reverse itself.

Resolution—At Last

Toward that end Mayor Wasicsko huddled with the city council behind closed doors for seven and a half hours, but his efforts to effect a compromise were in vain. Despite the imminent threat of layoffs of municipal workers and sharp reductions in city services, all of which had the potential to turn the tide of public opinion against the councilmen, the four were still walking tall. The next day they seemed to grow an inch or two, figuratively speaking, thanks to a decision by Westchester County district attorney Carl Veragari not to prosecute them. The emergency financial control board had sought Vergari's help on the grounds that the councilmen's actions had led to fines that represented unauthorized spending. Vergari had reservations about the "constitutionality of a statute which criminalizes the act of voting," and he also referred to Governor Cuomo's decision to await the U.S. Supreme Court's decision on whether to review the contempt rulings against the councilmen before removing them from office.[103] Unfortunately, Yonkers did not have the luxury of waiting, either for the Supreme Court or for the governor. By the end of the first week of September, the fines had reached a whopping million dollars a day! To continue paying them the city council had to authorize a transfer of funds from a litigation fees account to a judgment and claims account. They did so, but Councilman Fagan, whose bitter denunciation of Judge Sand shocked those in attendance at the council meeting, voted no and Councilman Spallone, who questioned whether a vote to facilitate payment of fines he deemed illegal would jeopardize the Supreme Court case, abstained. The vote was preceded by exhortations from residents to end the crisis by voting to comply with the housing plan. Faced with not only the specter of even more taxpayer dollars going toward fines and imminent major layoffs of municipal workers, even the People's Union, a group that had supported the four councilmen, now called for compliance. Clearly, the handwriting was on the wall. Something had to give and it had to give soon, lest the "Queen City of the Hudson" careen over the precipice and plunge into bankruptcy.

In the end, that dire fate was avoided, just in the knick of time, when two of the councilmen, Peter Chema and Nicholas Longo, voted, at a September 9 council meeting, to accept the housing plan. The two council members had sought a modification of the plan, but Judge Sand refused to consider changes until after the council voted to comply with his order to provide a thousand units of housing. By approving a zoning law permitting the erection of the new housing, the council finally brought the city into compliance, thereby averting mass layoffs and ending crushing fines. Within days, the city, together with the N.A.A.C.P., proposed changes to the plan. They included altering the number of sites for the two hundred units of low-income housing, changing the mix of housing, and providing social services for residents. Within the Yonkers N.A.A.C.P. there was some resistance to the changes because they included apartment houses that were likely to meet with resistance from residents of neighborhoods where they would be situated. An even bigger problem surfaced when Judge Sand proposed a site on Gramercy Avenue, near Central Park Avenue, as an alternative to the seminary site. The latter had been controversial because although the archdiocese had initially sanctioned its use, it later argued that this and nearby sites would place too many people in one parish. Ostensibly, that was the reason the archdiocese opposed condemnation of the property, but some Yonkers residents believed that pressure from Roman Catholic homeowners opposed to the low-income housing in their area was the real reason for the archdiocese's reversal. Ultimately, Judge Sand designated the Gramercy Avenue site as the replacement for the seminary site after the city council, in a politically expedient move, refused to propose an alternative site. According to *The Herald Statesman,* the judge's ruling on the Gramercy Avenue site was made at the conclusion of a hearing "at which the city argued that the Gramercy parcel was ill-suited and improperly zoned for public housing and would cost too much to develop."[104] The paper went on to observe that Judge Sand had characterized the city's arguments as a tactic in a "chess game" while refusing to recommend alternatives to the seminary site; quoting Abraham Lincoln, the judge said: "You can fool some of the people some of the time, but you can't fool all the people all the time."[105]

No matter what Judge Leonard Sand said, his detractors were waiting to object, and some went one step farther by suing the judge, claiming that he had exceeded his constitutional power by imposing the housing plan upon Yonkers. In late November, the Save Yonkers Federation, composed of more than a dozen groups opposed to the housing plan, filed suit on behalf of what it termed "petitioners" living near the seven sites slated for low-income housing.[106] At a news conference held by the federation to announce the suit, the organization's attorney declared that the plan involving one thousand housing units "violated the constitutional doctrine of federalism and separation of powers."[107]

New Year, New Challenges

Citizens suing the judge was fodder for the media, which had kept a watchful eye on Yonkers, frequently comparing the "Queen City of the Hudson" with the segregationist South of the pre–civil rights era but within months the city was moving ahead. In January 1989, the emergency financial control board loosened the strings on Yonkers, restoring most of the city's authority to spend. In February, the Yonkers Industrial Development Agency made a $40 million commitment to the Austin Avenue development site for a multiplex theater and hotel. Elsewhere in the city, developers were being sought to erect the four thousand units of new housing needed to yield the eight hundred units of subsidized housing required, under a 20 per cent/80 percent formula of subsidized to market rate units; although developers weren't lining up to take advantage of the inducements the city was offering, there was cautious optimism that progress would be made on this front. Of course, opponents of the court-ordered housing plan were in no hurry to see all of those new dwellings erected. Indeed, some of them were still hoping the whole thing would just go away, and that's why they were buoyed by the U.S. Supreme Court's decision, in March, to review the contempt citations against the four councilmen. Although the court turned down the city's appeal of the fines imposed upon it by Judge Sand, thus rejecting Yonkers's argument that the fines were unconstitutional, the city council seriously considered mounting a new legal challenge, but Peter A. Chema, one of the four housing opponents, refused to support it on the grounds that a new legal challenge should be postponed until the U.S. Supreme Court had heard the cases of the four councilmen. Chema cited the same reason for abstaining, a few days later, from a vote to appropriate funds for the purchase of sites for low-income housing. Since the emergency financial control board was empowered to approve this expenditure, however, the acquisition of the land was not in doubt.

At the same time that it was grappling with the site acquisition issue, the city council was dealing, none too successfully, with a mandate from Judge Sand, as part of the school desegregation plan, to erect two new schools. When the city council refused to approve spending $24 million for the schools, the emergency financial control board imposed a 1989–90 budget on Yonkers; it called for using a combination of spending reductions, transfers from various city accounts, and money from the city's surplus to erect the schools. Although school desegregation took second place to housing desegregation, it was an issue in the 1989 mayoral race already under way in the spring as the city endeavored to craft an acceptable budget. The race began on an April day when Henry Spallone told a crowd of seven hundred gathered at the Polish Community Center that he would challenge Mayor Wasicsko for the Democratic Party's nomination. Two weeks later, Spallone announced that he was switching parties and had received the endorsement of the Republican Party. In order to run for mayor, Spallone had to resign from the city council. This was a welcome move as far as some people were concerned because as a councilman Spallone was perceived as an obstructionist who was unwilling to negotiate. This led to his being excluded from the discussions preceding the site selection for the low-income housing. The end result was that four of the seven sites were originally in Spallone's district. When he announced that he would run for mayor, the sixty-two-year-old retired New York City detective, who earned a degree from Fordham University while working for the NYPD, did not bring up housing, but he and everyone else knew that it would be the hot button issue during the upcoming campaign. It also dominated the primaries. In addition to primaries for city council nominations, there was a contest for the Democratic mayoral designation. With the backing of the Yonkers Democratic leader, former city councilman Dominick Iannacone challenged Mayor Wasicsko. In an editorial endorsing the incumbent, *The New York Times* advised: "The first step to better government is to re-nominate Mayor Wasicsko"; as for the man running against him, in the opinion of the editorial writer, his experience notwithstanding, he "does lack conviction to carry out the judge's order."[108]

Mayor Wasicsko trounced his opponent, and interpreted his victory as a sign that the people of Yonkers really agreed with him about the need for compliance. The victory of Thomas A. Dickerson, who favored compliance, over Nicholas Longo in the council primary was another indication that the time had come to do what the judge had stipulated.

In the six weeks between the primaries and the November election, there were new developments in the four councilmen's appeals case resulting from a decision by the administration of President George Bush to ask the U.S. Supreme Court to uphold the fines imposed upon the four. Solicitor General Kenneth W. Starr, who would later figure prominently in the impeachment proceedings against President Bill Clinton, argued that the councilmen's defiance had compelled Judge Sand to impose the fines. When challenged by the attorney representing the councilmen to cite specific instances of a court ordering legislators to vote in a particular way, Starr could not come up with one example. *The New York Times* endeavored to shed light on this by stating in an editorial that U.S. Solicitor General Kenneth Starr "was hard pressed to cite any precedent"; the paper attributed this to the fact that the Yonkers City Council's "level of contempt" exceeded that of Southerners opposed to integration in the sixties.[109]

In another editorial, which appeared just before the election, the *Times* said that the way for Yonkers to move forward was by reelecting Mayor Wasicsko. The Yonkers Federation of Teachers fully agreed. The organization, which since the 1970s had supported union-endorsed candidates, sometimes in conjunction with other Westchester unions, and fearful of the impact a Spallone administration might have on the ongoing school desegregation efforts, launched a letter-writing and phone campaign on behalf of the incumbent. In the end, the efforts of the Save Yonkers Federation, which tenaciously underscored its members' belief that low-income housing would lead to depressed real estate values and a host of urban problems, were more effective than those of Mayor Wasicsko's supporters. In a close election, Spallone rode into city hall on the shoulders of Save Yonkers. Also fairly close was the approval of important changes in the city charter. The position of city manger was abolished and the mayor would serve for four years, with both changes taking effect in 1992, following the next mayoral election in the fall of 1991.

The next election may have seemed a long way off on election night 1989 when Nicholas Wasicsko addressed more than two hundred supporters who had gathered at the Polish Community Center. His message was clear. "Do not despair," he said, noting that he had been "there when the city needed" him and that he had "no regrets."[110] He proceeded to say: "I endured death threats and all sorts of abuse, but I think history, in the long run, will prove me right."[111] Gracious in defeat, Wasicsko pledged "my hand in support" to assist the mayor-elect.[112] Spallone responded, in his address at the Italian City Club, by saying that although he and Nick Wasicsko had been "on opposite sides of the arena . . . we will always work together."[113] To many residents of the "Queen City of the Hudson" that seemed too much to hope for but *The Herald Statesman,* in an editorial, was cautiously optimistic. After noting that the outgoing mayor had offered to help Spallone for the good of Yonkers, the paper's editor went on to say that Yonkers continued to grapple with the housing issue, finances, and other major challenges that the new mayor would have to address; the editorial ended by saying: "Our hope is that he will rise to the occasion and grow with the office."[114]

To an extent, that hope was based on the fact that the opponents of compliance had only a narrow majority in the new city council. Although Peter A. Chema and Edward J. Fagan Jr. were reelected and were joined in their opposition to the housing plan by Salvatore J. Sialiano, a newly elected council member, Nicholas V. Longo was defeated by Thomas A. Dickerson, who favored compliance, as did two additional new council members: Joe L. Farmer and John D. Spencer. Together with the new mayor, the councilmen would have to grapple with the housing issue and myriad other challenges. Just days before he left office Mayor Wasicsko enumerated some of them and declared, "There will be no running away for Mr. Spallone."[115] The mayor-elect's assessment of the situation was that the city would take a wait-and-see approach on housing until the Supreme Court ruled on the appeals of the fines and at the same time would be "working on bringing this city into the 21st century."[116] "We're thinking modern, we're thinking development," said the mayor-elect, adding "Yonkers is a great city, and when you look at it you realize some of the press we got was really undeserved."[117] In the next decade, Spallone and those who would follow him as mayor would make it their business to assure residents and outsiders alike that Yonkers was indeed a great city.

7

Toward the Millennium

The Nineties

Politics and Governance: Henry Spallone as Mayor

At his inauguration at the Polish Community Center, Henry (Hank) Spallone reiterated his intention to lead Yonkers into the twenty-first century, and on the housing issue he assured the approximately seven hundred supporters in attendance that his administration would abide by the decisions of the Supreme Court. "We had our fight, we'll get our decision and we'll join together and go forward," he declared.[1]

The new mayor didn't have to wait long for the Supreme Court ruling on the fines imposed upon the four councilmen whose negative votes had prevented the low-income housing from going forward. Ten days after Spallone's inauguration, the Court overturned the fines on the grounds that Judge Sand should not have imposed fines upon the city and councilmen simultaneously. The majority of justices on the high court felt that the judge should have waited to see whether the fines against the city would have been sufficient to persuade the councilmen to change their votes. The Court did not address the issue of whether local legislators enjoyed immunity from liability for actions taken in an official capacity, nor did the Court rule on the constitutional issue of violation of legislators' freedom of speech when they were compelled to vote as directed by a court. Despite the narrowness of the ruling, champagne corks popped in city hall as the new mayor and the vindicated councilmen celebrated their judicial victory, but Michael Sussman, the attorney for the N.A.A.C.P., was quick to point out that "the Yonkers remedy order is alive, well and will be implemented."[2] In his view, the decision was inconsequential. U.S. Solicitor General Kenneth Starr, who represented the federal government

271

in this case, concurred. While expressing disappointment, he emphasized that the ruling was "in no way, a victory for those who would roll back civil rights."[3] The editor of *The Herald Statesman* agreed. Noting that the decision was "a personal victory" for the councilmen, he pointed out that the housing order had not been altered and Judge Sand could still impose fines on the councilmen and the City of Yonkers.[4]

None of this deterred Mayor Spallone from asking the city's corporation counsel to research options for additional legal steps to prevent implementation of the housing plan. A prominent visitor to Yonkers, Martin Luther King III, son of the assassinated civil rights leader, declared, at a breakfast held at the Nepperhan Community Center on the eve of his father's birthday, that it was a "shame and disgrace" that Yonkers was still opposing the erection of low-income housing.[5] Within two months, the city council signaled its determination to keep on opposing the housing plan by replacing the attorney who had been the city's principal advocate on this issue by a team of three lawyers whose charge was to formulate new legal challenges to Judge Sand's mandate. Meanwhile, in the schools, where desegregation was proceeding, teachers, administrators, and support personnel went out on strike in June. The crisis was resolved when teachers and administrators accepted a new five-year contract, providing 9 percent increments in each of the last four years of the agreement. This fell a bit short of the 40 percent increase educators were seeking but it enabled them to make up for their previous contract's increments, which, because of the city's financial problems, were small.

Resolving the salary issue restored harmony in the schools, but on the housing front things were anything but harmonious. The city joined a suit filed by a Yonkers resident to stop the low-income housing on environmental grounds, but while the court required federal officials to assess the environmental impact of the housing, the judge determined that construction of the two hundred low-income dwellings could proceed, as could the planning process for the eight hundred subsidized units. The city council then dragged its feet on transferring title of the sites earmarked for the two hundred units. The matter was resolved when Judge Sand ordered the transfer to the company selected to build the initial units. At that point, everything seemed to be in place, but, lo and behold, opponents of the housing threatened to boycott banks providing financing to the developer! Ultimately, an out-of-state bank came through with a loan, although only after it had been promised federal protection in the event of any threats. Finally, construction of the low-income housing could get under way but as it was already November, groundbreaking was delayed until the following spring.

In the meantime, in December 1990, the four councilmen received an unpleasant surprise when a State Supreme Court justice in White Plains ruled, in response to a suit filed by Yonkers taxpayers, that the council members were personally responsible for the fines imposed upon the City of Yonkers because "their actions resulted in a waste of taxpayers' money, in violation of state law."[6] A month later, a formal contract signing for the construction of 142 of the two hundred low-income units on five sites took place. The signatories were DeLuxe Development, the designated builder, the U.S. Department of Housing and Urban Development, which was funding the construction of all two hundred units, and the Yonkers Municipal Housing Authority, which would ultimately take title to the units. On April 12, 1991, construction began, without any ceremony, at the Clark Street site across from Yonkers Raceway. City officials were conspicuously absent but Ken Barnes, an attorney for the U.S. Department of Justice who had initiated the lawsuit, was there. "This is a historic day for the city of Yonkers," he declared, adding: "People said it would never happen. By God, it's happening."[7] Ken Barnes's enthusiasm was not shared by some of the Clark Street homeowners who stopped by to gaze at the construction site. They vowed to continue the fight against court-ordered housing. That battle took the form of a lawsuit filed by five residents, each of them living near one of the five initial sites. They claimed that building permits had been granted without the approval of the planning board. This was not the only challenge that threatened to at least delay, if not derail, the housing plan.

Another problem was finding a developer to erect the remaining fifty-eight of the two hundred low-income units. Given the difficulties it had encountered in lining up financing for the first 142 units, DeLuxe did not want to tackle the rest of the job. Then there was the huge problem of finding developers to erect the four thousand units of housing of which 20 percent would be the required eight hundred subsidized dwellings. Despite the city's offer of tax abatements, developers weren't interested. The real estate market was weak at the time and even if that had not been the case, there was genuine concern that the 80 percent of tenants paying market rate rents would shy away from complexes where one-fifth of the units were subsidized. Above all, though, what deterred many developers was the ongoing opposition to the housing plan. Ultimately, Judge Sand would modify the housing order to allow the purchase of units in existing co-ops and condominiums in fulfillment of the requirement for the eight hundred subsidized dwellings but that would not happen until a changing of the guard had occurred at city hall.

As the all-important 1991 mayoral election approached, housing desegregation was a major issue, but, in a surprise development, the principal opponent of desegregation, the incumbent, Hank Spallone, was *not* on the ballot. Back in January, the executive committee of the Yonkers Republican Party had withheld its endorsement of the mayor. Then, in June, the Republican convention chose Peter A. Chema to be the party's candidate. Following legal challenges to the way the convention had conducted its business, a primary was held. In addition to Spallone and Chema, former mayor Angelo Martinelli was on the ballot. Spallone came in last in the three-way race. Chema was the top vote getter but his margin of victory over Martinelli was very small. Martinelli ran as an independent but Spallone's efforts to get on the ballot as an independent were derailed when a State Supreme Court justice ruled that he lacked the requisite number of signatures to run as an independent. Terence Zaleski, a former Yonkers teacher who had subsequently obtained a law degree and then served three terms in the New York State Assembly, was the Democratic candidate. Both the thirty-eight-year-old Zaleski and Martinelli favored compliance with the housing desegregation order. The election was close, but when all was said and done, Zaleski emerged victorious to serve a four-year term under the new strong mayor system. Despite his determination to resolve the housing matter and manage the city's government in a professional way, there were times when Zaleski may have felt that the title of Neal Simon's Pulitzer Prize–winning play, *Lost in Yonkers,* which opened in 1991, described the situation in city hall. In the play, set in 1942, the imperious Bella ruled her family, including two teenage grandsons temporarily left in her care, with an iron hand. Her fierce determination was not unlike that of Yonkers residents, both inside and outside of government, who opposed the housing plan, but with a new mayor at the helm as of New Year's Day 1992, the old maxim that "hope springs eternal" did not seem completely farfetched. Perhaps, like *Lost in Yonkers,* the housing crisis would have a happy ending, or, at least, an acceptable one.

The Zaleski Administration

By mid-1993 when the film version of *Lost in Yonkers,* which was shot in Kentucky, was released, Terence Zaleski was almost halfway through his four-year term. During that period, he had labored to promote a revised plan for the eight hundred units of subsidized housing required by the court. Although the proposal called for building 225 units of new housing, including some in southwest Yonkers, the remainder of the dwellings would be in existing co-ops and condominiums in the eastern and northwestern parts of the city. Residents of public or subsidized housing would be afforded the first opportunity to purchase units, with federal aid and mortgage subsidies. Opposition to the proposal came from the N.A.A.C.P., which concluded that it was too limited, and from the Save Yonkers Federation, whose members felt that it would have too great an impact upon affected neighborhoods. The N.A.A.C.P., however, was receptive to a compromise offer from the city calling for 709 rather than 625 units in existing co-ops and condos and an accelerated timetable of four rather than six years to provide the units. If the requisite number of apartments in existing complexes could not be acquired, the city agreed to undertake new construction. This plan, which was viewed as a giant leap forward, was approved by a four to three vote of the city council in April 1992.

The other component of the housing plan involving the construction of the low-income units was also moving along. With the first 142 units nearing completion, the Yonkers Municipal Housing Authority conducted orientation sessions for seventy-one families selected by lottery from among nearly four hundred families living in public housing in southwest Yonkers and another seventy-one families that had been on a wait list for public housing. Before moving into their new townhouses, the families received helpful information about maintaining their new homes and avoiding conflicts. When moving day arrived, nervousness, as well as excitement and optimism, was evident among the adults and children moving from the segregated southwest to the east side. By and large, residents of the surrounding neighborhoods did not stop by to welcome the newcomers, but in one instance the immediate neighborhood held a low-key party to welcome the new residents, and children already living in the neighborhood played with the youngsters who had just moved in. Strong friendships resulted in some instances.

With both parts of the housing plan seemingly falling into place, Mayor Zaleski turned his attention to fiscal matters, proposing a budget that called for a hefty increase in property taxes and cutting the city's workforce. This resulted in a work slowdown by municipal employees. Garbage went uncollected and police officers refused to get behind the wheel of patrol cars they claimed had mechanical deficiencies. The slowdown ended when employees were assured that, despite the budget cuts, they would receive salary increments. No sooner had municipal services gotten back to normal than the housing issue resurfaced. In early June, the N.A.A.C.P. indicated that it had reservations about the agreement hammered out a few months earlier. Concerned that co-op boards and owners of condominiums would be reluctant to sell to minorities and that the income levels were set too high to enable low-income residents to qualify for the subsidized housing, the N.A.A.C.P. withdrew its support from the plan. So, too, did the city council's majority leader, John D. Spencer, who had been one of the four council members voting for the plan in April. Spencer did an about-face because he was uncertain about the ongoing planning efforts by the Fair Housing Implementation Office, a city agency established by the court to construct, rather than purchase, subsidized housing. The agency had a mandate to plan for newly constructed housing before the compromise was worked out and it was simply following the judge's orders. This didn't satisfy John Spencer, nor did Judge Sand's decision, in July, to give the city four months to try out its plan to use existing housing. Citing the fact that the pilot program envisioned by the judge imposed limitations upon the city, for instance, a requirement that prospective residents of the newly acquired housing be chosen from a list compiled by the Fair Housing Implementation Office, Spencer seemed less enthusiastic than N.A.A.C.P. officials who viewed the pilot project as a way to pressure the city. If, after four months, the plan appeared to be faltering, the new construction the N.A.A.C.P. favored would take precedence over existing housing. In the end, the city had a year to line up apartments and minority residents eligible to purchase them, but not one family moved into a new home in that time.

Appearing before Judge Sand in June 1993, the city's attorney pinned the blame for the lack of progress on the court-appointed monitor of the implementation plan, who was accused of failing to provide up-to-date lists of eligible residents and unwillingness to work with the city in providing information sessions on financing the purchase of a co-op or condo unit. After listening to arguments from both sides, Judge Sand directed Yonkers, in July, to pursue new construction but instead of building seven hundred units simultaneously, he ordered the city to find developers for 168 units on three sites. Explaining the shift, *The Herald Statesman* noted that by emphasizing home ownership the judge said that Yonkers had "failed to address a need for rentals"; he, therefore, supported the mixed-income concept the oversight agency designated by the court embraced.[8] This revised plan, which required the city to find 250 apartments in existing complexes, was characterized by *The New York Times* as "an admirable effort to keep desegregation in Yonkers on track."[9] The judge had provided Yonkers space in which "to maneuver without letting it off the hook."[10]

Judge Sand wasn't letting Yonkers off the hook when it came to school desegregation, either. In August 1993, five months after School 32, one of the city's PEARLS (Program for Early and Rapid Learning) elementary schools, was designated a Blue Ribbon School of Excellence by the federal government, Judge Sand found that remnants of segregation were still evident in the public schools. Underpaid teachers, financial crises, and upheaval, both political and social, had thwarted attempts to completely eliminate segregation. What the Yonkers schools needed was an infusion of money. Mayor Zaleski indicated that the city was willing to provide more funding but that it could not remedy the situation alone. What was required was large-scale funding from New York State. Yonkers, together with the N.A.A.C.P., sought $600 million from the state. New York resisted, arguing that the situation in Yonkers was not unique to New York State but, rather, was found in other parts of the country as well. Attorneys for the state also blamed uncooperative teachers for the inadequate staff development in the Yonkers school system. Judge Sand ruled in 1993 that even if the state had been aware of the situation in Yonkers and had failed to address it, it still was not responsible for funding school desegregation. The N.A.A.C.P. and the Yonkers Board of Education appealed but the judge ruled again, in the spring of 1995, that the state was not liable. This was not the end of the matter, though, for yet another appeal was filed.

Before the school funding issue was resolved, the "Queen City of the Hudson" had to come to grips with some very troubling developments of a different sort. In October 1993, former mayor Nicholas C. Wasicsko took his own life. At the time it was said that he believed he was being investigated for his role as a board member and former chairman of the Yonkers Industrial Development Agency. Several months prior to Wasicsko's death, a secretary for the agency had admitted embezzling agency funds. She was eventually sentenced to one to three years in prison. As for Wasicsko, he had informed his brother that he was not guilty of any wrongdoing but he feared that his reputation would be tarnished nonetheless. Following Wasicsko's death, the Yonkers Police Department stated that the former mayor had not been targeted by the investigation. The police department had, however, been looking into suspected connections between some former Yonkers officials and organized crime. In 1992, in the midst of that investigation, which also involved the F.B.I. and the New York State Organized Crime Task Force, an attempt was made to assassinate Robert K. Olson, the city's police commissioner, who had left a similar position in Corpus Christi, Texas, to come to Yonkers in 1989. Fortunately, the bomb attached to his car malfunctioned, enabling the commissioner to avoid serious injury.

In 1993, the Police Department had to deal with another unusual crime when five youths wearing ski masks stormed a northbound train at the Glenwood station. Brandishing a gun, which was discharged into the floor of a railroad car, they robbed a half-dozen passengers before exiting the train. Two of the youths were arrested after police found a witness who had seen them donning ski masks before hopping on the train. Four years later, Yonkers detectives were dealing with another unusual and more tragic situation following a fire in the Yonkers apartment of Dr. Betty Shabazz, the widow of civil rights leader Malcom X. Dr. Shabazz died as a result of burns sustained in the conflagration set by her twelve-year-old grandson, who had previously been treated for psychiatric problems. Countless victims and massive destruction were the intended objectives of fires planned by a group of suspected terrorists. In June 1993, nearly a decade before the September 11, 2001, terrorist attacks that reduced the World Trade Center to rubble, claiming nearly three thousand lives in the process, Yonkers was one of several locations in the New York area where federal agents arrested members of a suspected Muslim terrorist group that was planning to set off car bombs at the Federal Building in lower Manhattan, the Lincoln and Holland tunnels, and the United Nations. The bombs the group was in the process of making were similar to the explosives detonated in the World Trade Center garage, killing six people and injuring more than a thousand, in February 1993. At the time the men were apprehended, federal authorities said that a Yonkers gas station owned by one of the arrested suspects was the source of the diesel fuel for the attacks planned for the summer.

Despite the best efforts of the Yonkers Police Department, sometimes with outside help from state and federal authorities, to keep the city safe, the police found themselves under fire as a result of abuse complaints. Two incidents in the early nineties showered the department with unfavorable publicity. In one case, police officers were indicted in the beating of two Irish immigrants while they were handcuffed. A jury acquitted the officers but the city paid $700,000 to settle a civil lawsuit filed by the men and their relatives. The other case involved a brawl among officers who claimed, falsely, that they had been attacked by an African American man. These incidents led to demands for a review board. In 1993, a police professional standards panel was created to review complaints against officers and, according to Mayor Zaleski, this Yonkers initiative quickly became a model throughout Westchester County and beyond.

Zaleski was also pleased that he had sought the assistance of the New York State Organized Crime Task Force to root out corruption in Yonkers. By early 1994, a former Yonkers planning commissioner had been indicted in the taking of bribes, and Zaleski's supporters, including Gail

Shaffer, New York secretary of state and chair of the Yonkers emergency financial control board, were convinced that his administration represented a major improvement in the way Yonkers was governed. That Ms. Shaffer had anything good to say about Yonkers is worth noting because in 1992 she and several of her staff had been jostled by union members after the control board rejected workers' demands for a wage hike. Ms. Shaffer's car also suffered thousands of dollars' worth of damage inflicted by angry municipal workers. Like Ms. Shaffer, former Yonkers mayor Alfred B. DelBello was in Zaleski's corner, predicting that the remainder of the mayor's term would be characterized by accomplishments in a number of areas. Former mayor Angelo Martinelli and city council majority leader John Spencer, on the other hand, were critical of Zaleski for what they claimed was his heavy-handed style of governance. In the summer of 1994 the city council attempted to thwart the mayor by rejecting his proposal to raise taxes by almost 10 percent, whereupon the mayor vetoed the council's proposal for a 5 percent increase. In the end, a budget calling for a tax increase of a little over 7 percent was passed by the council over the mayor's veto. Zaleski's opponents, who accused him of running the city "like an autocrat" and of failing to take charge when an electrical fire at the Buena Vista apartments left two thousand residents without a place to live, had some new ammunition by the fall of 1994 when the mayor and his wife were sued by the president of a public relations firm who claimed that his company had lost an advertising contract with the city because it had been unable to secure a publisher for a book written by Mrs. Zaleski.[11] The first lady of Yonkers was also accused of pressuring municipal officials to contribute to her husband's reelection campaign. Although no charges were filed following an investigation by Westchester County district attorney Jeanine Pirro, the mayor returned all contributions made by city employees. Both he and his wife, who stepped down as his campaign treasurer, contended that the investigation spearheaded by the Republican D.A. had been politically motivated. The matter was laid to rest from a legal standpoint, but it surfaced during the mayor's reelection campaign in 1995.

After surviving a primary challenge from Kevin T. Cacace, a restaurant owner, Zaleski ran against John Spencer, who himself had survived a primary challenge from former councilman Peter A. Chema. The previous year, Chema and the other three council members who had defied the court each agreed to pay $10,000 to settle a civil suit brought by four Yonkers taxpayers. With the contempt matter finally behind him, Chema hoped to move forward, but Spencer's margin of victory in the primary indicated that Republican voters wanted a change. The outcome of the general election confirmed the fact that the electorate as a whole favored change. In the weeks leading up to the election, each candidate spoke about his vision of the bright future awaiting Yonkers. On the issue of public education, both men advocated neighborhood schools as an alternative to magnet schools to which students had to be bused, but Mayor Zaleski took this one step further. He and Kenneth Jenkins, president of the Yonkers branch of the N.A.A.C.P., devised a plan for the city to take legal action, which, if successful, would allow Yonkers to decide whether to fund the current level of busing or to use some of the money for other educational purposes. Almost immediately, the attorney representing the N.A.A.C.P. in the desegregation case accused Kenneth Jenkins of failing to consult other leaders of the organization; the national organization then accused Jenkins of undermining the legal effort to desegregate the schools and suspended him as president of the Yonkers branch. Jenkins wasn't the only prominent Yonkers figure out in the cold. Terence Zaleski was, as well. All along, the Spencer camp didn't think Zaleski had a prayer, this despite the fact that the mayor, his wife and two children, one of them attired in traditional Polish dress, had met Pope John Paul II during the pontiff's visit to St. Joseph's Seminary in October 1995, only a month before the election. Although poised to celebrate its centennial in 1996, the seminary's fortunes, like those of Terence Zaleski, seemed to be in decline. Yet, despite the fact that fewer men were studying for the priesthood, the seminary remained viable, adding graduate education for lay people. Another Catholic institution of higher education, Elizabeth Seton College, however, closed in 1993, four years after its consolidation with Iona College.

Phasing out what didn't work was evident not only in education but in politics. If voters felt that an administration was functioning at less than optimal level, it was out with the old and in with the new. By handing an overwhelming victory to John Spencer, the electorate was indicating its desire for change, but there was a twist of irony in this. While a member of the city council, Spencer had railed against Zaleski's interpretation of the role of a strong mayor. Although the 1989 charter revision eliminating the city manager had created co-equal rule by executive and legislative branches of government, Zaleski was accused of being autocratic. Yet, at the same time that voters cast their ballots for his opponent, they approved a referendum giving the mayor control of the budget and conferring upon the executive branch power to appoint and set compensation for key municipal officials.

The Spencer Administration

During his first six months in office, the personable new mayor, who was praised by supporters for his ability to bring people together to work toward a brighter future for the "Queen City of the Hudson," was confronted with fiscal challenges. Criticizing New York State's formula for awarding aid to cities, the mayor concluded that a reduction in the city's workforce might be necessary to close a projected budget gap. At the same time that he was dealing with the budget, Mayor Spencer was focusing his attention on school and housing desegregation. He called for the gradual elimination of busing and the creation of a municipal housing office to supplant the federal entities supervising the creation of subsidized housing. Nine months into his term, Spencer received good news about school desegregation thanks to a decision by a three-judge panel of the United States Court of Appeals for the Second Circuit in Manhattan, which ruled that New York State "had helped perpetuate segregation in Yonkers in the 1960s and 1970s and must now pay a large share of the bill for narrowing the achievement gap between white and minority students."[12] Among the examples cited by the three-judge appeals panel were the role of state legislators in securing appointments to the board of regents of people who rejected the idea of busing, legislation prohibiting reassignment of students to achieve racial balance, and a reduction in state funding to assist with desegregation. In the wake of the appeals court ruling, Yonkers sought $500 million from New York State. Although the sum was significant, Governor George Pataki was equally concerned about the possibility that the Yonkers ruling would set a precedent whereby taxpayers statewide would be responsible for the actions of school districts and municipalities. For that reason, the Pataki administration decided to appeal the ruling to the United States Supreme Court.

In the meantime, there were some developments on the housing front. Mayor Spencer, the city council, Judge Sand, the U.S. Justice Department, the N.A.A.C.P., the New York State legislature, and Westchester County executive Andrew P. O'Rourke were all in agreement that a few acres of Rory O'Moore Park in northeast Yonkers should be used for thirty-four units of subsidized housing. There was a little problem, however. When the park property had been turned over to the City of Yonkers by Westchester County, there was a big string attached: a clause requiring that the land revert to the county should the city, at any time in the future, not use the property for park purposes. To circumvent this, the approval of the Westchester County Board of Legislators was needed, but after a heated debate during which some legislators underscored the need to preserve open space while others spoke about their commitment to home rule, the board voted to deny the use of the property for housing. Two months later, some of the legislators had a change of heart and the board agreed to allow the park property to be used. Gentle persuasion by Governor Pataki and State Senator Nicholas Spano, the Westchester Republican leader and a resident of Yonkers, seems to have played a role in the about-face. Still, the legislators who changed their votes put the best spin on things by pointing out that the proposal they decided to approve contained a provision for replacing the parkland that would be used for housing and a pledge that no additional parkland would become housing sites.

Soon after the parkland issue was resolved, Yonkers received some more good news. The U.S. Supreme Court, in June 1997, allowed the appeals court ruling holding New York State partially responsible for segregation in the Yonkers schools to stand. The task of figuring out how much the state should pay to rectify the situation fell to Dr. Joseph M. Pastore Jr., the court-appointed monitor overseeing school desegregation. After crunching the numbers for the period commencing with the appeals court ruling and extending through the upcoming 1997–98 school year, he came up with a figure of $35 million, but in the final analysis it was Judge Sand who determined how much and when the state should pay up. In October, the Judge ordered the state to give Yonkers $450,000, within ten days, as a preliminary payment for a segregation remediation effort that some estimates put at $300 million or more. Commenting on the judge's directive to the state, *The Herald Statesman* observed that it provided the funding required to, as Yonkers mayor John Spencer said, "engineer a new school district. We won't blow it."[13]

As for Governor Pataki's decision to file another appeal, the paper advised the governor to forget about it. In an editorial, the *Statesman* noted that "partly because of the state's intransigence," the city's high school students, for two generations, had been deprived of the benefits of the 1986 desegregation ruling.[14] The way to remedy this was for New York State to step up to the plate and pay 50 percent of the cost of desegregating the schools instead of contesting Judge Sand's order to do so. Although the paper praised Pataki for starting to address the inequity in state aid in order to ensure that school districts of similar size received the same assistance, it pointed out that the state aid issue was separate from the requirement to help pay for remedying decades of segregation. The editorial proceeded to castigate the state for "$150 million in legislative pork-barrel spending" plus discretionary funds of $425 million for the governor and legislative leaders; the bottom line was that the state "certainly can afford to accept its responsibility in the Yonkers case."[15]

In 1998, the state's responsibility expanded when Judge Sand ordered it to provide financial assistance to Yonkers for the purchase of apartments needed to satisfy the requirement for subsidized housing. The rationale for this was the fact that the state's Urban Development Corporation had sited its low-income housing in the heavily minority area of southwest Yonkers. This was music to the ears of Yonkers officials, especially Mayor Spencer, who more than a year before had worked with the N.A.A.C.P. on a revised housing plan for six hundred units over a period of six years, in existing complexes and new construction. To be eligible, families had to have incomes between $30,000 and $70,000 per year. Spencer envisioned this "middle-income and race-neutral" housing as a form of "natural integration" that would facilitate school integration.[16]

Things were looking up on the housing front but the mayor was clearly unhappy with the progress the city's public schools were making. He felt that test scores should have been higher and that students who did not make the grade academically should have been held back. Superintendent of Schools Reginald Marra, who had begun his career as a teacher in the city's school district, denied that unqualified students were being promoted, but the handwriting was on the wall and it was evident that the board of education, whose members were mayoral appointees, wanted to replace the superintendent. A search firm was engaged to identify candidates to replace Marra two and a half years before his contract expired. The mayor was accused of being behind this and some citizens wondered whether the executive branch of government was exerting too much authority. Marra, nevertheless, stepped down after accepting a severance package that included a stipulation that he not disparage the school district. Ironically, just at the time Marra left his post Saunders Trades and Technical High School was designated a Blue Ribbon school by the United States Department of Education. This was one of several positive developments in the "Queen City of the Hudson" in the late nineties.

Another was the disbanding of the Emergency Financial Control Board in July 1998. To guarantee that Yonkers would remain fiscally sound and thus capable of repaying bondholders, the New York State comptroller would monitor the city's finances until 2018, but by voting to dissolve itself, the Emergency Financial Control Board certified that Yonkers could, once again, become mostly independent from a fiscal standpoint. Mayor Spencer could not have been more elated. He was also delighted five months later when New York State agreed to give Yonkers $16 million to erect homes and apartments and provide low-interest mortgages. Eligibility was based on income and was not limited to minorities. However, in keeping with Judge Sand's finding that New York State's Urban Development Corporation had elected to construct subsidized housing in southwest Yonkers in the 1960s and 1970s, residents of low-income housing in that area were given preference for the new dwellings. This seemed to be a win–win situation. Yonkers would not have to bear the full cost of the housing, and Governor Pataki, who had initially opposed providing state funds to help the city pay for the court-ordered housing plan, was now able to breathe a sigh of relief knowing that the city would no longer be suing New York State. Mayor Spencer was pleased, but at the very time he was making positive comments about the forthcoming aid from the state, he was looking toward the day when the federal government would terminate the desegregation case. On the very day Judge Sand signed the agreement calling for the state to assist Yonkers in funding the housing plan, Spencer urged the federal government to "quite frankly leave us the hell alone"; annoyed because decades-old issues that were no longer relevant were being rehashed, the mayor declared: "It's time to get on."[17] In Yonkers, however, moving forward could take a good long while, in part because of differing perspectives.

This was apparent only a month after the agreement on state funding was announced. The N.A.A.C.P. questioned whether the city was doing enough to make residents of southwest Yonkers aware of the new housing opportunities and whether the income requirements were too high to enable them to qualify. Before long, those opportunities included a complex, on Tuckahoe Road and Cross Street, with twenty-two new condominiums, more than half of which were subsidized, with preference given to city residents who had lived in public housing since the early seventies. This complex, where the remainder of the units were market-rate housing, was not expected to have an adverse impact upon the value of real estate in the surrounding area. A study of subsidized housing and racial change in Yonkers published in 1993 noted that "even if the construction of subsidized housing did cause subsequent racial changes in Yonkers in the 1970s, there are several possible reasons why the causal links may have weakened in the 1990s"; these included an increase in "white tolerance for residential integration," the small scale and low density of Yonkers subsidized housing, and a New York area housing market that was "constraining the residential mobility of Yonkers whites."[18]

Another study, published in 1999 and conducted by researchers from Columbia, Harvard, and Michigan State Universities, revealed that housing values had held up in Yonkers. Using sales figures for more than three thousand houses between 1986 and 1998 and interviews with approximately seven hundred homeowners, the researchers concluded that for homes within a quarter-mile of the court-ordered housing, values had been maintained. Equally important was the fact that most of the people interviewed felt that it was time for their city to move ahead and strive for racial harmony. That was surely a favorable development, but reaching that point had been a long and painful process. In her critically acclaimed book *Show Me a Hero,* which deals with the housing portion of the desegregation case, *New York Times* writer Lisa Belkin describes the process and its impact upon individuals, both African American and Caucasian. In her conclusion she states:

> Yonkers is what will happen—is happening—everywhere, the result not of a court case, but of a demolition ball. In time, the townhouses will find their way into nearly every community and every neighborhood. . . . And one by one each of those neighborhoods will learn what that means for a nation whose people preach diversity, but who are most comfortable when surrounded by others like themselves.[19]

As time goes on, lingering doubts about desegregation will diminish. In the 1990s, however, there was still reason to be concerned not only because the occupants of the new townhouses were given the cold shoulder by residents of the surrounding neighborhood but because the ongoing challenges facing the "Queen City of the Hudson" extended beyond housing to the schools. In June 1999, a federal court of appeals ruled that the Yonkers school board and the N.A.A.C.P. had failed to prove that the achievement gap in the city's public schools was caused by segregation. In essence, the appeals court ruling invalidated Judge Sand's costly program for remedying segregation, which it asserted was based upon false evidence concerning the factors contributing to the achievement gap between white and minority students. In concrete financial terms, it meant that both New York State and the city would be required to contribute less to eliminate traces of segregation in the schools. This warmed the heart of many a taxpayer but, to everyone's surprise, the appeals court reversed itself five months later! In November 1999, after the N.A.A.C.P. appealed the June decision, the three-judge panel ruled that Judge Sand could prepare a new assessment to justify continued court supervision of the Yonkers schools and to retain or amend the plan requiring state and city funding.

Meanwhile, another issue affecting the schools surfaced. In October, teachers went out on strike to protest block scheduling, with its longer class periods, and what some perceived as the uncompromising management style of schools superintendent Dr. Andre Hornsby, a former administrator in the Houston school district who had succeeded Reginald Marra in 1998. From the very start of his tenure in Yonkers, Dr. Hornsby failed to win the support of the city's teachers. At an initial meeting with Yonkers educators, soon after being appointed superintendent, Dr. Hornsby attempted to impose a dress code for female teachers. They were told to wear stockings and heels. Sneakers were expressly forbidden. The dress code, which was unacceptable to Yonkers's educators, was not enforced. At the same time that he proposed the dress code, Dr. Hornsby informed the teachers that they were overpaid in comparison with educators in Houston, this despite the fact that the cost of living in Westchester County was considerably higher. As for the strike in October 1999, to the surprise of those who hoped Dr. Hornsby would be able to break the Yonkers Federation of Teachers, the community at large supported the teachers. Hundreds of citizens turned out for a big rally in the Chicken Island parking lot in downtown Yonkers. The strike was ultimately settled by negotiation. The resulting agreement called for additional staff development and a longer school day as well as postponing block scheduling pending teacher input. This didn't satisfy everyone, of course, but teachers and students returned to their classrooms hoping for better days ahead. For the superintendent of schools, however, the days ahead turned out to be far worse, because Dr. Hornsby and Mayor Spencer were on a collision course. Quite aside from the mayor's lingering dissatisfaction with the strike that had marred the beginning of the 1999–2000 school year, there was the matter of the 1999 federal court ruling that there were no vestiges of racism in the Yonkers schools. To Mayor Spencer this was good news, because he was eager to get the entire desegregation case behind his beleaguered city. The ruling, however, let New York State off the hook for almost $50 million in annual aid to narrow the achievement gap between minority and white students. In the next few years, the remaining issues in both the school and housing components of the desegregation case were resolved. A settlement agreement was reached and was accepted by Judge Sand in 2007.

Eye on the Economy: Focus on the Hudson

Just as Yonkers had moved ahead with the resolution of the desegregation case, it was also progressing on the economic front. Despite setbacks in the 1980s, the city soldiered on with its revitalization efforts in the final decade of the twentieth century, with some help from Westchester County.

In 1993 the county agreed to assist the city with viability studies for a waterfront aquarium and an outlet-type shopping center in the trolley barn. Façade improvements for buildings located on streets leading down to the river were also envisioned. That same year Yonkers was negotiating with the owner of the Port Imperial Ferry Corporation, which provided service from New Jersey to Manhattan, to run a high-speed ferry from the city pier to midtown. A new waterfront revitalization plan, developed by the firm responsible for the design of Battery Park City in Manhattan and Baltimore's Inner Harbor, was unveiled. Calling for gradual improvements over the course of seven to fifteen years, the plan was based upon the idea of carving out beautiful public spaces along the river and adopting a zoning formula for the area. Yonkers hoped that once all of this was in place, developers would be knocking on the door of city hall. Before long they were, and with their checkbooks open.

By early 1998 the city's office of waterfront development had whittled the list of potential developers down to three finalists; in March, Governor George Pataki came to town to join Yonkers officials in announcing that Collins Enterprises, a Connecticut developer, had been selected to build apartments, townhouses, offices, and stores on Pierpointe Street opposite the City Recreation Pier. Nearly a century old, the steel structure, which underwent top to bottom refurbishing thanks to a federal grant, was a vestige of an earlier age when people came down to the river to merely catch the breeze or to fish or get out on the water in a rowboat or aboard an excursion steamboat. In 1996, when the multimillion-dollar restoration was completed, the pier became a symbol of the waterfront's rebirth and a harbinger of things to come. Two years later, the Yonkers Comprehensive Plan stated in its goals section: "Capitalize on the City's downtown water-front access, existing Recreation Pier and proximity to New York City."[20] According to the plan, this could be accomplished in several ways, one being to "improve the quality of transportation facilities."[21] The restoration of the architecturally significant Getty Square railroad station to its Beaux Arts splendor was a step in the right direction. Good public transportation would be a factor in the unprecedented development of the waterfront, through both public and private initiatives in the first decade of the twenty-first century.

The Thruway Corridor: Till the Cows Come Home

In the meantime, another part of the city farther inland witnessed major economic development. In the 1990s, an area east of downtown, the Austin

Avenue industrial site, located along the New York State Thruway, became a centerpiece of redevelopment. This property, which had been a municipal garbage dump, had been eyed for development since the early 1980s. At that time the Morris Companies, New Jersey developers, entered into an agreement with the City of Yonkers and Westchester County, which owned the property jointly, to lease the land. The developers planned to build a $100 million office park, including a hotel, but when a federal grant for nearly $7 million did not come through in 1984, the Morris Companies shelved development plans. Then, in 1987, things were back on track thanks to the City of Yonkers and the County of Westchester, which provided funding for infrastructure enhancements. The money was actually a loan to be repaid from the rental income from the first building to rise on the site. Besides installing sewers and bringing municipal water to the elevated Austin Avenue location, Yonkers agreed to develop a park and reconstruct both Austin Avenue and Sprain Road. Westchester County assumed responsibility for building a four-way interchange on the New York State Thruway. With the necessary infrastructure assured, the Morris Companies planned to go full speed ahead, erecting seven mid-rise office buildings and a large hotel. Restaurants and stores were also part of the plan. Ultimately, after the market for office space evaporated in the late eighties, what materialized on the site were stores the likes of which Yonkers residents could have scarcely imagined. In 1993, Robert Morris, CEO of the Morris Companies, was actively promoting a new concept for the Austin Avenue site: megastores, starting with The Home Depot, which intended to make a foray into New York's northern suburbs by opening three super gigantic stores in southern Westchester. Besides Home Depot, the wholesale club Costco and one other still to be determined retailer would be coming to Yonkers, provided public opposition didn't sink the project. Citing traffic and other concerns, residents opposed to the megastores attempted to prevail upon the city not to rezone, from office to retail usage, the portion of the site envisioned for the big box stores. Their efforts were futile but four years later, with The Home Depot under construction and Costco set to go forward, a much bigger battle loomed, all because of the cows!

These were no ordinary bovines but, rather, the animated singing variety that graced Stew Leonard's, the Connecticut dairy store/supermarket. Shopping at Stew Leonard's was a little bit like visiting Disneyland. The place was clean and bright and there were surprises around every corner, just the sort of thing to lure customers, whether they had children or not. Stew Leonard's two Connecticut stores attracted shoppers from a wide surrounding area. They were truly destinations. A Yonkers store would be a magnet for shoppers from all over Westchester, the Bronx, and even from across the Hudson. Stew Leonard's didn't need much convincing to round up the cows and point them in the direction of Yonkers but the company did have one request, namely that a stretch of Sprain Road in Greenburgh, which had been closed down to prevent illegal dumping, be reopened in order to provide east-west access to the Austin Avenue site from Jackson Avenue. After all, was this too much to ask? Greenburgh supervisor Paul Feiner thought it was, and his views were shared by members of the Greenburgh/Yonkers Citizens Coalition. They were adamant about keeping Sprain Road closed but Stew Leonard's decided to commit to Yonkers anyway.

With eight million shoppers projected to flock to the Yonkers store annually, it just didn't make sense to pass up a chance to open a megastore in the "Queen City of the Hudson." Presumably, east-west access to the store took a back seat to the beautiful sound of ringing cash registers and tinkling cow bells. Yonkers city officials, elated at the prospect of seven hundred jobs being created, could also hear this new suburban symphony. They just couldn't wait for the cows to come home to Yonkers. In fact, they were so anxious that in 1997 when Mayor John Spencer, New York governor George Pataki, and Stew Leonard's executives made the official announcement that "the world's largest dairy store," according to *Ripley's Believe It or Not,* would be coming to Yonkers, two Holstein calves were imported for the press conference.[22] While the dignitaries spoke, the animals grazed contentedly on the lawn of city hall. Within months, the road dispute, which had initially threatened to keep Stew Leonard's out of Yonkers, was resolved when the city and the Morrises entered into an agreement with Greenburgh, which had filed a $150 million lawsuit to stop the Austin Avenue project, to use Sprain Road only for emergency access to the shopping center. Public access would be via the New York State Thruway, and the Thruway Authority would devise a comprehensive traffic flow plan for the center and surrounding region. That was all well and good but Ardsley, fearing that its local roads would become clogged by cars heading for the Thruway in order to get to the new shopping center, sued to have Sprain Road reopened. The suit was dismissed, as was the suit filed by a condominium on Jackson Avenue, which wanted to have nearby Sprain Road closed. Both Ardsley and the condo complex appealed.

While the fate of the road remained in judicial limbo, construction at the Austin Avenue site continued. In early September 1999, with Stew Leonard's nearing completion and The Home Depot and Costco well under way, the Morris Companies announced that the second phase of the project, consisting of office space and hotels, would begin and that two hotels would be completed the following year. This was welcome news, but most people were more impressed by the new Stew Leonard's, which was described as "a cross between Wal-Mart and Disney World" soon after it began welcoming customers in September 1999.[23] Within two months of the opening of Stew Leonard's, the ongoing road dispute was finally resolved when Greenburgh agreed to open Sprain Road until a new secondary road, financed by federal and state funds and built under the supervision of Westchester County, was completed.

Things were definitely looking up, and not just at the Austin Avenue site. In downtown Yonkers, the Nepperhan Valley Biotechnology Center was about to be launched thanks to a multimillion-dollar federal grant that enabled the city to transform an empty industrial building into a high-tech incubator. Maybe, just maybe, one or more of the businesses nurtured in the center would become for the Yonkers of the twenty-first century what Alexander Smith and Sons and Otis Elevator had been in the twentieth century. City officials weren't counting on it, but some of them couldn't help but do a little daydreaming. After all, stranger things had happened. The cows, albeit Stew Leonard's animated cows, had come home to the site of a former garbage dump where the land was so steep that it had once seemed inaccessible. Of course, what made it possible for all those customers to visit the cows and spend their money at The Home Depot and Costco, as well as at Stew Leonard's, was the new Thruway interchange. Absent this, the Austin Avenue property would have been about as accessible as Mars or the moon.

Win Some, Lose Some

Buoyed by the success of the Austin Avenue project, Yonkers extended a welcoming hand to businesses interested in setting up shop in the city. When Qwest Communications International, a broadband Internet company, leased the Saks Fifth Avenue distribution center on Tuckahoe Road in 2000 for use as a cyber center, Yonkers officials were elated. Reconfiguring the building's half-million square feet of space to meet the needs of the company required an expenditure of $100 million, but this did not seem to faze Qwest, which was delighted with the building's location a short distance from the fiber optic cable paralleling the New York State Thruway. Another attraction was the building's own electrical plant and space for backup generators, vestiges of the structure's original incarnation as a Western Electric plant that manufactured telephone equipment for AT&T. With everything falling into place, Qwest was anxious to begin reconfiguring the building and the city, eager to earn a reputation as an ideal location for Internet companies, pulled out all the stops to provide Qwest with a building permit in only six days. That was in November 2000. Six months later Qwest, which was sued by AT&T and ended up paying a huge percentage of its profits for the year 1999, halted construction, but indicated that it would not walk away from its twenty-five year lease for the building and would consider proceeding with its original plans in the future. Despite some setbacks in the 1990s, beyond the millennium the economy of Yonkers would benefit from a major contract awarded to Kawasaki Rail Car by the Port Authority of New York and New Jersey, the new Empire City Casino at Yonkers Raceway, a makeover of the Cross County Shopping Center, and the erection of the mixed use Ridge Hill complex.

Cleaning Up Yonkers: Infrastructure

In contrast with Ridge Hill or the modernization of the Cross County Shopping Center, some major construction projects in Yonkers were quite utilitarian and even unexpected. Such was the hasty rebuilding effort resulting from an accident that shut down the New York State Thruway, causing traffic nightmares throughout the New York metropolitan area and beyond. A little after midnight on an October night in 1997 when thick fog blanketed the region, an automobile hit a gasoline tanker truck bound for a Texaco station on Central Park Avenue. The car burst into flames as the truck driver neared it. The flames were so intense that the truck driver could not pull the driver of the car out of the burning vehicle. The accident, which occurred beneath a Thruway overpass, killed the driver of the car and caused severe structural damage necessitating the closing of the overpass for several weeks until a temporary bridge could be erected. Building a permanent overpass was expected to take a year but wonderful cooperation among agencies expedited the work. Mother Nature helped out as well, by providing mild winter weather, which enabled construction to proceed. The completion of the new overpass in the record time of under six months brought welcome relief to commuters and to Central Park Avenue merchants whose businesses had been impacted by the temporary traffic patterns in the area.

Another infrastructure enhancement, namely, the upgrading of the Yonkers sewage treatment plant, was not welcomed as enthusiastically in the 1990s. The project was preceded by a county study of the existing plant's ability to process more sewage and the impact this would have upon the environment. The study concluded that no serious environmental impact would result from enlarging the Yonkers plant to include a sludge dewatering component. Residents of Ludlow Park wanted a more comprehensive environmental study, but with the county facing fines of up to $60,000 a day for failure to submit an acceptable sludge disposal plan to the U.S. Environmental Protection Agency, the Westchester County Board of Legislators voted in 1990 to not only accept the study but to approve the erection of a $19 million sludge dewatering facility at the Yonkers sewage treatment plant. As a concession to Ludlow Park residents, the board agreed, unanimously, to spend an additional $20 million to cover the sometimes odiferous open tanks at the plant. Many members of the Ludlow Park Homeowners Association remained unconvinced that the county would actually made good on its pledge to cover the sludge facility. Skepticism grew when the county admitted, only two months later, that it had been illegally diverting sizable quantities of untreated sewage into the Hudson River for several years! County officials contended that at times when excessive rainwater entered sewage treatment plants, the facilities were allowed to empty some of the overflow into bodies of water. They pointed out that older sections of Yonkers had combined sewers that accommodated both waste water and rainwater and that during heavy downpours, there wasn't much they could do. Allowing the overflow to go into the Hudson had been deemed preferable to the alternative, namely, inundating the treatment plant and its adjacent parking lot. Although the county agreed to allow the plant to flood, if necessary, in the future, it also looked into getting a grit-filled control chamber back on line after a thorough cleansing. This seemed to be a more attainable goal than coming up with a permanent solution to the sludge problem.

Dewatering would be part of the solution but the problem of what to do with the residue remained. One option was to erect a special incinerator for burning sludge at the county's Peekskill solid waste facility; another was to build a sludge disposal plant in Yonkers; and a third possibility was to export the residue to the Putnam County town of Putnam Valley, where it would be transformed into agricultural lime. The process, developed by a Maryland sludge management company in partnership with a New York City construction company, was lauded by the Environmental Protection Agency but Liberty Waste Management, a subsidiary of the company operating the bus maintenance facility in Yonkers, Westchester's public buses, the county's garbage transfer stations, and its recycling plant located next to the Thruway in Yonkers, hoped to be selected to build the proposed Yonkers sludge plant. Residents of Ludlow Park wanted no part of Liberty, whose proposed sludge-drying process they feared would pose an increased health risk. The matter was settled in 1995 when the county entered into a twenty-five-year agreement to export dewatered sludge from the Yonkers plant to an out-of-state facility, initially in New Jersey and later in Pennsylvania, to be converted into fertilizer.

Final Thoughts

As the 1990s came to an end, infrastructure improvements and economic redevelopment were signs of a city on the move. Yet there was no denying that Yonkers and its people had endured much in the twentieth century, including the implosion of their city's once-thriving industrially based economy and the protracted desegregation case. There had been times when naysayers insisted Yonkers didn't have a prayer; and speaking of prayers, it should be noted that innumerable prayers were offered during two papal visits to Yonkers, the first of which occurred in 1995. As the thousands of people who gathered at St. Joseph's Seminary to welcome Pope John Paul II said prayers for themselves and their families, one suspects that some of the Yonkers residents on hand prayed for their city as well. Figuratively speaking, these people had kept the faith as they struggled to stem their city's decline from the mid-1900s until almost the end of the twentieth century when bold revitalization projects, some completed, some under way, and others still in the planning stage, promised to once again transform their metropolis into the "Queen City of the Hudson" and the "City of Gracious Living." To those who would say "Yonkers has had its day," the appropriate response two decades into the new century is: "Just you wait and see." A new day has finally dawned in the Empire State's fourth-largest city.

Notes

Preface

1. *The New York Times* (hereafter *NYT*), Aug. 22, 2011, 18.
2. Ibid.

Chapter 1. "Queen City of the Hudson"

1. *NYT*, Aug. 16, 1899, 3.
2. Ibid.
3. Ibid.
4. *Yonkers Statesman* (hereafter *YS*), Aug. 16, 1899, 1:3.
5. Ibid., Aug. 19, 1899, 3:1.
6. Michael P. Rebic, "Yonkers and the Public Bath Movement," *Westchester Historian* 62, no. 4 (Fall 1986): 107–13.
7. *NYT*, Dec. 15, 1899, 8.
8. *YS*, Dec. 15, 1899, 1:4.
9. Ibid., Feb. 10, 1908, 1:4.
10. *NYT*, Feb. 27, 1902, 6.
11. Jan Seidler Ramirez, "Paul Manship and Samuel Untermyer: A Sculptor and His Patron," *Westchester Historian* 63, no. 4 (Fall 1987): 100–14.
12. *Yonkers Herald* (hereafter *YH*) April 17, 1911, 4:1.
13. *NYT*, April 16, 1911, 12.
14. George P. Morrell, *The Millionaire Straphanger: A Life of John Emory Andrus* (Middletown, CT: Wesleyan University Press, 1971), 140.
15. Ibid., 141.
16. Ibid., 131.
17. Ibid., 136.
18. Ibid., 138.
19. Ibid.

20. Morrell, 156–57.

21. *NYT,* Aug. 4, 1905, 1.

22. *YH,* Nov. 30, 1900, 1:2

23. *YS,* Nov. 28, 1900, 1:4.

24. *YS,* Feb. 10, 1909, 6:4.

25. *NYT,* March 3, 1909, 1.

26. John Masefield, *In the Mill* (New York: Macmillan, 1941), 102.

27. Ibid.

28. Ibid., 103.

29. *YS,* June 10, 1903, 5:2.

30. *YH,* June 11, 1903, 4:1.

31. *NYT,* June 10, 1903, 3.

32. Ibid.

33. Ibid.

34. Ibid.

35. *NYT,* July 23, 1911, 4.

36. *YH,* Oct. 26, 1907, 1:3.

37. *NYT,* Oct. 28, 1907, 5.

38. *YS,* Jan. 26, 1903, 1:4.

39. *NYT,* Jan. 25, 1907, 2.

40. *YH,* Feb. 11, 1908, 1:1.

41. *NYT,* July 16, 1899, 1.

42. Ibid.

43. Ibid.

44. Ibid.

45. Yonkers Board of Trade, *Yonkers Illustrated* (Yonkers: Department of Publicity, Yonkers Board of Trade, 1903), 99.

46. "Country Living in Westchester," *Yonkers Historian* 13, no. 4 (Winter 2004): 1–4.

47. Ibid.

48. Ibid.

49. Ibid.

50. Ibid.

51. Ibid.

52. Ibid.

53. Ibid.

54. Ibid.

55. Ibid.

56. Ibid.

57. Ibid.

58. Ibid.

59. Ibid.

60. Ibid.

61. *NYT,* March 6, 1910, X:10.

62. *NYT,* April 26, 1908, RE:13.

63. Ibid.

64. Ibid.

65. Ibid.

66. Ibid.

67. Ibid.

68. *NYT,* March 6, 1910, X:10.

69. *YS,* Oct. 27, 1902, 5:4.

70. *NYT,* July 27, 1906 1.

71. Ibid.

72. *NYT,* Dec. 18, 1906, 7.

73. *YH,* Feb. 12, 1908, 1:5.

74. *NYT,* Sept. 24, 1903, 1.

75. Ibid.

76. *YS,* June 8, 1901, 4:1.

77. Ibid.

78. Katherine Maurine Winkler, "The Hollywood Inn of Yonkers: A Model Club for the Workingman," *Westchester Historian* 69, no. 2 (Spring 1993): 44–45.

79. *YS,* May 15, 1907, 1:4.

80. *YH,* June 15, 1913, 1:6.

81. *YH,* May 24, 1913, 1:3.

82. *YS,* Oct. 4, 1909, 1:1.

83. *YS,* Oct. 6, 1909, 6:1.

84. *YH,* Oct. 16, 1909, 4:1.

Chapter 2. The Great War and Its Aftermath

1. *YH,* Nov. 12, 1915, 1:6.

2. Ibid.

3. Purnell F. Harrington, *Yonkers in the World War* (Norwood, MA: The Plimpton Press, 1922), 63.

4. Ibid., 64.

5. Ibid., 65.

6. Rosalie Flynn, "The Carpet Shop: A History of the Alexander Smith and Sons Carpet Company in Yonkers, New York," MA Thesis, Manhattanville College, 1986, 39.

7. Harrington, *Yonkers,* 38.

8. Ibid.

9. Ibid., 29.

10. Ibid.

11. *YH,* Dec. 13, 1917, 1:4.

12. Ibid.

13. Ibid.

14. *NYT,* April 27, 1918, 6.

15. Ibid.

16. Harrington, *Yonkers,* 23.

17. Ibid.

18. *YH,* May 13, 1918, 1:1.

19. Harrington, *Yonkers,* 50.

20. Ibid., 49.

21. Ibid.

22. Ibid., 21.

23. *YH,* Nov. 11, 1918, 1:3.

24. Ibid.

25. Ibid.

26. "Yonkers Men Discuss the Votes for Women Problem," *Yonkers Historian* 14, no. 2 (Summer 2005): 4–8.

27. Ibid.

28. *YH,* May 27, 1913, 1:2.

29. *YH,* Aug. 26, 1913, 2:7.

30. Ibid.

31. *YS,* Nov. 6, 1915, 9:3.

32. Ibid.

33. Ibid.

34. *YH,* Nov. 9, 1915, 1:7.

35. Ibid.

36. *YH,* Aug. 26, 1920, 6:1.

37. *NYT,* June 21, 1929, 25.

38. *YH,* July 28, 1921, 1:1.

39. "The History and Architecture of Tibbetts Brook Park," *Yonkers Historian* 14, no. 3 (Fall 2005): 1–3.

40. *NYT,* June 21, 1925, RE2.

41. Ibid.

42. "Progress Changed Crestwood Forever," *Yonkers Historian* 10, no. 2 (Spring 2001): 3–4.

43. *NYT,* June 21, 1925, RE2.

44. *YH,* Feb. 2, 1925, 1:4.

45. John D. Agnillo, "William Boyce Thompson An Enduring Legacy in Yonkers," *Yonkers Historian* 8, no. 2 (Summer 1999): 6.

46. *NYT,* Jan. 4, 1924, 22.

47. *NYT,* July 7, 1919, 27.

48. Ibid.

49. Ibid.

50. *NYT,* Aug. 22, 1920, E6.

51. Ibid.

52. *NYT,* Oct. 3, 1920, 10.

53. *NYT,* Jan. 26, 1923, 1.

54. Ibid.
55. *NYT,* Feb. 26, 1923, 1.
56. Ibid.
57. Ibid.
58. *NYT,* Jan. 25, 1924, 1.
59. *NYT,* Jan. 28, 1924, 17.
60. *YH,* Jan. 30, 1924, 3:3.
61. *NYT,* Jan. 31, 1924, 14.
62. Ibid.
63. *NYT,* Feb. 9, 1924, 1.
64. Ibid.
65. Ibid.
66. Ibid.
67. *NYT,* Feb. 11, 1924, 14.
68. Ibid.
69. *NYT,* July 4, 1924, 12.
70. Ibid.
71. *NYT,* Sept. 11, 1924, 16.
72. Ibid.
73. Ibid.
74. *NYT,* Nov. 21, 1924, 1.
75. *YH,* Dec. 24, 1924, 1:2.
76. Ibid.
77. *NYT,* Feb. 2, 1925, 2.
78. Ibid.
79. *YH,* Feb. 2, 1925, 12:6.
80. *YH,* May 1, 1926, 1:1.
81. *NYT,* Nov. 17, 1927, 1.
82. *NYT,* Nov. 18, 1927, 8.
83. *NYT,* Nov. 17, 1927, 1.
84. *YS,* Oct. 29, 1929, 1:2.
85. *YH,* Oct. 25, 1929, 1:6.
86. Ibid.

Chapter 3. Years of Pain and Glory

1. *NYT,* March 16, 1930, RE2.
2. Ibid.
3. Ibid.
4. *NYT,* Feb. 15, 1931, 18.
5. *NYT,* Feb. 16, 1932, 14.
6. *NYT,* Dec. 27, 1934, 21.
7. Ibid.

8. Ibid.

9. "Model Farm, Example of Education," *Country Life and the Sportsman,* Aug. 1938, 42–43.

10. *NYT,* March 14, 1931, 3.

11. *YH,* March 14, 1931, 16:1.

12. Ibid.

13. *NYT,* Sept. 13, 1931, 2.

14. Ibid.

15. "Greek Gardens at Greystone," *Country Life,* May 1937, 59–62.

16. *The Herald Statesman* (hereafter *HS*), Nov. 22, 1932, 1:2.

17. *HS,* Jan. 25, 1933, 5:2.

18. Ibid.

19. *HS,* Jan. 25, 1933, 5:1.

20. Ibid.

21. Ibid.

22. *HS,* March 2, 1933, 1:5.

23. Ibid.

24. Ibid.

25. Ibid.

26. *NYT,* April 1, 1933, 29.

27. *NYT,* Sept. 5, 1933, 8.

28. Ibid.

29. Ibid.

30. Ibid.

31. *HS,* Sept. 5, 1933, 1:6.

32. Ibid., 14:2.

33. Ibid., 1:6.

34. *YS,* Nov. 17, 1930, 1:1.

35. Ibid.

36. "YB Dry: The Yonkers Brewery," *The Yonkers Historical Society Newsletter* 3, no. 2 (Fall 1994): 1–2.

37. Yonkers City Planning Commission, *Progress Report: 1934* (Yonkers: Gazette Press, 1935), 52.

38. Ibid., 51.

39. *NYT,* April 8, 1934, RE1.

40. *NYT,* Aug. 27, 1934, 25.

41. L. R. Chubb, "One City Takes Its Medicine," *American City,* Sept. 1935, 79.

42. *NYT,* Nov. 3, 1934, 17.

43. *NYT,* Nov. 16, 1934, 8.

44. Ibid.

45. *HS,* Feb. 24, 1934, 1:6.

46. Ibid., 13:3.

47. *HS,* May 14, 1934, 1:7.

48. Ibid.

49. Ibid.

50. *NYT,* Dec. 23, 1934, RE2.

51. Ibid.

52. *NYT,* June 7, 1936, 40.

53. Ibid.

54. Ibid.

55. Ibid.

56. Ibid.

57. Ibid.

58. Sophie F. Green, "The History and Development of the Carpet Industry in Yonkers," MA Thesis, Columbia University, 1938, 97.

59. *HS,* Feb. 14, 1937, 1:2.

60. Ibid.

61. Ibid.

62. *HS,* June 16, 1937, 1:8.

63. Ibid.

64. Ibid.

65. Thomas J. Shelley, *Slovaks on the Hudson: Most Holy Trinity Church, Yonkers and the Slovak Catholics of the Archdiocese of New York, 1894–2000* (Washington, DC: Catholic University of America, 2002), 185.

66. *HS,* July 19, 1937, 6:1.

67. Ibid.

68. Ibid.

69. Ibid.

70. Rhoda Breitbart, "Memories of a Yonkers Librarian," *Andrus Tatler,* Fall-Winter 1997, 6.

71. Ibid.

72. *NYT,* June 17, 1935, 19.

73. *HS,* June 17, 1935, 1:5.

74. Ibid., 2.

75. *NYT,* June 18, 1935, 6.

76. Ibid.

77. *HS,* June 18, 1935, 4:1.

78. *NYT,* June 21, 1935, 21.

79. *NYT,* June 24, 1935, 3.

80. Ibid.

81. Ibid.

82. *American City,* Aug. 1935, 17.

83. *NYT,* May 25, 1936, 21.

84. Ibid.

85. *NYT,* May 30, 1936, 17.

86. *HS,* June 22, 1936, 1:2.

87. *NYT,* May 26, 1937, 27.

88. Ibid.

89. *NYT,* July 13, 1937, 21.

90. Ibid.

91. *NYT,* July 21, 1937, 7.

92. *HS,* August 19, 1937, 2:7.

93. Phil Matthews, "The Yonkers Schoolboys' Race," *Yonkers History* 8, no. 1 (Spring 1999): 5–6.

94. "History of the Yonkers Empire City Racetrack," *The Yonkers Historian* 12, no. 3 (Fall 2003): 5–8.

95. "YCC History," Yonkers Paddling and Rowing Club, www.yprc.org/History.asp.

96. "Canoeing: Yonkers Club Shows How to Do It Safely," *Life,* July 15, 1940, 39–40+.

97. *HS,* July 19, 1937, 1:6.

98. *NYT,* May 1, 1939, 25.

99. *HS,* May 1, 1939, 1:2.

100. Ibid.

101. Bruce D. Haynes, *Red Lines, Black Spaces: The Politics of Race and Space in a Black Middle-Class Suburb* (New Haven: Yale University Press, 2001), 91.

102. *HS,* Aug. 14, 1939, 1:8.

103. Ibid.

104. Ibid.

105. Ibid.

106. *NYT,* March 23, 1940, 13.

107. *NYT,* March 28, 1940, 21.

108. *NYT,* July 21, 1940, 2

109. Ibid.

110. *NYT,* Nov. 22, 1940, 21.

111. *NYT,* Dec. 5, 1940, 27.

112. Ibid.

113. *NYT,* Feb. 19, 1941, 24.

114. *NYT,* May 7, 1941, 27.

115. T. T. McCrosky, "Only 216 Automobiles Cause Yonkers' Jam," *American City,* January 1938, 97.

116. *NYT,* Nov. 5, 1939, 46.

117. Tom Flynn, "Before Feminism, Yonkers Had Edith Welty," *Yonkers History* 8, no. 4 (Winter 1999–2000): 1–3.

118. *HS,* Nov. 15, 1939, 1:7.

119. *NYT,* Nov. 8, 1939, 1.

120. Marshall Beuick, "One Hundred Men and a City," *Nation's Business,* Nov. 1940, 66–69.

121. *NYT,* Nov. 8, 1939, 1.

122. *HS,* Nov. 8, 1939, 8:1.

123. *HS,* Nov. 15, 1939, 6:1.
124. *NYT,* Jan. 27, 1940, 9.
125. Flynn, "Before Feminism," 2.
126. *NYT,* Oct. 14, 1940, 7.
127. Ibid.
128. *NYT,* June 15, 1941, 35.
129. *NYT,* Aug. 25, 1942, 20.
130. Flynn, "Before Feminism," 3.
131. *HS,* Sept. 23, 1939, 2:4.
132. Ibid.
133. Ibid.
134. *HS,* Sept. 23, 1939, 1:8.
135. Ibid.
136. *NYT,* Sept. 26, 1939, 7.
137. *NYT,* Dec. 9, 1941, 36.
138. *HS,* Dec. 15, 1943, 13.
139. *HS,* Dec. 10, 1944, 1:1.
140. "Yonkers Blackout of 1942," *The Yonkers Historian* 13, no. 3 (Fall 2004): 8+.
141. Ibid.
142. Evelyn V. Warnock, "A Child in Yonkers During World War II," *Yonkers Historical Society Newsletter* 4, no. 4 (Winter 1995): 2–3.
143. *HS,* Dec. 30, 1942, 4:3.
144. Karolyn Wrightson, "Sugar Time on the Hudson," *The Yonkers Historical Society Newsletter* 4, no. 3 (Fall 1995): 1–2.
145. Ibid.
146. Consolidated Edison, "Interview with W. P. Edwards, Plant Manager, January 29, 1948," *The Story of Industry in Westchester County: A Unique Radio Series* (New York: Consolidated Edison, 1948), 5.
147. *HS,* May 25, 1945, 1:8.
148. Philip J. Matthews, "A World War II Remembrance: Operation Pluto," *Yonkers Historical Society Newsletter* 1, no. 2 (Summer 1992): 3–4.
149. Robert Glass Cleland, *The History of Phelps Dodge 1834–1950* (New York: Knopf, 1952), 265.
150. Ibid., 264.
151. Flynn, "The Carpet Shop," 39.
152. Shelley, *Slovaks on the Hudson,* 195.
153. *NYT,* April 12, 1945, 25.
154. *NYT,* Jan. 26, 1944, 38.
155. Ibid.
156. Ibid.
157. Ibid.
158. "No Strikes in Yonkers," *Nation's Business,* June 1944, 74.

159. *NYT,* Oct. 9, 1944, 28.
160. *NYT,* Oct. 2, 1944, 17.
161. Ibid.
162. Ibid.

Chapter 4. The Remaking of Yonkers

1. *NYT,* Aug. 28, 1946, 23.
2. *NYT,* Sept. 14, 1946, 4.
3. Ibid.
4. *NYT,* Nov. 30, 1946, 15.
5. Ibid.
6. *NYT,* Oct. 14, 1946, 23.
7. *NYT,* May 17, 1946, 11.
8. *HS,* May 17, 1946, 6:1.
9. Ibid.
10. *HS,* Jan. 2, 1948, 1:7.
11. *HS,* March 2, 1949, 1:7.
12. Ibid., 2:4.
13. Ibid.
14. *NYT,* March 6, 1949, 1.
15. Ibid.
16. Ibid.
17. *NYT,* March 7, 1949, 1.
18. *HS,* March 8, 1949, 1:7.
19. Ibid., 6:1.
20. Ibid.
21. *NYT,* March 9, 1949, 24.
22. Ibid.
23. *NYT,* March 12, 1948, 8.
24. *NYT,* March 8, 1950, 46.
25. *NYT,* Sept. 15, 1949, 1.
26. Ibid.
27. *HS,* Sept. 13, 1949, 6:1.
28. *NYT,* Sept. 15, 1949, 15.
29. Ibid.
30. Ibid.
31. "The Father of F.M.: The Tragic Story of Major E. H. Armstrong," yonkershistory.org/arms.html.
32. Ibid.
33. *HS,* Aug. 18, 1947, 1:1.
34. *NYT,* Oct. 30, 1948, 7.
35. Ibid.

36. *NYT*, Aug. 25, 1950, 12.

37. *NYT*, June 3, 1952, 24.

38. *HS*, Aug. 2, 1952, 2:3.

39. T. J. Friedman, "A Trail of Ghost Towns Across Our Land: The Decline of Manufacturing in Yonkers, New York," in *Beyond the Ruins: The Meaning of Deindustrialization*, edited by Jefferson Cowle and Joseph Heathcott (Ithaca: ILR Press, 2003), 43.

40. *HS*, June 26, 1954, 1:8.

41. *NYT*, June 29, 1954, 27.

42. *HS*, June 3, 1955, 1:8.

43. Ibid., 2:3.

44. Ibid.

45. *HS*, Oct. 2, 1951, 1:8.

46. Ibid., 13:3.

47. *America*, March 5, 1955, 578.

48. *NYT*, July 7, 1956, 15.

49. Ibid.

50. *NYT*, March 24, 1957, 46.

51. *NYT*, April 21, 1955, 25.

52. Ibid.

53. *HS*, Sept. 9, 1957, 1:3.

54. *NYT*, Sept. 6, 1957, 50.

55. Ibid.

56. *HS*, April 28, 1954, 1:4.

57. Ibid.

58. *NYT*, Sept. 14, 1954, 23.

59. *NYT*, Aug. 14, 1955, 54.

60. *NYT*, Sept. 9, 1955, 22.

61. Ibid.

62. Ibid.

63. *NYT*, Oct. 13, 1954, 33.

64. Ibid.

65. *NYT*, Oct. 24, 1953, 14.

66. *HS*, Sept. 1, 1956, 1:1.

67. *NYT*, Aug. 10, 1956, 19.

68. *NYT*, Sept. 15, 1959, 35.

69. *NYT*, May 22, 1948, 14.

70. *NYT*, May 25, 1948, 26.

71. *NYT*, April 28, 1950, 37.

72. *NYT*, July 27, 1958, S6.

73. Ibid.

74. Ibid.

75. *NYT*, Aug. 2, 1958, 14.

76. *HS*, Aug. 2, 1958, 10:6.

77. *HS,* Aug. 18, 1947, 1:1.
78. *NYT,* May 26, 1948, 27.
79. *NYT,* Nov. 18, 1956, 76.
80. Ibid.
81. *NYT,* Nov. 19, 1950, R1.
82. *NYT,* Aug. 26, 1956, R1.
83. *NYT,* Jan. 5, 1955, 23.
84. Ibid.
85. *NYT,* Feb. 16, 1955, 31.
86. Ibid.
87. *NYT,* April 18, 1955, 16.
88. *HS,* March 20, 1956, 4:1.
89. Ibid.
90. *NYT,* June 22, 1957, 17.
91. Ibid.
92. Ibid.
93. *NYT,* July 17, 1957, 28.
94. Ibid.
95. *NYT,* April 21, 1955, 25.

Chapter 5. An Urban/Suburban Metropolis

1. *HS,* Dec. 2, 1963, 1:4.
2. *HS,* Sept. 11, 1973, 1:1.
3. *HS,* Sept. 23, 1976, 1:1.
4. Ibid.
5. Ibid., 12:3.
6. Ibid., 10:1.
7. *NYT,* May 3, 1964, R1.
8. Ibid., R18.
9. Ibid.
10. *HS,* May 10, 1965, 22:1.
11. Ibid., 1:7.
12. Yonkers Department of Development, *Getty Square Development Program* (Yonkers: Dept. of Development, 1973), 6.
13. *HS,* July 27, 1973, 1:7.
14. Ibid., 22:1.
15. *HS,* Sept. 12, 1973, 21:1.
16. Ibid., 1:1.
17. *NYT,* April 9, 1978, WC22.
18. Ibid.
19. Ibid.
20. Ibid.

21. *NYT,* April 15, 1979, WC1.

22. *NYT,* Oct. 11, 1963, 29.

23. Ibid.

24. Ibid.

25. Ibid.

26. *NYT,* Dec. 24, 1969, 24.

27. *HS,* Jan. 30, 1970, 1:3.

28. Ibid.

29. *NYT,* Jan. 7, 1971, 37.

30. *NYT,* Oct. 15, 1972, 53.

31. *HS,* January 2, 1974, 16:1.

32. Jeff Canning and Wally Buxton, *History of the Tarrytowns* (Harrison: Harbor Hill Books, 1975), 219.

33. *NYT,* Dec. 19, 1974, 47.

34. Ibid.

35. *NYT,* Nov. 14, 1975, 19.

36. *HS,* Nov. 15, 1975, 1:3.

37. Ibid., 16:1.

38. *HS,* Dec. 13, 1975, 1:1.

39. *NYT,* Dec. 16, 1975, 43.

40. *NYT,* Dec. 17, 1975, 97.

41. Ibid.

42. *NYT,* Dec. 26, 1975, 30.

43. Ibid.

44. Ibid.

45. *NYT,* Jan. 10, 1976, 24.

46. *NYT,* Jan. 11, 1976, 42.

47. *HS,* Feb. 17, 1976, 1:1.

48. Ibid., 10:1.

49. *NYT,* Oct. 5, 1976, 93.

50. *HS,* June 20, 1977, 1:4.

51. *HS,* July 2, 1977, 1:3.

52. *NYT,* Oct. 30, 1977, 379.

53. Ibid.

54. Ibid.

55. Ibid.

56. Ibid.

57. *NYT,* Jan. 8, 1978, WC1.

58. Ibid.

59. *HS,* March 18, 1978, 1:1.

60. *HS,* June 24, 1978, 1:1.

61. *HS,* Nov. 27, 1978, 1:3.

62. *NYT,* Nov. 27, 1978, B2.

63. *NYT,* July 1, 1979, WC3.

64. *HS,* April 22, 1969, 1:5.

65. *HS,* March 8, 1969, 1:3.

66. *NYT,* Jan. 4, 1972, 40.

67. *NYT,* Jan. 7, 1972, 29.

68. *NYT,* Sept. 30, 1975, 28.

69. *NYT,* March 16, 1976, 44.

70. *NYT,* Aug. 6, 1976, 23.

71. *NYT,* July 10, 1976, 22.

72. Ibid.

73. *HS,* Sept. 8, 1977, 1:6.

74. Ibid., 16:1.

75. M. Villecco, "Technology—First U.S. Systems—Built Highrise, Futura in Yonkers," *Architectural Forum,* Nov. 1971, 68–70.

76. *HS,* Oct. 18, 1964, 1:5.

77. *HS,* Aug. 9, 1979, 22:1.

78. *HS,* Aug. 10, 1979, 1:3.

79. Ibid.

80. Ibid.

81. *NYT,* Feb. 22, 1967, 58.

82. *HS,* June 3, 1961, 4:1.

83. Ibid.

84. *HS,* Nov. 12, 1962, 1:1.

85. *HS,* Oct. 28, 1963, 23:1.

86. Ibid.

87. *NYT,* May 14, 1978, WC7.

88. *NYT,* May 13, 1979, WC3.

89. Ibid.

90. *NYT,* Feb. 26, 1978, 58.

91. Ibid.

92. Ibid.

93. Ibid.

94. Maury Allen, *China Spy* (Yonkers: Gazette Press, 1998), 112.

95. *HS,* Aug. 4, 1970, 17:5.

96. Ibid.

97. Ibid.

98. *HS,* Dec. 21, 1965, 3:6.

99. *HS,* Dec. 22, 1965, 10:1.

100. Ibid.

101. *NYT,* Feb. 12, 1966, 14.

102. *HS,* June 13, 1967, 1:1.

103. *HS,* Aug. 12, 1977, 3:2.

104. *NYT,* Aug. 12, 1977, A1.

105. *HS,* Sept. 8, 1975, 1:1.

106. *NYT,* Oct. 14, 1975, 41.

107. Ibid.
108. *HS,* May 15, 1965, 1:1.
109. Ibid.
110. Ibid.

Chapter 6. A City in Transition

1. *HS,* Dec. 10, 1982, 1:5.
2. Ibid.
3. Ibid.
4. *NYT,* Dec. 12, 1982, WC1:5.
5. Ibid.
6. *NYT,* March 6, 1983, WC3:1.
7. *HS,* Nov. 9, 1984, 18:4.
8. Ibid.
9. *NYT,* April 17, 1987, B1:2.
10. *NYT,* March 13, 1988, WC1:5.
11. Ibid.
12. *NYT,* June 29, 1986, WC12.
13. Ibid.
14. Ibid.
15. *NYT,* June 29, 1986, R1:2.
16. Ibid.
17. *NYT,* July 10, 1983, WC1:1.
18. *NYT,* Oct. 18, 1987, 25:1.
19. *NYT,* June 26, 1988, WC1.
20. Ibid.
21. *NYT,* Oct. 18, 1988, B4:1.
22. Ibid.
23. Ibid.
24. Ibid.
25. Ibid.
26. Ibid.
27. Ibid.
28. "CU Buys a New Testing Center," *Consumer Reports,* March 1989, 144.
29. *NYT,* Sept. 7, 1980, WC1.
30. Ibid.
31. City of Yonkers Planning Bureau, *City of Yonkers Local Coastal Management Program* (Yonkers: City of Yonkers Planning Bureau, 1980), 12.
32. *NYT,* Feb. 10, 1980, WC1:2.
33. *NYT,* Feb. 7, 1988, WC1:1.
34. *NYT,* Nov. 1, 1987, WC40:5.
35. Ibid.

36. *NYT,* Jan. 2, 1980, B2:1.

37. Ibid.

38. *NYT,* Feb. 15, 1982, B1:1.

39. Ibid.

40. *NYT,* July 29, 1983, B3:1.

41. *NYT,* April 6, 1984, A34:1.

42. Michael V. Yazurlo, "Desegregation: Yesterday, Today, and Tomorrow: A Case Study of Yonkers Public Schools," PhD dissertation, Fordham University, 1990, 10.

43. *HS,* June 28, 1980, 10:2.

44. Ibid.

45. *HS,* Dec. 2, 1980, 1:6.

46. *The Washington Post* (hereafter *WP*), Sept. 10, 1981, A17.

47. Ibid., Sept. 18, 1981, A13.

48. Joseph M. Pastore Jr., *Monitor's Final Report to the U.S. District Court for the Southern District of New York Reflecting on the Monitoring and Settlement Processes Re: United States V. Yonkers,* Aug. 2005, 8.

49. Ibid.

50. *NYT,* Aug. 3, 1983, B1:5.

51. Ibid.

52. Ibid.

53. *HS,* Feb. 6, 1984, 12:1.

54. *U.S. v. Yonkers,* 624F.Supp.1276, 1985 U.S. Dist. Lexis 13713.

55. *NYT,* Nov. 21, 1985, A1:3.

56. *U.S. V. Yonkers,* 624F op. cit.; *NYT,* Nov. 21, 1985, B12.

57. *NYT,* Dec. 7, 1985, 26:1.

58. Ibid.

59. *HS,* April 17, 1986, 1:3.

60. *HS,* April 23, 1986, 1:2.

61. *U.S. v. Yonkers,* 635F.Supp.1538, 1986 U.S. First District. Lexis 15686; *NYT,* May 15, 1986, B3.

62. *NYT,* June 4, 1986, A26:1.

63. Ibid.

64. *HS,* June 11, 1986, 1:3,4.

65. *NYT,* June 11, 1986, B13:5.

66. *HS,* June 13, 1986, 10:3.

67. *NYT,* May 3, 1987, WC1:1.

68. *NYT,* Dec. 1, 1987, B1.

69. Ibid.

70. Ibid.

71. *NYT,* Nov. 8, 1987, WC1:1.

72. *NYT,* Nov. 25, 1987, A26:1.

73. Ibid.

74. *NYT,* Dec. 25, 1987, B4:6.

75. Ibid.

76. *U.S. v. Yonkers*, 837F.2d1181, 1987 App. Lexis 17054; *NYT,* Dec. 29, 1987, A1.

77. Ibid.

78. *NYT,* Dec. 29, 1987, B2:1.

79. Ibid.

80. *NYT,* June 12, 1988, 35:1.

81. Ibid.

82. *HS,* June 17, 1988, 16:1.

83. Ibid.

84. Ibid.

85. Ibid.

86. *NYT,* July 27, 1988, B1:2.

87. *HS,* Aug. 2, 1988, 1:1.

88. *NYT,* Aug. 3, 1988, A22:1.

89. *HS,* Aug. 3, 1988, 16:1.

90. Ibid.

91. Ibid.

92. Ibid.

93. *NYT,* Aug. 6, 1988, 24:1.

94. Ibid.

95. *NYT,* Aug. 10, 1988, B2:1.

96. Ibid., A1:1.

97. Ibid.

98. *HS,* Aug. 10, 1988, 1:4.

99. *NYT,* Aug. 16, 1988, B1:2.

100. Ibid.

101. *HS,* Aug. 30, 1988, 1:1.

102. Ibid.

103. *NYT,* Sept. 7, 1988, B1:2.

104. *HS,* Oct. 18, 1988, 1:3.

105. Ibid.

106. *NYT,* Nov. 30, 1988, B2:1.

107. Ibid.

108. *NYT,* Sept. 2, 1989, 22:1.

109. *NYT,* Oct. 7, 1989, 22:1.

110. *HS,* Nov. 8, 1989, 1:5.

111. Ibid.

112. Ibid., 10:1.

113. Ibid.

114. *HS,* Nov. 8, 1989, 18:1.

115. *NYT,* Dec. 26, 1989, B3:1.

116. Ibid.

117. Ibid.

Chapter 7. Toward the Millennium

1. *NYT,* Jan. 2, 1990, B2:6.
2. *HS,* Jan. 1, 1990, 1:4.
3. Ibid.
4. *HS,* Jan. 11, 1990, 10:1.
5. *NYT,* Jan. 15, 1990, B3:1.
6. *HS,* Dec. 15, 1990, 1:1.
7. *HS,* April 13, 1991, 5:4.
8. *HS,* July 14, 1993, 5:1.
9. *NYT,* July 17, 1993, 18.
10. Ibid.
11. Charles Mahtesian, "Terence Zaleski: Opening Up of Yonkers," *Congressional Quarterly* 8, no. 3 (December 1994): 17.
12. 96F.3d600, 1996, U.S. App. Lexis 24856; *NYT,* Sept. 26, 1996, B6.
13. *HS,* Oct. 9, 1997, 1:1.
14. *HS,* Oct. 10, 1997, A16:1.
15. Ibid.
16. *NYT,* Jan. 28, 1997, B1:5.
17. *JN,* Dec. 2, 1998, 1:2.
18. George Galster and Heather Keeney, "Subsidized Housing and Racial Change in Yonkers, New York," *Journal of the American Planning Association* 59, no. 2 (Spring 1993): 172–94.
19. Lisa Belkin, *Show Me a Hero* (Boston: Little Brown, 1999), 326.
20. Yonkers Department of Planning, *Connections: Yonkers Comprehensive Plan* (Yonkers: City of Yonkers Planning Department, 1998), Executive Summary, 2.
21. Ibid.
22. *NYT,* Dec. 7, 1997, WE4:3.
23. *NYT,* Oct. 8, 1999, A1:3.

Bibliographic Note

Published material on the history of Yonkers is found in a wide variety of books, periodicals, and newspapers. A good starting point for readers interested in pursuing the history of New York State's fourth-largest city is *Then and Now: Yonkers,* produced by the Yonkers Historical Society and the Blue Door Artist Association. Published in 2008 as part of Arcadia Publishing's series on American municipalities, it is a delightful pictorial history juxtaposing historic and contemporary illustrations of buildings and other scenes. With substantive captions for each illustration, acknowledgments by Jeffrey Williams, president of the Yonkers Historical Society, and an introduction that includes highlights of the city's history and information about the Yonkers Historical Society and the Blue Door Artist Association, the book is a pleasure to navigate. Each of the six chapters covers a different geographic section of the city, thereby enabling the reader to travel around the "Queen City of the Hudson" with ease. Undoubtedly, many people who pick up this appealing book will want to learn more about the history of Yonkers. For them the next logical step would be to access the website of the Yonkers Historical Society (www. yonkershistory.org).

The Yonkers Historical Society's homepage has links to an extensive array of excellent articles, some of which have appeared in *Yonkers History,* the society's quarterly. *Yonkers History* itself is a superb publication covering every epoch in the city's history. Of particular interest for the study of twentieth-century history are articles on Alexander Smith Cochran (Spring 2006), women's suffrage (Summer 2005), Mayor Edith Welty (Winter 1999–2000), Prohibition (Fall 1994), the Yonkers brewery (Fall 1994), Tibbetts Brook Park (Fall 2005 and Winter 2005), Yonkers Raceway (Summer 1992 and Fall 2003), World War II (Summer 1992, Fall 1995, and Summer 2005) and the Polish Community Center (Spring 2001). The Yonkers Historical Society is also the repository for the tapes of oral history interviews conducted in conjunction with the twentieth-century book project. The society's office and archives are located in the Grinton Will Library, and researchers who go there to access the society's collections are but a short elevator ride away from the Will Library's reference department, where one can view microfilms of *The Journal News, The Yonkers Herald, The Yonkers Statesman,* and *The Herald Statesman.* Spanning a period of more than a century, these papers are also available on microfilm at the Riverfront Library in downtown Yonkers.

In addition to its newspaper collection, the Riverfront Library has an impressive array of primary and secondary sources on Yonkers history. This material is housed in a spacious room overlooking the Hudson. Of particular interest are the John Flynn Archives, arranged by subject and covering the senator's long political career. In addition to the Flynn Archives, the Riverfront Library has extensive files on Yonkers industries, schools, politics and government, population, youth, transportation, the Hudson River, and other subjects. Voluminous material on housing and legal documents pertaining to the desegregation case are also part of the Local History Collection as are city directories, minutes of the Common Council, city budgets, and documentation pertaining to various urban revitalization projects. In addition to specialized material on Yonkers, the Local History Collection includes such standard works on Westchester as Robert Bolton's *A History of the County of Westchester from Its First Settlement to the Present Time* (New York: Alexander S. Gould, 1848), Alvah P. French's *History of Westchester County, New York* (New York: Lewis Historical Publishing Company, 1925), J. Thomas Scharf's *History of Westchester County, New York* (Philadelphia: L. E. Preston and Co., 1886), Frederick Shonnard and W. W. Spooner's *History of Westchester County* (New York: The New York History Co., 1900), and Susan Cochran Swanson and Elizabeth Green Fuller's *Westchester County: A Pictorial History* (Virgina Beach: The Donning Company, 1982). These volumes contain useful information about the "Queen City of the Hudson" and serve as a good introduction to Charles Elmer Allison's *The History of Yonkers* (New York: Wilbur B. Ketchum, 1896), Frank L. Walton's *Pillars of Yonkers* (New York: Stratford House, 1951), and Joseph P. Madden's *A Documentary History of Yonkers* (Bowie, MD: Heritage Books, 1992). For a more thorough understanding of various aspects of the city's twentieth-century history, the following works are recommended:

Allen, Maury. *China Spy.* Yonkers: 1998.
Ameer, John P. *Assyrians in Yonkers: Reminiscences of a Community.* Piscataway, NJ: 2008.

Archer, Allan F. "Holy Trinity Russian Orthodox Church, Yonkers, New York: Biography of a Parish." ThM thesis. St. Vladimir's Orthodox Theological Seminary, Yonkers, 2003.

Arcus, Sam G. *Deja Views of an Aging Orphan: Growing Up in the Hebrew National Orphan Home.* New York: 2000.

Austin, Rory A. "Seats That May Not Matter: Testing for Racial Polarization in U.S. City Councils." *Legislative Studies Quarterly* 27, no. 3 (August 2002): 481–508.

Belkin, Lisa. *Show Me a Hero: A Tale of Murder, Suicide, Race, and Redemption.* Boston: 1999.

Boyd, Robert L. "Race, Labor Market Disadvantage, and Survivalist Entrepreneurship: Black Women in the Urban North During the Great Depression." *Sociological Forum* 15, no. 4 (December 2000): 647–70.

Briggs, Xavier N. De Souza. "Brown Kids in White Suburbs." PhD dissertation, Columbia University, 1996.

———, and Joe T. Darden. *In the Wake of Desegregation: Early Impacts of Scattered-Site Public Housing on Receiving Neighborhoods In Yonkers, New York.* Cambridge: 1997.

Brown, Henry Collins. *Old Yonkers 1646–1922.* New York: 1922.

Built on the Rock, 1869–1969: A History of Saint John's Evangelical Lutheran Church, Yonkers, New York. Yonkers: 1970.

Cleland, Robert Glass. *The History of Phelps Dodge 1834–1950.* New York: 1952.

Corporate Centennial Anniversary, 1835–1935. Asbury Centenary M. E. Church, Crestwood, Yonkers, New York, 1771–1935. Yonkers: 1935.

Corrigan, Hugh, *100th Anniversary, the Church of St. Mary's of the Immaculate Conception, 1892–1992.* Yonkers: 1992.

Cowle, Jefferson, and Joseph Heathcott, eds. *Beyond the Ruins: The Meaning of Deindustrialization.* Ithaca: 2003.

Dee, Eddie. *Getty Square: The Village and Other Yonkers Memories.* Yonkers: 2005.

Esannason, Harold A., and Vinnie Bagwell. *A Study of African-American Life in Yonkers from the Turn of the Century.* Elmsford, NY: 1993.

Flynn, Rosalie. "The Carpet Shop: A History of the Alexander Smith and Sons Company in Yonkers, New York." MA thesis, Manhattanville College, 1986.

Flynn, Tom. *Yonkers Life in 1900.* Yonkers: 2000.

Fried, Marc L. "Residential Segregation: Where Do We Draw the Lines? A View of *United States v. Yonkers Board of Education* and Democratic Theory." *Columbia Journal of Law and Social Problems* 23, no. 4. (Fall 1990): 467–85.

Friedman, Tami J. "Communities in Competition: Capital Migration and Plant Relocation in the United States Carpet Industry, 1929–1975." PhD dissertation, Columbia University, 2001.

Gaffar, Safeera. "A GIS Analysis on the Capacity of Green Roofs to Reduce Stormwater Volume in the Yonkers, New York Combined Sewer Areas." MS thesis, Pace University, 2008.

Galster, George, and Heather Keeney. "Subsidized Housing and Racial Change in Yonkers, New York." *Journal of the American Planning Association* 59, no. 2 (Spring 1993): 172–94.

Gelormino, A. Gerald, and Margaret Gotti. *The Italian Heritage in Yonkers.* Yonkers: 1984.

Goodwin, Jason. *Otis: Giving Rise to the Modern City.* Chicago: 2001.

Green, Sophie F. "The History and Development of the Carpet Industry in Yonkers." MA thesis, Columbia University, 1938.

Greenberg, Ira A., Richard G. Safran, and Sam G. Arcus. *The Hebrew National Orphan Home: Memories of Orphanage Life.* Westport, CT: 2001.

Halliburton, Warren J. *A Pictorial Story of Yonkers and Its People.* Yonkers: 1987.

Hankins, Grover. "Like a Bridge Over Troubled Waters: New Directions and Innovative Voluntary Approaches to Interdistrict School Desegregation." *The Journal of Negro Education* 58, no. 3 (Summer 1989): 345–56.

Harrington, Purnell F. *Yonkers in the World War.* Norwood, MA: 1922.

Haynes, Bruce D. *Red Lines, Black Spaces: The Politics of Race and Space in a Black Middle-Class Suburb.* New Haven: 2001.

———. "The Social Construction of a Black Suburban Community: A Case Study of Runyon Heights, Yonkers, New York, 1912–1994." PhD dissertation, City University of New York, 1995.

Howe, Julia. "Energy Polyculture." MA thesis, Rhode Island School of Design, 2008.

Hubert, Warren G. *History of the Baptist Church of the Redeemer, Yonkers, N.Y.* Yonkers: 1913.

Jackson, Pamela I., and Gail E. Marhewka. "Black Visibility: Early Political Victories and Income Inequality." *Journal of Black Studies* 17, no. 1 (September 1986): 33–48.

Johnson, Yolanda, Mary E. Lawson, Lillian Reilly, Loraine Spencer, Ethel Thibault, and Emelyn Webster. *Yonkers Through the Years.* Yonkers: 1962.

Kohn, Alan. "Circuit Panel Sustains Finding of Discrimination by Yonkers: Imposition of Housing, Education Remedies Upheld." *New York Law Journal* 198, no. 124 (December 1987): 1.

Liotta, Marie Elena. "The Four Great Strikes of Yonkers Teachers: An Historical Analysis of Conflict and Change in Urban Education." EdD dissertation, Fordham University, 2002.

Mahtesian, Charles. "Terence Zaleski: Opening Up Yonkers." *Congressional Quarterly* 8, no. 3 (December 1994): 17.

Masefield, John. *In the Mill.* New York: 1941.

Matheson, James D. *A History of Warburton Avenue Baptist Church.* Columbus, GA: 1970.

McCue, Deborah K. *Dunwoodie: The Heart of the Church in New York.* Yonkers: 1997.

McGrath, Brian, and Claire Weisz. *New Urbanisms/New Workplace: Yonkers Nepperhan Valley.* New York: 2000.

Morrell, George P. *A Life of John Emory Andrus.* Middletown, CT: 1971.

Pastore, Joseph M. Jr. *Monitor's Final Report to the U.S. District Court for the Southern District of New York Reflecting on the Monitoring and Settlement Processes Re:* United States v. Yonkers. Yonkers: 2005.

Piscareta, Geraldine. "The Effect of Court-Ordered Busing for Desegregation and The Creation of Magnet Schools on Student Achievement." EdD dissertation, Fordham University, 1998.

Radcliff, John P. *Souvenir History of Yonkers, 1872–1922.* Yonkers: 1922.

Rayner, George. *Yonkers Illustrated.* Yonkers: 1903.

Rebic, Michael P., James D. Keen, and Doris B. Keen. *Landmarks Lost and Found: An Introduction to the Architecture and History of Yonkers.* Yonkers: 1986; 2nd Ed., 2008.

Reed, Thomas H. *A Brief Financial and Administrative Survey of the City of Yonkers, November and December, 1933* New York: 1934.

———. *Report on the Financial Condition of the City of Yonkers, New York.* New York: 1934.

Salerno, Rachelle M. "Segregation, Northern Style: A Political History of Non-Policy Making in Yonkers." PhD dissertation, Fordham University, 1985.

Schaumburg, Harry W. "Liberating the People of God." Thesis, New York Theological Seminary, 1988.

Scheuring-Leipold, Malissa A. *Job Satisfaction: A Study of High School Teachers in An Era of Educational Reform.* New York: 2008.

Seixas, Peter C. *Shifting Sands Beneath the State: Unemployment, the Labor Market, and the Local Community, 1893–1922.* New York: 1993.

Shelley, Thomas J. *Slovaks on the Hudson: Most Holy Trinity Church, Yonkers, and the Slovak Catholics of the Archdiocese of New York, 1894–2000.* Washington, DC: 2002.

————. *Dunwoodie: The History of St. Joseph's Seminary, Yonkers, New York.* Westminster, MD: 1993.

Smith, Catherine R. *These Years of Grace: The History of Westminster Presbyterian Church, Yonkers, New York, 1858–1964.* Yonkers: 1965.

Steigman, Arnold L. "Mayor-Council Government: Yonkers New York 1908–1939: A Study of Failure and Abandonment" DPA dissertation, New York University, 1967.

The Story of Industry in Westchester County: A Unique Radio Series. New York, 1948.

Sussman, Michael H. "Discrimination: A Unitary Concept." *Minnesota Law Review* 80, no. 4 (April 1996): 875–900.

Tanzone, Daniel F. *Slovaks of Yonkers, New York.* New York: 1975.

Tolhurst, Desmond. *St. Andrew's Golf Club: The Birthplace of American Golf.* Rye Brook, NY: 1989.

Tupper, Jack A. "The Impact of the Relocation of the Alexander Smith Carpet Company upon the Municipal Government of the City of Yonkers, New York." MPA thesis, New York University, 1963.

U.S. v. Yonkers 624F.Supp.1276 (1985).

Walsh, Amy. "The Yonkers Case: Separation of Powers as a Yardstick for Determining Official Immunity." *Fordham Urban Law Journal* 17, no. 2 (July-August 1989): 217–55.

Walton, Frank. *The Cedar Knolls.* Bronxville: 1960.

Warburton Avenue Baptist Church, Yonkers, N.Y. Valley Forge, PA: 1954.

Westchester County Department of Environmental Facilities: 1895–1992. White Plains: 1992.

Wiese, Andrew. "The Other Suburbanites: African American Suburbanization in the North Before 1950." *The Journal of American History* 85, no. 4 (March 1999): 1495–1524.

Willcox, Walter F. "The Distribution of Immigrants in the United States." *The Quarterly Journal of Economics* 20, no. 4 (August 1906): 523–46.

Williams, Gray. *Picturing Our Past: National Register Sites in Westchester County.* Elmsford: 2003.

Wolters, Raymond. *Right Turn: William Bradford Reynolds, the Reagan Administration, and Black Civil Rights.* New Brunswick: 1996.

Yazurlo, Michael V. Sr. "Desegregation: Yesterday, Today, and Tomorrow, A Case Study of the Yonkers Public Schools." EdD dissertation, Fordham University, 1990.

Although books, dissertations, and articles in scholarly journals shed considerable light on Yonkers history in the twentieth century, articles appearing in *The Herald Statesman, The Yonkers Statesman, The Yonkers Herald, The*

Journal News, The New York Times, Architectural Forum, Nation's Business, Country Life, Consumer Reports, and the *Westchester Historian* are also helpful; these are referenced in the notes for the various chapters. Finally, the Westchester County Historical Society, which publishes the *Westchester Historian,* has both primary and secondary sources on Yonkers in its superb library and archives housed at the Westchester County Records Center in Elmsford. For research on any community in the county, the Westchester County Historical Society is the place to begin.

Yonkers Speaks

Excerpts from Oral History Interviews

Mary Hoar: On Nodine Hill in the Early 1900s
(Chapter 1—The Working Class)

My mother's family grew up in Nodine Hill. . . . When my mother first moved there . . . her family were the only Irish Catholics on the street. There was an Italian family who lived next door . . . but everyone else was Scottish and it was considered to be the Scottish neighborhood back in the nineteen-tens, nineteen-twenties.

Mary Hoar: On the Building of the Bronx River Parkway
(Chapter 2—Parks and Parkways)

My grandfather came over as a teamster. He actually rented horses when they built the Bronx River Parkway so part of his team of horses he had in his stable helped to build the Bronx River Parkway.

John Romano: On the Great Depression
(Chapter 3—Brother, Can You Spare a Dime?)

No one really had anything of substance. There were hundreds of houses that were vacant . . . the people couldn't afford the money they owed the banks. It was a struggle . . . but one thing we had. We had each other. Yonkers people worked together.

Mary Hoar: On World War II
(Chapter 3—Doing Without)

He [father] loved horseback riding. They actually had a small stable in Yonkers . . . near Van Cortlandt Park which his father . . . took care of, ran it for him. There were actually pictures of my brother . . . in the paper when they were having the gasoline shortage during World War Two. There's my brother, six months old, riding a horse.

Joan Cahraman Hull: On World War II
(Chapter 3—Doing Without)

We got along fine with the rationing. . . . In terms of food . . . we just adapted to the conditions, ate a lot of peanut butter, took a lot of peanut butter to school but I like peanut butter anyway. . . . My mother became an air raid warden and made sure that everybody in the apartment had their blinds closed. We didn't see any lights . . . and then later there was another family in the apartment house; the father worked for the Weather Bureau for the Navy and he said he needed somebody and so she [Hull's mother] went to work. That was at Columbia University and so she drew weather maps for the Navy during the war.

Arlene McCann Reden: On World War II Rationing
(Chapter 3—Doing Without)

I remember coupons, World War Two coupons, and my mother used to save bacon fat in the kitchen in tin cans and you would bring it to Gristede's down at the end of the car line and redeem it for coupons.

Arlene McCann Reden: On the Hitler Image in the Palisades
(Chapter 3—America at War)

From the bottom of Roberts Avenue you could see across . . . to the Palisades and around the time of the rise of Hitler his face appeared and just around the time that he disappeared, there was a landslide and he's gone. . . . It's almost like it was drawn by a cartoonist . . . like chiseled in but a natural chiseling with the nose and mustache. It was unbelievable.

John Rossell: On Factory Employment and World War II (Chapter 3—Hands and Hearts at Work)

Everybody had a job just about. There was no shortage of jobs. If you didn't work for Otis or Habirshaw, there was Anaconda in Hastings and there was Polychrome. There was an awful lot of work here but the majority of people worked in Alexander Smith's. At their height there was about eight thousand people. During the war [World War II] they made blankets for the Navy. They made very little carpet during the war. . . . My mother worked on the blankets.

Nobody had anything so we were all in the same boat. Everybody was satisfied.

Walter Hlewicki: On Alexander Smith and Sons (Chapter 4—The Silence of the Looms)

I remember as a child the carpet shop. It seems like everybody at one time or another worked there. My parents worked there. My grandparents worked there until they started businesses. . . . I can always remember, especially in the summertime, when the windows were open, you could hear the looms and you would hear the click, click of the looms.

Stephen Macknowski: On his Childhood Home (Chapter 4—The Silence of the Looms)

I lived in a cold water flat. . . . My mother was immaculate. . . . Every year the dining room had to be painted and the kitchen had to be painted. The old black woodstove. We didn't use coal. Coal was on Christmas, Easter. Special days you'd put the coal and the gas, your meters, you'd put a quarter. . . . We were in an environment that molded us the right way and we had the right parents, too.

John Rossell: On Living on Moquette Row
(Chapter 4—The Silence of the Looms)

The apartment was five rooms. . . . After the war [World War II] they sold the apartments for two hundred dollars a room. . . . There were three bedrooms upstairs, one large, two small. We had the dining room and living room and kitchen and the basement, which we called the cellar. That was where the bathroom was. . . . Everybody had a backyard. Some people grew tomato plants and some just had grass but everybody had their own backyard. . . . A lot of the houses had trees so if you wanted to put up a hammock you could.

Stephen Macknowski: Otis Elevator
(Chapter 4—What Goes Up Must Come Down: Otis Elevator)

Otis was a very good place to work, one of the best around. Slowly, after the G.I. Bill and after maybe ten years or so things were falling into place real good. The economy was coming around.

[Referring to his twenty years as a machinist at Otis]: They had an incentive system there; the more pieces you could put out, the more you got paid.

Walter Hlewicki: On Recreation
(Chapter 4—Cruisin' Down the River)

We did a lot of crabbing and fishing at the foot of Ludlow Street near where oil companies had piers . . . and when the barges weren't in they would allow us to go down and fish off their piers. . . . At that time the river was pretty clean.

Leonard Winstanley: On Childhood Pastimes
(Chapter 4—Cruisin' Down the River)

When I was a kid I went down to the Hudson . . . used to walk from Lawrence Street . . . and walk all the way down to Ludlow and we would fish for crabs. . . . It was amazing when these spring runs came up how many fish we would catch.

No one had cars and we just hung around and played stickball . . . and box ball and all the things that you hear about or read about. The block was everything.

Jeremiah Jerome: On Boat Trips up the Hudson and to Rockaway (Chapter 4—Cruisin' Down the River)

We would go down to Yonkers pier . . . and we would take the Dayliner. We'd go up the river. . . . There was a stop at Bear Mountain. We didn't get off at Bear Mountain but people did and then they [the Dayliner] would go to Poughkeepsie, then turn around and come back down and one other day they would have a boat there [Yonkers pier] that would take you to Rockaway. . . . We'd pack big lunches and bring the sandwiches and soda water and it was a good life.

Edward Petti: On an Adventure on the Other Side of the Hudson (Chapter 4—Cruisin' Down the River)

My most memorable experience in West Yonkers was me and my best boyhood friend one day we . . . decided to get on the trolley car and we took it to Getty Square and we decided we were going to climb Palisades Mountain. So what that meant was . . . getting on the ferry, taking the ferry across. . . . We got there. . . . I can't believe it; we climbed up. . . . I don't know how far we climbed; we probably were where we shouldn't have been. We were sliding.

Edward Petti: On Saturday Afternoons at the Movies (Chapter 4—Strolling Through the Park)

Our entertainment was the Kent Theatre. The Kent Theatre is on McLean Avenue. . . . We would go there every Saturday afternoon, see a movie. I think it was twenty cents and . . . a double feature, cartoon, newsreel. Could you beat that for twenty cents? It was a four or five hour outing.

Gerald Loehr: On Growing Up in Yonkers
(Chapter 4—Strolling Through the Park)

I grew up on Warburton Avenue. I lived across the street from Trevor Park. . . . I could look out my bedroom window and see as soon as two or three people arrived down on the baseball field. . . . As really young children we lived in the park and the park drew people from all over. . . . You could be in that park when the Dayliner would go by and everybody would leave the ball field, run across the tracks, take their clothes off and jump in the water to get the waves. The water wasn't too clean back then but it was fun. . . . As you got a little older, whether you played Little League or you started to play school sports, then that's when you really met people from all over the city because the games were against the other city schools.

We used to walk everywhere. . . . We used to walk from Warburton Avenue down to the movies in Getty Square or to Loew's, which was even further down, by St. Joseph's Hospital.

My Boy Scout troop . . . used to go on overnight camping trips right by the Yonkers/Hastings line. There's all condominiums now but it was woods then. . . . You could hear the trains and the tugboats. We went crabbing; we went fishing. . . . We built rafts out of old railroad ties. It was a good place to grow up, lots of sports.

Symra Brandon: On Growing Up in Yonkers
(Chapter 4—Backyards and Barbecues)

I lived in Yonkers . . . from the age of one. I was born in New York City. Right after that period of time my parents moved to Cottage Place Gardens which is on Warburton Avenue. . . . I basically grew up in public housing . . . it was a great community. It was a series of about ten buildings, about three stories high. I can remember it all because I still live in Yonkers and I live exactly one block from where I grew up. . . . Going back to those days, it was a very small community. Everybody knew everybody. Everybody was your mother and your father. . . . The neighborhood took care of itself and we went to the local school, which is School Six. . . . It was really . . . a friendly neighborhood where . . . you were able to play outside without fear. . . .

We really didn't go out of our neighborhood. The church was . . . right at the border of public housing where we lived. You had the barber shop, the grocery store. The drug store was on another side of the complex so when you went outside of your neighborhood it was either because you were sent somewhere or your parents or your mother . . . took you to Getty Square or you were venturing out with a little group . . . so you really stayed and did everything around the neighborhood.

It was a great place to live at the time and at the time it was also integrated housing. It wasn't just people of color. . . . Back then public housing was a place where families started out and then they moved on.

I started School Six in kindergarten and . . . it was a pleasant experience. . . . I remember parents coming in and out of the school and the teacher was always right back then. . . . If the teacher said you did something, you actually did it.

The best thing about growing up in Yonkers was you always had a support system. The support system was in the schools. The support system was in your neighborhood. The support system was in your religious organization. . . . You had . . . this big, gigantic family and all your friends and life was safe and wonderful.

Joan Cahraman Hull: On Recreation (Chapter 4—Backyards and Barbecues)

I would ride my bike up Broadway, North Broadway. This is when I was about twelve. The Julia Andrus Home, orphanage, had some cows. I would take my lunch in a paper bag and sit on that wall and look at cows. To me that was the biggest Saturday adventure that you could have.

Joan Jennings: On Getty Square
(Chapter 5—Urban Renewal)

My father was . . . a butcher in the Getty Square area. In those days women stayed at home and they walked into the Square and did their shopping and they went to the butcher shop and they went to the curtain store and they went to Genung's and they went to Mimie's for their dresses.

My father was in a very active butcher shop so he knew everybody in Getty Square and everyone knew him and from the time I was about seven or eight I was allowed to walk down Elm Street to Getty Square and hang out because everybody would keep an eye on me.

Everybody was basically on foot, walked all over the place from the Square or took the trolley or took a bus. . . . There were thriving mom and pop stores. You went to your individual providers. People had their favorite meat markets and their bakeries and lunch counters. . . . The Square was a thriving place. My mother knew all the shopkeepers; they knew who she was but with the advent of the car and the popularity of the car and then you had Cross County Shopping Center, it was a novelty to drive to go shopping.

Arlene McCann Reden: On Getty Square
(Chapter 5—Urban Renewal)

[Grandfather owned commercial buildings in Getty Square and elsewhere in Yonkers.]

We also owned Nine Main Street, which was probably better known in the 1900s as Genung's. It was originally Marshall Matheson's Department Store at the time he (grandfather) bought it. . . . Around nineteen thitry-five it was rented to Genung's and it was one of the few stores to open during the Depression. Now my mother was a buyer for Stern's down in New York City . . . and they cut back their days . . . and she said it was hardly worth the . . . trolley and train fare to go down to the city and she said she was walking home from the train station one night . . . and she saw a sign at Marshall Matheson . . . they were hiring and she went in and when they realized she was a buyer for Stern's they hired her immediately. Now this was right next to the warehouse [owned by the McCann family]. They shared an alley . . . and that's how she met my father because he worked in the warehouse.

Now to Getty Square—as a child, it was quite fashionable on a Sunday afternoon to go down and stroll around looking in the shop windows. There was the Clermont. . . . That was in one of our Broadway buildings. [The proprietor of the Clermont] made his own ice cream; he made his own chocolate and we would go into the back of the building, which backed onto Mill Street, and there were a couple of floors with small rooms and I remember wooden slats on the floor and they were hardly bigger than a telephone booth and there would be a woman in there making the chocolates. . . . At Easter he [proprietor of the Clermont] would send the children in the McCann family huge Easter rabbits and jelly beans.

Jeremiah Jerome: On Childhood Experiences:
Going to Getty Square
(Chapter 5—Urban Renewal)

It was good . . . in Yonkers then when I was a kid growing up. As a young kid I would go up to Getty Square with my grandmother on the trolley . . . and go to the meat market. . . . Getty Square was where you went. That's where the movies were; that's where the restaurants were. That's where the shops were.

Leonard Winstanley: Observations of a Former Councilman
(Chapter 5—Urban Renewal)

I've been involved in the City of Yonkers for a long time. . . . A lot of the plans which we thought would revitalize the city have gone astray. It's a shame . . . very frustrating. . . . They'd start a project and all of a sudden the economy would go.

People forget to realize we're the fourth largest city in New York State. My sister used to call it "the biggest hick town in the world." Everybody knew each other.

Gregory Arcaro: On Urban Renewal
(Chapter 5—Urban Renewal)

Urban renewal did some good things to the extent that some of the neighborhoods in which there was old, deteriorated, dilapidated structures, housing, inadequate type facilities, they were eliminated. The reuse of this new vacant land . . . came to be in most cases affordable housing. Good news is a lot of good people got a chance to have a decent place. The downside from the commercial end was that the people who lived there, who were eligible to live there, were restricted in income so with a limited income they did not have a lot of disposable income so two things were going on which appeared in conflict: revitalize the downtown without any consideration of the waterfront commercially and urban renewal reuse is income restricted housing . . . so therefore there were years when nothing happened commercially.

Alfred DelBello: On His Election as Mayor
(Chapter 5—Playing Politics)

In nineteen sixty-nine when my term [as councilman] was coming to an end, I remember coming home and saying to my wife: "There's no point in running again for councilman. You can't make a change in this city". . . . She just said to me: "Look, why drop out? Run for mayor. If you get elected, change it; if you don't get elected, you're out anyway." So in sixty-nine I ran for mayor against the incumbent, James F. X. O'Rourke, and I really ran on very much of a reform platform pointing out . . . the political patronage system . . . and the corruption that existed . . . and that's when I got elected and I was the youngest mayor, first Italian American, first Democrat in thirty-two years. . . . The night of the election was extremely exciting. Actually the people came out of their homes and started parading in the streets. . . . The citizens knew about the corruption. There were public hearings, newspaper articles pointing out what was wrong with Yonkers.

Alfred DelBello: Summarizing His Most Important Achievement as Mayor (Chapter 5—Playing Politics)

I think the most important thing was taking the city from the old patronage-driven system of running government into the new, more modern system of professional government, professionalizing the government. I think that's unquestionably the most challenging, the most important thing that could happen.

Gregory Arcaro: On the Colonnade (Chapter 5—A *New* Day Dawning?)

I was there when we designed the Colonnade. There was a developer named Taubman. . . . There was discussion that he wanted to build his mall up at Boyce Thompson and there were wonderful planners and politicians who said no. We saw what happened to the downtown. . . . The local merchants felt as if no one would come out of this mall [proposed downtown mall], that they needed something exciting, something different, so that's how the Colonnade came to be, something that was very different, very exciting that would bring people out of the mall onto the street. Everybody thought it was worth a shot so there was great support for it. Then Taubman's development doesn't go through and these Colonnades looked kind of silly hanging out there and people who didn't know the background said: "What are these people, crazy?". . . . I think, unfortunately, people didn't realize the history . . . and just saw it go up and said this is crazy.

George Rutledge: On the Results of Collective Bargaining (Chapter 5—A *New* Day Dawning)

There was a time when we'd [Yonkers police] try to negotiate salary increases. One year, it wasn't a raise. It was a benefit in our contract. What we gained that year was . . . that . . . in the summertime we could take off our ties and open up the top button on our shirt.

Jennie Tritten: Student Unrest in Yonkers (Chapter 5—Reading, Writing, 'Rithmetic + Rallying and Protesting)

You did not have any fires . . . because of the . . . coalition of black ministers that met and black people from the community that kept Yonkers from burning down. I went to some of those meetings. I was not allowed to record them. They wanted me there to listen. . . . What they did accomplish . . . (was) getting the board of education to include Black Studies into their curriculum and they marched on the board of education and that's where the kids were guided to go and to protest. . . . Muriel King Taylor . . . assistant principal from Gorton High School . . . had assemblies that I attended. She just preached to these kids that no good comes from burning down the school. . . . The rumor was that they were going to burn Gorton High School down.

Jeremiah Jerome: On Yonkers School Strikes (Chapter 5—Reading, Writing, 'Rithmetic + Rallying and Protesting)

I transferred [as a teacher] from there [Longfellow Junior High School] to Lincoln High School in nineteen sixty-three and then we began the push right after that for the union. The union had been around since about forty-seven–forty-eight but we reinvigorated it. . . . The first union vote you had to have a majority and there were people absent and we won but we didn't get a majority and then there was a second election and we defeated the YTO (Yonkers Teachers Organization) and we became the bargaining agent for the teachers of the City of Yonkers and I was one of the original executive board. . . . We were out on strike, I think, three or four times. . . . First time we were out . . . was a very, very bitter strike. . . . I think the union had done great things for the city because it brought more money to the city . . . more programs, more staffing, class size, and things that we enjoy today and everybody could use the union as a whipping boy. The politicians loved it . . . but it (the union) . . . improved the city education system tremendously and we have a number of . . . excellent schools.

Jeffrey Williams: On Busing
(Chapter 5—Reading, Writing, 'Rithmetic + Rallying and Protesting)

Because of the location of this community [Runyon Heights] . . . when I was going to school, the city was attempting to make some changes in terms of trying to desegregate the schools before it went to court and so this community always took the brunt because it was always this pocket that was getting transferred out to all these remote places where . . . some years you'd go, people just didn't want you there. I mean they really didn't want you there. . . . I went to five different schools in five years. . . . The reception was horrible. . . . [At] Walt Whitman it was just a miserable year. They just didn't want us out there and . . . they would look down their nose a little bit at you. . . . I guess they thought they were better than we were. We had to tell them: "Look, you guys, . . . you all are living in apartments. Folks out here own their own homes. Don't look down your nose at us."

Jeffrey Williams: On the Origins of Runyon Heights
(Chapter 5—Home Sweet Home?)

The . . . thing that's interesting about Runyon Heights is just the way it's laid out. The section of Runyon Heights where I grew up was nothing but dead end streets, which . . . meant our parents felt free to let us go out. . . . They knew where you were going and how far you were going. There really is a hugely strong sense of community.

Sylvia Banks: On the Runyon Heights Community Center
(Chapter 5—Home Sweet Home?)

This building was built because of the desire of our parents. . . . They saved money by having barbecues and card parties . . . until they were able to purchase the land.

John Rossell: On His Work on the Committee Formed to Secure the Release of Hugh Redmond
(Chapter 5—The Tragic Case of Hugh Redmond)

We met with Secretary of State John Foster Dulles . . . and while he said he would do everything he could, there were no guarantees or no promises of any sort.

Mrs. Redmond kept her fight up right up to the end. She always kept trying to get her son out.

Hughie Redmond was married to a Russian woman. . . . From what I understand it was a marriage of convenience. . . . I met her once at Mrs. Redmond's home. . . . My understanding from Mrs. Redmond was that Hughie was supposed to board a ship within an hour and at that time he was picked up. . . . Whether she [Redmond's wife] turned him in or not, I'm not sure. If she turned him in, I don't think she would have been welcome there [Mrs. Redmond's Argyle Terrace home].

He [Hugh Redmond] supposedly committed suicide . . . but nobody believed it.

George Rutledge: On the Creation of the Police Museum
(Chapter 5—Unspeakable Crimes)

I was a police sergeant and around nineteen seventy-eight I went to an individual's home. . . . He was complaining about noisy neighbors. I listened to the complaint and I assured him we'd give special attention to the area and then when I started to walk away he said: "You don't know me, do you?" And I said: "No, sir; I'm sorry." He said: "You wouldn't but I spent thirty-five years in the Yonkers Police Department and the day that I left was the last time anybody in the police department ever spoke to me . . . and the same thing is going to happen to you, kid." . . . That really stuck with me and little by little I started to think about ways that we could make sure that the men who served for so long are remembered and with that I started collecting things that I saw, old police memorabilia. . . . I asked the police commissioner at the time and they gave me a little room . . . so I had to sheetrock the room up myself with my money and paint the room with my money. I bought and built some wooden display cases with plastic see-through tops on them and got some other display cases from jewelry stores. . . . I started to put my collection out . . . and at the same time I decided we would run a picnic and gather back as many of the retired as we could once a year. We called it old timers' picnic. In nineteen seventy-eight in September we had our first annual old timers' picnic and we had, I think . . . maybe fourteen or fifteen retirees . . . and now we have about a hundred and fifty retirees come year after year from all over the U.S.

Mario Caruso: On the City's Architecture, Particularly City Hall (Chapter 6—A *New* Day Dawning?)

There's really great architecture all over the city, not just downtown. Architecturally, Saint Joseph's Seminary is a very impressive building with a series of turrets. City hall itself is really an impressive building going back to classical architecture and that's really how city hall was built out of that style . . . and I love clock towers. It has a mix of good architecture and a four-sided clock tower. A co-worker and I . . . in ninety-four or ninety-five . . . happened to see the door on the fourth floor of city hall open in the center of the hallway . . . so we darted up the stairs. . . . It's staircase after staircase and you're in line with these clocks that have to be ten feet wide and then you get above that. Then there's windows for all four sides and you can see all the way down to the Statue of Liberty and the Empire State Building. It's a great view. That was really the thought behind placing city hall on top of the tallest hill in downtown.

Angelo Martinelli: On the Development of the Waterfront (Chapter 6—The Mighty Hudson)

For years as a young boy growing up in Yonkers we would hear about plans to redevelop the waterfront and to broaden our economic base and for years nothing ever happened because there were constant changes in administrations in the city, constant bickering back and forth between elected officials and also constant financial crises. . . . So there was very little long-term planning. It was a triage method of running government by crisis. We're finally turning the corner there. We're seeing development in every corner of the city, smart development which will not negatively impact the quality of life of our neighborhoods but will bring much needed change . . . particularly the project in Chicken Island, the west side of our city. I was very proud to secure the money to daylight the Saw Mill River. I was able to secure twenty-four million dollars to daylight the river and ultimately we will have a riverwalk with restaurants and shops around a river that for decades was covered over.

Angelo Martinelli: On Yonkers Raceway
(Chapter 6—Down Time)

Yonkers Raceway has continued to be part of the history of the City of Yonkers. It is one of Yonkers's largest employers. More important than that it stands out as a beacon, a light on the Thruway. It really represents what Yonkers is all about.

Sal Prezioso: On His Experiences as City Manager
(Chapter 6—Familiar Face, Familiar Problems)

Politics was the biggest thing in Yonkers that ever happened. They crossed one another. They were friends with one another. They were enemies with one another but somehow or other when they got to a real purpose that they were both interested in, they all came together.

Rhoda Breitbart, who was a librarian at the Carnegie Library
(Chapter 6—Familiar Face, Familiar Problems)

One of the most heartbreaking moments was watching that old Carnegie Library come down. It broke my heart and it shouldn't have happened. . . . When we talked to the mayor he said it was too late to change the plan and they were running a state highway right through the building.

Gregory Arcaro: On Affordable Housing and the Desegregation Case (Chapter 6—Background of the Case)

As a planner, my sense of it was that we in the City of Yonkers built more affordable housing than the whole rest of Westchester added up. Good news: it helped people. Bad news: we tended to locate it all around Getty Square as part of the urban renewal process. In every case, every building certainly received local support. . . . In every case it received either federal or state support. Then the federal government . . . said to us: "This is inappropriate; this is wrong," but in every step of the way each building had federal support. On the face of it they're certainly absolutely right. . . . As a local professional planner in government, we would have felt better if the Pound Ridges and Bronxvilles of the world also somehow received a citation for not participating in that responsibility . . . and yet if you drive around this community, no community has done more for affordable housing than Yonkers.

The desegregation case, did it have merits? Yes, but it didn't seem equitable because other communities didn't even provide anything. We thought we provided something and we got punished for that.

John Romano: On Housing in Southwest Yonkers Funded by H.U.D. (Chapter 6—Background of the Case)

They've taken the poor. They corralled them. . . . Instead of saying, as I believe, they should have built two-family houses and say: "Here's the key." Given a sense of responsibility, that would pull you out but unfortunately someone in Washington (said) it's better to build projects.

Gerald Loehr: On the Desegregation Lawsuit (Chapter 6—Background of the Case)

When the lawsuit was first filed . . . I was just in office. I made inquiry of the government; I went to Washington to inquire as to what was their ultimate goal. . . . I believe they were looking for either eighteen hundred or two thousand units, which was disproportionate and I told them so because at that point in time Yonkers, which had roughly twenty-five percent of the population, had thirty-four to thirty-five percent of the low-income housing in the county, and the rationale for the housing's location in Yonkers was really driven by property values. The land on the east side never fit the governmental formulas that would allow the government programs to purchase that real property and use it for housing. The older section of town that had ... deteriorating housing qualified for acquisition for low income housing. . . . The housing was built where it was because that's where the land could be acquired.

Many of us thought that the proper defensive posture for the City of Yonkers was a regional approach, which would have meant that the surrounding communities which had no low income housing would have been put in the same boat as Yonkers and then there would have been a true distribution, and that was my understanding of the way it was going to be defended until I was replaced and my successor . . . didn't want to follow that. I was deposed in connection with that case and I was not represented by the city. . . . I had a lot to say but neither side saw fit to use my testimony. . . . I had a little bit different view than the polarizing views that a lot of people were putting forth. They just made a bad case worse the way it was handled.

Sylvia Banks: On Perceptions of Discrimination
(Chapter 6—Background of the Case)

When I was growing up here in Runyon Heights there was no neighborhood school any more so . . . from the time you went to school you had really kind of different experiences. . . . You were in a school where you were in the minority and then you came home and that wasn't an issue.

Jeffrey Williams: On Discrimination
(Chapter 6—Background of the Case)

[Referring to instances of discrimination]: We're raised to know that these things were going to happen but it was never an excuse for us not to excel or do the right thing. . . . That was not going to be allowed.

Angelo Martinelli: On the Desegregation Case (Chapter 6—Post-Election Blues)

And then in the eighties we had the desegregation case. I was the man telling people you ought to settle this case. I went to the judge. I went to the board of education. . . . We can go down there, I said to them, like if I'm in business and the IRS comes and says we're auditing your business. This was a businessman's approach to this thing and . . . they come back and say these are our findings and I say you're wrong there . . . but you know, maybe you've got a point in this one. So instead of saying, I'm going to fight you, I'm going to say, here's the areas I think I can beat you and this is the area I think you might have a shot at me. Let's make a deal . . . I'm willing to settle this thing. . . . I'm willing to say this if you're willing to say that and so that's what I did in the desegregation suit. I said let's make a deal. We'll take X amount instead of the total amount of the low income housing. We'll take X amount of it and we will do . . . a modified neighborhood school. . . . We almost had . . . a modified neighborhood school and what happened was they turned it down. We lost it by one vote in the city council. . . . We had the N.A.A.C.P., the Justice Department, and board of education. Each voted for this modified neighborhood school. . . . The council didn't have to vote in favor of the plan. All it had to do was vote the money for the plan. It cost eleven million to do the capital work for the magnet program . . . but we lost it by one vote . . . and then . . . all hell broke loose.

In nineteen eighty-seven I went out and said to the people: "Look, you've always trusted me; you've trusted my advice." Now, all of a sudden, I'm the bad guy because I'm supporting settling this case. I said I want to be able to get up in the morning, be able to look myself in the mirror and say: "I said what I honestly believed in and so I said I can tell you what you want me to tell you, what you want to hear. . . . I know what you want to hear. You want me to say to you I'm going to fight this case till my death. I'm going to go to the Supreme Court," I said, "but I know in my heart that's wrong. I'm only leading you astray."

In eighty-eight, they signed the consent decree. They gave away the store. There was no negotiation. I got a call the next day, two days later from the Justice Department. I had dealt with them . . . I got a call which said Angelo, Mister Mayor, you know they gave us everything. He said, you know they could have negotiated half of it out. They gave us the whole ball of wax. Then they (the city council) reneged on that and the judge came in and fined then and then they finally had to go with it anyway.

We're living today . . . with the vestiges of the housing and the schools. . . . It could have been over in nineteen eighty-five. The devastation that it caused. . . . We had a plan to rebuild the waterfront and we were moving. Well, there were developers. . . . The first phase of the development of the waterfront was building an old power house into a high rise condominium. They sold those units for four hundred thousand dollars. . . . In nineteen eighty-eight, four hundred thousand dollars was a lot of money. . . . They had a showing early in January nineteen eighty-eight. Now I left office . . . They got . . . one hundred and nineteen verbal commitments. Then . . . the city goes into this thing where they signed the consent decree and they defied the judge. All the headlines . . . all around the country saying Yonkers was a big racist city and all of a sudden the hundred and nineteen went down to thirty-nine units that were sold and that killed the project and that would have been the catalyst for the revitalization of downtown Yonkers at that time.

John Favareau: On the Strong Mayor Form of Government (Chapter 6—New Year, New Challenges)

In the forties, interestingly enough, both the Democratic Party and the Republican Party in Yonkers wanted proportional representation thrown out. The professional pols, I'd say, feared losing control of the political process. I'd also guess that some of them were quite unhappy with the city manager form of municipal government here, which came in with proportional representation and which replaced the "strong mayor" form of government. There was a persistent attempt, at any rate, to restore the strong mayor. Election after election in the seventies and eighties, the ballot would include a proposed change to the city charter, replacing the city manager form of government with the strong mayor form of government. Problem for the pols was, the proposed charter change had to be approved by the voters, and the voters kept voting it down. Finally, the strategy of "heads I win, tails we flip again" paid off. In the election of nineteen eighty-nine, the voters approved a change to the charter restoring the strong mayor form of government. It was a momentous occasion. Because to my mind, whether one favors the massive development projects that are now under way here, or whether—like me—you cast a cold eye on them, nothing on this scale could have been undertaken were it not for the return of the strong mayor.

But the history of this thing raises a question: Why did the voters, having rejected the strong mayor form of government in nineteen eighty-seven, vote in favor of it just two years later? Here's my hypothesis. I offer it to any grad student who needs a dissertation topic. In terms of tension and emotions, nineteen eighty-eight was the height of the deseg case—the contentious zenith of the whole quarter-century-long case. The election of nineteen eighty-nine, I'd say, has to be seen in light of that. The man who was elected mayor in nineteen eighty-nine was Henry Spallone, the one person on the city council who was widely seen as willing to defy Judge Sand to the bitter end. My hypothesis is that many voters mistakenly thought that by bringing in the strong mayor form of government in nineteen eighty-nine that they would at the same time be making Henry Spallone the first strong mayor of Yonkers. What they failed to realize was that there was a two-year "delay" written into the legislation, so that the first strong mayor would be the man elected not in nineteen eighty-nine, but in nineteen ninety-one.

Joseph Pastore Jr.: On Toleration
(Chapter 7—The Spencer Administration)

The case was not about getting people to socialize. The case was about allowing individuals, independent of ethnicity, race, to live where they want to live. That's really what it's about. . . . It's not so much about coming together. It's about tolerating.

Symra Brandon: On the Court-Ordered Housing
(Chapter 7—Politics and Governance: Henry Spallone as Mayor)

I was in office when they opened up the first units and matter of fact I got to pick out of the lottery someone's name . . . who moved into the first set of public housing on the east side. I think once the housing was put up and people moved in they blended into the community. I don't think it was as problematic as some people portrayed it to be. I remember the housing unit on Midland Avenue. Sarah Lawrence became involved and offered amenities, such as you can use our playground. . . . There was a lot of benevolence in terms of the new people moving in.

John F. Prill: On Public Education
(Chapter 7—The Spencer Administration)

People outside of Yonkers really don't know what a great city it is and I hope that the school system is organized to the point where it's really acceptable. The school situation could be resolved. I hear a lot of good things but it's the funding of it that's skewed. . . . I do wish and hope that the educational system improves mightily. It has improved greatly since we moved here, absolutely. That's really the biggest thing. I thing we have to get the educational quality resolved. I think that'll make a big, big difference because now starter families moved into the neighborhood, for instance our neighborhood, but they're very transient. When they have children they move out.

Andrew Romano: On Perceptions of Yonkers
(Chapter 7—Final Thoughts)

I think as a result of the efforts of a lot of people Yonkers has evolved over the past half century. It's much more tolerant of people. What's interesting is Yonkers has always been an immigrant town where one group of immigrants would come in and they would do well and would move up. . . . Now the Albanians, Indians, and Pakistanis are moving in and Spanish, whether it's Guatemalans or Mexicans. . . . They're doing great. If you work, you're going to do well in this town.

Royden Letsen: On Perceptions of Yonkers
(Chapter 7—Final Thoughts)

It is a city of industry and business and most of Westchester County sort of looked down on Yonkers as not being comparable to Rye, Scarsdale, and White Plains, et cetera.

Angelo Martinelli: On a Big, Little City
(Chapter 7—Final Thoughts)

It's a very big city and it's a city made up . . . of little villages almost. . . . Any section in Yonkers, they're little villages in a way.

Alfred DelBello: On Perceptions of Yonkers
(Chapter 7—Final Thoughts)

I think Yonkers has totally turned the corner and is now taking off.

Nicholas Spano: On Impressions of Yonkers
(Chapter 7—Final Thoughts)

Yonkers continues to be a big city but a very small town with many different neighborhoods with many different ethnic groups who have a great deal of pride in where they came from as well as a love for the city they live in.

John Romano: On His Fondness for Yonkers
(Chapter 7—Final Thoughts)

There'll never be another place like Yonkers. . . . It's fascinating. It's a great city.

John F. Prill: On East Side/West Side in Yonkers
(Chapter 7—Final Thoughts)

There is Yonkers enthusiasm on the west side that is not on the east side, except in certain pockets but that's probably the problem of Yonkers in that there are a lot of pockets and it's not unusual in big cities. I lived for quite a while in Minneapolis and I even lived in the suburbs but we all thought of ourselves as Minneapolitans whereas people deny that they live in Yonkers in certain areas, mostly on the east side, and that's very bad.

John Favareau: On Perceptions of Yonkers
(Chapter 7—Final Thoughts)

What gets lost in a lot of the optimistic talk about development is the cost of all these things. With increased development you're going to incur an increased demand for all kinds of city services, the most obvious ones being police, fire, and sanitation, not to mention all kinds of changes that have to be made to the infrastructure. So at the end of the day, I would not be surprised if Yonkers is not very much better off financially after all this development takes place than it is right now. If, moreover, everything that's being proposed now were to get built, I think that in about ten years from now you'd have a radically different Yonkers from anything known during my lifetime. On the west side, certainly, it will be much more like certain parts of Manhattan. I call it "Manhattan-Lite." It's almost sure, too, to bring in a very different sort of resident. Yonkers has historically been a place where one could come in as a person with little experience or little education and find a decent niche for oneself and one's family. I'm not sure that this is going to be true any more of the kind of place they're planning to turn Yonkers into, here on the west side, anyway. The "tone" of Yonkers and the tone of Manhattan have been antithetical up to this point, and if we make Yonkers into a "Manhattan-Lite" the old Yonkers will be gone forever.

Mary Hoar: On Perceptions of Yonkers
(Chapter 7—Final Thoughts)

I see Yonkers going back to its roots of being a bedroom community, particularly with all of the new development that we have. We don't have the major employers the way we used to so more and more people are working outside of Yonkers. People will be walking out of their homes or their apartments (near the river) . . . walking the two blocks down to the train station, getting on the train and going into New York City so I see us going back more towards that. I suppose it's fine as long as we have the tax dollars. . . . We have such wonderful resources available to a city, just the view alone . . . and the history of Yonkers is priceless. It's filled with funny, quirky stories. People say: "Well, that's Yonkers." Well it is and I think it's time that people became proud of who we are, what we were and what we're going to be.

The Interviewees and Dates of the Interviews

Arcaro, Gregory: Executive Director, Yonkers Community Planning Council (May 25, 2006)

Banks, Sylvia: (June 23, 2008)

Brandon, Symra: Minority Leader of the Yonkers City Council (May 5, 2006)

Breitbart, Rhoda: Yonkers librarian (October 25, 2006)

Caruso, Mario: Principal Planner and Grants Manager, City of Yonkers Planning and Development Department (June 22, 2006)

DelBello, Hon. Alfred: Mayor of Yonkers, 1970–73; Westchester County Executive; New York State Lieutenant Governor (November 5, 2007)

Favareau, John: Reference librarian, Riverfront Library, Yonkers (June 23, 2008)

Flynn, Tom: (April 23, 2008)

Hlewicki, Walter: (March 29, 2006)

Hoar, Mary: Educator and President of the Yonkers Historical Society (June 21, 2008)

Hull, Joan Cahraman: (April 20, 2006)

Jennings, Joan: (June 22, 2006)

Jerome, Jeremiah: Educator and trustee of the Yonkers Historical Society (May 2, 2008)

Letsen, Hon. Royden: New York State Senator from Yonkers (September 20, 2006)

Loehr, Hon. Gerald: Westchester County Court Judge; Acting Justice of the New York State Supreme Court; Mayor of Yonkers, 1980–81 (November 19, 2007)

Macknowski, Stephen: (October 18, 2006)

Martinelli, Hon. Angelo: Mayor of Yonkers, 1974–79, 1982–87 (May 27, 2006)

Pastore Jr., Joseph: Professor Emeritus, Lubin School of Business, Pace University (May 23, 2007)

Petti, Edward: (September 20, 2006)

Prezioso, Sal: City Manager of Yonkers, 1982–83 (March 16, 2006)

Prill, John F.: (May 19, 2008)

Reden, Arlene McCann: (March 31, 2006)

Romano, Andrew: (June 21, 2008)

Romano, John: (May 19, 2008)

Rossell, John: (May 9, 2007)

Rutledge, George: (April 28, 2008)

Spano, Hon. Nicholas: Member of the New York State Assembly, 1978–1985; Member of the New York State Senate, 1986–2006 (May 6, 2008)

Tritten, Jennie: (June 29, 2008)

Williams, Jeffrey: Commissioner of Planning, City of Mount Vernon; Commissioner of Planning and Development, City of Yonkers; President of the Yonkers Historical Society (June 23, 2008)

Winstanley, Hon. Leonard: Member, Yonkers City Council (May 25, 2006)

Donors

The Yonkers Historical Society gratefully thanks the following donors for their assistance in helping us preserve Yonkers History.

Historian

Hudson Valley National Foundation

Preservationist

Stephen Byrnes
The Thomas and Agnes Carvel Foundation

Benefactor

Mr. and Mrs. William E. Griffin
The Col. Troster Fund

Patron

Mr. and Mrs. John P. Abplanalp
Ecco Development, LLC
Allan Eisenkraft
Adam Ifshin, DLC Management
Kathleen and Dan Kelleher

Mr. and Mrs. James J. Landy
Stephen Macknowski, Yonkers Canoe Club
Queen's Daughters Day Care Center, Inc.
Mr. and Mrs. John A. Pratt Jr.
Gregory Holcombe, Precision Valve Corporation
Michael Spicer, Saint Joseph's Medical Center
Iris Walshin

Donor

East Yonkers Rotary Club
Robert Kern
William Plunkett

Supporter

Robert Altman
Mr. and Mrs. Stephen R. Brown
City and Suburban
Mr. and Mrs. James M. Coogan
Joan Cunningham
Mr. and Mrs. Maurice Curran
DLC Management
Mr. and Mrs. Carl A. D'Angelo
Mr. and Mrs. Jay Dupay
Rosalie Flynn
George Friedberg
Leon Geller
Mary Hoar and Ira Goldman
Mr. and Mrs. Gregory Holcombe
Mr. and Mrs. George Homer
Mr. and Mrs. Martin Hopwood
Hon. and Mrs. Royden Letsen
Barry Levites, Baron Associates
Luther Burbank Garden Club
Arthur Maggiola
Mr. and Mrs. Michael Maloney
James Mannion
Hon. and Mrs. Angelo R. Martinelli

Hon. and Mrs. Michael A. Martinelli
Mr. and Mrs. Philip Matthews
Mr. and Mrs. William J. Mulrow
Carl Petrillo
Dorothy Rosner
Mr. and Mrs. Ronald Sylvestri
Mr. and Mrs. Craig S. Thompson
Philip Wanderman
Jeannie Martinelli, Yonkers Chamber of Commerce

History Book Committee

John F. Prill, Chairman
Mina Crasson
Benedetto "Ben" Ermini
John Favareau
Rosalie Flynn
Tom Flynn
Teresa Hennelly
Mary Hoar
Joan Jennings
Jeremiah Jerome
Elizabeth McFadden
Richard Moore
Andrew Romano
George Rutledge
Deirdre Hoare-Rylander
Jennie Tritten
Jeffrey Williams
Robert Wilson
Leonard Winstanley
Marianne Winstanley

Index

Abplanalp, Robert, 138
Adams, Benjamin, 36
Adler, Fred J. (city manager), 178–79
A.F.L. (American Federation of
    Labor), 132
A.F.L.-C.I.O. (American Federation of
    Labor and Congress of Industrial
    Organizations), 134, 225, 263
African Americans, 101–2, 235,
    242, 259–60. *See also* busing;
    desegregation
alcohol, 77–78. *See also* breweries;
    Prohibition
Alders (Boyce Thompson Estate), 67
Alexander Smith and Sons Carpet
    Company (Alexander Smith
    Company), 139–42
    closing of Yonkers plant, 141–42
    Congress of Industrial
        Organizations (C.I.O.) and, 140
    Eva Smith Cochran and, 10–11
    expansion, 96
    Frederick B. Klein and, 140
    Halcyon Skinner and, 11
    John Masefield at, 12–13
    labor relations, 140–41
    productivity, 67
    profit sharing, 67
    strike, 141
    unionization, 94–95

Warren B. Smith and, 10
William C. Ewing and, 140–41
World War I and, 46, 48
World War II and, 123
Alexander's Department Store, 151,
    169
Alioto, Robert F., 196, 197
Allen, Commissioner James E., Jr.,
    165
Allied Stores Corporation, 231–32
Almog, Zvi, 216
American Federation of Labor
    (A.F.L.), 132
American Federation of Labor
    and Congress of Industrial
    Organizations (A.F.L.-C.I.O.),
    134, 225, 263
American Real Estate Company
    Great Depression and, 79
    Park Hill and, 23
American Sugar Refining Company,
    15
Amtrak, 205
Anderson, William, 70–77
Andrus, John Emory
    bequests, 81
    birthday pronouncements, 59
    burglary at residence, 69–70
    death, 80
    Great Depression and, 80

Andrus, John Emory *(continued)*
  as mayor, 8–9
  as millionaire straphanger, 8–10
  Surdna Foundation and, 58
  taxes, 59
  theater and, 59
  women's suffrage and, 58
Andrus Planetarium, 207
annexation of Yonkers by New York
    City
  in early 20th century, 7–8
  in 1930s, 90
Anti-Saloon League, 9, 70–77
anti-shorts crusade, 96–99
Apple Tree Gang, 208
Armour Villa Park, 65
Armstrong, Edwin Howard, 138
Arthur G. Blair, Inc., shipyard, 121
Asbury Methodist Church, 129
Ashburton Urban Renewal Area, 230
Atlas, Sol, 146, 169
AT&T, 290–91
Austin Avenue industrial site, 206,
    239, 241, 256, 266, 288–90
auto racing, 30–33
  at Empire City Track, 30–31
  New York to Paris auto race, 32–33
automobiles. *See also* highways
  advent of, 27–33
  speeding, 28
  Yonkers-Catskill Highway, 30
automobiles accidents, 30

Baekeland, Leo Hendrick, 138
bakeries, 228–30
Barnes, Ken (DOJ attorney), 273
Barnes, Mayor Benjamin F., 99, 107,
    111, 117–19
Bassons Industries, 144
bathhouses, public, 3–4
Batory (Polish Gdynia-American Line
    ship), 113–14
Beall, Judge Joseph H., 30

Belkin, Lisa, 285
Benedict, Mrs. Albert, 69–70
Benson and Hedges, 144
Berger, Martin, 224, 228
Berkowitz, David, 217–19. *See also*
    Son of Sam
Black Hand (secret society), 51
blacks. *See* African Americans
boating, 206
boating accidents, 38–41, 62–63
bootleggers, 77–78
Borkowski, Eustacy (captain of
    Batory), 113
Borrazzo, Edward, 227
Boyce Thompson Institute for Plant
    Research, 120, 170
  founding of, 67–68
Brandt's Theatre
  teachers' strike, fiscal crisis and,
    197
breweries, 40, 73–74. *See also*
    Underhill's Brewery
bridges. *See under* Hudson River
Brogan, Thomas A., 178
"Brother, Can You Spare Dime?"
    (song), 79
Browne, Thomas A., 30
Bryn Mawr Ridge apartments, 164
Buddhism. *See* Zen Buddhism
busing, 199–200, 248, 249, 252–55,
    280, 281
Butler, James F., 34
  death, 100
  Empire City Racetrack and, 34

Canoe Club. *See* Yonkers Canoe Club
CANOPY (Citizens and Neighbors
    Organized to Protect Yonkers),
    263
Caramadre, Thomas J., 235–36
Carey, Governor Hugh, 172
Carr, Sam, 218
cars. *See* automobiles

Carter, Jimmy, 249
Carvel, Tom, 138
Casey, J. Emmet (city manager), 182, 184–86
Castaldo, Vincent (city manager), 185, 187, 189–91
Cedar Knolls, 65
Celtic Park, 38
Chamber of Commerce. *See* Yonkers Chamber of Commerce
Charter Revision Commission, 237–38, 241
Chateau Fleur de Lys, 104
Chema, Councilman Peter A., 234, 258, 265, 266, 269, 274
Church of the Immaculate Conception, 129
churches, 129
citizens, leading, 58–61
Citizens and Neighbors Organized to Protect Yonkers (CANOPY), 263
city hall, 119, 129–30, 262
  building a new, 9, 26, 43
  demonstrations at, 133, 195, 197
  a woman's touch in, 136–37
city manager form of government, 108–9
city managers, 184–86. *See also specific city managers*
City Recreation Pier, 287
civil rights, 261, 272. See also *Yonkers Board of Education, United States v.*
Civil Rights Division of Justice Department, 249
Clark, William H., 33
Clean Water Act, 233
Clearwater (sloop), 234
Clearwater, Inc., 234–35
clubs, community, 38
coal, soft
  health problems from, 15–16
Cochran, Alexander Smith, 10
  bequests, 61
  death, 61

Cochran, Eva Smith
  Alexander Smith and Sons Carpet Company and, 10–11
  bequests, 10
  blindness, 11
Cochran, William F., 38
Collins Enterprises, 287
colonnades, 176, 230–31
Committee for Industrial Organization (C.I.O.), 95, 263. *See also* Congress of Industrial Organizations
Committee of One Hundred, 108–9
Committee of Organizations Meeting to Preserve Law in Yonkers (COMPLY), 263
Committee to Free Redmond, 213–14
Common Council. *See* Yonkers Common Council
community centers, 38
COMPLY (Committee of Organizations Meeting to Preserve Law in Yonkers), 263
Comprehensive Plan. *See* Yonkers Comprehensive Plan
Condon, Senator William F., 133, 135
Condon-Wadlin Act, 132, 134, 135
Congress of Industrial Organizations (C.I.O.), 123, 130, 132, 134, 140, 142. *See also* Committee for Industrial Organization
Consumers Union, 231
corruption, 179, 180, 278–79
Costco, 288, 289
Country Life magazine, 23–24
Coyne, Mayor Frank
  New York Central Railroad and, 20–21
  Yonkers Street Railway Company and, 16
Crestwood, 65
  explosion at Thomas Porter's home in, 201

Crestwood Citizens Association, 84–85
  opposition to New York Central
    Railroad fare increase, 21
Crestwood Lake Apartments, 162
crime, 68–70, 215–19, 277–79. *See
  also specific crimes*
Cronin, Richard, 176
Cross County International
  Automobile Show, 148
Cross County Parkway, 107, 117, 151,
  153, 204
Cross County Shopping Center, 146–
  49, 151, 169, 202, 220, 221, 232,
  243, 291. *See also specific stores*
Cross County Square Mall, 232
Cuomo, Governor Mario, 183, 226,
  261, 262
Curran, Charles L. (city manager),
  137, 165, 178–79

D'Agostino, Robert J. (deputy assistant
  attorney general), 249
death rate in Yonkers, 4
Defense Rangers. *See* Yonkers Defense
  Rangers
DelBello, Alfred B., 170, 175
  Angelo Martinelli and, 181
  as county executive, 181, 239
  finances and, 203–4, 226, 239, 243,
    244
  Getty Square and, 175
  as lieutenant governor, 226, 243, 244
  as mayor, 175, 179–80
  Terence Zaleski and, 279
DeLuca, Neil J. (city manager), 258
DeLuxe Development Company, 273
DeSantis, Nicholas (acting city
  manager), 243, 247
desegregation, 235. *See also* busing;
  *Yonkers Board of Education, United
  States v.*
Devereux, Colonel Frederick, 106
Dewey, Governor Thomas E., 127,
  133, 139, 141

Dickerson, Thomas A., 267–69
Divine, Father (Reverend M. J.
  Divine), 101–2
Dollar Land Holdings, 169
downtown redevelopment, 230. *See
  also* urban renewal
  Dean J. Grandin, Jr. and, 230
downtown Yonkers. *See* Getty Square
drugs. *See* alcohol
Dunwoodie Golf Course, 154

earthquakes, 101
education. *See* schools; teachers;
  Yonkers Board of Education;
  *Yonkers Board of Education, United
  States v.*
Eker (steamship), seizure of, 77
Elizabeth Seton College, 280
Emergency Financial Control Board,
  283
Empire City Casino, 291
Empire City Race Track, 33, 100,
  156. *See also* Yonkers Raceway
  auto racing, 30–32
  Jockey Club allocation of meeting
    dates, 34
  during World War II, 117–18
entertainment, 207–8. *See also*
  recreation
environmental protection, 62
Environmental Protection Agency
  (EPA), 223, 234, 292
Ewing, William, 140–41
Excelsior Transparent Bag
  Corporation, 223

Fagan, Councilman Edward J., Jr.,
  264, 269
Fair Housing Committee. *See* Yonkers
  Fair Housing Committee
Farkas, George, 151
Farmer, Joe L., 269
Farrell, Frank, 33
Fay, Judge Martin, 97

Federal Sugar Refining Company, 15
    permanent closing, 94
    temporary closing, 67
Federation of Teachers. *See* Yonkers
    Federation of Teachers
financial crisis, deepening, 186–89
firefighters
    New York State Firemen's
        Association Convention, 1–3
    strike, 238–39
First National Bank, 86
Flynn, John E. (Chippie)
    as mayor, 178, 203
    as state senator, 188, 244
Fogarty, Mayor John F., 81
Fokine, Vera, 104
Food Stamp program, 104
Fox, Eugene (acting city manager),
    237, 238
Frank, Mayor Curtiss E., 134

gambling, 111, 178
Gateway, The (apartment complex), 200
General Bakelite Corp., 138
German newspapers outlawed during
    World War I, 50–51
Germany, 93
Getty, Robert P., 11
Getty House Hotel, 11
Getty Square, 125, 174, 175
Gimbel's Department Store, 148, 169
Ginsburg-Taubman Associates, 175–77
Glassman, Bernard, 228, 229
Godin, Tawny Elaine, 219–20
golf, 35–37, 208
governance, 108–12, 271–74. *See also*
    specific topics
Great Depression, 79–85
    Alexander Smith and Sons Carpet
        Company and, 94–95
    American Real Estate Company
        and, 79
    and building for the future, 92–96
    communist rally during, 82

Crestwood Citizens Association and,
    84, 86
hitting bottom, 88–92
hope springs eternal, 85–88
John Andrus's observations of, 80
National Municipal League and, 89
stock market crash of 1929 and, 78,
    79
Thomas A. Burke real estate
    company and, 79
unemployment during, 81–82
Works Progress Administration and,
    93–94
Great Oriental Land Development
    and Industrial Company, 68–69
Greater New York Fair and
    Exposition, 41–42
Greyston Bakery, 228–29
Greystone (estate), 5–7
    erection by John T. Waring, 5
    fundraisers, 84, 93
    offered to Yonkers, 102–4
    open grounds week, 103
    purchase and restoration by Samuel
        Untermyer, 5–6
    purchase by Governor Samuel J.
        Tilden, 5
    Richard Croker's visit of, 6
    transfer to Untermyer children, 59–60
Grinton I. Will Library, 207
Guilette, Randy, 189
Gunter, Elder (city manager), 179
gypsies, 22

Habirshaw Cable and Wire
    Corporation, 121–23
Habirshaw Division of Phelps Dodge,
    96, 116, 145, 171
Handy, William Christopher (W. C.
    Handy), 161
Havemeyer, John C.
    death, 60
    meeting with labor leaders, 13–15
    objections to smoking, 60

Hearth-Stone Development, 162
Hebrew National Orphan Home, 163
Hello, Dolly!, 219
Hendrick Hudson Hotel, 23, 66
  fire, 23
highways, 149–53, 204–5. *See also
  specific highways*
Hillview Reservoir, 206
Hodgman, Walter W., 36
Hollywood Inn, 38
Home Depot, 288, 289
Hornsby, Andre, 286
horse racing, 33–35, 209–12
  horses from Soviet Union, 212–
    13
hotels, 11, 23, 66
housing, 200–204, 284–85. *See also*
  suburban homes; *Yonkers Board of
  Education*
  low-income/subsidized, 163, 164,
    200, 235, 248, 255–57, 260,
    265–68, 271–75
    Spencer administration and, 281,
      283, 284
    Zaleski administration and,
      274–76
Housing and Urban Development
  (H.U.D.), U.S. Department of,
  251, 252, 255, 257, 273
housing assistance, 105. See also
  Yonkers Board of Education
Housing Authority. *See* Yonkers
  Municipal Housing Authority
housing discrimination, 200–201. See
  also *Yonkers Board of Education*
Hudson-Fulton Celebration, 42–43
Hudson River, 61–64, 159–61,
  233–36
  accidents, 39, 40, 62–63
  Bill (Bojangles) Robinson birthday
    celebration, 160–61
  City Recreation Pier, 287
  ferry to Manhattan, 287
  ice, 62

pontoon bridge, 63–64
proposed bridge, 233
Hudson River Day Line, 160
Hudson River Museum, 220, 239
  addition of Andrus Planetarium,
    galleries, and branch library, 207
Hudson River Sloop Clearwater,
  234–35

Iannacone, Dominick, 185, 189
income taxes, 186, 193, 242, 247
industrial elite, 10–12
Industrial Exposition (1913), 41
Industrial Organization, Committee
  for. *See* Committee for Industrial
  Organization
Industrial Organizations, Congress
  of. *See* Congress of Industrial
  Organizations
industry, 66–68. *See also specific
  companies*
infrastructure, 204–6, 288, 291–93. *See
  also* highways; *specific topics*
Iona College, 280
Iridium Gold and Platinum Company,
  68
Irwin, Rodney H. (city manager), 243

Japan, 227
Jenkins, Kenneth (president of
  N.A.A.C.P. Yonkers branch), 280
Jerome Knitting Mills, 95
Jewish Community Center Fire
  arrest and conviction of Thomas
    Alfred Ruppert, 217
  rescue of children by Lucille Sacks,
    215
  Zvi Almog's testimony, 216
Jockey Club, 34
Joseph Kaplan and Sons, 144
Joseph Love, Inc., 96
Julia Dyckman Andrus Memorial, Inc.,
  163
Justice, U.S. Department of, 248–49, 281

Kawasaki Heavy Industries, 226–27
Kawasaki Rail Car, 291
Keith, Herman, 194, 235
Kennedy, Thomas V. (city manager/
    city controller), 131, 142
Kennedy family and Yonkers Bus
    Company dispute, 105–6
King, Martin Luther, III, 272
Klein, Frederick B., 140
Kristensen, Mayor Kristen, 137
Krupa, Gene, 215
Ku Klux Klan (KKK), 102

labor relations. *See also* strikes; unions;
    workforce
  during World War II, 123–24
Larkin, Mayor Thomas F., 66
Larkin Plaza, 66
Lawrence Park West, 65
Leake and Watts Children's Home,
    202
Lehman, Governor Herbert, 111
Lennon, Mayor James
  and ice in Hudson River, 62
  women's suffrage rally and, 57
Levitt, Arthur (New York State
    comptroller), 192
Liberty Bonds, 50, 51
Liberty Lines, 233
Liberty Waste Management, 292
libraries, 9, 11–12, 207
Lockwood Lumber Company, 230
Loehr, Councilman Gerald E.
  firefighters strike and, 238–39
  as mayor, 193–94, 237–40
  municipal budget and, 238–39
Loehr, Mayor Joseph F.
  annexation of Yonkers by New York
    City and, 90
  Yonkers Better Housing Committee
    Model House and, 92
Longo, Minority Leader Nicholas V.,
    254, 265, 268, 269
Loral Corporation, 172–73, 227

Loral International, 227
Lost in Yonkers (Simon), 274
Ludlow Park, 234, 292–93

Maritime Oil Company, 131
Marra, Reginald (school
    superintendent), 283
Martinelli, Mayor Angelo, 181–84
  and City Council attempt to
    reduce power of mayor, 191
  defeated by Gerald Loehr, 194
  defeated by Nicholas Wasicsko, 247,
    256
  defeated Gerald Loehr, 240
  defeated John R. Morrissey, 181
  fiscal crisis and, 182–85, 187, 192
  income tax proposal, 193
  labor negotiations, 193
  as mayoral candidate, 274
  municipal budget and, 242
  Otis Elevator Company and, 172
  redistricting, 241–42
  reelection, 245
  United Technologies Corporation
    and, 225
  U.S. v. Yonkers Board of Education
    and, 256–58
  Yonkers-Alpine ferry and, 233
  Yonkers Plan and, 243
Masefield, John
  at Alexander Smith and Sons
    Carpet Company, 12–13
  as England's Poet Laureate, 12
  return visit to Yonkers, 85–86
McInerney, Thomas (assemblyman),
    192
media. *See* newspapers
Miss America, Tawny Elaine Godin
    crowned, 219–20
Montgomery, Robert Craig (city
    manager/city controller), 130, 131
Morelite Construction Company, and
    downtown redevelopment, 177
Morris Companies, 288, 289

Morrissey, John R., 181
Mulford Gardens, erection of, 105
Music Hall. *See* Yonkers Music Hall

narcotics, use of, 202–3
Nathan's Famous, 169
National Association for the
    Advancement of Colored People
    (N.A.A.C.P.)
  complaint filed by, 247–48
  housing, segregation, and, 247–48,
    251–53, 255, 262, 265, 275–77,
    281, 283–85
  Yonkers chapter, 194, 247–48, 262,
    265, 280
National Guard, 239
National Municipal League, 89
National Recovery Administration, 87
National Sugar Refining Company, 15
  World War I and, 48
Nazi Germany, 93
Nepperhan Valley Biotechnology
    Center, 290
New Deal programs, 86, 90, 93
New York, Boston and Westchester
    Railroad, 106
New York Central Railroad
  accidents, 20
  fares, 20–21
  service complaints, 21
  Yonkers Bus Company dispute and,
    106
New York City. *See* annexation of
    Yonkers by New York City
New York State Firemen's Association
    Convention, 1–3
New York State Thruway, 150–53, 170
  Austin Avenue industrial site and,
    288, 289
  construction, 150
  overpass accident, 291
New York State Urban Development
    Corporation, 232, 283, 284
Newman, Judge J. O., 261

Newman, Oscar, 255, 257
newspapers. *See also specific newspapers*
  German, outlawed during World
    War I, 50–51
Noble, G. Clifford, 81
Normandy, invasion of, 122–23

oil crisis of 1973, 205
Oldfield, Barney, 30–31
Oliver, John W., 4
Olson, Robert K. (police
    commissioner), 277
One Hundred, Committee of, 108–9
Operation Pluto, 122–23
O'Rourke, Andrew P., 239, 281
O'Rourke, Mayor James F. X., 178–79
Otis Elevator Company, 142–45,
    171–72, 224–25
  departure from Yonkers, 224–25
  explosion at, 121
  Great Depression and, 96
  plan to transfer production from
    Yonkers, 171
  plans for new facility in Yonkers,
    171–72
  site purchased by Port Authority
    of New York and New Jersey,
    225–26
  strike, 142
  United Technologies Corporation
    and, 224–25
  World War I and, 47
Oxman, Harry, 254

papal visits to Yonkers, 293
Park Hill, 22–26
  American Real Estate Company
    and, 23
  development, 23–25
  Father Divine and, 101–2
  Hendrick Hudson Hotel and, 66
  proposed apartment hotel in, 66
Park Hill Theatre, tear gas explosions
    in, 207

parks, 64–66, 153–55
parkways, 64–66, 204. *See also* Cross
    County Parkway; Saw Mill River
    Parkway
Parsons, Florence, 97
Pastore, Joseph M., Jr., 249–50, 254,
    282
Pataki, Governor George, 281, 282,
    284, 287, 289
peace theme, 128–29
Peacock, Eulace, 100
Pearl Harbor attack, reaction to, 115
Pei, I. M., 174, 175
Penn Central Railroad, 205
Permanent Peace Day (December 18),
    128–29
Petersen, LeRoy A. (CEO of Otis
    Elevator), 143
Peterson, John (city manager/city
    controller), 131, 132, 135
Phelps Dodge, Habirshaw Division of,
    96, 116, 121–23, 145, 171
Philipse Manor Hall, 43
    anniversary, 85
    as New York State historic site,
    43–44
Phillipse Towers, 173
Pierpointe-on-the-Hudson, 235–36
Pluto, Operation, 122–23
Police Department. *See* Yonkers Police
    Department
Polish Community Center, 94–95,
    114, 118, 132, 140, 267, 268, 271
Polychrome Corporation, 170–71
pontoon bridges, 63–64
Port Authority of New York and
    New Jersey, 160, 225–26, 233,
    291
Port Imperial Ferry Corporation, 287
Porter, Thomas, 201
Portman, Merrill A. (acting city
    manager), 179
Powell, Eleanor, 65
press. *See* newspapers

Prezioso, Sal J. (city manager), 240–42
Prince Alert (race horse), 33
Proctor Paint and Varnish Company,
    225
Proctor's Theater, explosion at, 90–92
Prohibition
    bootleggers and rumrunners, 77–78
    raids, 88
    seizure of steamship *Eker*, 77
    State Cereal and Beverage
    Company and, 77
    Underhill's Brewery and, 77, 89
    William H. Anderson, Anti-Saloon
    League, and, 70–77
property taxes, 104, 183, 193, 196,
    241, 243–44, 247, 275
Public Service Commission, 17
Public Works, Department of, 129–30
Pupin, Michael, 138
Putnam Division of New York
    Central Railroad, 232
    Yonkers Bus Company dispute and,
    107

Qwest Communications International,
    290–91

raceways. *See* Empire City Race
    Track; Yonkers Raceway
railroads, 20–22, 106, 107, 232. *See
    also* Yonkers Street Railway
    Company
Ravo, Pat T. (city manager), 191, 193,
    237
Raymond, Joan, 252–54
Reagan, Ronald, 249, 252
real estate, 162, 200–201
    post–World War II construction,
    162–63
real estate taxes, 88, 130, 164, 230,
    232
recreation, 37–41, 206–9
Redmond, Hugh Francis, Jr., 213–14
Refined Syrups and Sugars, 223–24

Reynolds, William Bradford, 249
Ridge Hill, 291
Ridge Hill Rehabilitation Center, 203
Rio Lages (British cargo steamer),
    bombing of, 45
Robert Martin Company, 224, 228
Robinson, Bill (Bojangles), 160–61
Robitaille, Joseph P., 248
Rooney, John, 211
Rooney, Timothy J., 236
Roosevelt, Franklin Delano, 86
    visit to Yonkers, 86
Roosevelt, Governor Theodore, 1–3
Roosevelt High School, double
    sessions at, 166
Rory O'Moore Park, 281
Rosenshein, Bernard, 232
Rosenwaser, Morris (city manager),
    130
Ross, Winston, 247
rumrunners, 77–78
Ruppert, Thomas Alfred, 217
Russians and horse racing, 212–13

S/E Asset Development and
    downtown redevelopment, 177
Sacks, Lucille, 215
Saegkill Golf Club, 36
Saks Fifth Avenue distribution center,
    170
sales tax, 131, 166, 183, 243
Salute to Yonkers Industrial exhibition,
    145
Samuel Untermyer Park and Gardens,
    154–55
Sand, Judge Leonard B., 248–61,
    264–67, 276, 286
sanitation workers' strike, 132–36
Sarah Lawrence College, 196
Saunders, Ervin, 11
    bequests, 11–12
    death, 11
Saunders Trade and Technical High
    Schools ("Saunders"), 12

Save Yonkers Federation, 263, 266,
    268, 275
Saw Mill River Parkway, 107, 150
Scher, Seymour (city manager), 180,
    181
School 32, 276–77
schools, Yonkers, 12, 164–67. See also
    teachers
    busing proposal, 199
    closings, 198
    compared with other Westchester
        County school districts, 194
    finances, 244–45
    sit-ins, rallying, and protesting,
        194–99
    staff reductions, 198
    survey of, 166
sea lion, escape of, 78
Seabiscuit (race horse), 100
Sedition Act of 1918, 50
segregation, 235. See also
    desegregation; National
    Association for the Advancement
    of Colored People
sewage
    dewatering plant, 234
    Liberty Waste Management, 292
    pollution charge by N.Y. State
        Health Commissioner, 62
    sludge dewatering, 291–92
sewage treatment plants
    Ludlow Park Homeowners
        Association's opposition to, 234
    updating of North Yonkers and
        South Yonkers, 205
Shabazz, Betty, 278
Shaffer, Gail S. (New York Secretary
    of State), 262, 278–79
Shanker, Albert, 197
shopping centers. See Cross County
    Shopping Center; Cross County
    Square Mall
Sialiano, Salvatore J., 269
Sikes, Ralph, 133

Skinner, Halcyon
  Alexander Smith and Sons Carpet
    Company and, 11
  hit by train, 11
Slater, Alderman William, 96–99
Smith, Warren B.
  Alexander Smith and Sons Carpet
    Company and, 10
  death, 10
Smith Carpet. *See* Alexander Smith
  and Sons Carpet Company
Son of Sam, 217–19
Soviet Union and horse racing, 212–
  13
Spallone, Henry (Hank), 264
  as councilman, 258, 267
  as mayor, 267–69, 271–74
Spano, Senator Nicholas, 282
Spencer, John D.
  as councilman, 269, 276
  as mayor
    administration, 281–86
    election of, 280
  Terence Zaleski and, 279
sports, 35–38, 100
  legal challenge to banning Sunday,
    35–37
  running and rowing, 99–101
Spreckels, Claus A.
  and closing of Federal Sugar
    Refining Company, 67, 94
  industrial sabotage, 15
Spreckman, Bernice, 245
St. Andrew's Golf Club, 208
  founding, 35
  75th anniversary, 208
St. John's Getty Square, Thanksgiving
  service at, 125
St. Joseph's Church, 129
St. Joseph's Seminary, 129, 293
Starr, U.S. Solicitor General Kenneth
  (Ken) W., 268, 271–72
State Cereal and Beverage Company,
  77, 89

Stern's (department store), 231
Stew Leonard's, 288–90
Stilwell, Benjamin W., 116
Stilwell, Colonel John, 116, 150
Stilwell, General Joseph W., 116, 127,
  150
stock market crash of 1929, 78, 79
Strand Theatre, 91, 135
  transformed into Yonkers Playhouse,
    207
strikes, labor, 141, 142, 171, 188, 197,
  211, 238–39. *See also* sanitation
  workers' strike
  strikers and strikebreakers, 15–22
  teacher strikes, 196–98, 285–86
Sullivan, Vice Mayor James A., 128,
  130–31
Summer of Sam (film), 219
Surdna Foundation, creation of, 58
Sussman, Michael (N.A.A.C.P.
  attorney), 250
Sutherland, Mayor Leslie
  New York State Firemen's
    Association Convention and, 1
  as witness at wedding of John W.
    Oliver, 4

Taiwan, 226–27
Taubman Corporation, 169–70
tax cuts, 3, 84, 89, 230
tax exemptions, 104, 154, 204, 241
tax increases, 84, 130, 186, 192, 193,
  230, 241, 242, 244, 247, 275, 279
tax strike, call for, 89
taxes, 71, 89–90, 143, 165, 179, 230,
  232
  income, 186, 193, 242, 247
  John Andrus on, 80
  property, 104, 183, 193, 196, 241,
    243–44, 247, 275
  on racetrack admissions, 156–57,
    159
  real estate, 88, 130, 164, 230, 232
  sales, 131, 166, 183, 243

Taylor, Harold, 129
teachers. *See also* schools
   collective bargaining and Yonkers
      Federation of Teachers, 194
   salary reductions, 198–99
   strikes, 196–98, 285–86
tercentennial, 127–29
terrorism, 278
Thanksgiving service at St. John's
   Getty Square, 125
Thompson, Colonel William Boyce
   Boyce Thompson Institute for Plant
      Research and, 67–68
   death, 81
Tibbetts Brook Park, 153, 154
   anti-shorts crusade and, 99
   dedication, 65
Tice, Walter, 197
Tilden, Governor Samuel J., 5
Triangle Shirtwaist Company
   Triangle Shirtwaist Factory fire,
      13
   Yonkers factory, 13
trolleys, 83, 149, 150
   accidents, 18–19, 83
   transfers, 19
Troster, Oliver J. (chair of
   Tercentennial Commission), 128
Truman, Harry S., 139
Truth, Sojourner, 235
Tudor Woods Apartments, 200
Tylenol mystery, 245–47

Underhill, Edward, 40
Underhill's Brewery, 77, 89, 177
unemployment during Great
   Depression, 81–82
unions, 94–95. *See also* strikes
United States Department of Housing
   and Urban Development
   (H.U.D.), 251, 252, 255, 257,
   273
United States Department of Justice
   (DOJ), 248–49, 281

United Technologies Corporation
   (UTC), 224–25
United Textile Workers Union, 94
Universal Indian Alliance of America,
   meeting of, 87
Untermyer, Irwin, 155
Untermyer, Samuel
   on annexation movement, 8
   Black Hand and, 51
   death, 103
   driving at excessive speed, 27–28
   First National Bank and, 86
   fundraisers at Greystone, 84, 93
   and German language press during
      World War I, 50–51
   at Liberty Bonds rally, 50
   National Recovery Administration
      and, 87
   Nazi Germany and, 93
   observations of Great Depression,
      83–84
   offered Greystone to Yonkers, 102–
      4
   open grounds week at Greystone
      and, 103
   purchase and restoration of
      Greystone, 5, 6
Urban Development Corporation.
   See New York State Urban
   Development Corporation
urban renewal, 173–77. *See also*
   downtown redevelopment
   beautification of Getty Square, 174
   Chicken Island and, 174
   colonnade and, 176
   N.Y. State Division of Housing and
      Community Renewal and, 173
   Phillipse Towers and, 173
   proposed I. M. Pei buildings and,
      174, 175

V Brand Systems, Inc., 227
Vergari, Carl (district attorney), 178,
   264

Wagner, Donald C. (city manager),
135, 137
Wall Street Crash of 1929, 78, 79
Wallachs, 147
Walsh, William, Jr., 179
Walsh, William A.
as city manager and director of
public safety, 111–12
as mayor, 65
Walt Whitman Junior High School, 166
Walton, Frank, 208, 220–21
Wanamaker, John, 146, 147
Waring, John T., 5
Waring Hat Company, 48, 67
Wasicsko, Mayor Nicholas C., 231
1989 mayoral race and, 267–68
defeat of Angelo Martinelli, 247, 256
Henry Spallone and, 267–69
suicide, 277
U.S. v. Yonkers Board of Education
and, 256, 258, 260, 262, 264
waterfront redevelopment, 235–36
Collins Enterprises and, 287
Weller, Ralph, 172
Welty, Edith, 129
city manager form of government
and, 108–10, 112
as mayor, 136–37
Westchester County Fair (1981), 236
Western Electric, 144
Whitney, Raymond J. (city manager),
110–11
Wilmorite mall (proposed), 232
Wilson, Governor Malcolm, 133, 203
Windell, J. T., 14
women
attire. See anti-shorts crusade
suffrage, 56–58
in workforce, 124
work life during World War II, 121–25
workforce, 121–25. See also labor
relations; unemployment during
Great Depression; World War I;
World War II

working class, 12–15
Works Progress Administration, 93–94
World War I, 45–55
armistice, 55–56
industrial output during, 46–48
Sedition Act and, 50
volunteer work during, 47–49,
52–54
World War II
Alexander Smith and Sons Carpet
Company and, 123
America at war, 114–16
civil defense during, 116–19
enemy aliens and, 120
Eustacy Borkowski and, 113
labor relations during, 123–24
"mutiny" on the Batory, 112–14
Operation Pluto and invasion of
Normandy, 122–23
Polish Gdynia-America Line ship
detained, 113–14
rationing during, 119–20
work life during, 121–25

Yonkers
1988 as the annus terribilis of,
258–60
as a city on the move, 3–5
longevity of residents in, 4–5
nicknames, 1, 128
300th anniversary. See tercentennial
Yonkers-Alpine ferry, 38, 63, 119, 160,
235
Angelo Martinelli and, 233
anti-shorts crusade and, 97
cessation of service, 160
music on, 101
Yonkers Better Housing Committee,
model home of, 92–93
Yonkers Board of Education, 244
Yonkers Board of Education, United
States v. (desegregation case), 285
and 1988 as Yonkers' annus terribilis,
258–60

Yonkers Board of Education, United States v. (desegregation case) *(continued)*
  appeal, 254–55
  background, 247–49
  decision, 251–54
  N.A.A.C.P. and, 247–48, 253, 255, 262, 265
  and post-election blues, 256–58
  resolution, 264–66
  showdown, 260–64
  Yonkers on trial, 249–51
Yonkers Bus Company, 106–7
Yonkers Canoe Club, 100
Yonkers-Catskill Highway, 30
Yonkers Chamber of Commerce, 176, 235
Yonkers City Hall. *See* city hall
Yonkers Common Council, 109–12, 131, 135–37, 164–66, 197
Yonkers Comprehensive Plan, 287
Yonkers Defense Rangers, 118
Yonkers Fair Housing Committee, 201
Yonkers Federation of Teachers, 194–97, 263, 268, 286
Yonkers Herald, The, 55–56
Yonkers Marathon, 37–38, 99, 208–9
"Yonkers Means Business" advertising blitz, 224
Yonkers Municipal Housing Authority, 163, 273
  Cottage Place Gardens, 163
  Mulford Gardens, 105
Yonkers Music Hall, 13–15
Yonkers-Oklahoma delegation, 128–29
Yonkers Plan, 243–44
Yonkers Police Department, 277–78
  sick out, 188

Yonkers Public Library
  Ervin Saunders's bequest to, 11–12
  opening of the first, 9
Yonkers Raceway, 155–59, 236–37. *See also* Empire City Race Track
  fiberglass caps and, 157
  foreign dignitaries and, 159
  investigation of, 157
  renovation, 158–59
  riot at, 210
  Russians and, 212, 213
  sale of, 156
    to John Rooney by Tannanbaum Family, 211
  strike at, 211
  theft at, 212
  virus outbreak at, 210
Yonkers Sports Hall of Fame, 100
Yonkers Street Railway Company
  Frank Coyne and, 16
  strikes, 15, 17
  takeover proposal, 18
Yonkers Tercentennial Commission, 128
Yonkers Teutonia, 38
"Yonkitis," 238
Young Men's Christian Association (Y.M.C.A.), 53–55
Young Men's Hebrew Association (Y.M.H.A.), 52
Young Women's Christian Association (Y.W.C.A.), 53–54
Young Women's Hebrew Association (Y.W.H.A.), 53–54

Zaleski, Terence (mayor/assemblyman), 226, 274–80
Zen Buddhism, 228–30